NEW ARCHITECTURE IN THE EMERGING WORLD

Projects by Andrew Bromberg, Aedas

NEW ARCHITECTURE IN THE EMERGING WORLD

Projects by Andrew Bromberg, Aedas

prologue and epilogue by **larry rouch**
foreword by **ralph lerner**
introduction by **aaron betsky**
essay by **joseph giovannini**
edited by **oscar riera ojeda**

OSCAR RIERA OJEDA
PUBLISHERS

The attainment of the Promised Land, at least in the version promised to the descendants of Abraham, has proven elusive. Periods in the wilderness, mountaintop sojourns, and the building of pyramids often interfered. The Promised Land for architects and designers is, likewise, elusive – we keep moving in search of new worlds with fertile ground for new opportunities, material developments, and enlightened patrons who appreciate our contributions. Today, the site of the Promised Land has returned to Asia – not western Asia between the Nile and Euphrates (with the notable exception of the Emirates), but rather the most eastern regions of Asia. Andrew Bromberg, the immensely talented designer at the Hong Kong Office of Aedas, arrived in the Promised Land ten years ago, and the projects he has carried out from this base have reached far and wide, to well beyond the region.

Andrew Bromberg was raised in the American West – an earlier vision of the Promised Land. At the start of this book, he presents us with an introductory autobiographical photo essay of his wide ranging Grand Tour leading up to his joining Aedas and his residency there (see Larry Rouch's essay, Shadow Boxing). His photographs and drawings are more than a travelogue – rather, they illustrate a personal point of view: the important forms (boats), sites (water spaces), regions and people that Bromberg is drawn to. He also makes a point of including himself in various different contexts, and provides sketches, notebooks etc., in order to link his intellect, and selected sites and forms, to his creative imagination. It is from this experience that his hunger to directly interact with his clients, their cultures, customs, and idiosyncrasies seems to have arisen. Bromberg's cultural and intellectual background is also a critical factor in understanding his journey, and his motivation to discover efficient and simple ways to build seemingly extravagant forms is not without its own history.

Architects in the United States have generally shown a tendency to see design as an apolitical act, and have glossed over the link between form and ideology. While this may have worked well earlier, today's era of globalization of architectural practices brings the evaluation of this important linkage to the foreground in architectural practice particularly because of the increasing number of architectural firms whose offices are unfettered by the restrictions of national boundaries. For Bromberg, Hong Kong is only the base camp. It was through accepting the separateness of ideology from form, along with the tension between the America of rugged individualism (particularly in the American West) and the America that suppressed individuality within the confines of corporate structures, that large-scale architectural practices as we know them today were born. In fact, these large American architectural firms became synonymous with the 'American Way.'

Bromberg was educated in America, where the establishment of large corporate design practices took place in an era of extreme optimism following the Second World War. The country had just emerged as the dominant world power, every boundary seemed permeable and the victorious army was welcomed home to the Promised Land after its trials in the wilderness of global war. The new scale of architectural practices that emerged in that period, accompanied by the technical prowess of American architecture as it harnessed advanced technologies developed during the war, was accepted as a natural consequence of the ascendancy of modern architecture in the context of a country physically separate from the ideological founts of modernism in Europe. A new global form of practice was emerging to facilitate big building projects at home and abroad and this quickly led to the projection of America's new role as a world leader in architecture. This became a predominant model, one which explains a firm such as Aedas – whose own roots lay elsewhere.

East Asia is awash in celebrity culture when it comes to architecture, and the most prominent stars of the recent Beijing Olympics and the national pavilions at the Shanghai Expo are structures that signify the emergence of China as a world power. Aedas' success and the very high quality of its projects, however, are based upon an emphasis on its ability to provide expertise and a full range of professional services, without tying itself exclusively to the work and ideas of any single one of the talented individuals working in the firm – for the most part, its designers remain anonymous – except for Andrew Bromberg. Bromberg's subtle wordless introduction is complimented by three analytical essays that examine several elements of this paradox: Aaron Betsky (Curving and Swerving Through Sprawl: Andy Bromberg Makes Architecture in the Global Continuum); Joseph Giovannini (Aedas: Building the Future); and Larry Rouch (Shadow Boxing). Together, they fill in blanks by providing readers with three distinct points of view on Bromberg, and the forms and meaning of his work. All three also touch upon the story of the phenomenal growth of China in the last twenty-five years – which needs no re-telling here.

While Bromberg may not yet be a household name comparable to Gehry, Koolhaas, or Foster, I see his place among designers working on their own or in the context of large international firms, as being that of an important 'Early Adopter' of a particularly important form of global practice. Others have followed. Increasingly, important architects and designers are now moving themselves, and/or their practices, to East Asia: OMA; UNstudio; Foster + Partners; etc. The region is filled with astounding opportunities for designers of Bromberg's caliber – those willing to adapt to the way practices are organized here, and who are also wide open to, and hungry for, new ideas.

As Dean I am often asked the difficult question about how best to categorize and evaluate the overall work of large architectural firms and their relationship to idiosyncratic design voices within their organization. There are a limited number of large firms where the primary designer's voice routinely employs easily identifiable, or sometimes truly exceptional characteristics and in some cases a firm's work slowly evolves along a consistent trajectory of closed formal concerns, and demonstrates innovation within the category of a single building type, or through the identification of the firm with an iconic project. Perhaps the difficulty lies in the assignment of significantly greater value to the creation of a distinctive brand, rather than to the quality and value of simply making things well.

Bromberg's global platform is the Hong Kong office of Aedas. In my view, the firm is exceptional for demonstrating the value of emphatically supporting the voice of an individual designer within the operations of a truly global practice. In East Asia the question is even more pressing because of the culture's heavy emphasis on the material value of a distinctive brand, which stands in contrast to the prevalent tradition of extreme frugality. Most interestingly, the exceptional work of Andrew Bromberg thrives in this paradoxical condition.

---

ralph lerner, Chair Professor of Architecture – Ralph Lerner FAIA HKIA, B. Arch., the Cooper Union; M. Arch., Harvard University – is the Dean of the Faculty of Architecture at the University of Hong Kong. Prior to joining the University he was George Dutton '27 Professor of Architecture and Dean of the School of Architecture at Princeton University (1989-2002). His professional practice, Ralph Lerner Architect PC, is located in Princeton, New Jersey USA. His research and professional work is the result of over twenty-five years of practice – resulting in a portfolio including a wide variety of project types – architecture, urban design, historic preservation, exhibitions, furniture, and the organization of national and international design competitions. He is the recipient of first awards for several international architectural and urban design competitions, including the Indira Gandhi National Centre for the Arts (New Delhi, India). More recently he participated in the design of one of five proposals for an Olympic Village as part of New York City's bid for the 2012 Olympic Games, the Great Falls Park Design Competition, and the Hoboken 9/11 Memorial Competition. He has been awarded numerous international design commendations. Lerner's work has been published in numerous architectural journals and has been exhibited at the National Building Museum, the Institute of Contemporary Art in London, and MoMA.

1.

To get to Andrew Bromberg's office, you have to undergo a very Asian experience. Take a subway to Quarry Bay, arrive at the bottom of an older building on a street with stores packed close together, cross an elevated walkway and walk into an air-conditioned maze of corridors that cut through the bases of a group of high-rise towers. Escalators negotiate rises and falls in floor levels, shops sprout out of the angled intersections of different structures, art blossoms on granite walls, and glimpses of older residential buildings reflect off the expanses of glass. Find your way to the right elevator bank, push the button to make the right conveyance appear, rise up to a high floor and find yourself in a world of white walls, curtains, receptionists poised over ledges and monitors beaming out the latest news. Walk into the design studio, and you find row after row of a polyglot collection of mainly very young architecture enthusiasts staring at screens while outside cargo ships make their slow way between the steep green hills from which needles of human habitation rise. This is Hong Kong, and this is the world in which Andrew Bromberg and his team work.

It is a world with certain important characteristics. First, it is, obviously, urban, but it is a city whose scale and intensity far exceed the ones for which, until very recently, traditional rules, theories and models existed. Second, it is a sprawling urbanism: not only out towards the periphery and into the landscape (Hong Kong and Shenzhen are already almost one city, and soon the whole Pearl River Delta will be one agglomeration), but also internally, as the traditional borders between functions, buildings and districts blur. The city no longer consists of objects that together create a much larger object, but of interpenetrating zones and forms whose intensities ebb and flow.

Third, the spaces most people inhabit in such cities are conditioned. This is literally true as much of the globe's most intense growth has occurred in zones with a hot climate, but also socially and certainly economically speaking. Your use of the city is dependent on your economic function, but also on how you are dressed and behave. The city's interiors are reserved for those who belong, and the sliding glass doors admit only those who have a proper place within. Those who do not belong roam the streets; outsiders even if they are in the city's core.

Fourth, the urban environments that have grown up in this manner necessitate dense and intense moments of use. At the core of the city is the computer screen, fed with an array of data; the store or restaurant, which are the end-point of often global distribution systems; the bedroom, nurtured and cocooned by myriad technologies; and the place of spectacle, where more technological and economic struggle produces moments of visual intensity. The containers for these controlled explosions are shrink-wrapped in cocoons as tight and cheap as the designers and developers can make them. They advertise themselves by appearing slick and minimal; as they are, while sporting the sort of inhuman, robotic appearance that can only come out of the same sort of systems which have precisely these characteristics.

Finally, this urban environment is generic in that it consists of elements that are present around the world. The competition for these things, whether they are goods or buildings, is intense, and marks the struggle between different urban areas to define themselves. While some of the largest and most successful cities, which have grown exponentially in the last few decades, are enlargements of existing megalopolises, most of them, from Hong Kong to Singapore to Dubai, are almost instant phenomena that have grown up out of what were, a century ago, small villages outside of the major areas of development. While this is true of every generation of cities produced by the industrial revolution, whether they be Manchester, Liverpool, the Ruhr area, Detroit, Cleveland, Los Angeles or Tokyo, the speed and scale of the expansion of this latest crop of urban centers, as well as their distance from traditional centers of growth, has been of a different order.

It is within this city, perhaps unrecognizable as such for those looking for the likes of New York or Chicago, let alone London or Paris, that Andrew Bromberg works. He sees his task as contributing towards the growth and success of these cities, while delivering an efficient package that is still recognizable as an architectural product. To do this, he must use the logic of the technology, global culture and sprawling form that has produced the urban fields in which he operates.

2.

As I noted above, the combination of conditioned intensity and sprawl is central to this environment. On the one hand, buildings are increasingly defined by the need to create as efficient an environment as possible. On the other hand, they appear not only in a physically dispersed space, but also as nodes within networks of transportation and data dispersal and thus are, in a sense, three-dimensional storage and retrieval systems. The question, then, is how they should appear. What contribution can architecture make to an almost automatic process of condensation and so reduce the anonymity of such containers?

On top of these two questions, an architect such as Andrew Bromberg, who is based in Hong Kong and whose work appears mainly in the "new" cities that have arisen out of these forces, has to figure out whether he can find an identity or sense of place in these sprawling collections of nodes which seem to be the same everywhere. What imagery can he draw on, what will make the products his team creates distinctive and saleable, while also responding to whatever traditions, specificities or futures he might be able to draw on in the locations for which he designs?

If we look at the first of these conditions separately, we might notice that what we think of as architecture is hard to find. First, creating an efficient space means maximizing the amount of square footage of a quality that is safe and usable with the minimum amount of capital investment. There are, quite simply, formulas for this. On top of the traditional calculations of floor area to core ratios, come safety regulations, and bubble diagrams. Architects these days must contend with software that tells them how to maximize area and minimize material use, not to mention the calculations that developers use before they even hire a designer. Floor and even whole building configurations become standardized, their variations predetermined by a meta-calculation of relations between all of the financial and contextual formulas to which they must respond. Towards the end of the process, value engineers and other cost cutters tend to leech anything to which a use value cannot be assigned out of the design.

The only thing saving buildings from complete and interchangeable anonymity is that fact that developers in particular are often driven as much by ego and risk-assumption as they are by rational considerations. Bromberg's clients, in particular, are quite often entrepreneurs, rather than the sort of anonymous corporations that today dominate more saturated markets. They believe that they can find value where others have not, and are often enough successful.

They also believe that they must create a "product" that is distinctive, both in terms of how it appears and what it delivers in terms of space and amenities. Architecture thus becomes a kind of validation of place on the one hand, and a clever way of creating recognizable products on the other.

In terms of building in sprawl, developers must thus identify the location for the next node. This used to be a question of building near ports, the entrance to mountain passes, river crossings, or major intersections of natural travel routes. Then it was a question of looking for major highway interchanges, the presence of flat land suitable for development, balancing distances between previous developments, shifting demographics, and even such arcane issues as the presence of major power sources or golf courses. Now, optimal locations are even more difficult to ascertain, especially in the new cities of Asia and the Middle East. What makes the issue even more difficult is that sites are quite often designated by governments. This has been true in Hong Kong for many decades, and is also the case in Singapore. In cities such as Dubai, the rulers let a few firms compete against each other, but only in zones they have assigned. It is within such areas that sub-developers must find ways of distinguishing their product without any natural or man-made references. In rare cases, the overall developer needs a strategy like Emaar's production of the ridiculously inefficient, but highly noticeable, Burj Khalifa.

Bromberg's 2005 design for the Boulevard Plaza next to the Burj Khalifa is in this case more typical, as it involves a pair of buildings whose height and placement are the result of overall development considerations (the twin towers are part of a build-up towards the central exclamation point, and also serve as one of the circular development's gateways). Given this starting point, the buildings must have enough character for the developer to market them with some conviction and success.

The placement of such buildings in what is – at least from the developer's perspective – a tabula rasa, means that their function must also be interchangeable. Why is one building a condominium, a hotel, or a set of rental apartments? Or why is it an office building, either for headquarters or back-office support? Could it even be some sort of storage facility for data or goods? The possibilities are in some cases completely open, and the function an architect assigns to a given plot depends on a combination of market analysis and guess-work.

At the intersection of these concerns lies the fact that such speculative structures have to be part of an overall picture of dynamic development. The proliferation of Free Trade Centers in the 1980s started this trend: governments designated specific zones where nodes within global sprawl would be placed, and these areas had to serve business people with a variety of structures, including not only office buildings and storage areas, but also hotels, longer-term residences, shopping, restaurants, and even recreation. All of these pieces had to be related and connected. This was also true for newly designated urban areas such as Canary Wharf in London or the various planned developments around the Bay in Tokyo.

In such a situation, which Hong Kong and Singapore again pioneered in the 1970s, a building is in essence a fragment of a whole, but that whole has no coherence other than its containment in a given site. Moreover, the buildings have to be recognizable as being part of the international network: they have to proclaim the fact that they are modern, efficient, conditioned, secure, and plugged into infrastructure. Collectively, they have to look like a node. They also have to contain the sort of spaces that the people who control (through demand or development) such facilities, recognize. Not only do the office floors and hotel rooms have to be standard, so that in the middle of the night the jet-lagged traveler knows where the bathroom is, but there also has to be a food court, swimming pool and a branch of a well-known purveyor of suits or shirts.

Thus the architecture is, again, to a large degree pre-determined, and it is no coincidence that most such developments are designed by a relatively small collection of "alphabet soup" firms (companies whose name is made up of the initials of the original or current partners). It is only in smaller, local developments that other designers have a chance to obtain commissions, and some deviations in function or character are possible. In most cases, however, the locals are trying to look and act exactly like their international models. All this, by the way, comes without mentioning the monocultures of mass housing developments that make up the anonymous meat of much sprawl, whether they be suburban homes in the United States or the apartment slabs of Asia. These developments feature, quite simply, no architecture whatsoever. There is only the environmentally and socially unsustainable production of dreary space.

The one place where the nature and thus the character of new construction is not either completely automatic or generic, is in the creation of the infrastructure that ties all these nodes together. Airports and high-speed train stations have become the locations for the most heroic and monumental architecture of the early 21st century, eclipsing government or business headquarters, as well as cultural institutions. This is where identity is set and where money must be spent on something more difficult to define than work, living or even play, namely the gathering, waiting and entertaining of large groups of people. These nodes become celebrations of the very nature of sprawl.

A subcategory of such nodes consists of attractors that do not just facilitate movement, but act as a kind of counterpoint to all that to and fro, while also giving locations an image to go with the node. These include the new display centers, such as multiplex cinemas, concert arenas, theaters, sports venues, and the new breed of mega-churches. Each of these pregnant volumes, only filled part of the day, or sometimes part of the year, serve as visual anchors within sprawl, and generate a host of ancillary activities and thus structures around them. They are fundamentally different from previous entertainment venues in that they integrate such functions more and more into their actual structures. In that manner, they are more like medieval churches, with houses built into their flanks and commerce occurring within their side aisles.

What is most remarkable is that these new gathering spots have as little connection to their place as any of the new skyscrapers that serve as beacons, the masses of residential and office development, or the shopping malls which form the backdrop and the catchment areas for such exceptions. As a result, there is a fundamental disconnection between form and content. These structures are speculative in the most fundamental sense of the word, built in the hope of attracting, however fleetingly, inhabitants to sleep, work, or recreate within them. They do not come out of a community, nor do they, in any concrete sense, create one. They only make a temporary gathering place for a particular attraction that will be gone in a moment.

Community, then, exists in a kind of limbo state, in which everything is the same, and everything is movement. If meaning, coherence, or even mere persistence appear, it is as if by chance. These new attractor cores are also symbols of the world they serve. They create a false and ephemeral sense of belonging. What remains instead, more than anything else, is what humans can (so far) not control: the geography and climate that frame distant vistas, determine the vegetation decorating the fringes of these structures, create fissures within the fabric in the form of mountains or rivers, and in general remind one that they are still in a particular place with a specific, though often suppressed, reality.

3.

This, then, is the landscape within which an architect such as Andrew Bromberg works. It is one of sprawl, with a coherence that is fleeting, forms that are generic, filled with conditioned spaces and yet unmistakably urban in its density, and haunted by a specificity of place. It is a lot like where he works physically. In the decade that Bromberg has devoted to this space, he has tried to develop methods to make a meaningful architecture out of just such a situation.

To do so means, first respecting the rules of engagement. Bromberg prides himself on his ability to deliver office buildings, residential towers and now infrastructural nodes that are as efficient as anything that exists in the cities, such as Hong Kong, Dubai, and Singapore, in which he works. As a result, each of his buildings balance an experiential pursuit with a tightly packed container of conditioned space whose form is defined as much by international regulations (from standardized building codes to the formulas developers use to determine optimal floor area ratios, occupancy loads, and costs) as it is by the whims of any designer.

Bromberg's response has been to stretch, twist, mix up, and deform the elements he knows must be his building blocks in order to rearrange or transform what are otherwise standardized parts. In trying to escape from the confines of the parameters within his work, he uses his own design skills, coming up with strong forms. He then utilizes the same technology of standardization, which is in the main the result of computer aided design and construction programs, to further develop these designs. In this, his technique is fundamentally different from that of those architects who either mainly concentrate on creating exception structures such as cultural institutions, or who see their task as adding something different to the structure – an unusual skin, a cloud of ancillary program, or a non-functional structure. Instead, his work has more in common with the manner in which the makers of such standardized buildings, themselves often multi-nationally operating firms of a large size, attempt to distinguish their products. This in itself is not that surprising, as Bromberg directs a small studio that exists within the much larger Aedas design firm. Yet his ambitions are to be able to manipulate his conditions in a way that will enable him to achieve the same

sort of startling results as some of his more exception-elaborating peers, such as Zaha Hadid, Asymptote, or Jean Nouvel.

Some of Bromberg's most impressive and innovative designs are, in fact, exceptional. As a result, some of them remain speculative, as in the Arabian Performance Venue he designed in 2006 for Dubai Creek. Here the whole structure resembles a flower unfolding over the desert, its curves so daring and its engineering so extreme that one might wonder whether it could actually be built. If one looks more closely at the design, however, there is a logic to it: the main performance hall blossoms from a stem that serves not only as support, but also as a lift for the scenery, while the petals surrounding this curved block house offices and provide shade. A large forecourt, raised off the ground to catch breezes and take advantage of the same shade as the petals, could be used to seat an audience during open air performances. It is not practical, but it is logical, and the references to desert blooms, as well as the acknowledgment of thermal conditions, would make this building a true icon for the place.

One gets the sense that such schemes provide Bromberg with opportunities for research and development, in the same manner that cultural icons play symbolic rather than functional roles in these global urban nodes. Similar approaches reappear in the proposed mixed used project in Jeddah (Towers of Arabia, 2009), where they become more believable as towers that curve in towards each other before reaching up thousands of feet into the sky. Bromberg claims local imagery (the Arabian arch) and practical considerations (each of the towers could be developed separately), guided him in the design but this remains an extreme product of his imagination.

These ambitions, however, reappear in structures that can and will exist, such as Dubai Marina's Pentominium Towers and the Empire Towers in The Shams of Abu Dhabi (both 2006), in the Marina district of Dubai. The curves of Empire Tower bundle together, melding into a structure whose slenderness and deformation stretches what appears to be economically feasible or efficient in order to produce a slightly extreme result (larger apartments stacked up on a small site) within an area in which it is difficult for the developer to support such gestures. In the interesting hybrid of the Corporate Towers, designed for Bangkok (2006), the curves would have stood in a composition of three towers, as in the Jeddah project. Similar forms curve to the ground to become the roof of the West Kowloon Terminus, currently under construction in Hong Kong.

It would seem that Bromberg has hit on a fruitful strategy for working in the conditions with which he is presented: a delamination of constituent constructional and mass elements, which he then streamlines to create forms that have a smoother and at the same time less monolithic appearance than one might otherwise expect. He and his team can manipulate these curves and swerves to fit or bring out what they see as the essential properties of a site, to create a bulge for a particular programmatic density, to highlight what they think is an important program element, to provide – in their delamination – extra corners or balconies, to accommodate or accentuate structure, or to otherwise twist the buildings into something out of the ordinary, without affecting the fundamental logic under which they are constructed.

In larger-scale projects, such as the master plan for Xian (un-built, 2005), or the various schemes for Moscow (currently on hold , as is the case with the majority of projects in Moscow with the current recession), these curves become completely independent objects. Bromberg strews them around the landscape to accentuate or bring out its characteristics, or to respond to specific traits, such as the railroad tracks on the site in Xian or to provide views in the Aerostar project. Their massing then adapts to their particular position, both within the development and in relation to climatic or geographic cues. They can become higher or lower, often within the same curve, can turn towards the sun or away from the wind, and can accentuate views in certain directions. By controlling these relationships, Bromberg can also create an overall coherence to the grouping, as if they were all drops of the same stream, distilled, and congealed into apartment buildings or office blocks.

The most monumental of these exercises, the Asia Asia Hotel, planned for Dubai in 2008, would have been a kilometer-long, undulating bundle of such curves, so large as to be an artificial landscape form in its own right. It recalled the dunes that once made up this landscape, while also recalling the dreams modernist architects once had of bringing all human habitation together into mega-structures.

Not all of his forms, however, are smooth. Bromberg has a fondness for large buildings that appear as shards or fragments, their edges cut off as if by a divine razor blade, jutting from the edges of harbors or sites. The Khor Dubai Wharfage (2005), a row of three office buildings by the side of Dubai Creek, is probably the best example of this technique. The buildings would have stood like abstract pieces of sculpture, each gesturing to the other and recalling the cranes on marine loading docks. The aim here appears to have been to make something memorable and distinct, again connected to the site through evocative imagery, but also removing itself into a realm that would have been aggressively and self confidently new.

When such schemes enter the realm of the buildable, the gestures become, in my opinion, a bit too tame to be truly effective, being more like a superficial skin-covering and slight adaptation of type than a true rethinking of what is possible. Such is the case with the Russian projects, but also the U-Bora Tower, currently under construction in Dubai. Though the form is elegant enough; it is clearly a rationalized version of one of the three Khor Dubai structures, it has no resonance, and is not aggressive enough to be truly distinctive. As Bromberg has recently developed new parametric modeling tools within his studio, however, and continues to develop his elements and strategies, one hopes that he will be able to push his forms closer to his original intentions in future buildings.

The strongest redesign of standardized types that Bromberg has proposed is a rearranging of components into literal stacks, held in place by cores that serve as both visual and structural stabilizers. Here, the ideal prototype is the Media Tower, again for Dubai (2007), while the realized example (flipped on its side), is the convention center building and hotel currently under construction in Pazhou.

The Media Tower is a product of impeccable logic, namely that Bromberg decided it would be more rational to give each of the recording and performance studios that were central to the program their own box, and then to pile these up on top of each other. Each studio appears independently, and the whole is an extremely efficient use of the ground space. The composition is masterful, balanced between off-kilter instability and the impression of a cubist collage turned into a skyscraper.

The Convention Center has no such special program. Its base is, in fact, a completely generic volume: an extreme example of the conditioned anonymity global sprawl produces. Convention centers have to be big, open boxes that can be filled with traveling salespeople and goods for limited periods of time and must be as flexible as possible. Bromberg left this box alone, turning it into a tightly skinned volume, though he did try to make it appear less massive by fracturing the ends. He then stacked two towers on top of the two blocks of the base. One is a hotel, while the other is intended as offices. Both perch at the edge of the base box and the site, preserving the aggressive stance of some of Bromberg's prow designs. Each also consists of a stack of tubes. Unlike in the delaminations, the tubes here are straight, and Bromberg clearly delineates each piece. The space in between becomes a public atrium, and their cut-off, unfinished appearance makes it look exactly what it is; a fragment of a global system made concrete in one arbitrarily selected place.

With the swerves, curves, delaminations, stacks and drops, Bromberg has reached the limits of what is possible within the world of office and residential structures. Like most self-respecting architects, he aspires to do more than this, and it is not surprising that he has turned recently to the creation of iconic nodes within the sprawl. The two commissions he has won show how he hopes to take his techniques of curving away from and pulling apart generic elements into the realm of a more symbolic and anchoring architecture.

The West Kowloon Terminus is by far the largest of these commissions, and certainly the most important in Bromberg's still short career. The station's immense size hides, like an iceberg, mainly underground, leaving the structure and entrance visible above grade. Bromberg's original design was a clear and simple one: bundles would trace the line of the tracks, twist and curve up and out, rotating upwards to become separate office or residential towers and to hold the trusses reaching up over the main public halls. The whole would be a landscraper with the prowing entrance building, being completely accessible from above and filled with vegetation, rising up out of a park covered by bulbous canopies recalling Bromberg's Dubai Performance Center design and gesturing to the skyscrapers of Hong Kong Central.

After Bromberg and his team won the competition, they had to develop the project in a manner that would accommodate the many acts of standardization that are part and parcel of the design process, especially for such a large public tender. The towers disappeared from their immediate purview and the base became constrained by the necessity of making room for a regular grid of columns to support towers possibly designed by others. In the interior, many spaces became full of functions, and every possible surface will probably be given over to advertising. The part of Bromberg's vision that will undoubtedly remain is the singular gesture of a leaping bundle of structural beams arching over a very large public hall whose space will lead one down past ticket offices, security gates and other functions, or upwards, all the while maintaining the excitement of the sheer scale of this piece of infrastructure.

In Singapore, Bromberg is designing an important civic mixed-use development that will function as a 5000 seat theater but will also be available for rental to one of the project's owners as a religious gathering point for their congregation. Here, he has condensed his prows into a single object wearing a cowl of translucent okalux panels. The skin is bent, fractured, and extrudes out, forming a loose fit over the main auditorium and sheltering secondary gathering spaces within its folds. The objects float, like many of Bromberg's objects, off the ground, and he has kept its shopping mall base as open as possible, allowing thin sheets of glass to drape down from the main object and angled columns to shoot up overhead. The Center is both dense and open, tracing the movement and gathering of people in the fluid way appropriate to the landscape of sprawl.

4.

Thus Bromberg seems to be seeking ways to apply his curves and swerves, his stacks and his blocks, his prows and his angled objects, to the places where people gather. He will, no doubt, continue to create large objects in which people will work and live, and improve his ability to shape them – within the constraints of the economic, social, and cultural system in which he works. It seems as if he will focus, however, on the creation of moments where formal deformation is not just a deviation from a norm, but a celebration of the state of time and space within the world of sprawl. He will create objects that tend towards dissolution while maintaining recognizable form, that want to sprawl, while remaining icons, that move away from the familiar, but draw us into their folds.

The approaches that Bromberg has developed should be able to maintain their coherence and they will have to if he continues to work for the clients that now employ him. He may continue to be constrained by the realities of financial limits and not always controllable execution. Or they may cut loose and become fragments, snakes slithering through sprawl and rising up above our current skyscrapers, artificial stones stuck into the smooth flows in order to stop and make us think, intimations of past forms hovering on the facades of sleek corporate packages, or moments of structural intensity that celebrate our ability to make.

As you sit and wait for Andrew Bromberg to appear from the rows of desks where he works with his team, you find yourself in a conditioned cocoon, nestled into large chairs while those televisions offer news, music videos and sports from around the world. Below, a real Hong Kong is visible, in all of its complexity, and yet you are not completely sure of where you are in the labyrinth the latest generation has etched onto that place. You are in limbo, fed by technology, waiting for architecture to somehow make sense of all this, perhaps if only for a moment, through fragments or gestures. Certainly this is what Andrew Bromberg, sitting in the middle of it all, is employing his considerable knowledge and skills to do.

aaron betsky is the Director of the Cincinnati Art Museum. Previously, he was Director of the Netherlands Architecture Institute (2001-2006) and Curator of Architecture and Design at the San Francisco Museum of Modern Art (1995-2001). In 2008, he directed the 11th International Architecture Biennale Venice. Mr. Betsky is the author of over a dozen books including *False Flat: Why Dutch Design Is so Good*, *Landscrapers*, and *Architecture Must Burn*. He is currently preparing a volume on modernism and a collection of his essays. He writes regularly for both lay and professional publications, and lectures on art, architecture and design. Mr. Betsky lives in Cincinnati with his partner, the artist Peter Christian Haberkorn.

media tower, 2006, dubai, uae

shadow boxing

2

3

"The real voyage of discovery consists not in seeking new landscapes, but in having new eyes."
Marcel Proust

For as long as anyone can recall, pilgrimages have been rites of passage for architects. Le Corbusier's travels in Italy, the Balkans, Greece and Asia Minor between 1907 and 1911 crystallized the idea of the Grand Tour for subsequent generations, but the tradition is as old as architecture itself. Initially though, a pilgrimage was not a privilege undertaken for the sake of broadening one's architectural horizons, but a necessity one endured to learn how it is possible for buildings to become what they are.

4

5

6

7

8

9

10

13

14

15

16

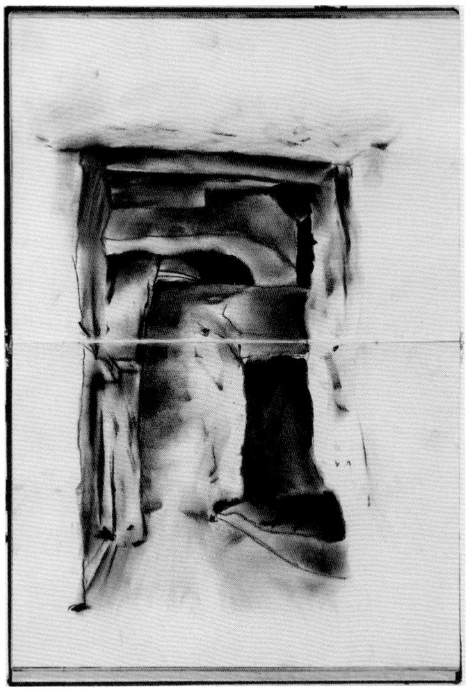

17

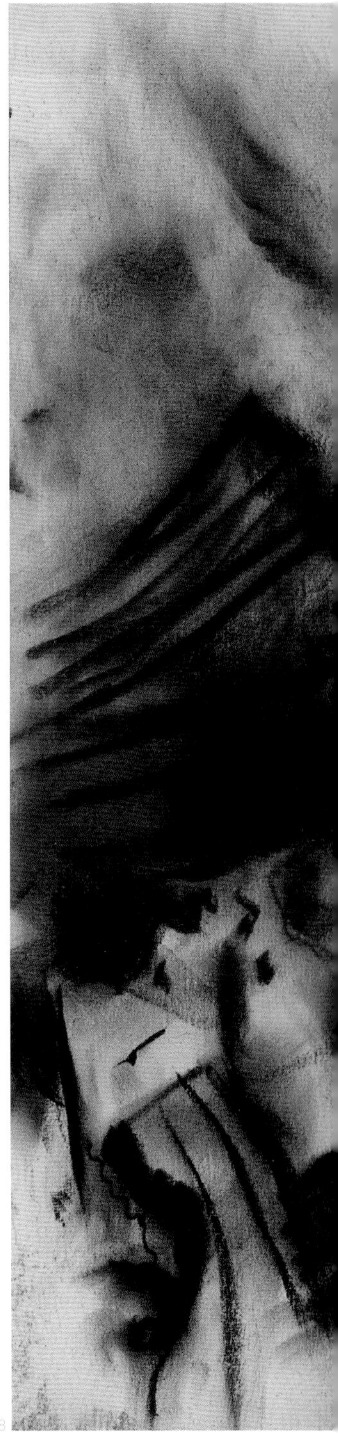

18

20

21

For example, we understand from Vasari that Michelangelo's father beat him for wanting to be an architect, thinking the profession unworthy of the family. Brunelleschi's father intended for him to go into Law. Instead he went to Rome with Donatello at the age of twenty-five to study architecture, selling a farm to provide funds. When these were depleted he took up gem-setting to maintain himself. Bramante was not able to visit Rome until the age of fifty, when he had saved enough to settle there solely to study. Falconetto spent twelve years studying ruins, living by working for other painters two to three days a week. He and the others, including Raphael, Alberti, Peruzzi and Fribolo, studied architecture by sketching buildings in the early mornings, before they left to fulfill their obligations as apprentices to various crafts and trades. [Falconetto] "... and to the end that each of us might have drawings of every work, we did not copy the same thing on the same day, but different ones, and when night came we copied each other's drawings for the purpose of saving time, and also to advance our studies; nor did we ever breakfast in the morning, except on what we ate while standing, and that very frugally." Brunelleschi's love for beautiful old things was so intense that on one occasion when he was told by Donatello of an antique marble vase at Cortona, he rushed there from Florence as he was, "... in his mantle, his hood, and his wooden shoes, without saying a word where he was going." [Cortona is seventy-two miles from Florence.]

The romantic notion of the Grand Tour usually connotes embarking on a sweeping tour of the great cities and monuments of Europe in one way or another. For the fortunate it was managed with luxe, calme et volupté, but for the less fortunate it often began with a knapsack, raw gumption and a hoped-for dose of luck. Either mode was and still is elixir for the architect's soul, remaining key to the development of the architect's ideas and projects for his or her lifetime.

22

23

24

25

28

29

30

31

32

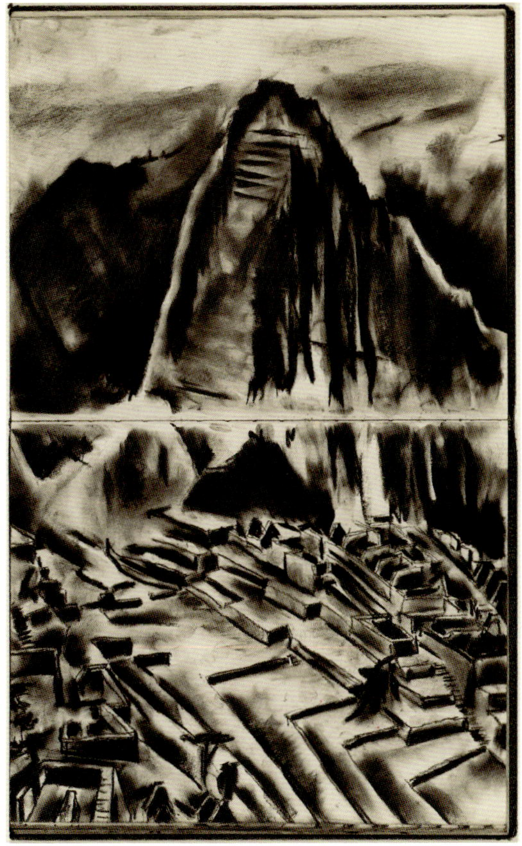

33

For all the romance associated with sojourns to Europe, there has always been a persistent stream of architectural pilgrims who ventured East as well as West. Frank Lloyd Wright and Antonin Raymond in Japan circa 1920 and Bruno Taut in 1933, also in Japan, come to mind. Although the 'twenties and 'thirties might not seem so long ago from a Eurocentric perspective, it is important to recall that the People's Republic of China was racked by civil and international war from 1927 until 1950, and even though Japan was heavily industrialized (and militarized) by 1920, it was successively at war with China, Russia and the Allied Forces from 1931 until 1945. Pilgrims who ventured to the East in the 'twenties and 'thirties were pilgrims indeed!

34

35

36

37

38

39

If travel today is more predictable than it used to be it can still be revelatory, especially for the adventurous. By any measure Andrew Bromberg has led a peripatetic and adventurous life, having traveled frequently to areas where luck and karma served him better than maps and itineraries ever could. Beginning in his late teens Andrew went on several tours of Europe, including Greece, Turkey and North Africa. During and after university he undertook extended tours 'elsewhere', to Singapore, India, Nepal, Vietnam, Peru, Myanmar, Thailand, Cambodia, Hong Kong, Brazil, Kuala Lumpur, Japan, Sydney, Mexico and, after re-locating to Hong Kong in 2000, to Korea, Macau, The Philippines, Portugal, Hungary, Russia, the UK, Kazakhstan, Poland, Belgium, China, the UAE, Oman, Lebanon, Egypt, Jordan, Norway and Finland. Certainly most of the later trips were related to business, but the excursions prior to Andrew's relocation to Hong Kong stemmed from Andrew's abiding interest in being directly engaged in the rhythm of vernacular peoples and cultures, especially those furthest from his own.

So what, you may fairly inquire, may we surmise is the takeaway from these adventures for an architect whose projects today are global, enormous and, for the most part, driven by relatively narrow development priorities? From conversations one can see that, despite the formal and very masculine vigor apparent in Andrew's projects, he designs with the pedestrians and inhabitants of the projects principally in mind, primarily

44

45

46

by weaving circuitous byways and pathways through the projects as extensively as possible, traversing layers and levels in hopes of offering experiences for users akin to micro-journeys in mega-structures. Though these gestures are inherently subordinate to the architectural superstructure, they are conceived as liberating and invigorating experiences in contrast to building programs that are frequently conventional and functionally mono-dimensional. One hopes that these may become dominant rather than subordinate gestures in forthcoming work. Then formal and kinesthetic vigor may embrace each other with reciprocal fervor!

Lastly, though apparent to a much lesser degree, is Andrew's hope that his large, primarily commercial projects can be indexed, to some degree, with the locales where they occur. This desire, which must be familiar to most international architects, is an almost impossible challenge when the projects themselves are meant by their developers to be typologically, functionally and symbolically nearly placeless. Regardless, there is always an attempt to find attributes of a project that resonate with attributes of the locale. [1000M Dubai tower!]. When Andrew's project types broaden to include cultural and institutional buildings that inherently have more content, so to speak, he will be challenged to make definitive connections between site, program and architectural concept that are largely not possible in the commercial genre he has mainly worked in up to this point of his career. Such projects are presently in Andrew's studio in Hong Kong. Once complete, they shall illustrate how adventure and aspiration, locale and ambition may finally tie the threads of a serendipitous, peripatetic life into a coherent, persuasive and inspiring body of work.

larry rouch (MArch Univ. of Washington, Seattle) established Larry Rouch Co. in Seattle after producing large commercial and public projects for other firms. The firm has designed notable residences and commercial and interior projects throughout the Western United States, including the 55,000 square foot San Francisco exhibition: "Toshimitsu Imai – Ka Cho Fu Getsu." Larry Rouch Company projects have been featured in publications including: *Architectural Record, Progressive Architecture, ID Annual Design Review, Interiors, Ottagono* (Italy) and *Worldspace Design* (Japan).Larry also has taught graduate design at the University of Washington and SCI-ARC, and has been a guest instructor or critic at Otis College of Art & Design, the University of British Columbia, Tulane University, Columbia University, California College of Arts and Crafts, Washington State University, the University of Idaho and the University of Oregon.

1 desert outside jaisalmer, india 1995
2,3,4 kalaw, myanmar 2000
5 hong kong 1998
6 mexico city 2000
7 hong kong 1988
8,10 inle lake, myanmar 2000
9,11 lago sandoval, peru 1998
12,42,47 varanasi, india 1995 1997
13 trujillo, peru 1998
14 rome, italy 2000
15 alghero, sardinia, italy 1993
16 segesta, sicily, italy 1993
17 atrani, italy 1993
18,48 outside amalfi, italy 1993
19 ubein bridge, amarapura, myanmar 2000
20, 23 amarapura, myanmar 2000
21 angkor, cambodia 2000
22 outside mandalay, myanmar 2000
24 outside kalaw, myanmar 2000
25 kalaw, myanmar 2000
26 hill tribe village above kalaw, myanmar 2000
27 yangon, myanmar 2000
28 guanajuato, mexico 2000
29 saigon, vietnam 1997
30 urubamba valley, peru 1998
31 bhaktapur, nepal 1995
32 moray, peru 1998
33 machu picchu, peru 1998
34 angkor thom, cambodia 2000
35 phnom phen, cambodia 2000
36 chiang mai, thailand 2000
37 jaipur, india 1995
38 salinas, peru 1998
39 lake titicaca, peru 1998
40,44,45 yangon, myanmar 2000
41 jaisalmer, india 1995
43 my son, Vietnam 1997
46 ravello, italy 1993

47

selected projects

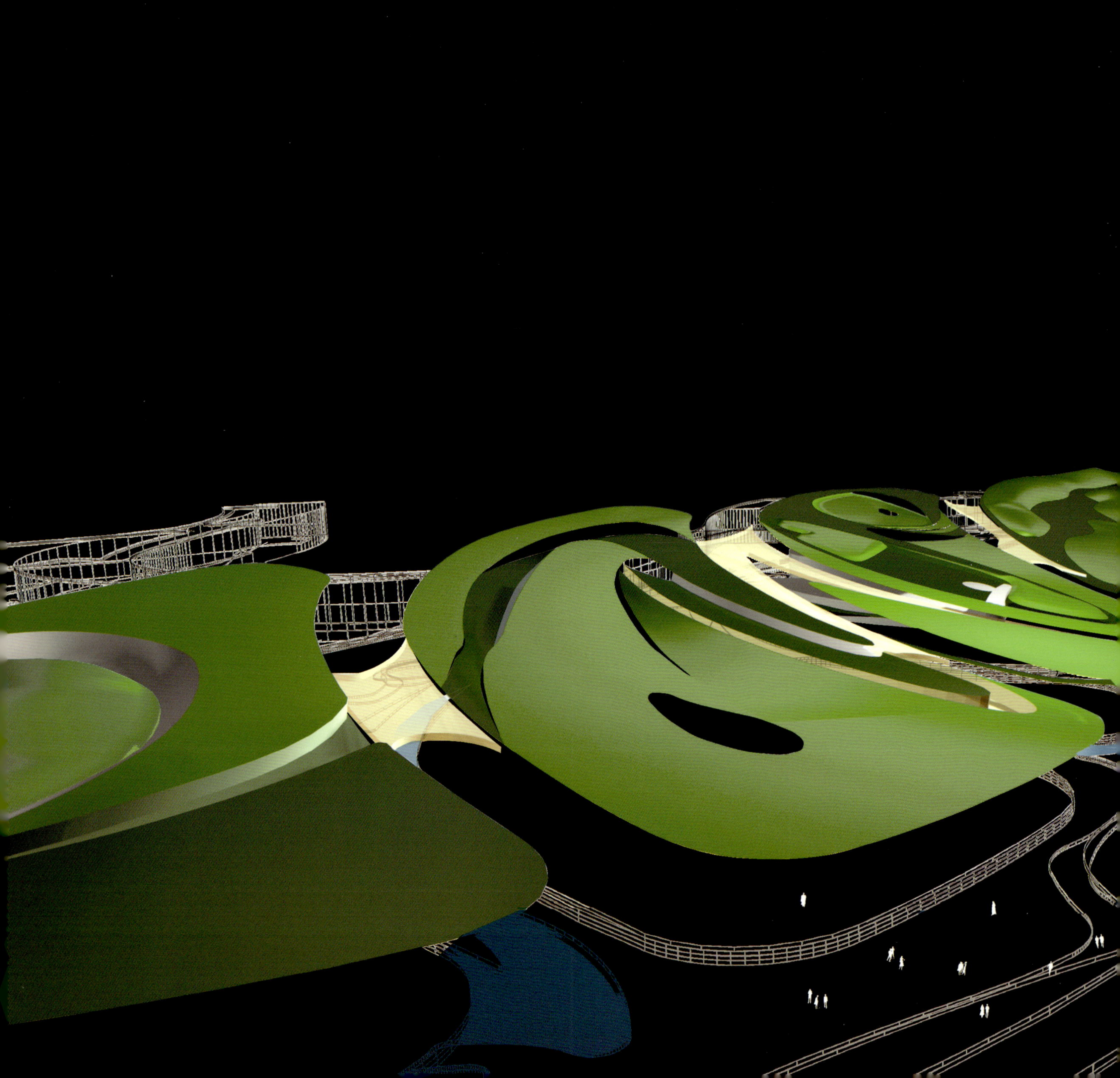

west kowloon cultural district

west kowloon cultural district

master plan

client: sunny development ltd.

location: hong kong, china

site location

size/scale

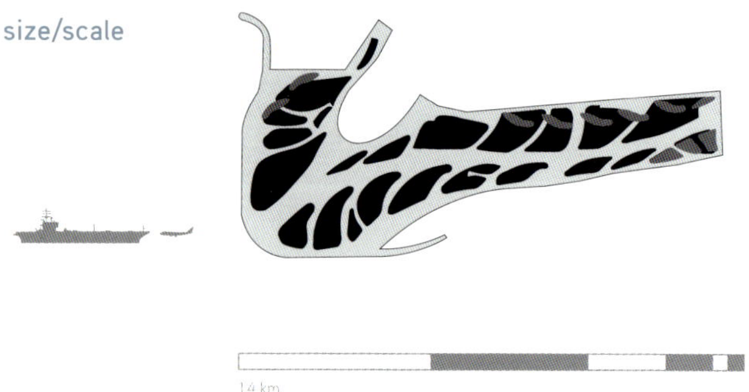

project description

The West Kowloon Cultural District will become Hong Kong's communal heart, bringing unparalleled life and energy to the urban waterfront. It will transform the city both culturally and economically: With this transformation will come a new identity that will reflect the vitality of a city's people, its history and its future. As a true city of the world, Hong Kong's strength, desire and vision will continue its role as the gateway to Asia.

description of the 'green space'

On one level this will be a cultural district. On another level it will be a 40-hectare park, physically threaded into the life of the city and the harbourside. This new, urban open space will be as large as the sum of all three of Hong Kong's existing city parks: Hong Kong Park, Victoria Park and Kowloon Park. It will be a new place in the urban landscape – one where people can play, discover, learn and explore. This is a park in the sky, an undulating landscape affording all who visit – whether by day or by night – amazing views of the harbour and Central District's glittering citadels.

The park grows like the coastline from the water, rising naturally at the southern end and growing over the facilities underneath toward the north. Spectacular canyons give the park a natural and dynamic relief. In the majestic openings of these canyons are the performing arts venues, and the theatres and museums where Hong Kong's cultural heart is going to make its home. Six piazzas grow from natural widenings in the canyon floors. Each has its unique style and grace, and each is a performing arts venue in its own right, with the lights, sound systems, seating and refreshments equipment to support performances. There are 90,000 square metres of these piazzas – enough to delight casual visitors...or the cultural pilgrim.

goals

To push high density urban tissue back to save all waterfront for public use.

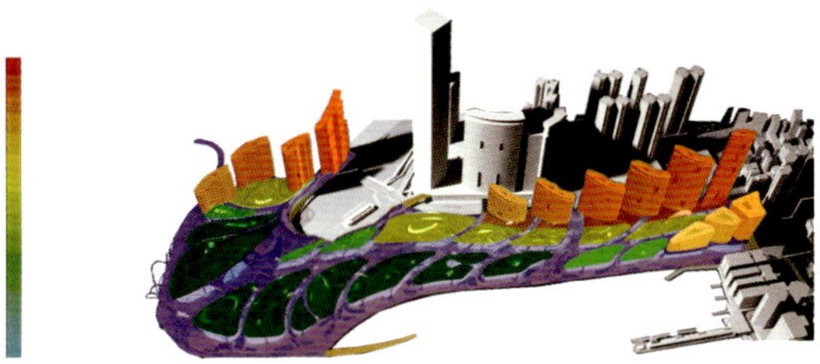

challenge

The canopy suspended above the whole park area.

play

To activate public space at night time.

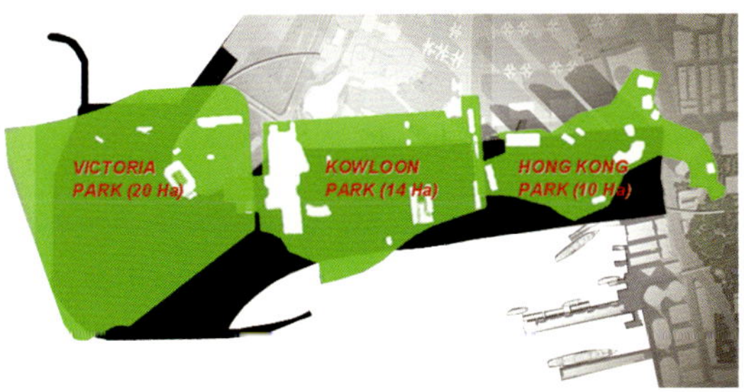

process

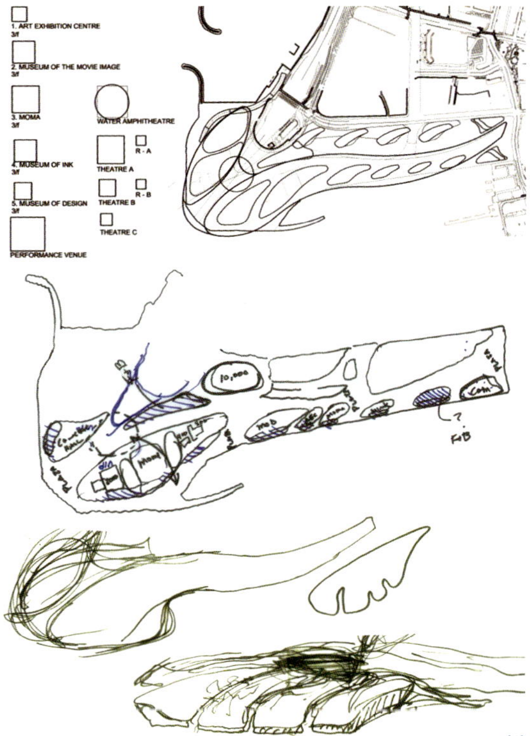

week1

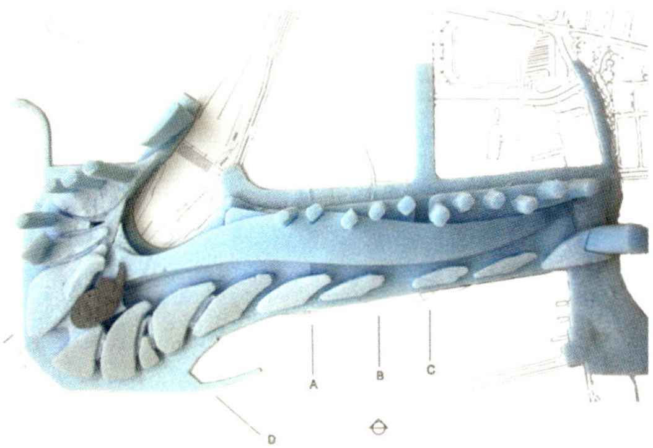

week2

usage

residential
829530 m2 8928987 sqf

hospitality
95650 m2 1029568 sqf

office
138458 m2 1490350 sqf

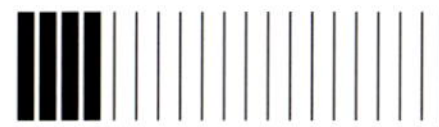

retail + f&b
171550 m2 1846549 sqf

landscape
400000 m24305564 sqf

art&culture/others
465930 m2 5015229sqf

total area: 1,731,871 m2
18,641,700 sqf

| = 50,000 m2 /538195 sqf

status

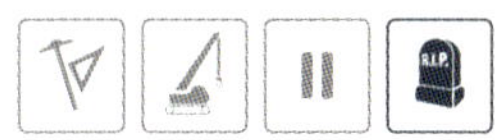

shortlisted 2005,
project re-tendered 2009

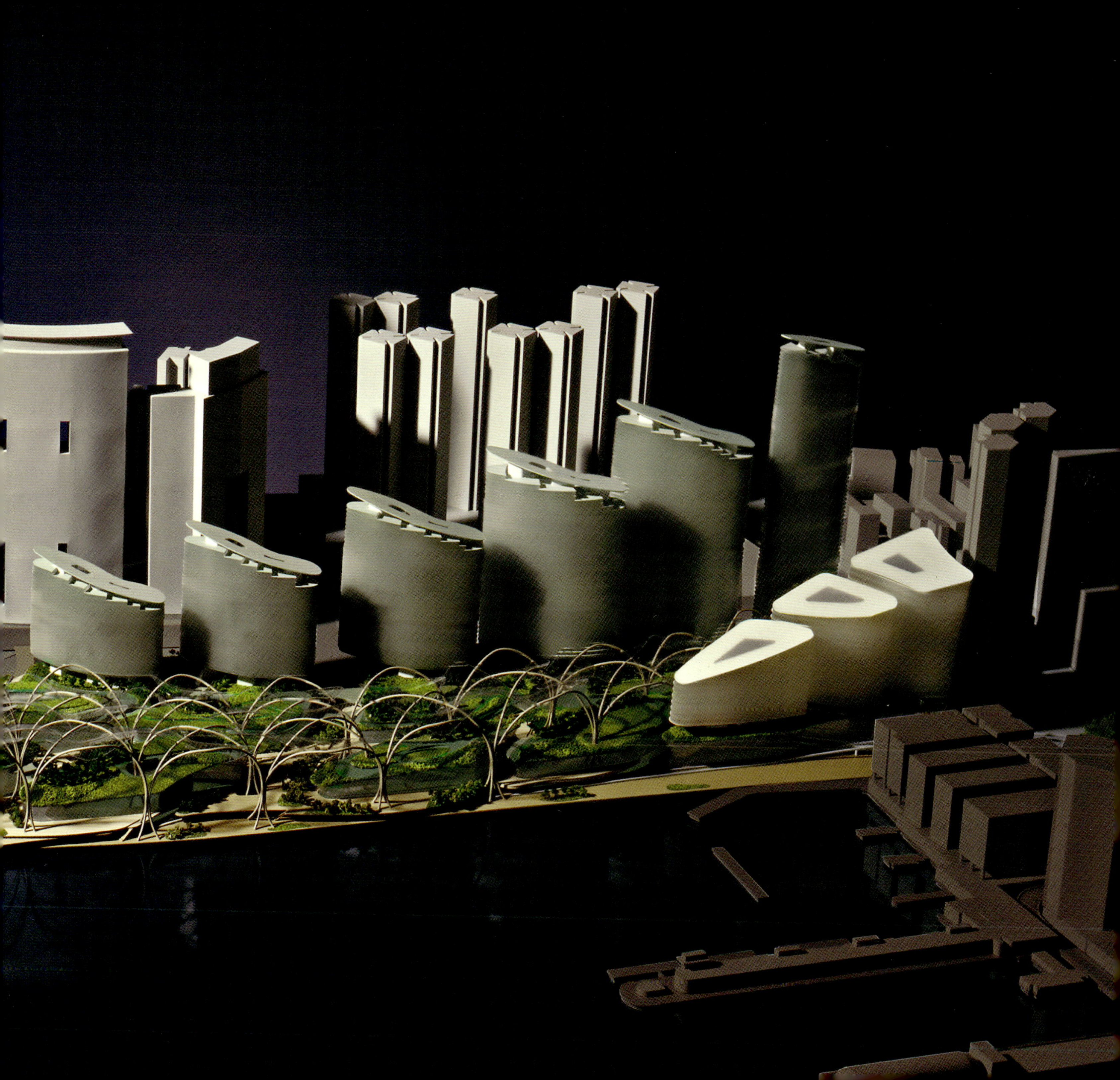

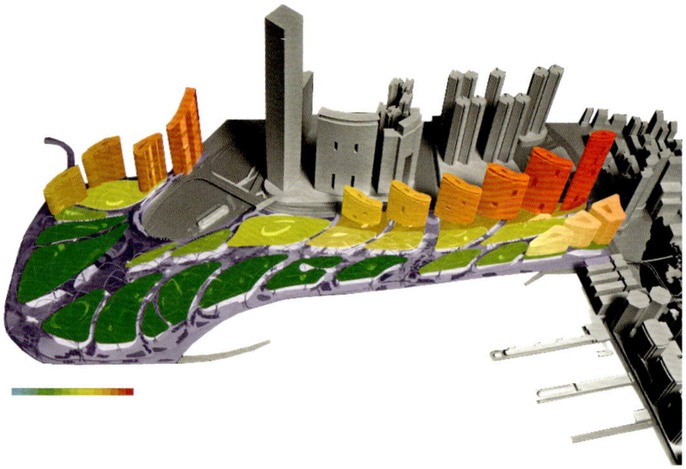

area density

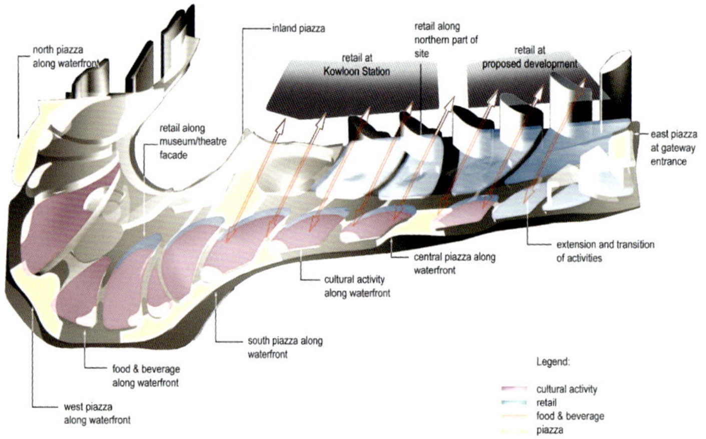

activity linkages

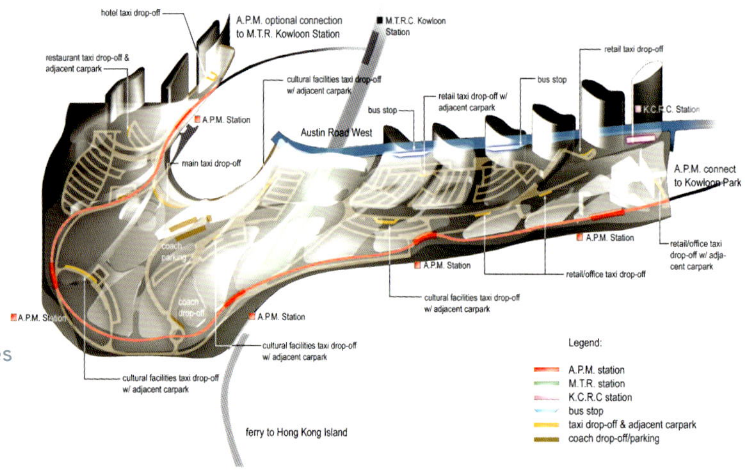

transportation linkages

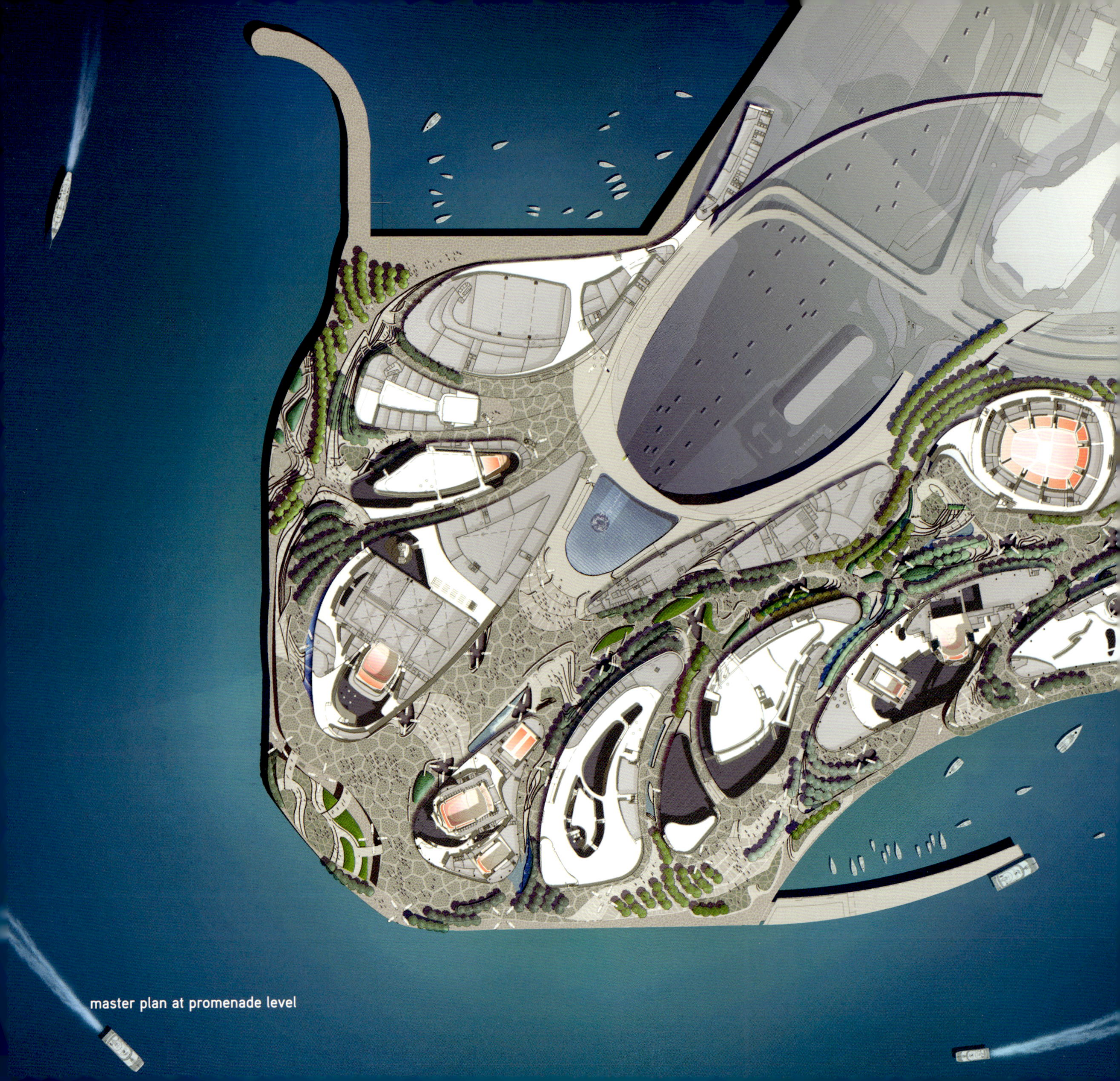

master plan at promenade level

introduction to the cultural assets

The organic building shapes emulate the rills and tidal pools created by natural erosion. The central promenade naturally organizes east to west movements whilst the canyons and valleys lead from piazza to piazza, and from waterfront walkways to the cultural caverns of the interior.

Within these caverns there will be museums and performance venues purposefully intermixed to feed off each other's specific, optimal time and operation periods. A concert hall and an education centre have been designed into the master plan as additional components.

cultural assets

The core performing arts cultural facilities will consist of:

- Theatre A (2000 seats);
- Theatre B (800 seats);
- Theatre C (400 seats);
- Performance Arena (10,000 seats);
- Water Amphitheatre (5,000 seats);
- Concert Hall (1,750 seats);
- Recital Hall (350 seats);
- Education and Resource Centre;
- Six performance-enabled piazzas.

The WKCD will contain four museums and an art exhibition centre:

- MOMCA–the Museum of Modern and Contemporary Art;
- MITS–the Moving Image and Technology Studios;
- MINK–the Museum of Modern Ink Painting;
- CLAD–the Centre for Living Arts and Design; and
- AEC–the Art Exhibition Centre.

The performing arts venues are distributed throughout the district intermingled with four museums and an Art Exhibition Center. There are a total of 6 principal venues: 3 theatres of 2000, 800 and 400 seats, as well as a 1750-seat state-of-the-art concert hall, 10,000 seat performance arena and the Water Amphitheatre. The large theatre and the concert hall, are the jewels of the performing arts complex. They sit on the prow of the headland, a symbolic gateway from the sea. The 2000 seat Theatre A will be used for dance and musical theatre. Classical and jazz music will be facilitated in the Concert Hall. Adjacent to the Concert Hall, to the east, are the MITS and the MOMCA; these are the two biggest museums.

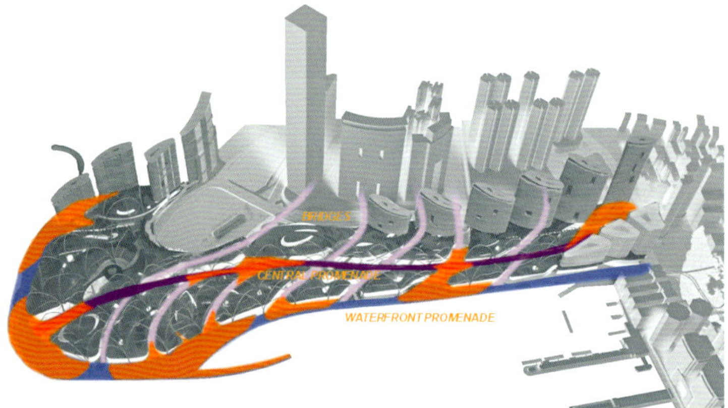

promenade level - open space/pedestrian circulation

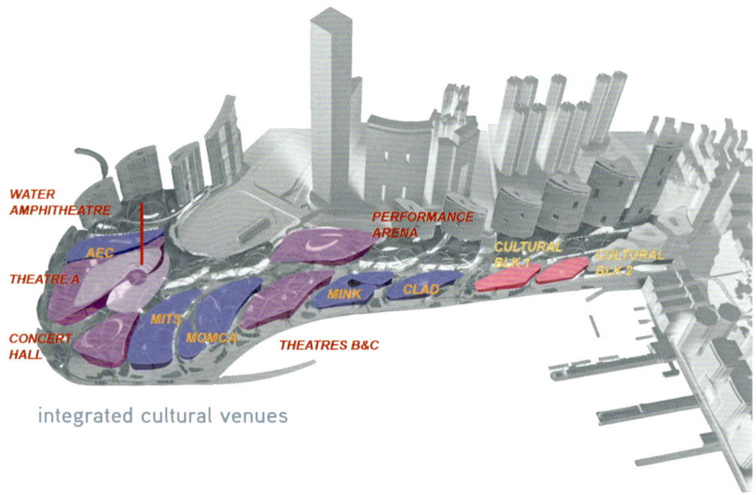

integrated cultural venues

commercial and retail "activators"

24-hour time cycle disposition

water amphitheatre

performance arena - central promenade

core arts and culture - waterfront

central promenade

All these theatres and museums cluster between the waterfront and the central promenades and have frontage to at least one major piazza. The Performance Arena was located deliberately to the north to benefit from a close proximity to the existing Kowloon Mass Transit Railway station for ease of access and egress.

the master plan: strategic planning

Powerful, iconic architectural forms rise up out of the central promenade, revealing the diverse cultural activities inside. Great care has been taken to ensure that the West Kowloon Cultural District will not become a localized cultural ghetto, but a genuine district, where the diversity of use creates activity that starts in the morning and spreads long into the night.

Activities have been added which would best extend the hours of use. More than 12 resident artistic companies will be given luxury purpose-designed facilities in the district, and these will bring with them the normal artistic activities – daytime activities of rehearsal and set, building and discussion – as well as the normal evening activities associated with many performing arts groups. The museums and other venues have been designed with great airy spaces in the foyers and halls and galleries. This will give them opportunities in the evenings and nights to host parties and receptions as well as large galas.

Even with the increase in the evening activities of the museums they still have primarily a daytime cycle of activity whilst the 140,000 square meters of performance venues would see their major excitement at night. Mixing the two types of venue into a single cultural cluster will create an energy that will extend far into the night.

other buildings and facilities

The landscape is formed into three areas – the north headland area of hotels, a conference centre and residential developments; the lively eastern area, a place for shops and homes, and the central cultural area itself.

Food and beverage outlets line the waterfront promenade, and are intermixed with the cultural venues. An automated rail transport system runs beneath the waterfront promenade, commanding its own views across the harbour. Five stations serve the five piazzas off the waterfront promenade and the line continues onwards to make a connection with the Kowloon MTR.

Reinforcing the vibrancy and diversity of this special place, there are four linked retail malls to the north of the central promenade and the central promenade itself becomes a kilometer-long pedestrianised shopping street with shops, restaurants and entertainment. The retail experience continues into all the venues as well with museum shops, restaurants, cafes, bars and venue-themed gift stores.

Momca. Museum Of Modern And Contemporary Arts
33,700 sqm

Mits. The Moving Image And Technology Studios
22,800 sqm

museums

art exhibition centre	11500 sqm
moving image and technology studios	22800 sqm
museum of modern ink painting	20700 sqm
centre of living arts & design	14000 sqm
museum of modern and contemporary art	33700 sqm

performance venues

theatre a	2000 pers
theatres b&c	1320 pers
concert hall	1750 pers
performance arena	10000 pers
water amphitheatre	5000 pers

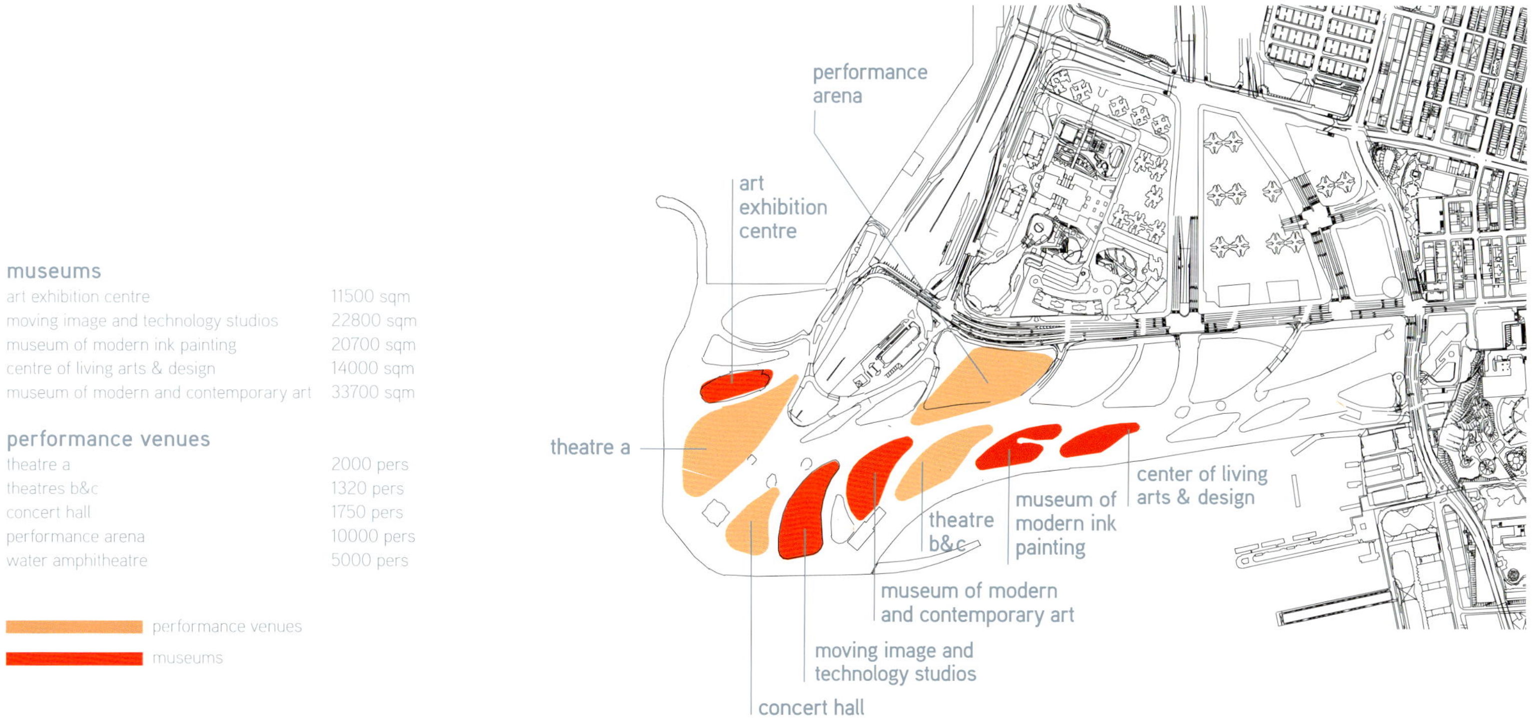

Clad. Centre Of Living Arts & Design
14,000 sqm

Theatre A. Art Exhibition Centre

master plan at park level

In addition to all this cultural and retail activity there will be 138,000 square metres of grade-A office space on the eastern edge of the project and 128,000 square metres of luxury hotel and conference space just off the northern piazza. There will also be 1,200,000 square metres of residential units designed to actively knit the West Kowloon Cultural District into the urban skyline.

the canopy

The pedestrian shopping area and the park are sheltered from the rain and weather by a unique and visionary canopy. This transparent canopy vaults high over the park, and above the streets and buildings. The canopy will provide both sun-protection, and rain-protection as well as helping to funnel cooling breezes off the ocean. This mighty 22-hectare construct will be the 8th wonder of the world and a magnificent icon for Hong Kong.

The canopy flows like waves on water. It rises up from the east toward the headland before dipping down as a symbolic gesture of greeting to those entering into Hong Kong's harbour. Covering over 58% of the development area, the canopy is structurally independent from the building below and intentionally designed to maximize its uses. Apart from its being a new icon for Hong Kong, it has great climatic benefits – the canopy will provide protection over the majority of piazzas, the pedestrian shopping street as well as a significant area of the waterfront promenades.

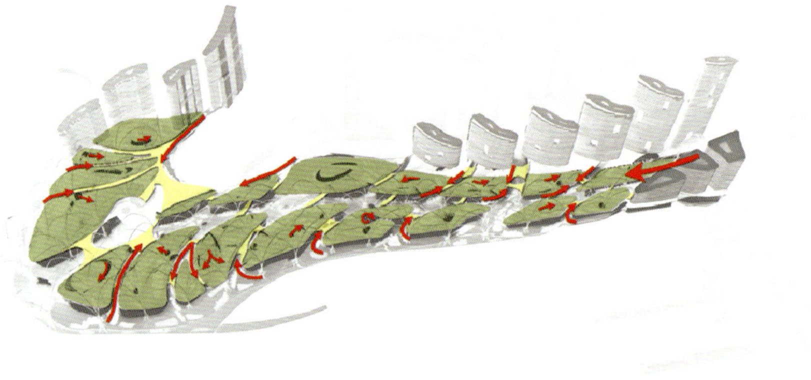

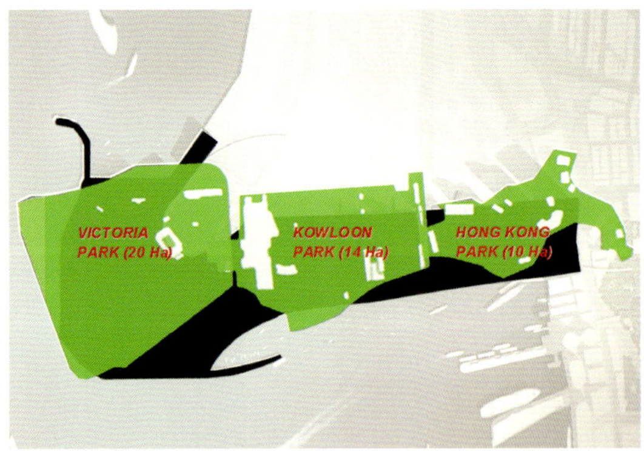

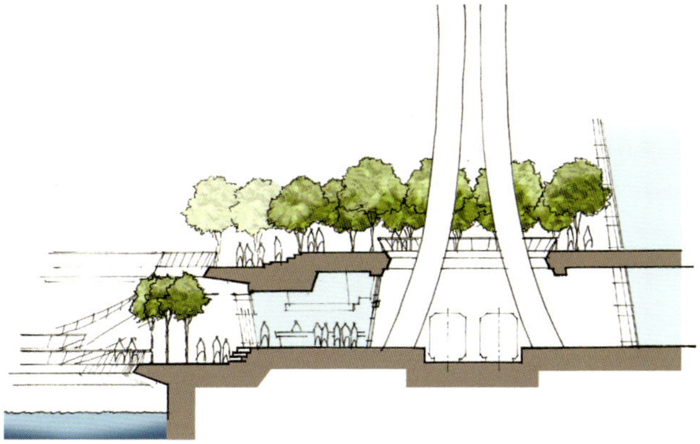
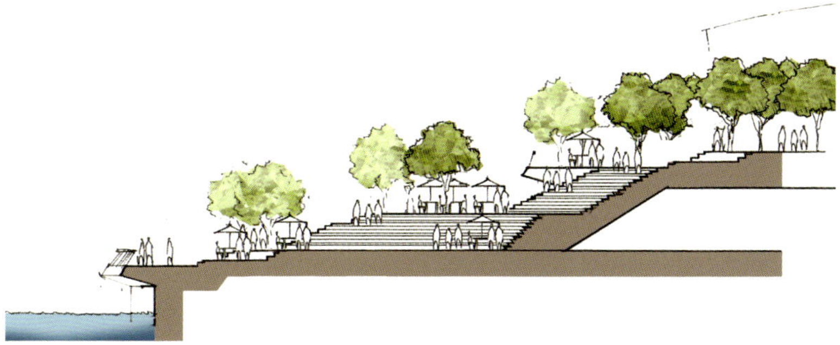

park in the sky

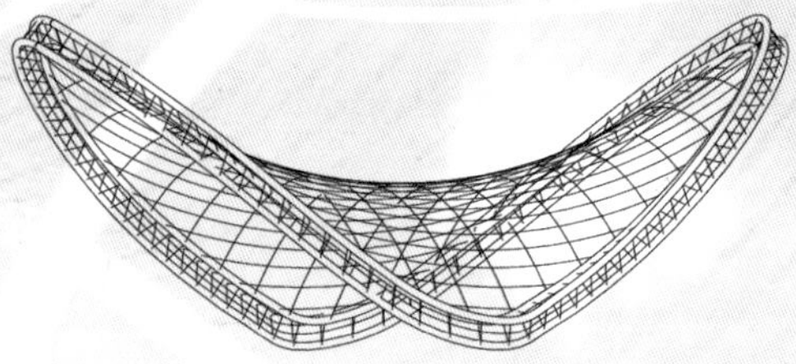

Side Elevation

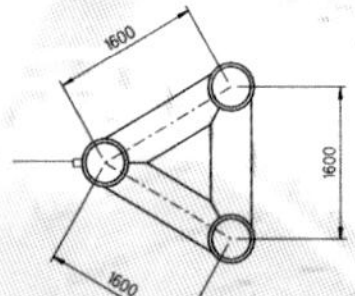

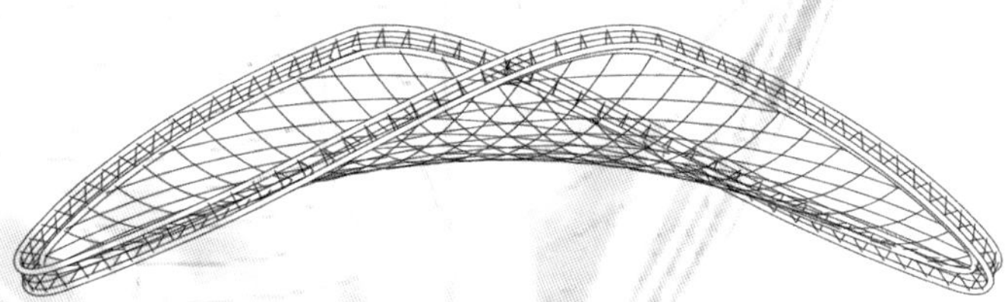

Front Elevation

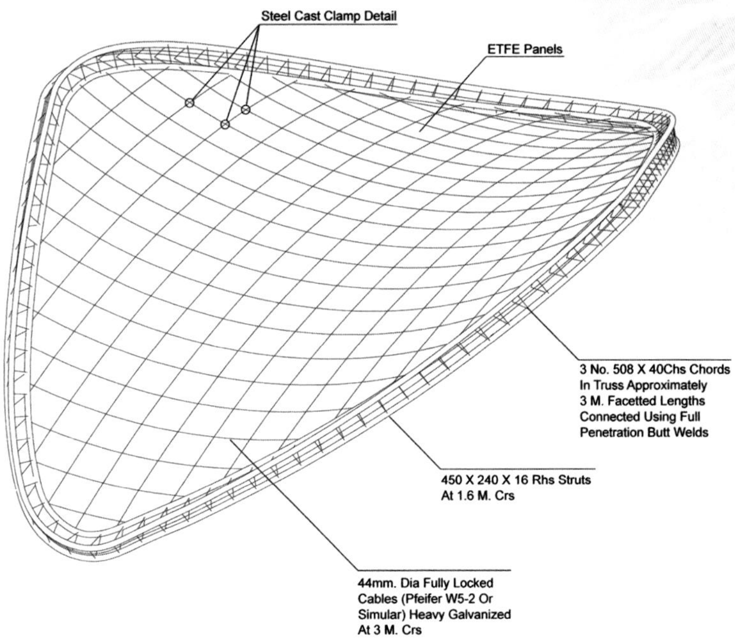

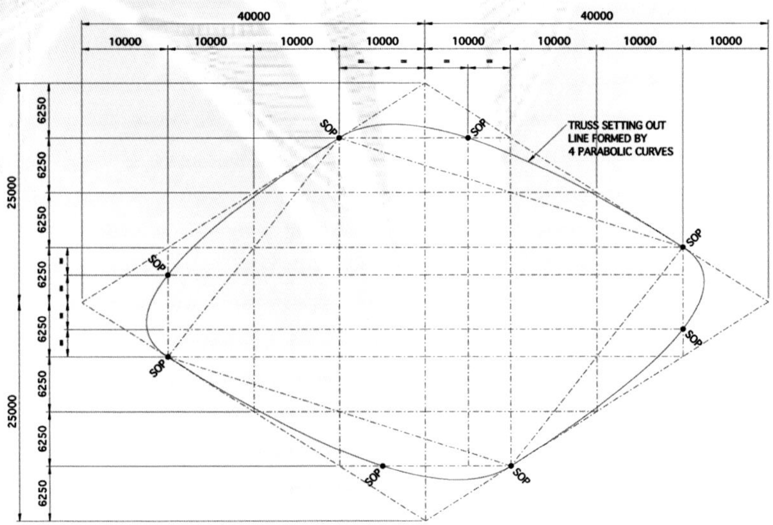

As one of the landmarks of the design, the canopy will be a new signature of Victoria Harbour. Together with the park in the sky, the canopy will provide continuity along the waterfront as it floats uninterrupted over the buildings and park it covers.

conclusion

The West Kowloon Cultural District will be a true 'Civic' setting which will present the pride of Hong Kong's people to the rest of the world. This is a project that will enable Hong Kong to rise up among the ranks of the great world cities. It becomes an integration of 'world class' cultural facilities along with necessary supporting and complementary programs. The district will be one of energy and vibrancy – a place for cultural growth and learning. As the landscape, of the urban park permeates throughout all levels of the senses, a new language for experiencing city fabric is created. This new public realm empowers and elevates one to new heights, allowing for both discovery and renewal.

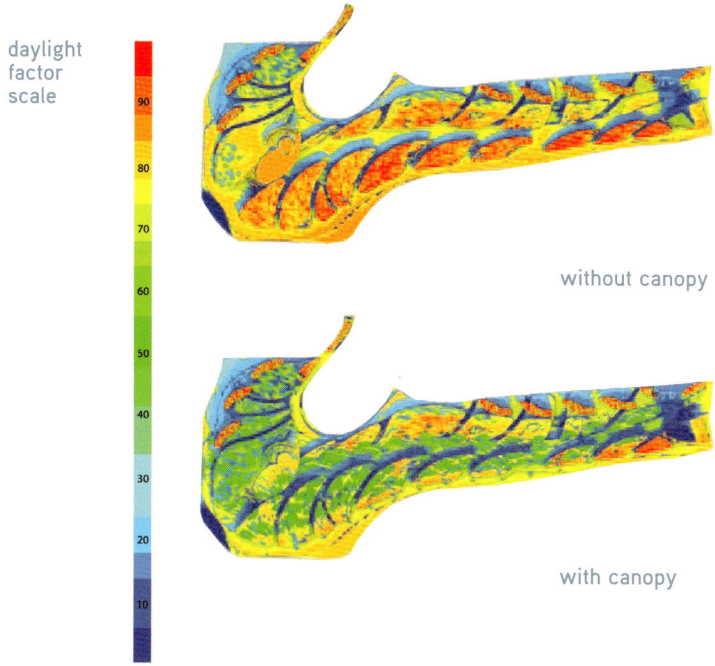

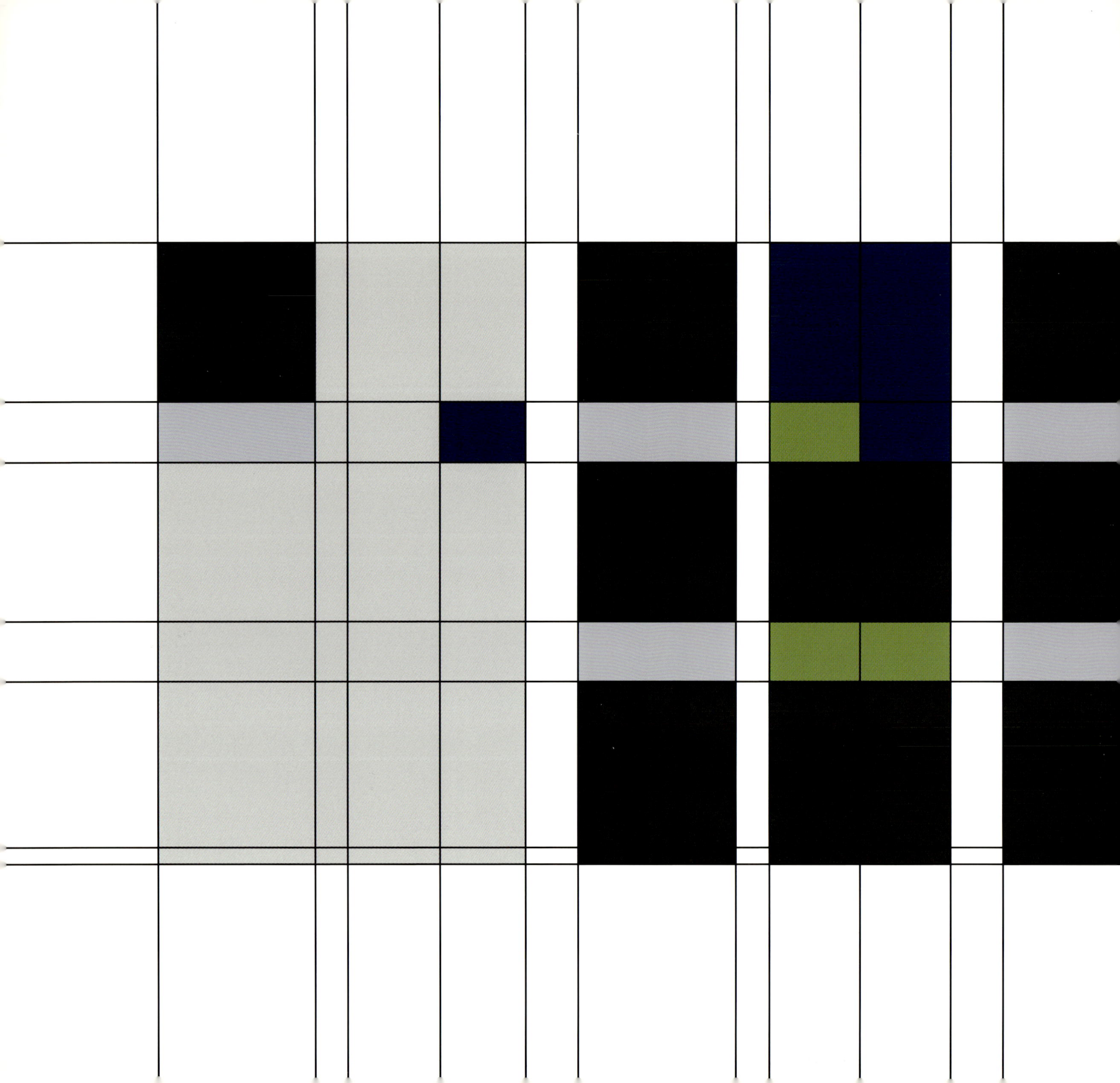

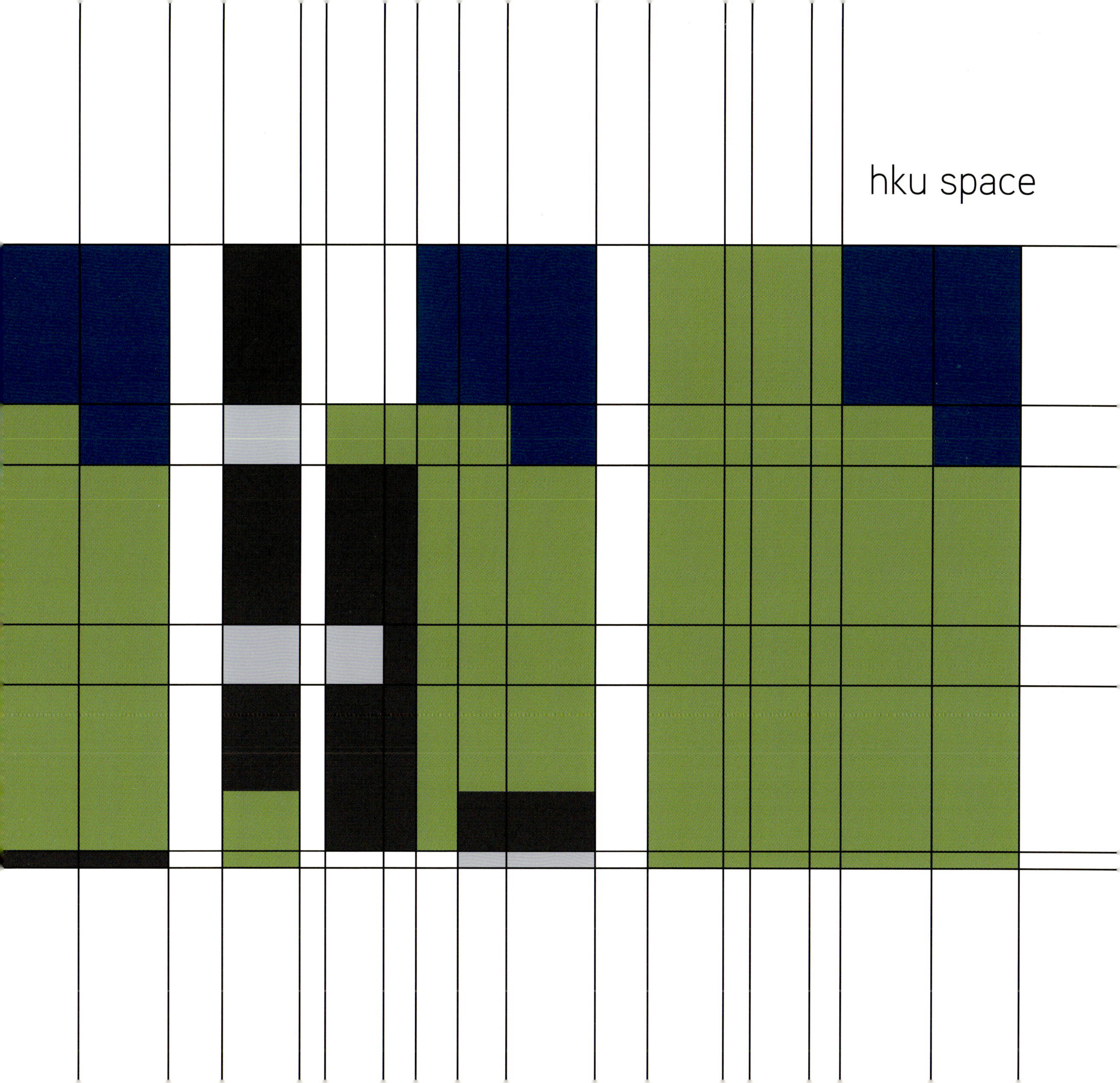
hku space

hku space

institutional
client: hong kong university
location: kowloon bay, hong kong, china

site location

size/scale

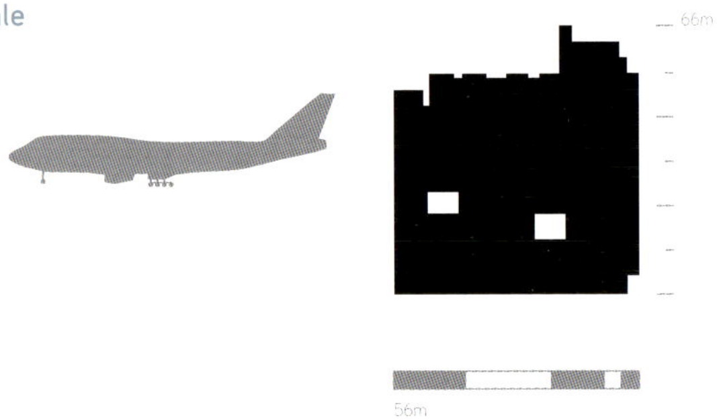

project description

This institutional client in Hong Kong strives to deliver higher education throughout Hong Kong conveniently for those who cannot afford to commute across town or take time off from their daily obligations. Most of its students are older than the typical university student and have jobs and families to support. Consequently, the university has acknowledged, in order to entice this group, it needs to cater to its specific needs by building facilities throughout the city and thus providing convenience, allowing students to take courses during their lunch breaks as well as after the family is fed. This often leads to the buildings being built in very urban and more economically viable areas of the city as is the case for this project – built in Kowloon Bay, a dense industrial warehouse district in Hong Kong.

It was felt to be important that although this was a stand alone building within an industrial area, the project should try and achieve a campus environment for the university – vertically. In this regard, the building attempted to simulate varying levels of density, interconnections, interrelationships, and degrees of public privacy, both internally and externally.

The larger more public facilities such as the auditoria, library, cafeteria and lecture halls were located within the podium densely but with a simple circulation street allowing for way-finding and facilitating social interaction between students and faculty. Intermixed with smaller "pocket gardens" these spaces ramp up the site to the top of the podium, where the gymnasium and recreational open space are located.

process

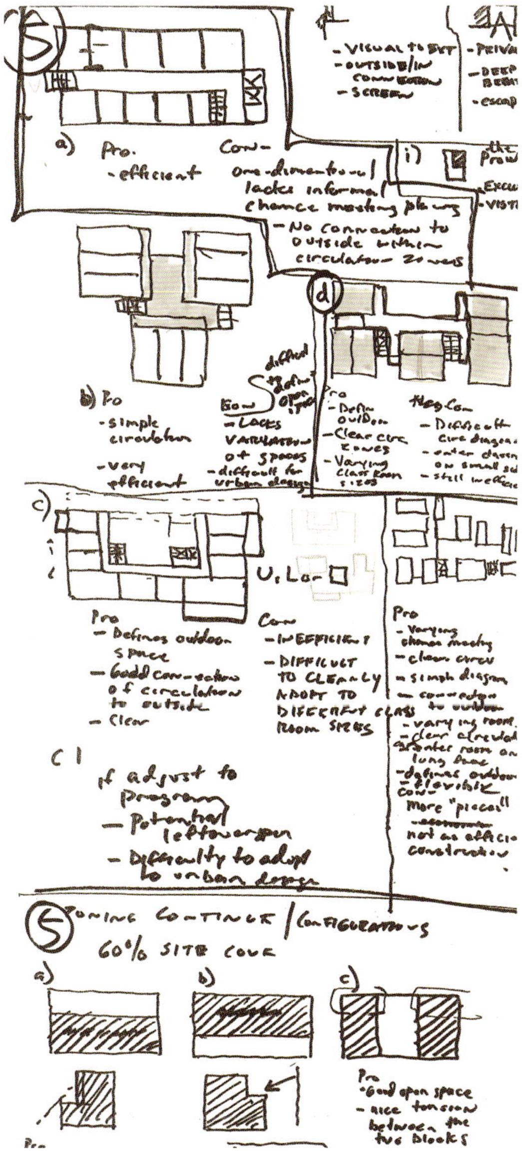

goals

To break down the traditional Hong Kong single volume urban university into an interwoven vertical campus – intermixing facilities with varied open space.

challenge

To activate a "vertical campus" within the existing density of the site and with the adjacent contextual constraints of traffic noise and limited available daylight and views.

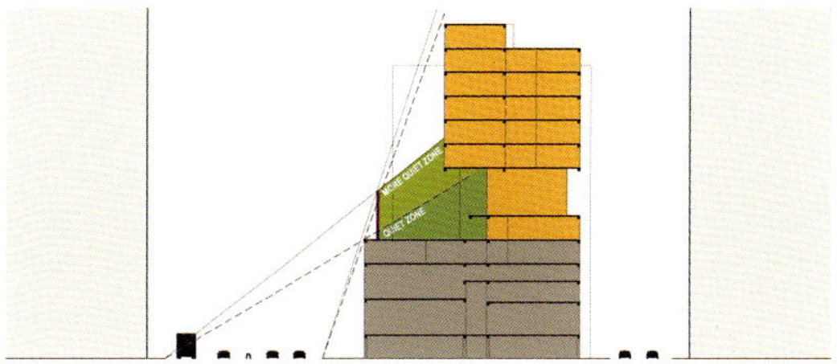

play

The building as an object for discovery – interweaving a varying tapestry of formalized and informal semi-public spaces within the constraints of a highly programmed educational facility.

usage

residential
0 m2 0 sqf

hospitality
0 m2 0 sqf

office
0 m2 0 sqf

retail + f&b
0 m2 0 sqf

landscape
1300m2 139993 sqf

institutional
15370 m2 165441 sqf

total area: 15,370 m2
165,441 sqf

| = 2500 m2 / 26910 sqf

status

competition runner-up

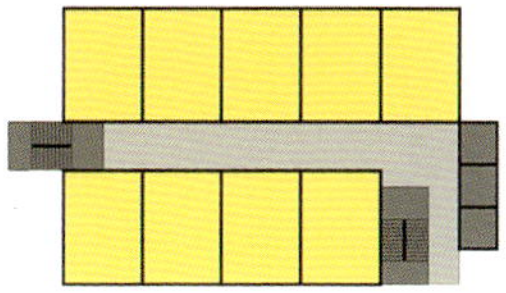

option a

++ efficient
-- one dimensional, lacks informal chance meeting place
-- no connection to outside within circulation zones

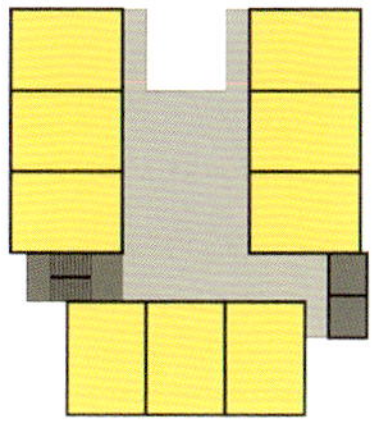

option b

++ simple circulation
++ very efficient
-- lacks variation in spaces
-- difficult for urban design
-- difficult to define open spaces

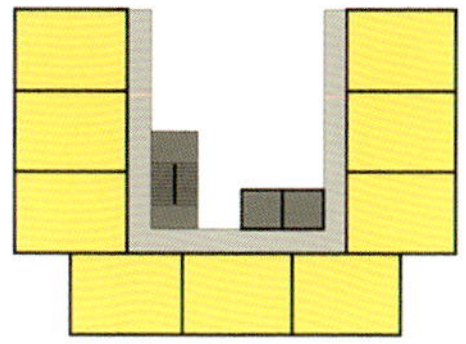

option c

++ defines outdoor space
++ good connection of circulation to outside
++ clear
-- inefficient
-- difficult to clearly adapt to different class room sizes

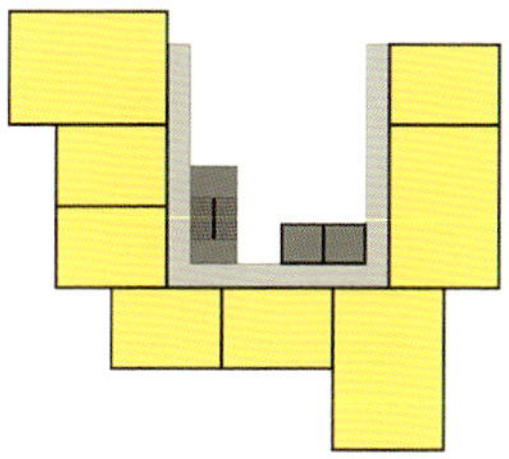

option c1

if adjusted to program
-- potential leftover space

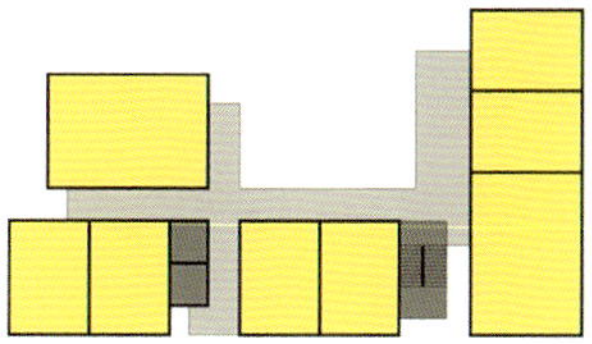

option d

++ defines outdoor space
++ clear circulation zones
++ varying classroom sizes
-- difficult circulation diagram
-- enter classroom on smaller side
-- inefficient

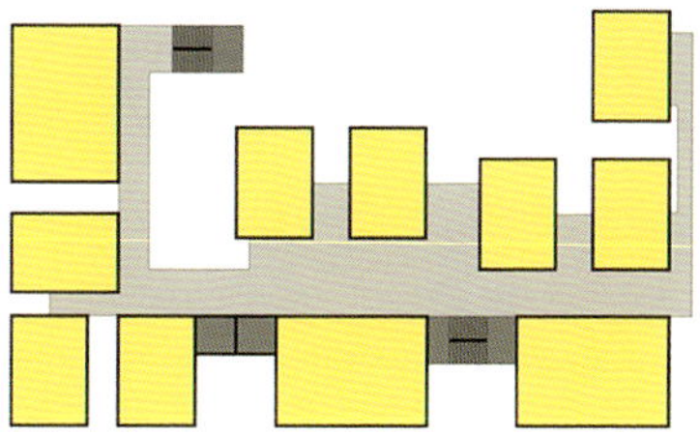

final configuration

++ varied places for chance meetings
++ clear circulation
++ simple diagram
++ connection to outdoors
++ varying sizes of the rooms
++ enter rooms on long side
++ defines outdoor spaces
++ flexible
-- more "places"
-- not a 100% efficient construction

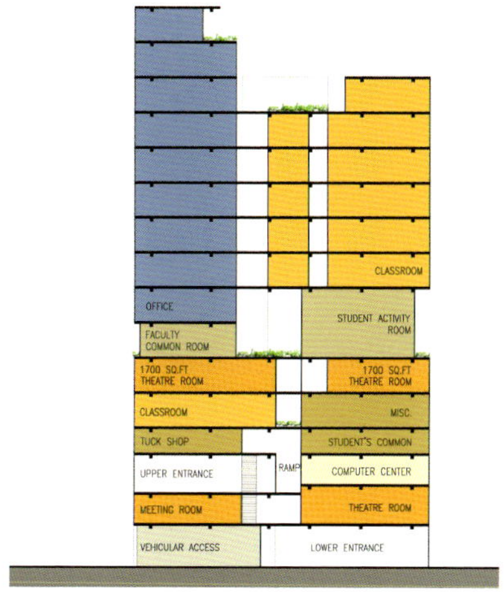

section

- office
- classrooms
- function rooms
- theatre rooms
- common areas
- garden

The more private classrooms are located floating above this semi-public zone. Attention was given to the design and position of these facilities. A simple circulation pattern was necessary due to the volume of students and the limited time allowed between classes. The classrooms was designed to be able to be combined and separated maximizing necessary flexibility for classroom sizes. Orientation of these classrooms was studied to maximize day-lighting and they were positioned in relation to the podium to minimize noise distraction from the street below. The density and efficiency of the classrooms were then balanced in the belief that impromptu chance meeting semi-public spaces were important and should exist throughout the development.

These classrooms and semi-public spaces were then positioned to define the recreational open space below. The administrative core was placed at the most active corner of the site. This gave the long term employees of the facility, opportunities for views and openness within the dense environment. It also provides direct access to the classrooms on every floor and further shelters the student spaces from the urban noise beyond, however briefly, a sense of being a part of a campus environment with students enjoying all of the social and educational intangibles campus life affords.

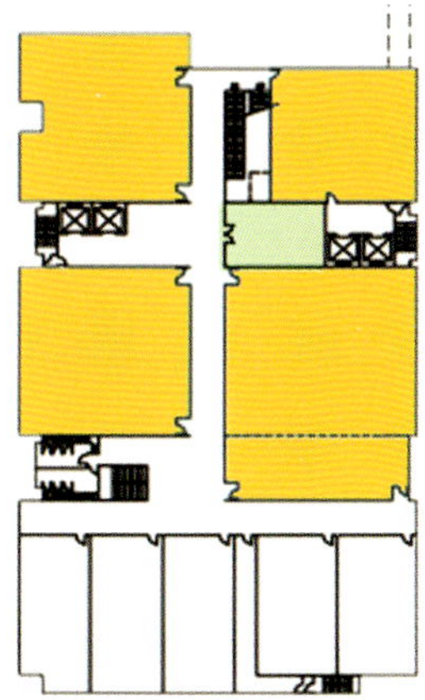

level 1 plan

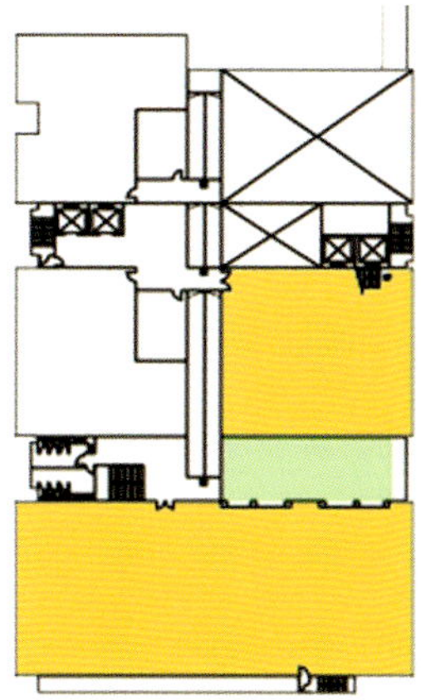

level 3 plan

scenario b

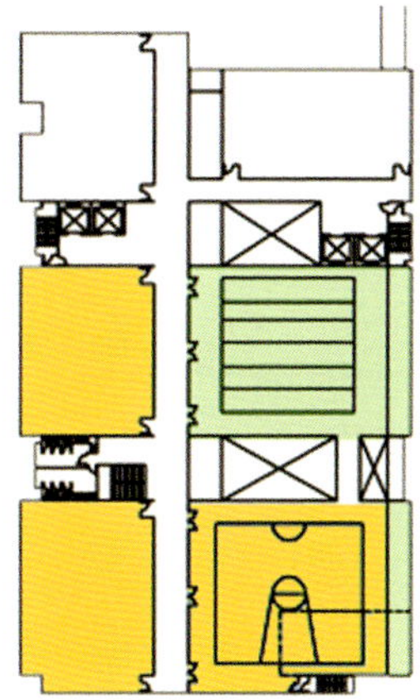

level 5 plan

scenario a

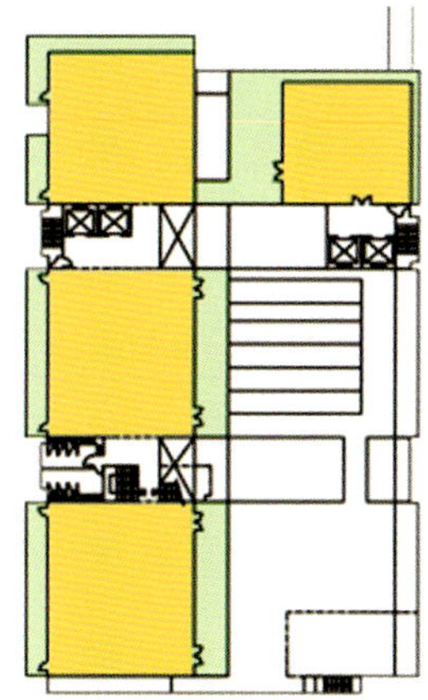

level 7 plan

scenario c

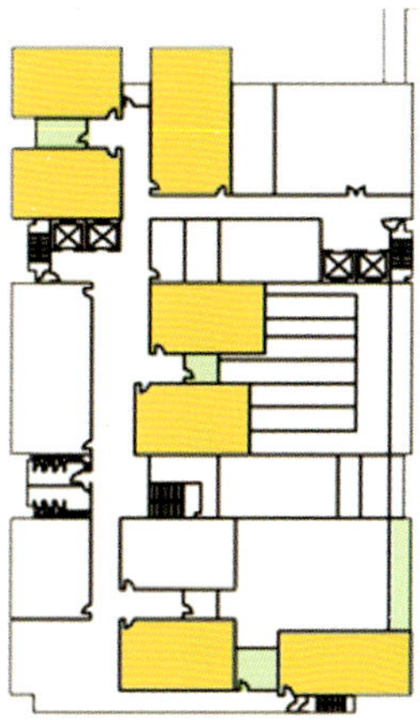

level 9 plan

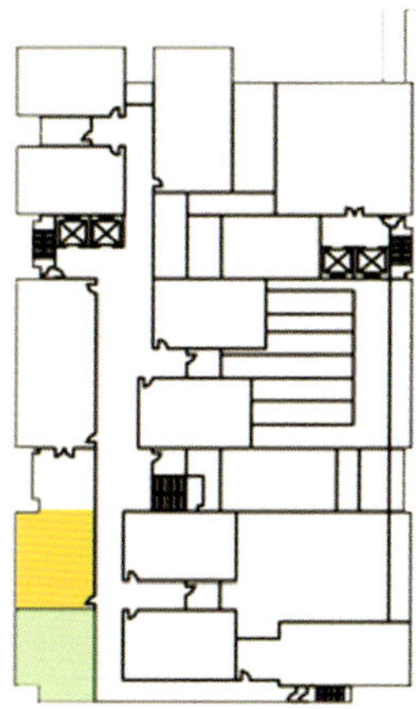

level 13 plan

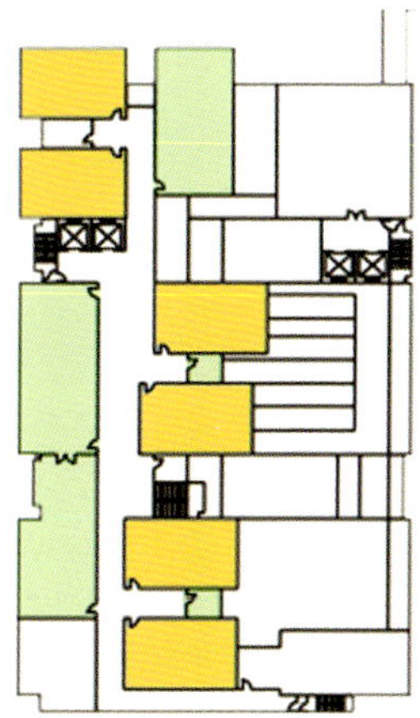

level 14 plan

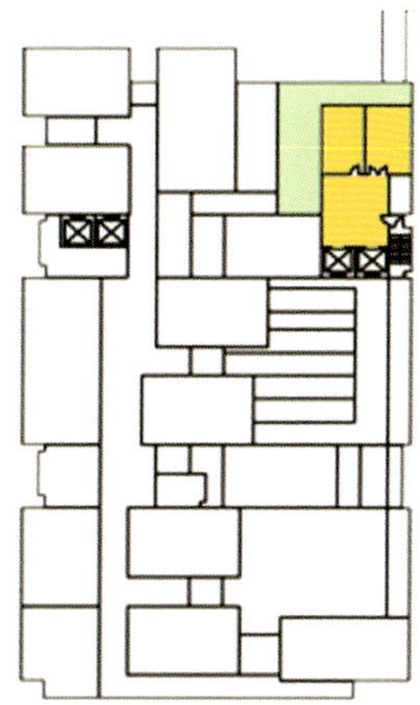

level 16 plan

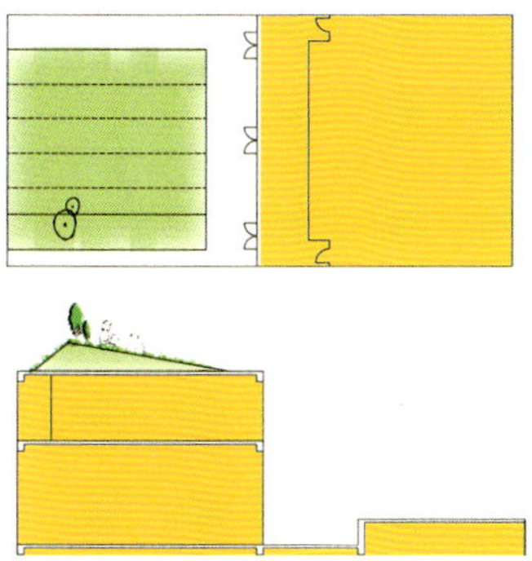

scenario a

green, exposed and open landscape deck

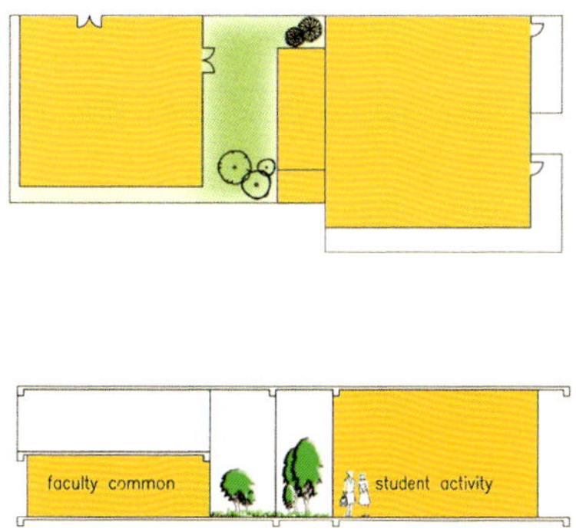

scenario b

cool, quiet and intimate courtyard
desirable enviroment for meditation

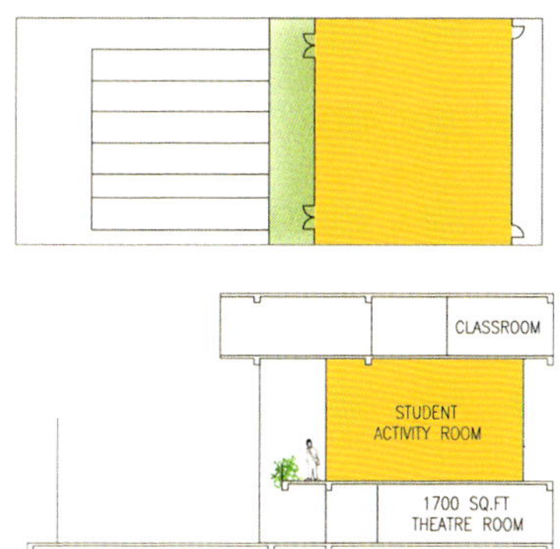

scenario c

balcony
- quick breath of fresh air
- reminder of reality beyond the walls

xian master plan

xian master plan

residential master plan

client: aedas, beijing ltd.
location: wei yang district, xian, china

site location

size/scale

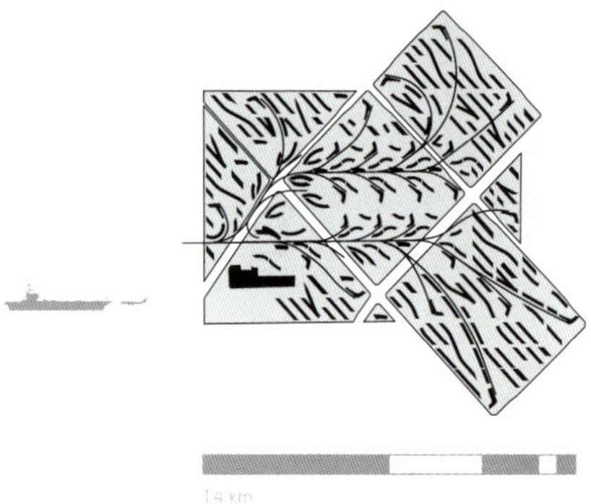

project description

the site

When looking at the site, four main forces jump out as defining characteristics. Rather than resisting these forces, we have, chosen to find a balance and harmony between them in our design.

force number one:

THE WALL. Historically, walls have often been an important element in the creation of a city. They serve to create a protected inner world for their inhabitants, allowing them to grow and exist freely.

force number two:

THE TRACKS. The rail tracks that run through the site are an important element. They are the arteries of a city, the element that links the site to the outside world.

force number three:

THE BUNKERS. These bunkers, which exist within the site, are to become the core activity centers. They are the elements within the landscape that become nodes of identity.

force number four:

THE GRID. The imposition of the larger city grid upon the walled inner city forces a dialogue between its history and progress.

the growth of the tracks

The imprint of the city grid on the site compromises the integrity of THE WALL. Like stalks of wheat, THE TRACKS strive to grow outwards, reaching into the farthest corners.

THE BUNKERS as nodal points

THE BUNKERS will expand beyond the inner world to provide communal nodes within the surrounding sites linking back to the project center.

process

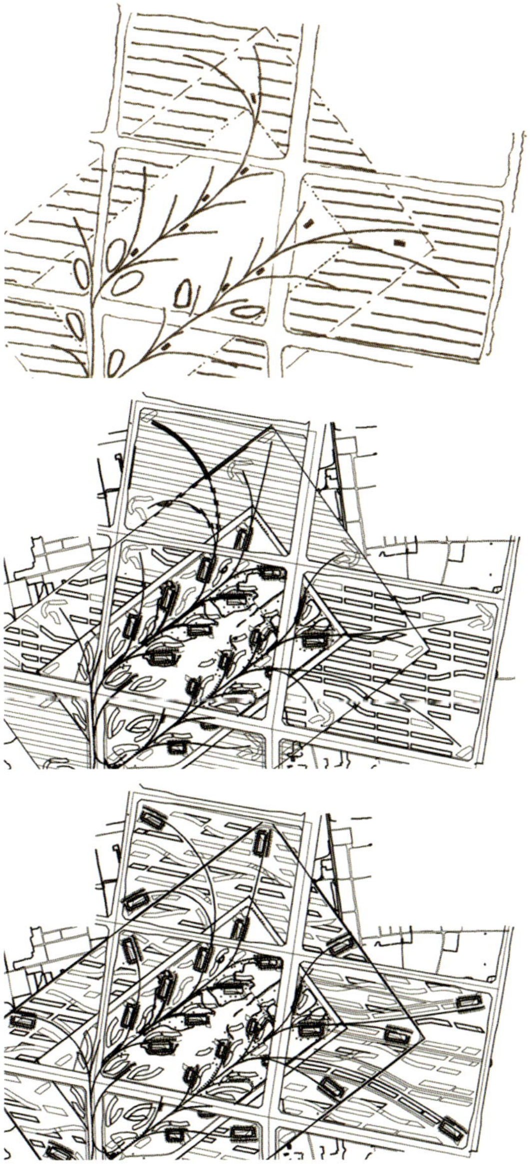

goals

Maintaining characteristics of the site defined by 4 forces: bunkers, tracks, city grid, the wall.

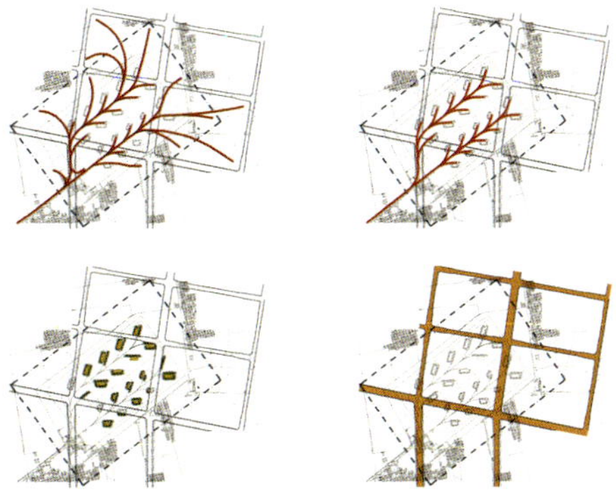

challenge

Utilize existing tracks within master plan.

play

To create harmony between the grid and the wall.

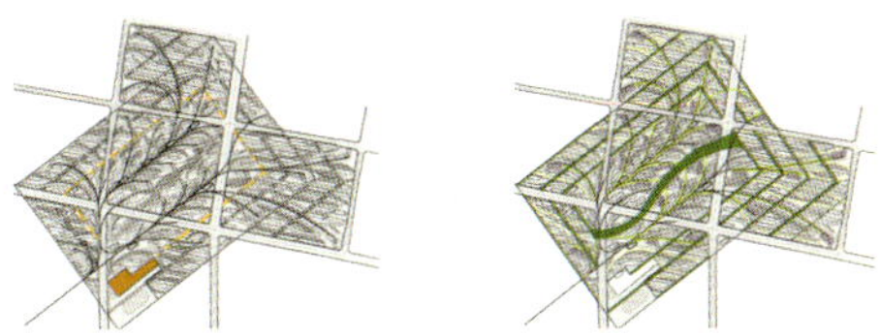

usage

residential
2000595 m2 21534230 sqf

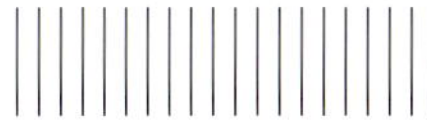

hospitality
0 m2 0 sqf

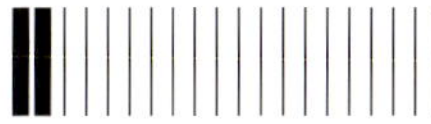

office
93061 m2 1001700 sqf

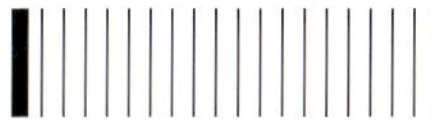

retail + f&b
56557 m2 608775 sqf

landscape
6710000 m2 72225840 sqf

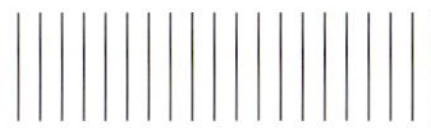

other
0 m2 0 sqf

total area: 8,860,214 m2
95,370,550 sqf

= 50,000 m2 /538195sqf

status

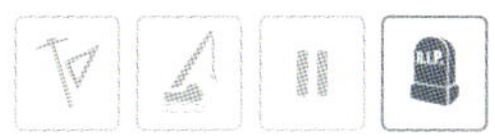

competition winner

blocks that reinforce the grid

The residential blocks respond to the urban grid and southern light in the most efficient manner possible. This helps reinforce the urban grid. When the blocks meet the city wall they stop as if the wall were absorbing these forces to protect the inner world.

harmony between grid and wall

As the "old" elements continue to grow into the new city block, the city grid continues to exert itself. The wall is absorbed into these forces, remaining with the urban blocks or becoming a memory in between. The existing facility in the wall will be readapted and will house the school.

the ring roads

The wall resonates beyond its physical setting, creating a ripple of ring roads that in turn balance the city grid. This is reminiscent of Beijing's ring roads, and like those, the ring roads will be both the main pedestrian walkways and traffic routes through the site.

the inner world

With the existence of the protective Wall, the inner world is allowed to grow freely and the blocks extend from the crossroads of its main arteries.

bending motion

With the ring roads cutting through its site, the city grid blocks are broken. The urban blocks are then allowed to respond and flow toward the energy of the inner world.

objects in the landscape

As the blocks around the bunkers increase in height, the bunkers then seek to reassert themselves as objects within the landscape, growing to rise above the surrounding blocks.

markers

Taller blocks also develop throughout the site as identifiable markers in the landscape.

the landscape

Similar to the development of the blocks, the landscape, follows and reinforces these forces, growing freely and shaping the movement of people within the wall.
As it extends outside the wall, it adapts to the city grid, as well as the relatively freer nature of the tracks. It is tamed in its expression, but flows around the site, creating pods and community spaces for each of the plots.

a cycle

This dialogue between the forces on the site, in which they absorb and respond to each other, completes a cycle that results in a complete harmonious environment.

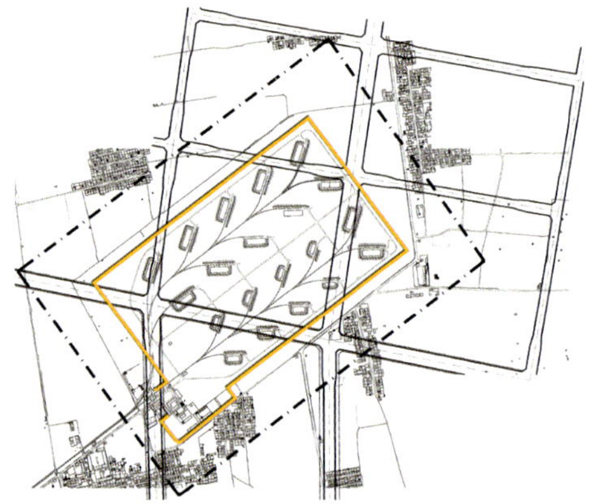

force one: the wall

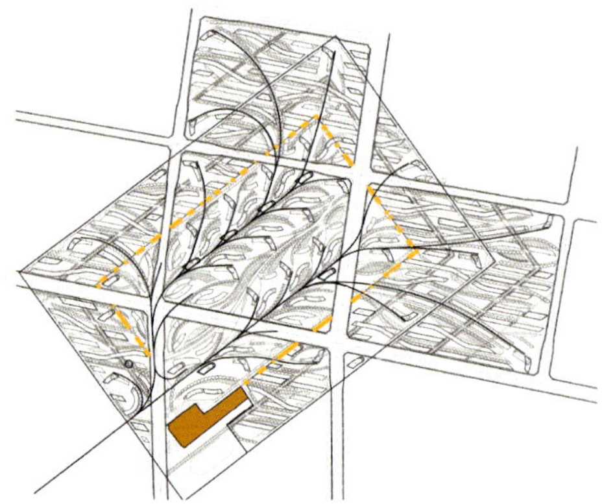

harmony between grid and wall

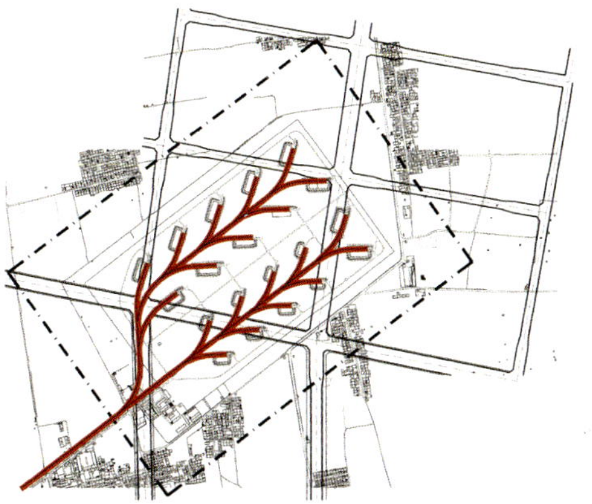

force two: the tracks

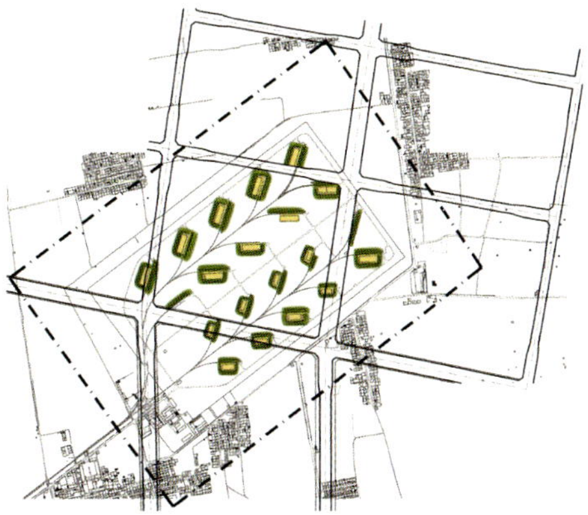

force three: the bunkers

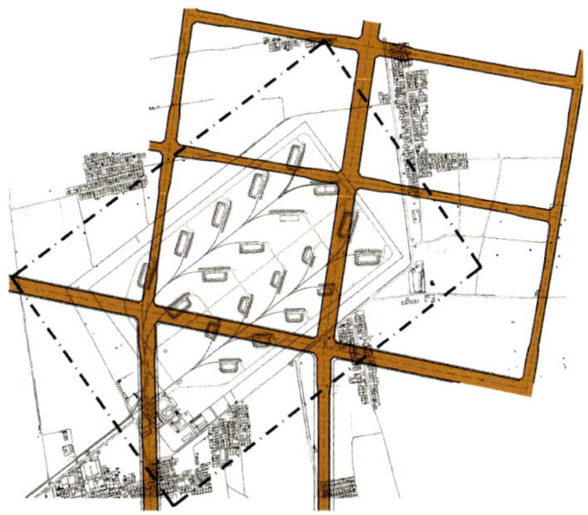

force four: the grid

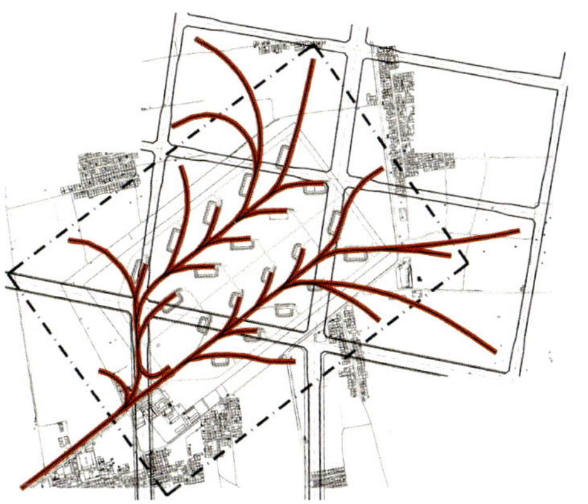

the growth of the tracks

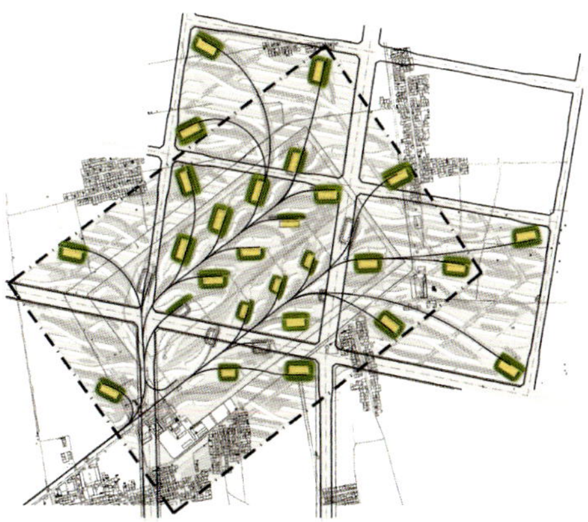

the bunkers as nodal points

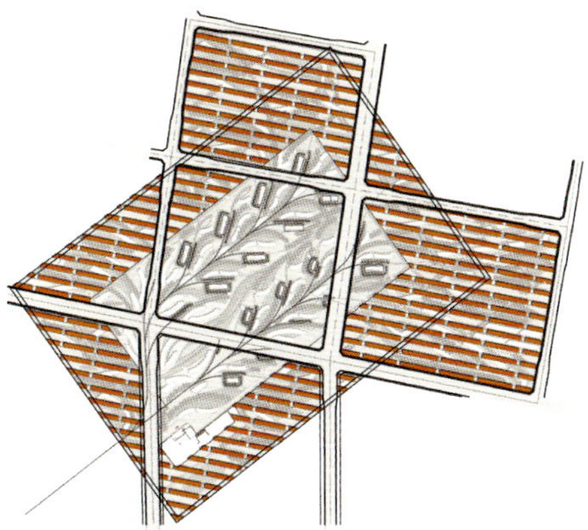

blocks that reinforce the grid

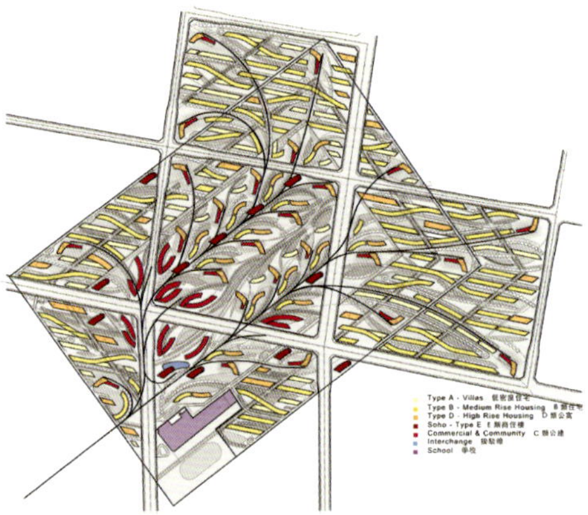

land use

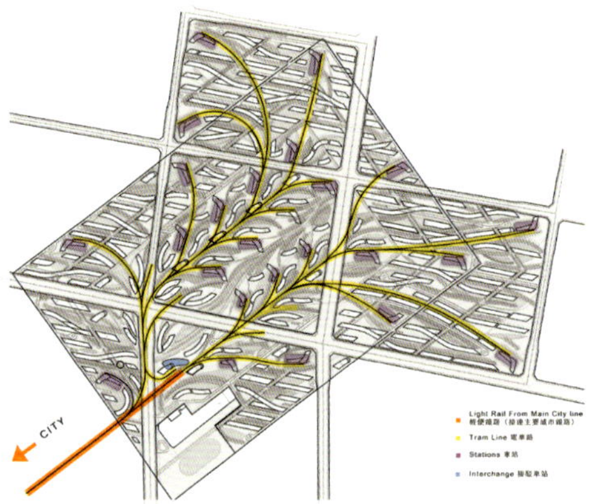

regional traffic

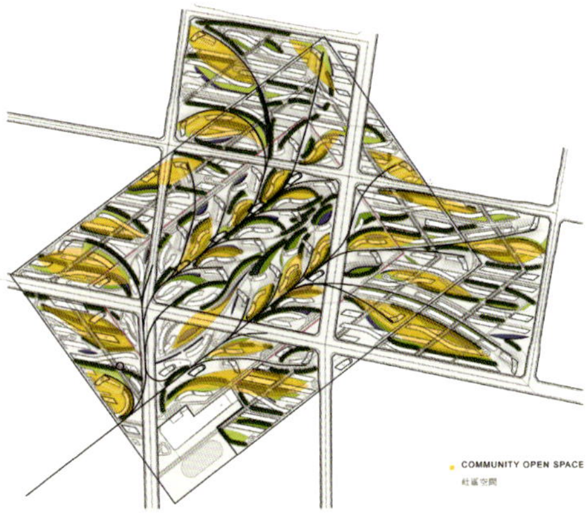

landscape

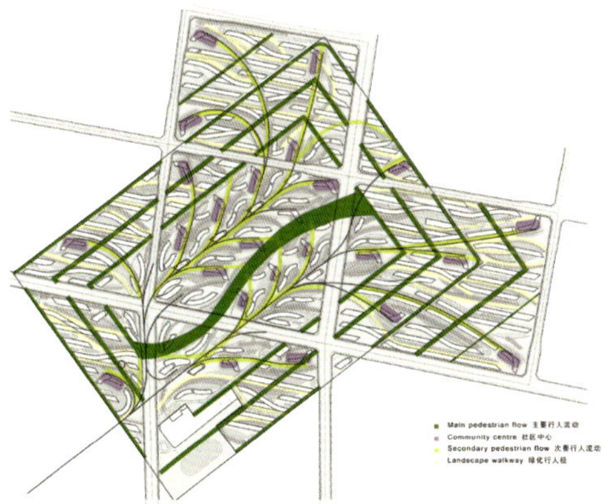

pedestrian flow

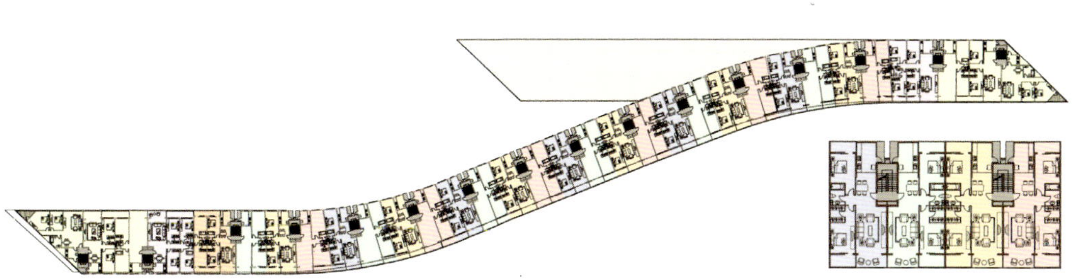

type B

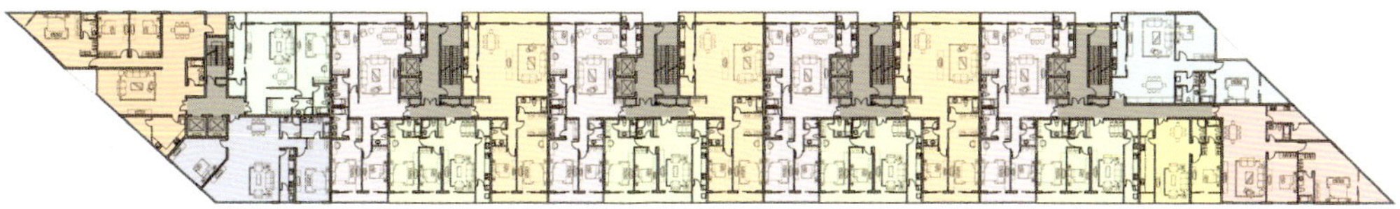

type D

sheth headquarters

sheth headquarters

offices

client: sheth developers pvt ltd.

location: mumbai, india

site location

size/scale

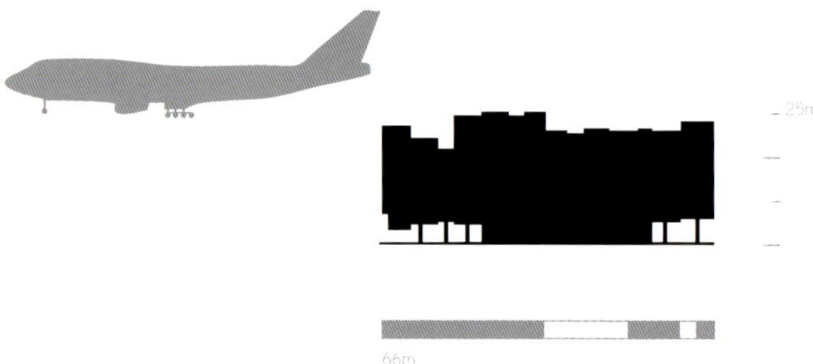

project description

As a headquarters for a small developer with a very complex internal organization, this design strove to provide a unified vision while still responding appropriately to the individual needs, requirements and expression of its three equal owners – who also happen to be brothers.

This challenge was compounded by the requirement that the design response for the project adhere to Vastu principles. These principles ended up dictating both the formal response to the site as well as the basis for inner office organization, which also needed an outward expression.

When examining the goals of the client to have impressive volumes of space for both the reception area and their project showcase gallery, it became clear that the lack of available space to build in this tight site was going to be one of the major obstacles. With the height limit restricted, the overall use of the site needed to be very efficient. This is where the Vastu challenge forced a creative response to the site.

Vastu principles dictate an orthogonal relationship based on cardinal orientation. In this instance, the site is rectilinear rotated 10 degrees off of this orientation. Consequently, if a large rectilinear block respecting Vastu was placed in this site, a considerable amount of site area would be lost. In response to this, the volume of space was sliced into a modular structural grid and expanded to the boundaries. The building was thus able to maximize its use of the site and carve out sufficient excess areas internally to achieve the desired volumes of space.

The next major challenge came up with the notion of the "power zone" in Vastu where the Chairman's corner office is located. In this instance, the design broke the project down in plan and section, so all three brothers had their own "power zone" corner on different floors in an attempt to avoid any sibling rivalry in this regard. The location of their offices was then set in relation to the different departments which they ran individually.

process

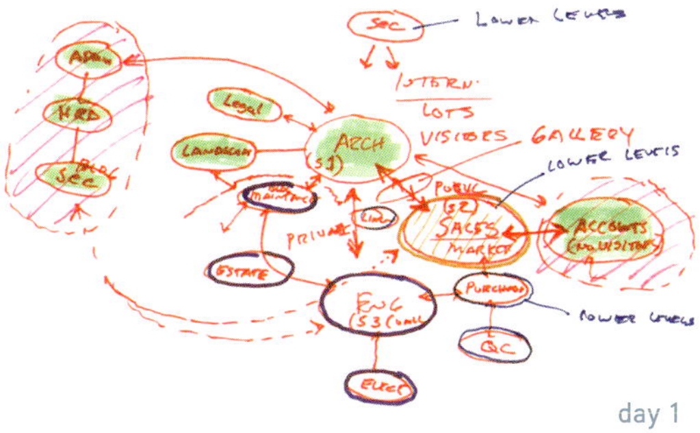

day 1

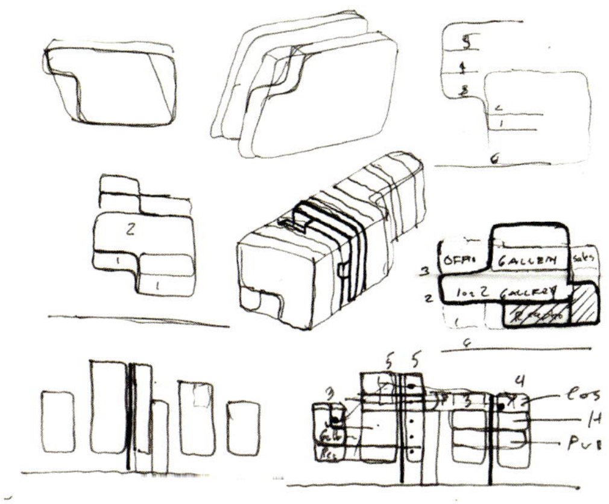

day 2

week 1

goals

To provide a facility with a unified vision for a small but very complex developer owned by three independent and strong minded brothers.

challenge

The client request that the building keep strictly to "Vas-tu" philosophy and design restrictions based on cardinal directions contrasting to the orientation of the site.

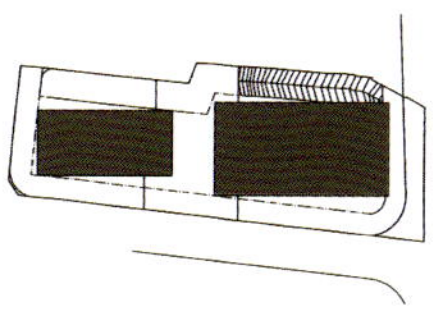

baseline

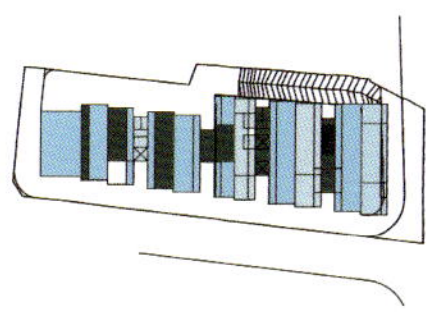

proposed

play

Within Vastu – a building has one corner which is considered the "power zone". The project was designed with three power corners in order to try and keep peace between the three brothers.

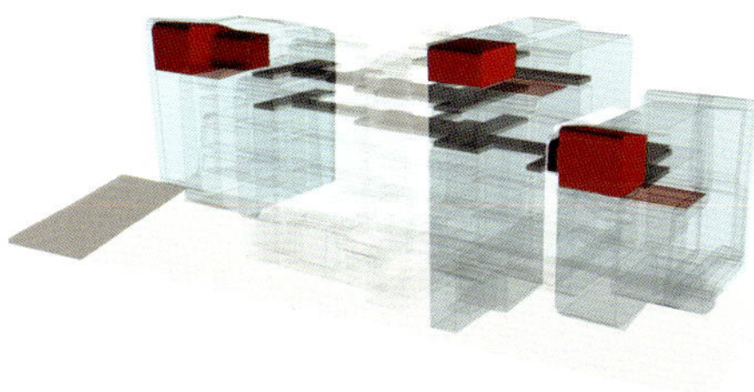

usage

residential
0 m2 0 sqf

hospitality
0 m2 0 sqf

office
4073 m2 43841 sqf

retail + f&b
630 m2 6781 sqf

landscape
368 m2 3961 sqf

exhibition
263 m2 2830 sqf

total area: 4,966 m2
53.453 sqf

| = 2500 m2 / 26910 sqf

status

client did not acquire land

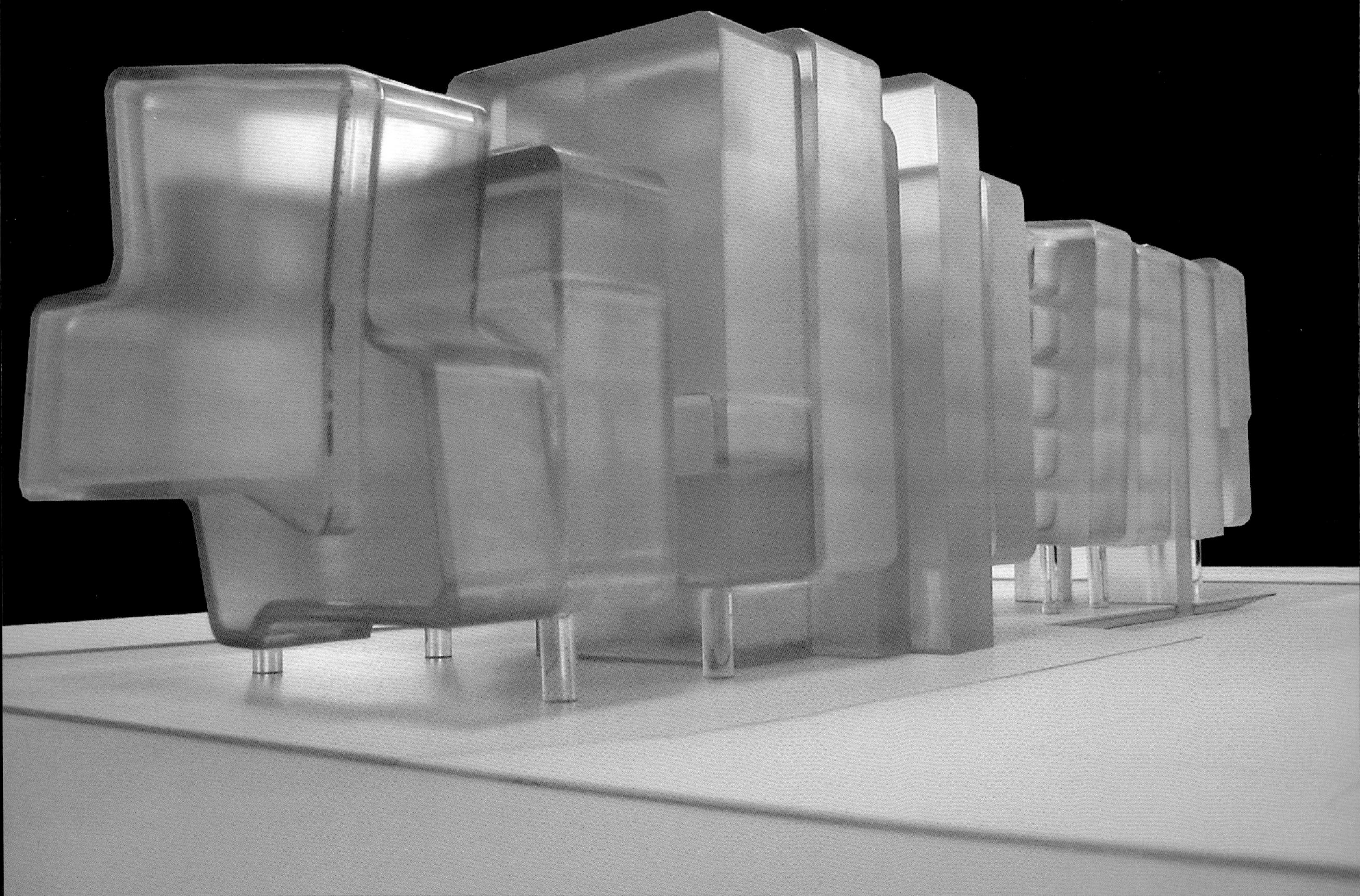

3 brothers' offices in "power zone" according to vastu principle

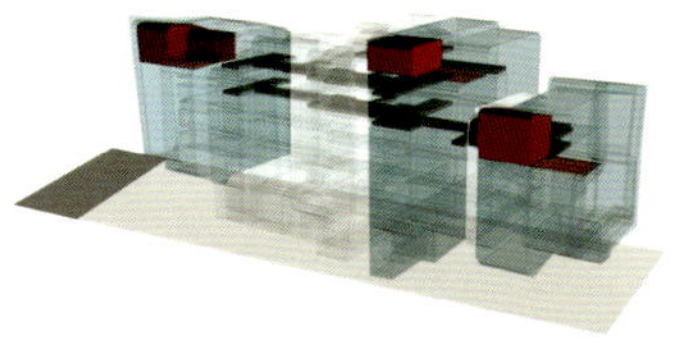

ashwin sheth: architecture, liaison, legal and accounts.

vallabh sheth: admin, estate, security, HR, maintenance, purchase, QS and engineering

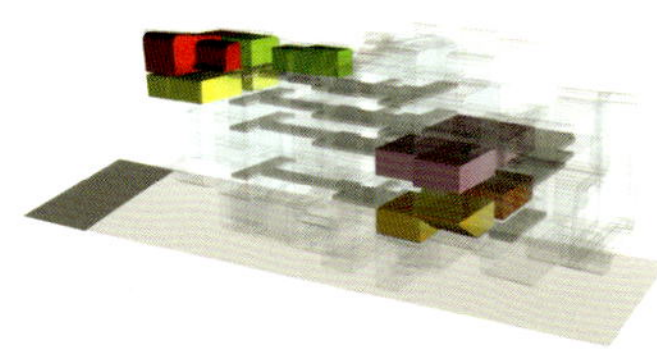

jitendra sheth: sales and gallery

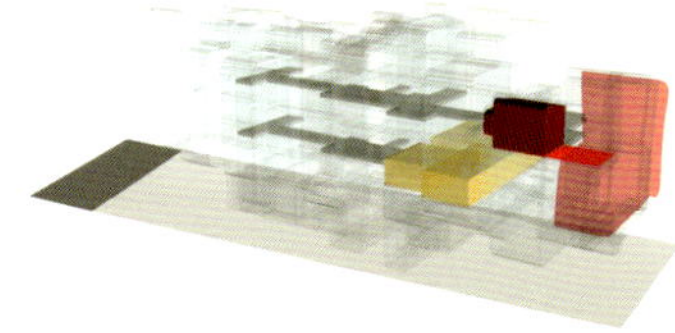

circulation

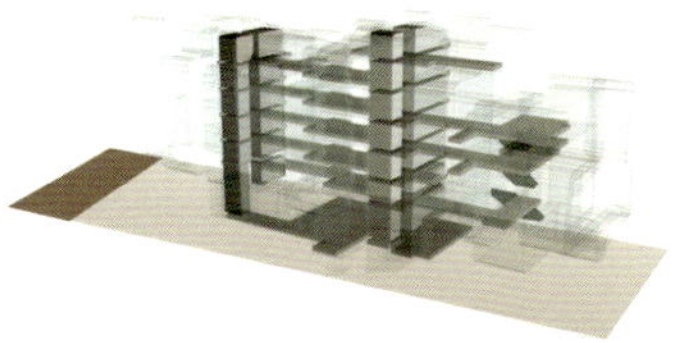

entrance, waiting area and gallery

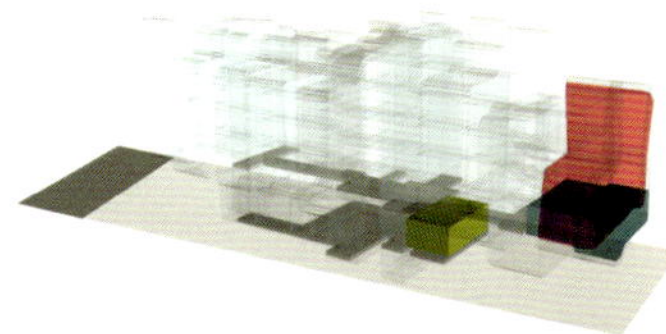

utilities: canteen and conference rooms

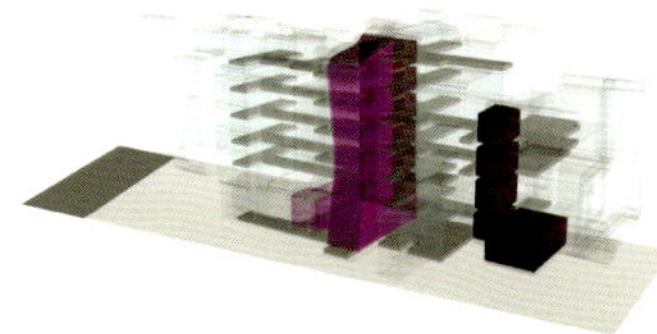

architecture and engineering

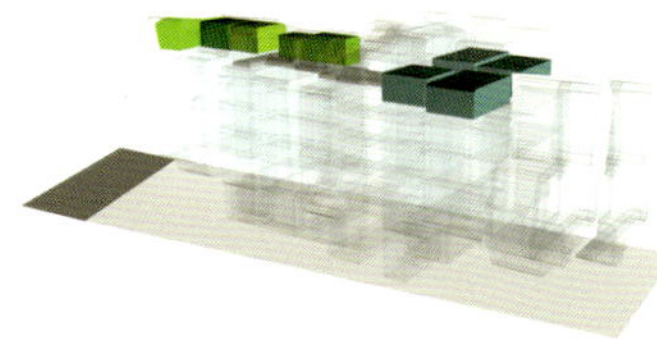

admin, security, estate, accounts, architecture, legal and liaison

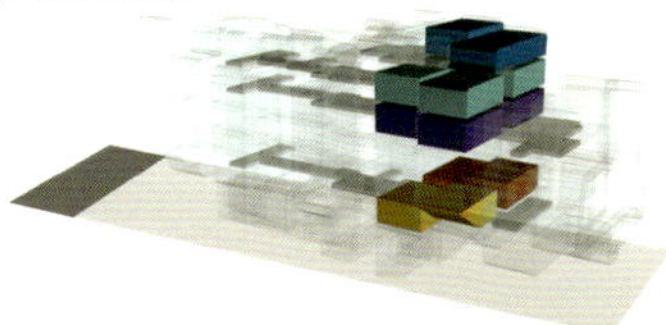

sales, accounts and architecture

general offices and expansion

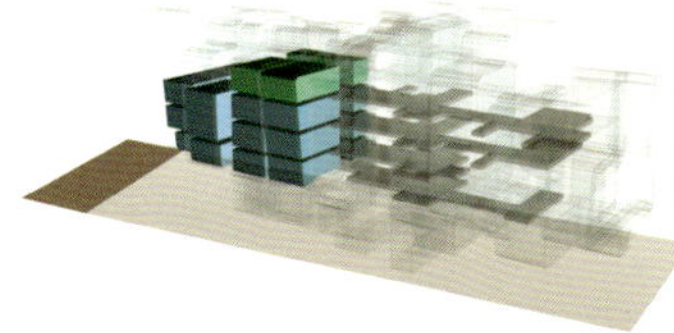

sales and gallery

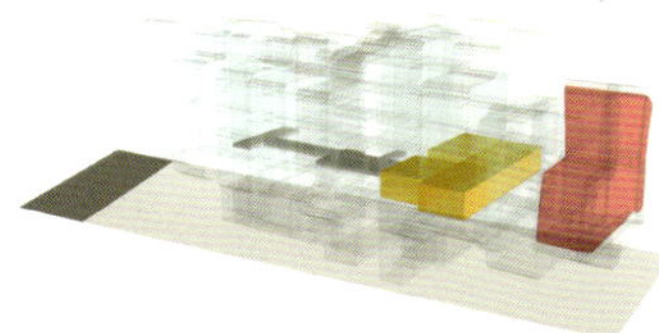

option 1: rear courtyard

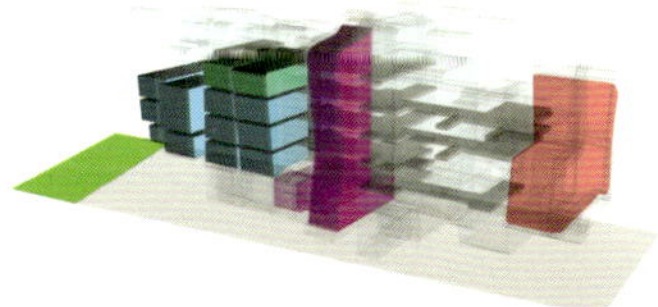

option 2: center courtyard

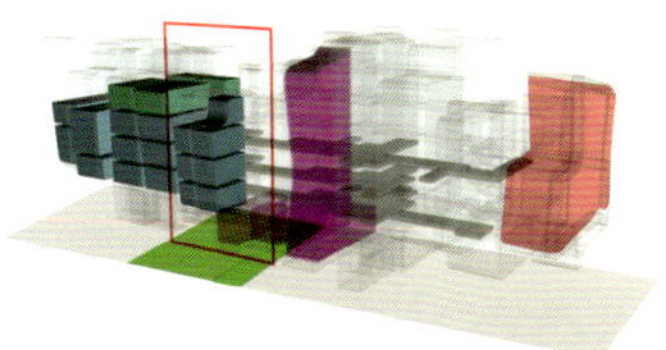

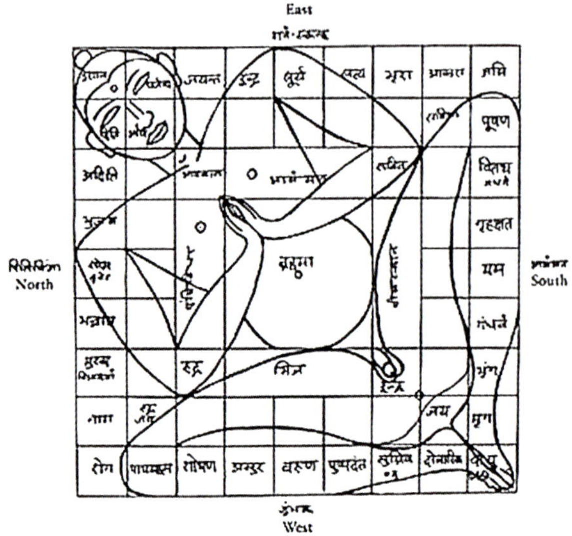
East
North
South
West

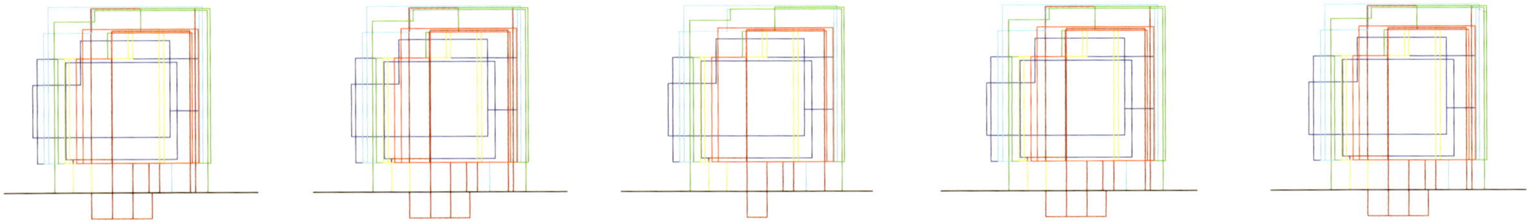

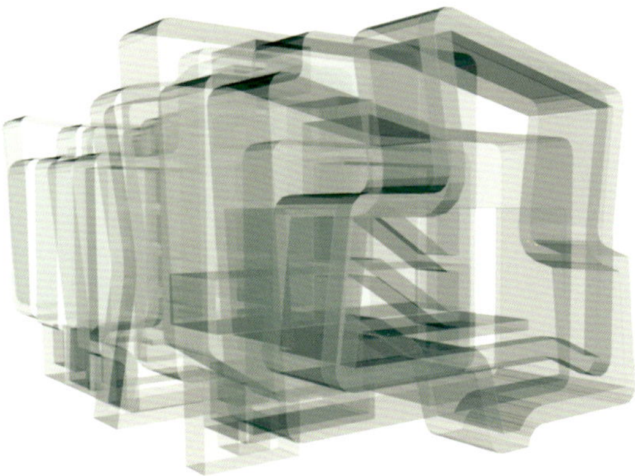

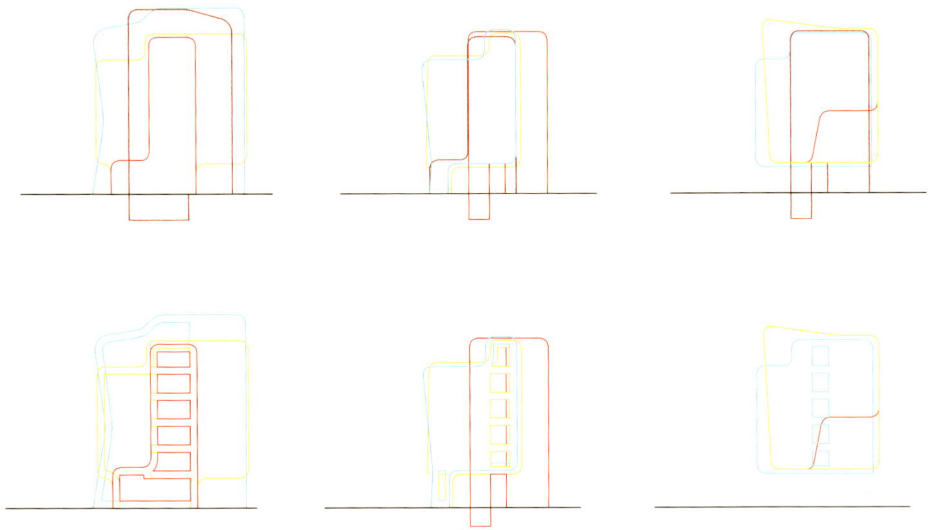

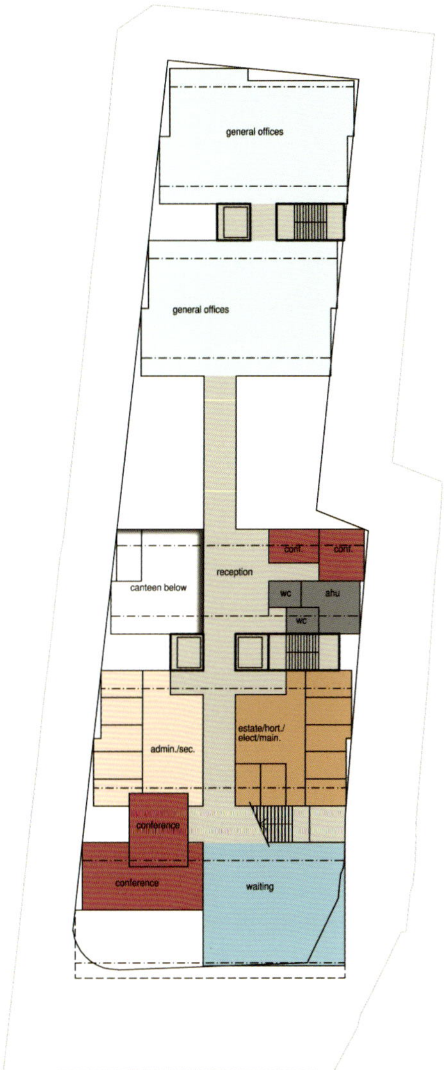

level 1

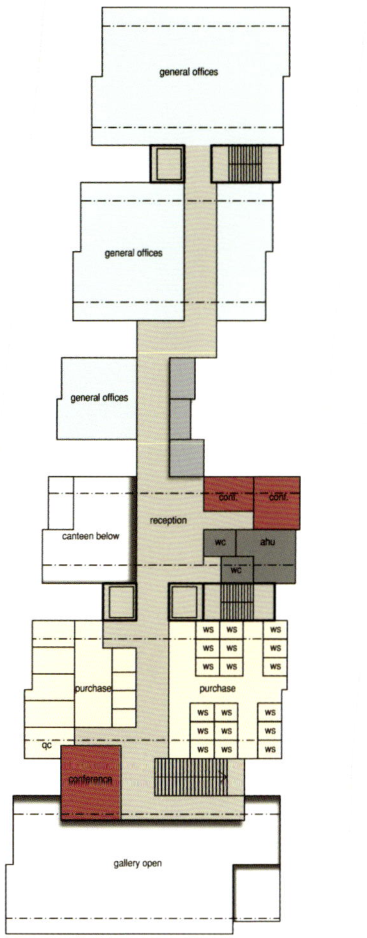

level 3

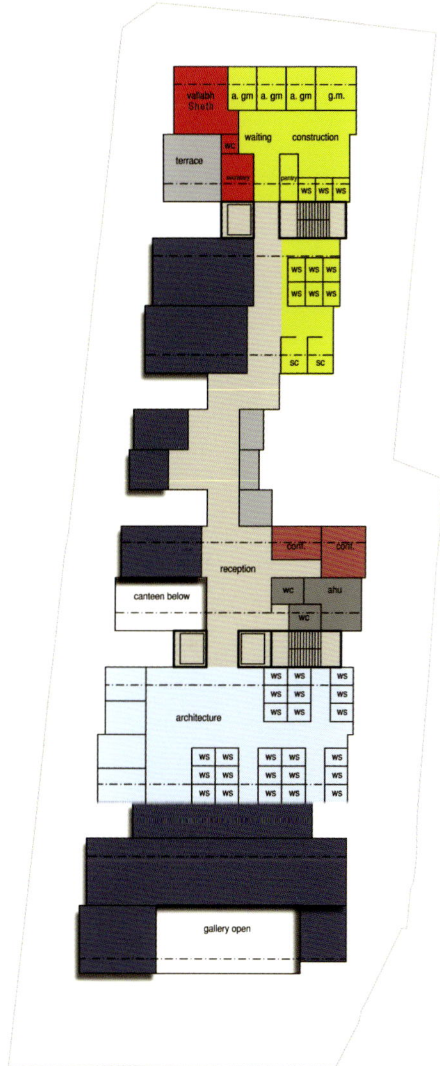

level 5

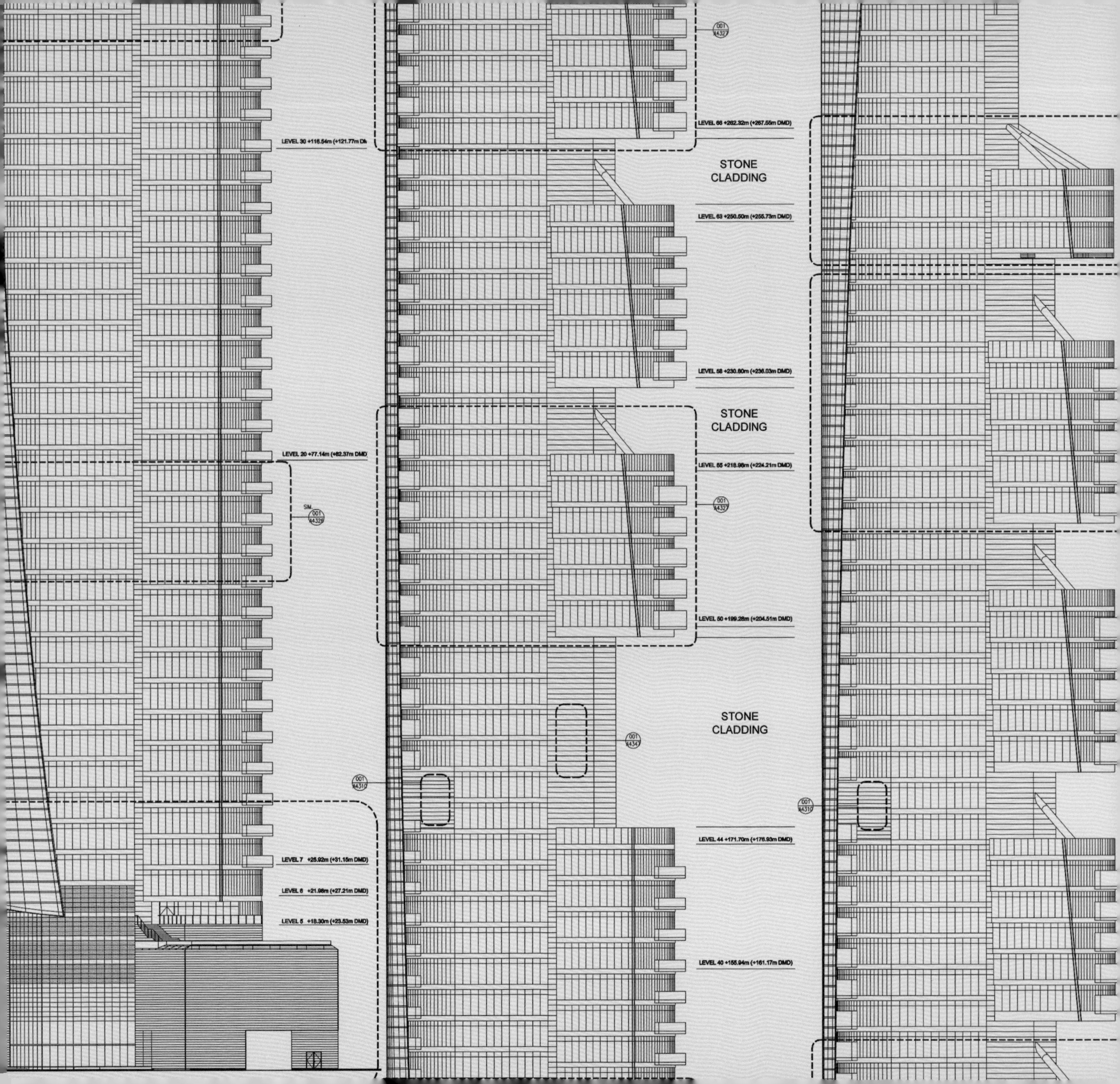

LEVEL 30 +116.54m (+121.77m DM
LEVEL 20 +77.14m (+82.37m DMD
SIM.
001
A4326
LEVEL 7 +25.92m (+31.15m DMD)
LEVEL 6 +21.98m (+27.21m DMD)
LEVEL 5 +18.30m (+23.53m DMD)
001
A4310
001
A4327
LEVEL 66 +262.32m (+267.55m DMD)
STONE CLADDING
LEVEL 63 +250.50m (+255.73m DMD)
LEVEL 58 +230.80m (+236.03m DMD)
STONE CLADDING
LEVEL 55 +218.98m (+224.21m DMD)
001
A4327
LEVEL 50 +199.28m (+204.51m DMD)
001
A4347
STONE CLADDING
LEVEL 44 +171.70m (+176.93m DMD)
LEVEL 40 +155.94m (+161.17m DMD)
001
A4310

pentominium

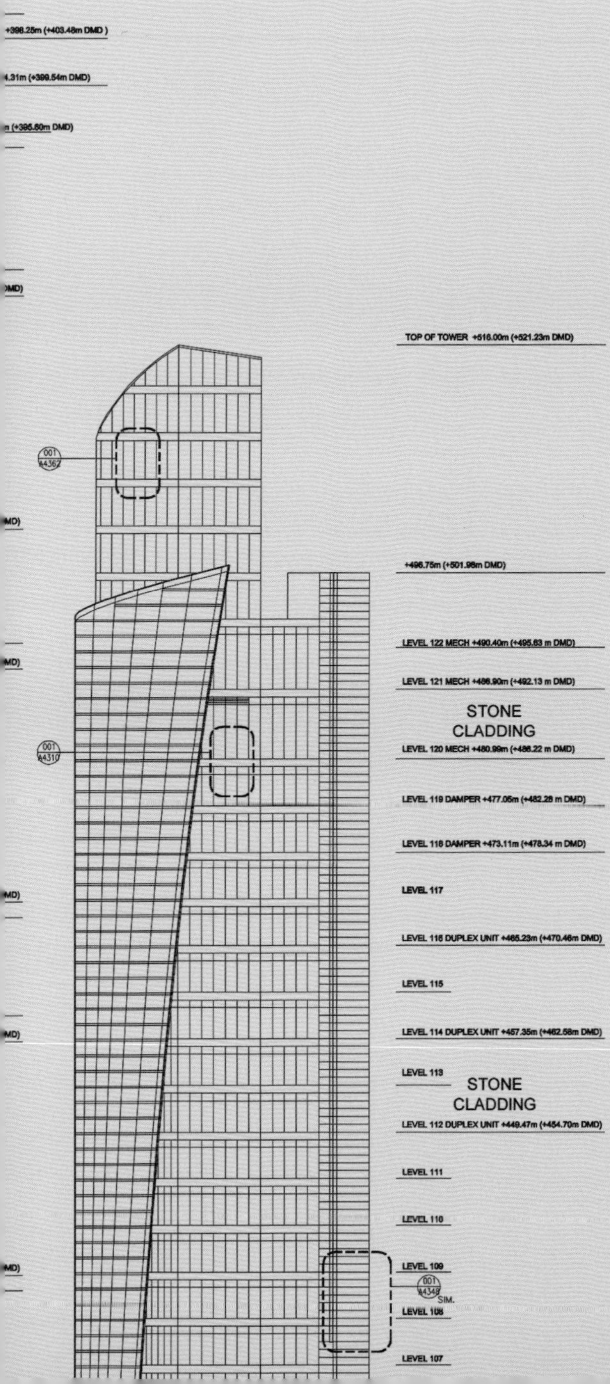

pentominium

residential

client: trident international holdings

location: dubai marina, dubai, uae

site location

size/scale

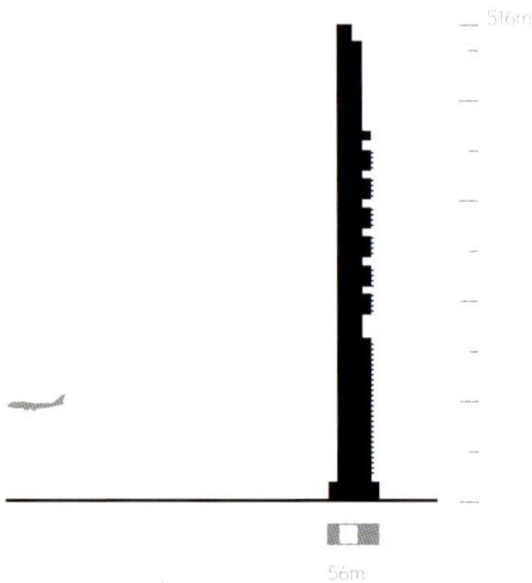

project description

This 518 meter high luxury penthouse and residential tower had a unique challenge. Its neighbor is also very tall, at 380 meters, but located only 20 meters away. The project was designed to fit comfortably into this context by concentrating on the negative space between the two towers.

Immediately adjacent to this extruded neighbor, 9 five-story pods cling to the core with 7 meter high vertical garden oases separating them. Constructed from lightweight steel, the loads of these pods are transferred back to the core to allow a free and flowing space between them – thus enabling the tower to breathe next to its dense context.

The shape of the tower, with only two 600 sm units per floor, was curved and bent to look past its orthogonally located neighbors. By introducing the gardens on the one side, the other, more viable side ends up with 87 of the 147 units.

The asymmetric top of the building and the "texture" the pods provide on the one face surface significantly break up the wind strength and frequency at the top of the building, reducing forces exerted on the tower, thus taking pressure off of the structural system.

In transferring the pods back into the core, the slenderness ratio becomes enormous, with a minimum of 1 to 15 in the center of the plan, tapering down on the sides. To achieve this, bridge technology is used vertically with stress bars introduced; similar to "rubber bands" they stretch from the top down to the ground through the shear walls. This allows the tower to behave structurally as if it were heavier than it is – and thus able to resist the shamal wind forces.

The result is a very thin, lightweight 122 story tower which sits lightly in its setting of extruded neighbors and powerfully maintains its presence through this contrast.

process

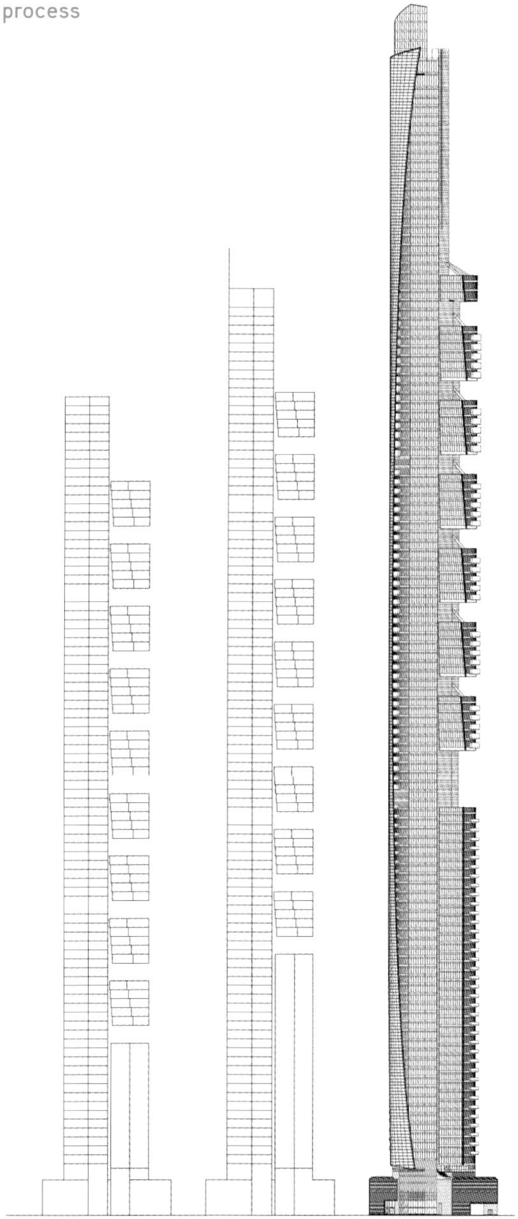

goals

Balcony per unit, disperse wind load, reduce solar gain, introduce common, semi-private areas.

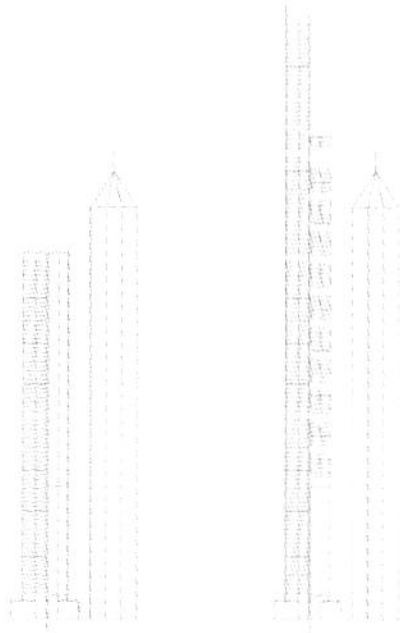

challenge

Stack effect (or increasing pressure) in the 500 meter continuous lift shafts due to temperature and outdoor differentiating pressures experienced due to the building's height.

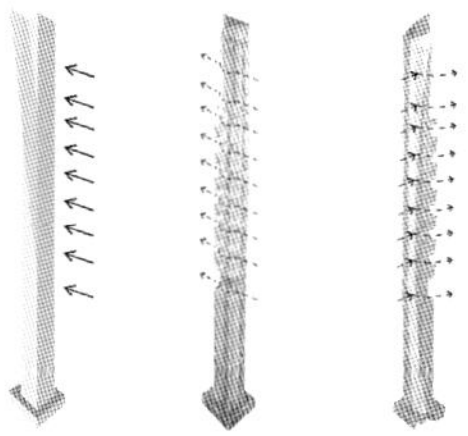

play

Sky Gardens

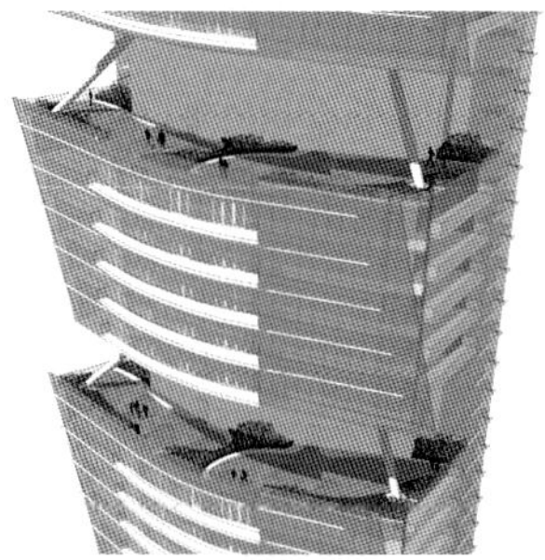

usage

residential
108119 m2 1163783 sqf

hospitality
0 m2 0 sqf

office
0 m2 0 sqf`

retail + f&b
0 m2 0 sqf

landscape
0 m2 0 sqf

recreational
6424 m2 69147 sqf

total area: 114.543 m2
1.232.932 sqf

= 2500 m2 / 26910 sqf

status

projected completion: 2012

Concept of repositioning area from one side of building to the other where views are more open. Sky gardens are then introduced on the opposite side to give more value to units with less view.

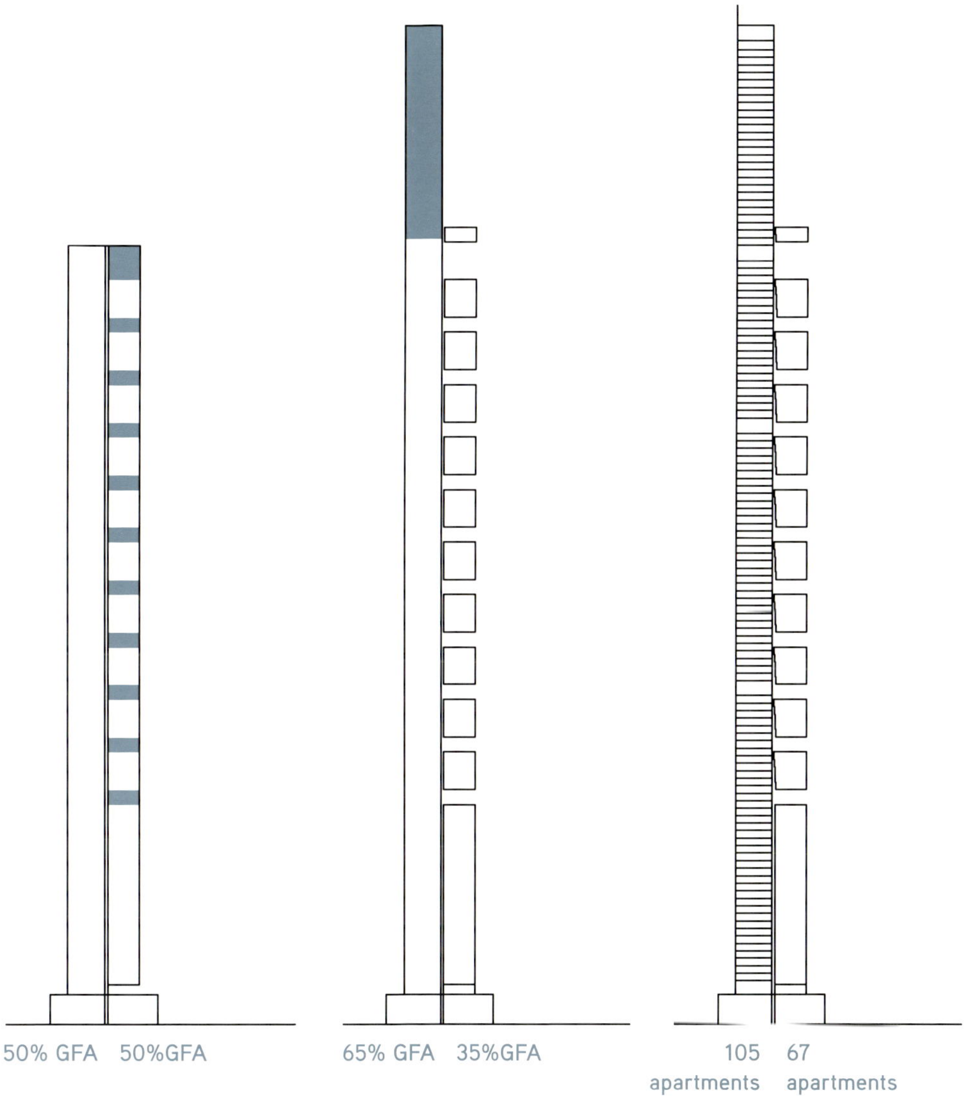

Lower carved out volumes added to the tower crown resulting in extra value units offering panoramics views over adjacent buildings
Gardens enhance the living quality offering unique outdoor space for tenants adding value to the PODs units
Area carved out to provide more comfortable distance from adjacent building
Area carved out to allow building to breath next to adjacent neighbour

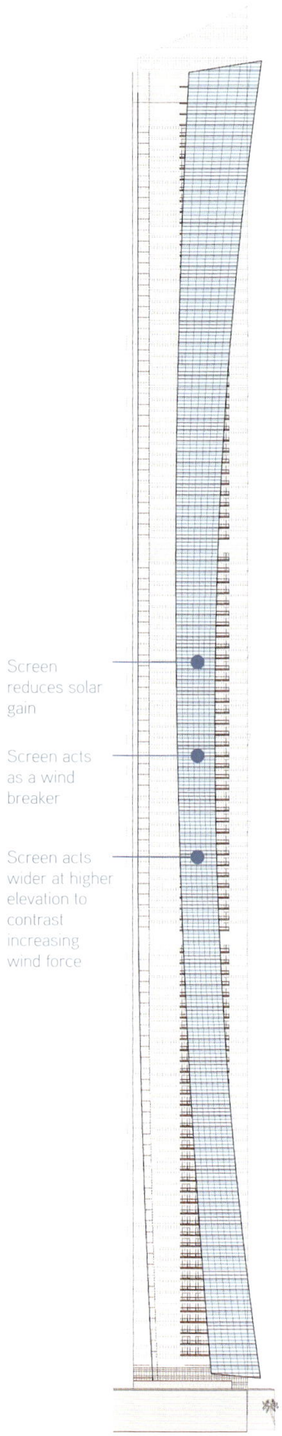
Screen reduces solar gain
Screen acts as a wind breaker
Screen acts wider at higher elevation to contrast increasing wind force

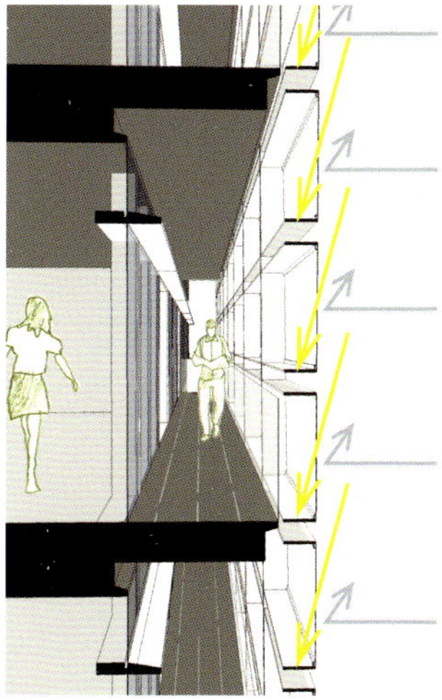

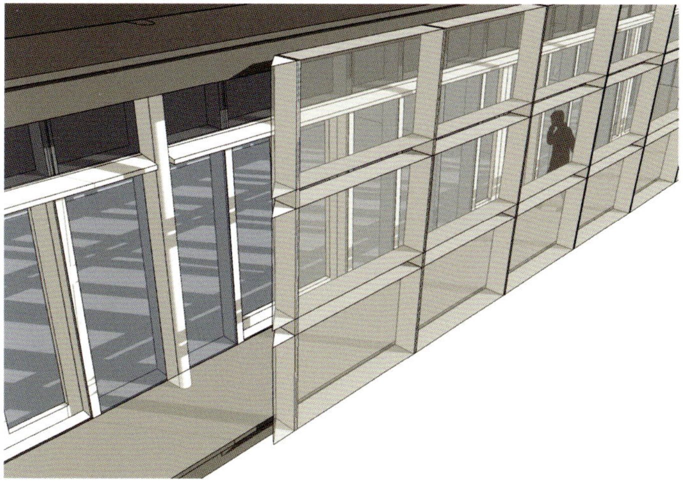

less wind force = less structure = less concrete

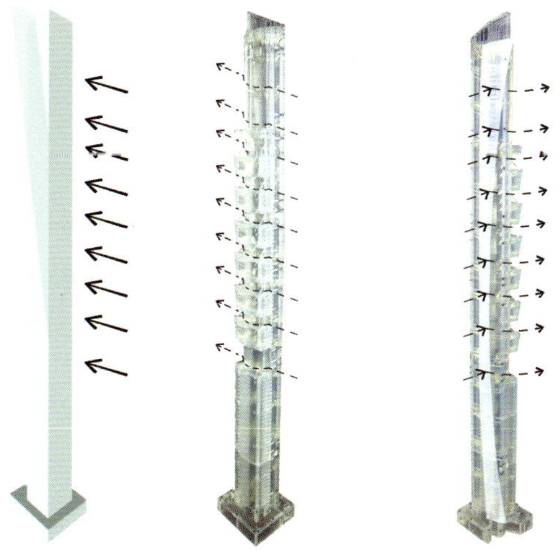

conventional building

effect of pods reduces wind force on building

effect of screen reduces wind pressure on building

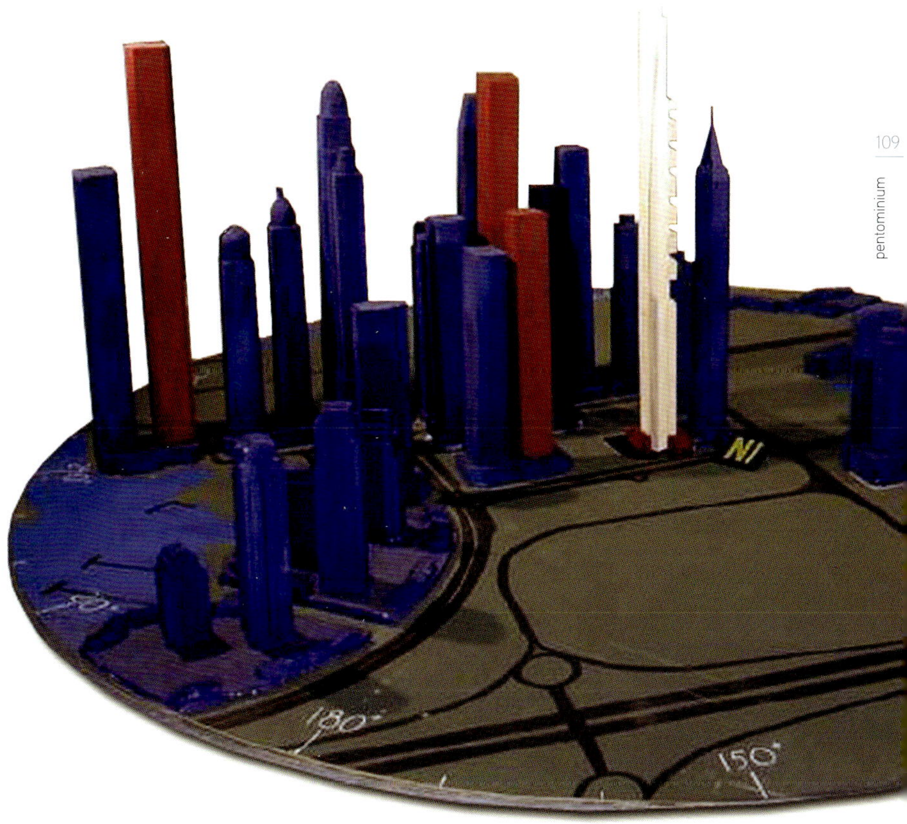

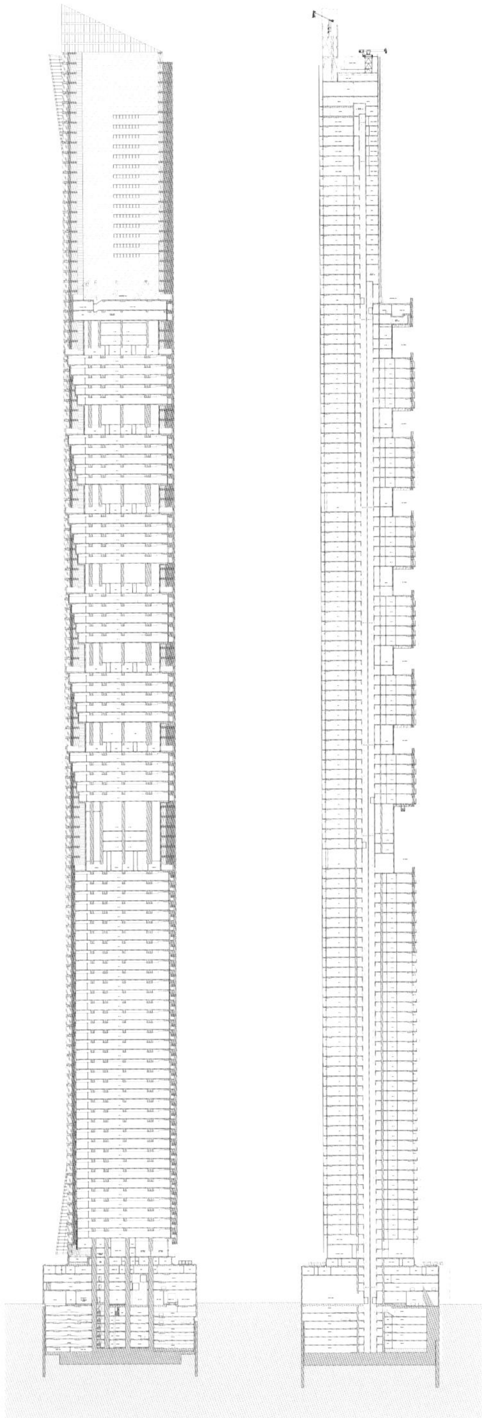

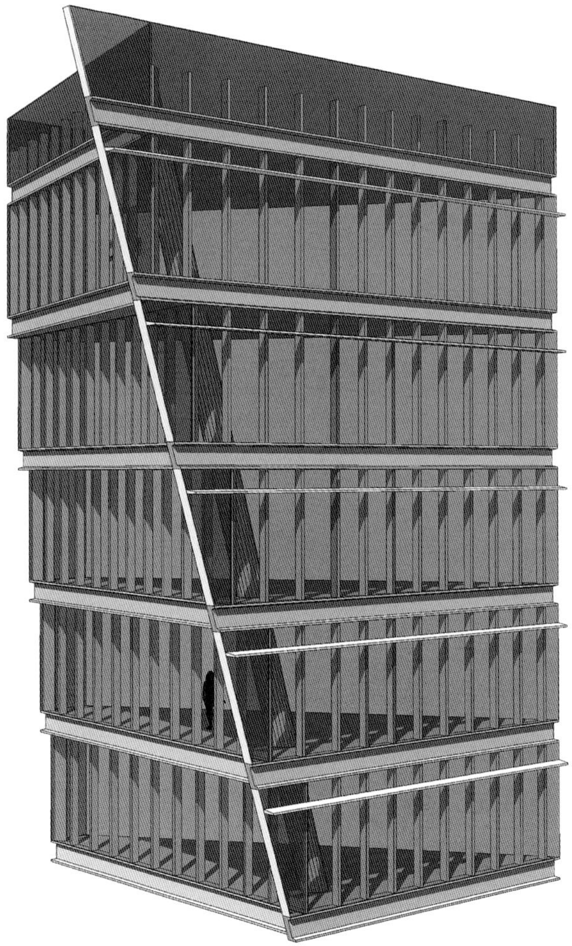

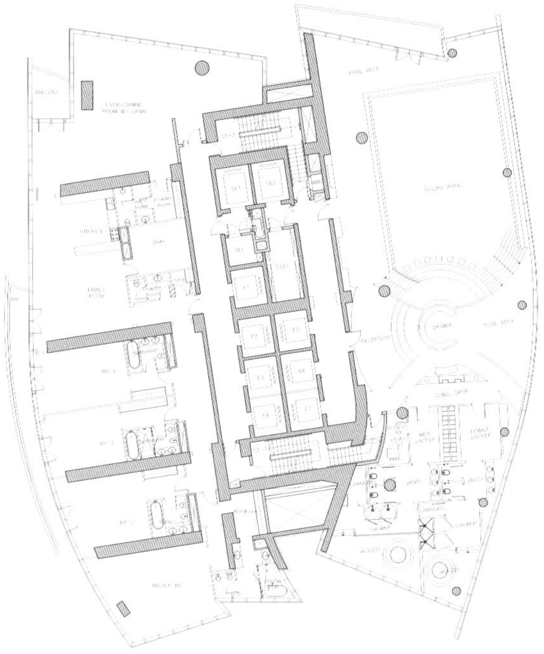

swimming pool level

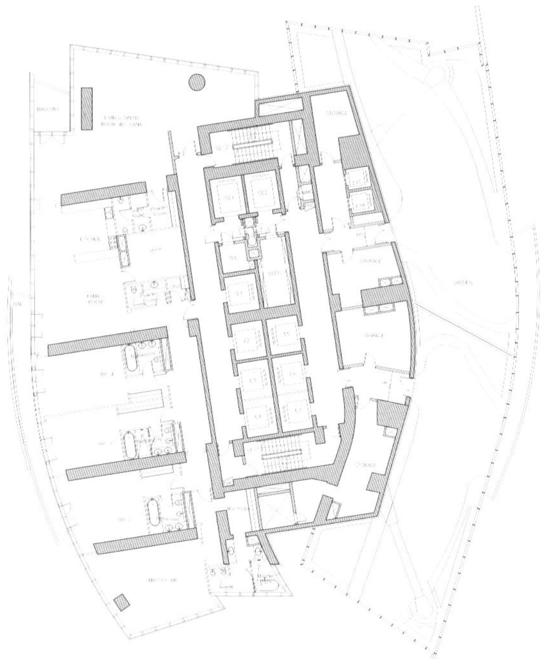

terrace level

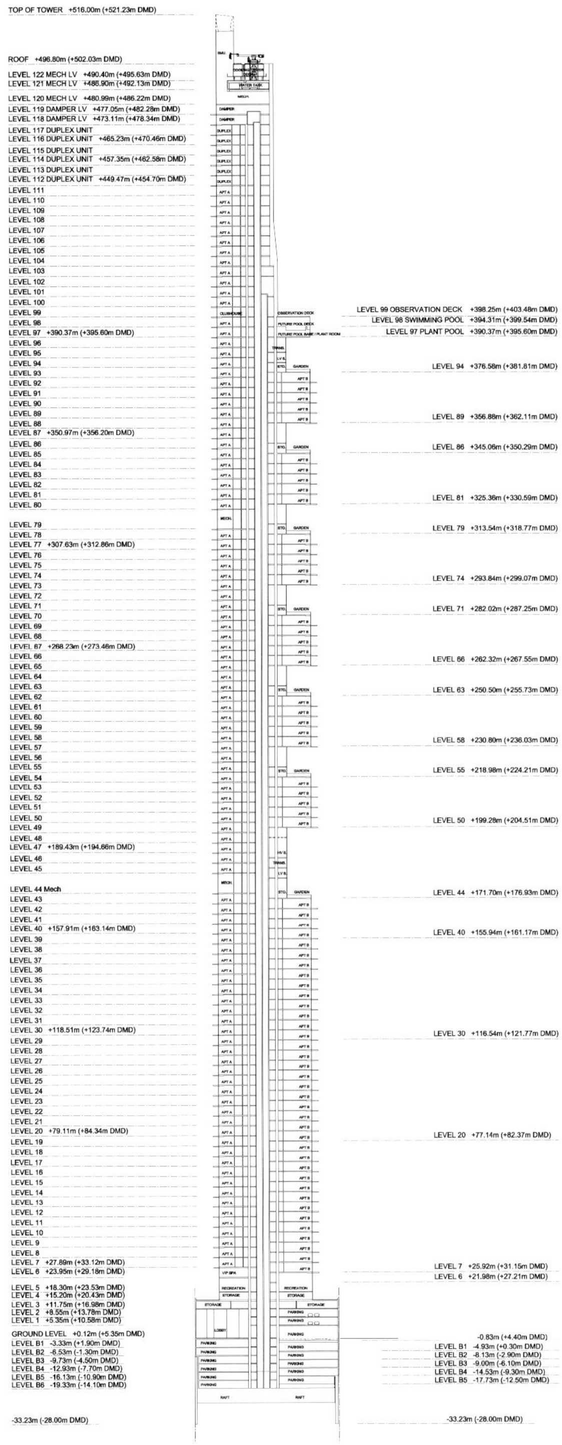

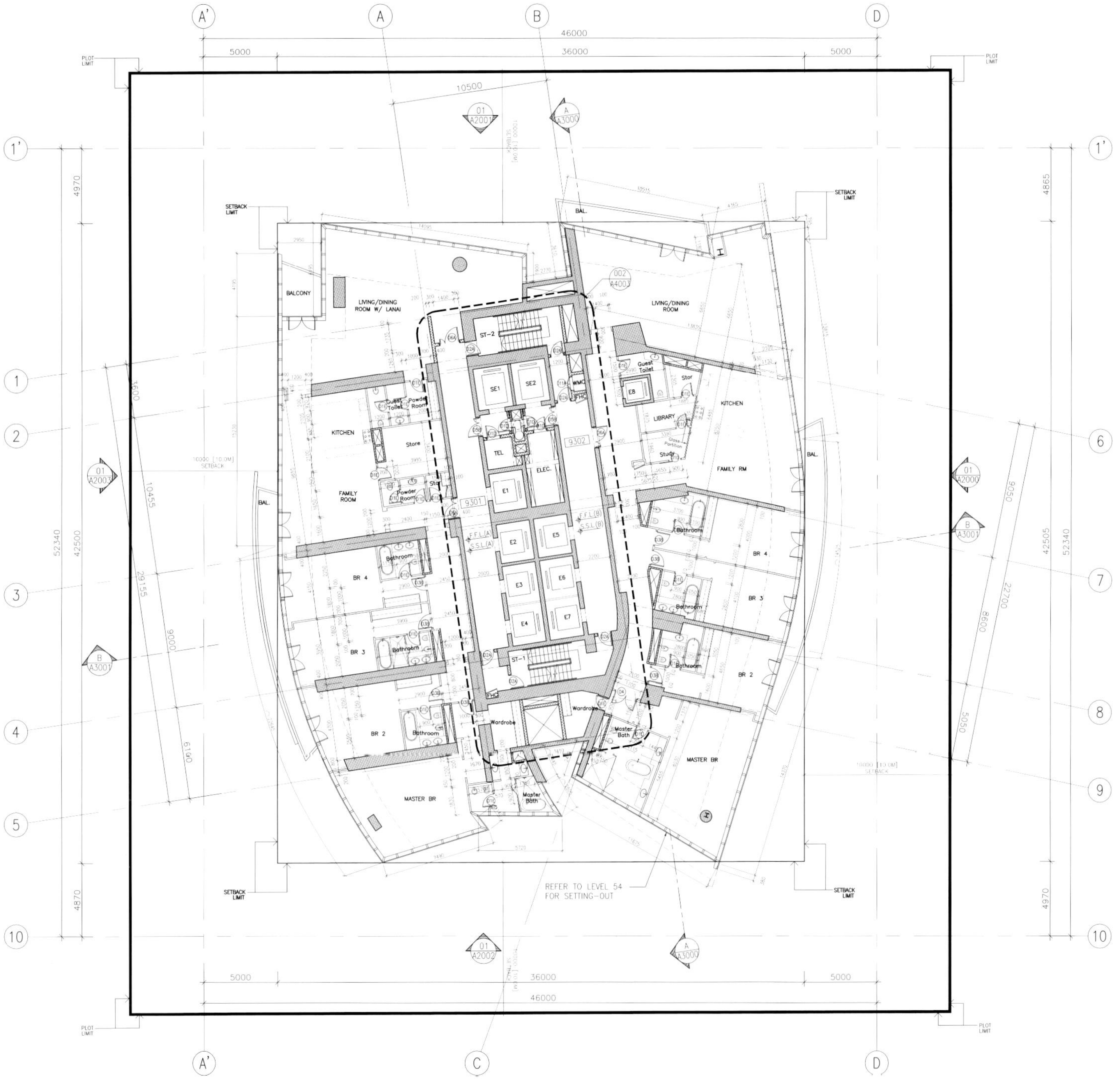
PLOT LIMIT
SETBACK LIMIT
46000
36000
5000
10500
LIVING/DINING ROOM W/ LANAI
BALCONY
LIVING/DINING ROOM
BAL.
KITCHEN
Guest Toilet
Powder Room
Store
FAMILY ROOM
Bathroom
BR 4
BR 3
BR 2
MASTER BR
Master Bath
Wardrobe
ST-2
ST-1
SE1
SE2
TEL
ELEC.
WMC
FHC
E1
E2
E3
E4
E5
E6
E7
E8
9301
9302
F.F.L.(A)
S.S.L.(A)
F.F.L.(B)
S.S.L.(B)
LIBRARY
Study
Stor
FAMILY RM
10000 [10.0M] SETBACK
REFER TO LEVEL 54 FOR SETTING-OUT
52340
42500
42505
4970
4865
4870
A'
A
B
C
D
1'
1
2
3
4
5
6
7
8
9
10

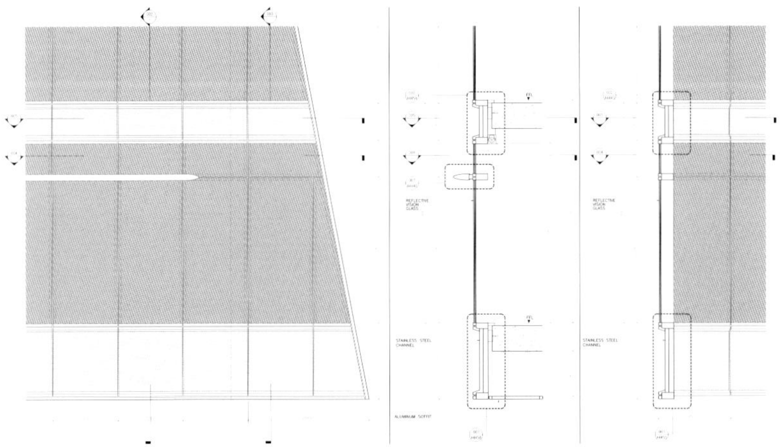

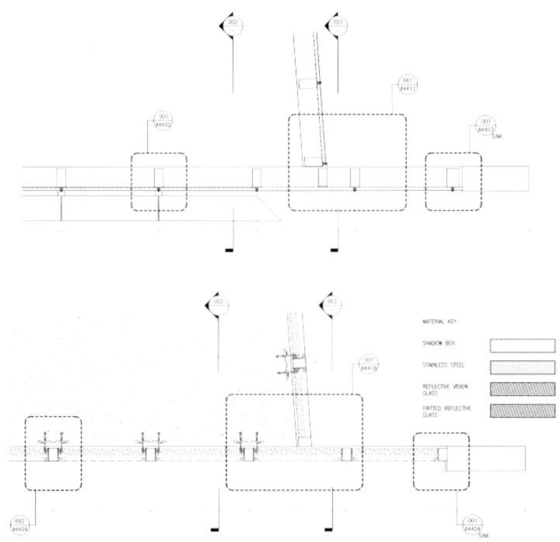
MATERIAL KEY:

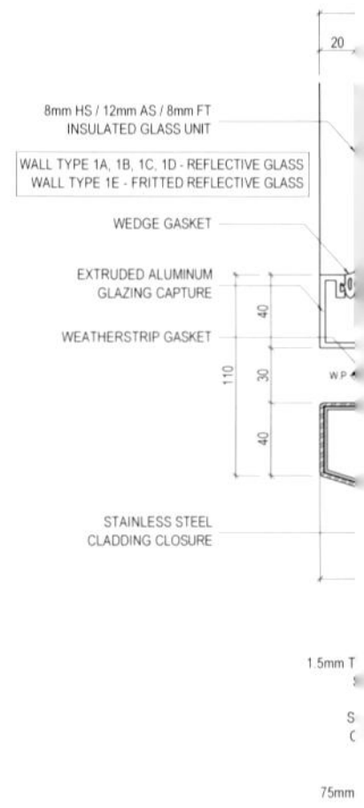
8mm HS / 12mm AS / 8mm FT
INSULATED GLASS UNIT
WALL TYPE 1A, 1B, 1C, 1D - REFLECTIVE GLASS
WALL TYPE 1E - FRITTED REFLECTIVE GLASS
WEDGE GASKET
EXTRUDED ALUMINUM
GLAZING CAPTURE
WEATHERSTRIP GASKET
STAINLESS STEEL
CLADDING CLOSURE

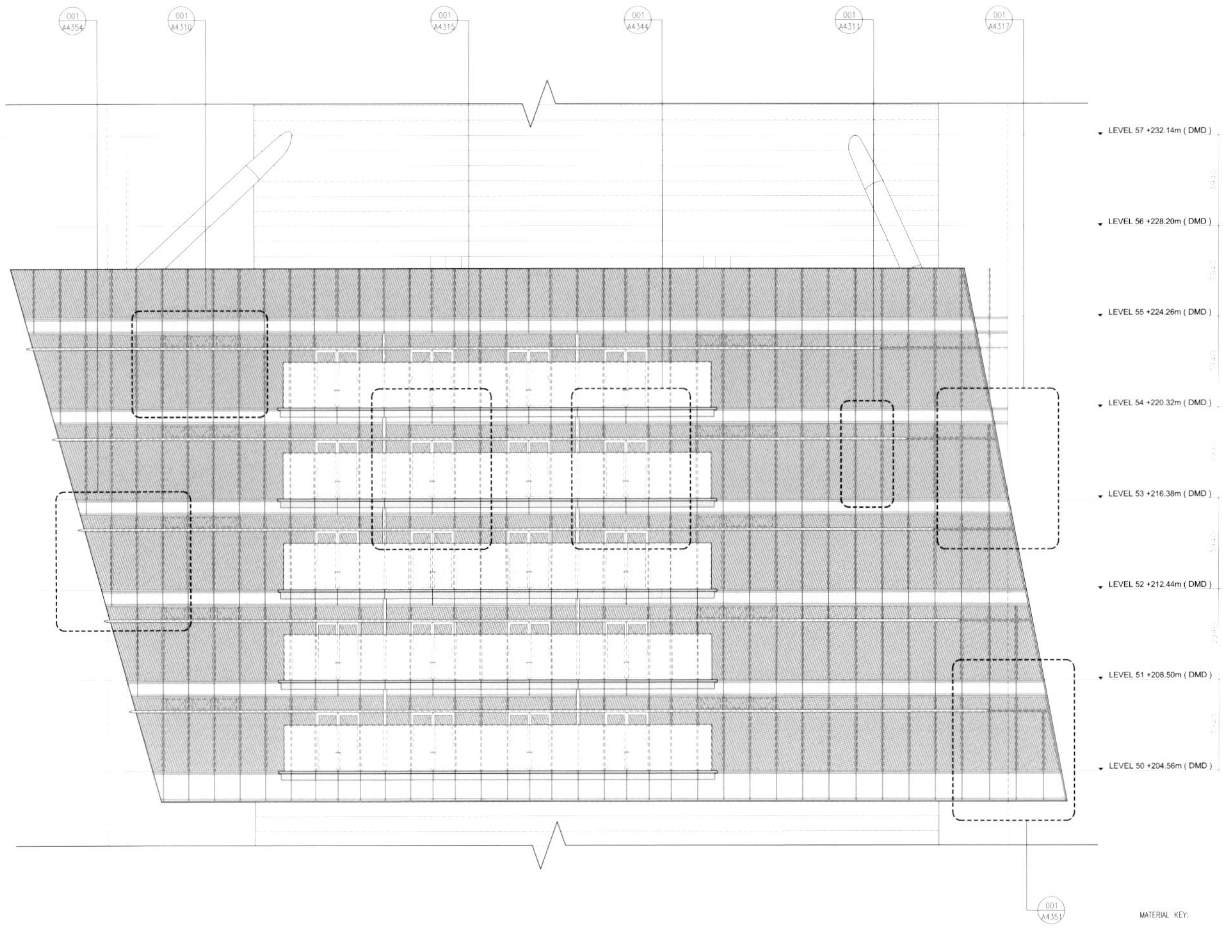
001
A4354
001
A4310
001
A4315
001
A4344
001
A4311
001
A4317
LEVEL 57 +232.14m (DMD)
LEVEL 56 +228.20m (DMD)
LEVEL 55 +224.26m (DMD)
LEVEL 54 +220.32m (DMD)
LEVEL 53 +216.38m (DMD)
LEVEL 52 +212.44m (DMD)
LEVEL 51 +208.50m (DMD)
LEVEL 50 +204.56m (DMD)
001
A4351
MATERIAL KEY:

SEALANT @ ENDS
STAINLESS STEEL
CLADDING CLOSURE
THERMAL BREAK
WEATHERSTRIP GASKET
EXTRUDED ALUMINUM
GLAZING CAPTURE
8mm HS / 12mm AS / 8mm FT
INSULATED GLASS UNIT
1A, 1D, 1E - FRITTED REFLECTIVE GLASS
1B, 1C - REFLECTIVE GLASS
EXTRUDED ALUMINUM
TRANSOM

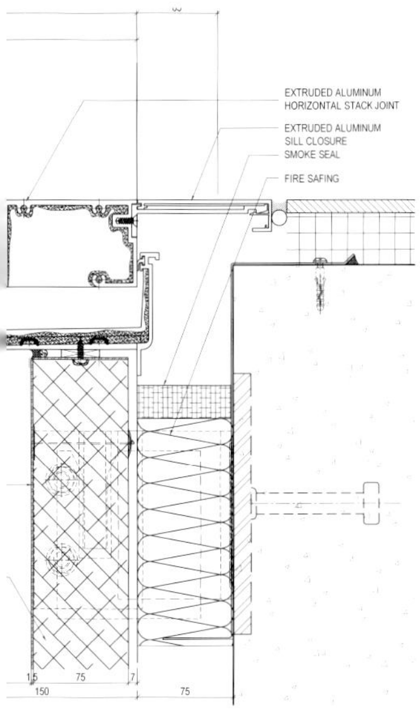
EXTRUDED ALUMINUM HORIZONTAL STACK JOINT
EXTRUDED ALUMINUM SILL CLOSURE
SMOKE SEAL
FIRE SAFING

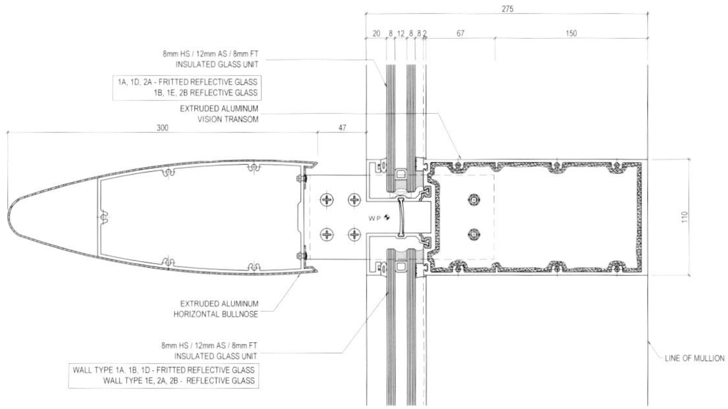
8mm HS / 12mm AS / 8mm FT INSULATED GLASS UNIT
1A, 1D, 2A - FRITTED REFLECTIVE GLASS
1B, 1E, 2B REFLECTIVE GLASS
EXTRUDED ALUMINUM VISION TRANSOM
EXTRUDED ALUMINUM HORIZONTAL BULLNOSE
8mm HS / 12mm AS / 8mm FT INSULATED GLASS UNIT
WALL TYPE 1A, 1B, 1D - FRITTED REFLECTIVE GLASS
WALL TYPE 1E, 2A, 2B - REFLECTIVE GLASS
LINE OF MULLION

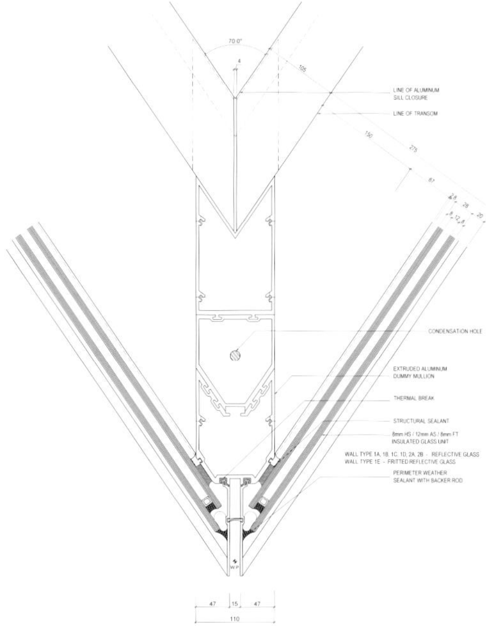
LINE OF ALUMINUM SILL CLOSURE
LINE OF TRANSOM
CONDENSATION HOLE
EXTRUDED ALUMINUM DUMMY MULLION
THERMAL BREAK
STRUCTURAL SEALANT
8mm HS / 12mm AS / 8mm FT INSULATED GLASS UNIT
WALL TYPE 1A, 1B, 1C, 1D, 2A, 2B - REFLECTIVE GLASS
WALL TYPE 1E - FRITTED REFLECTIVE GLASS
PERIMETER WEATHER SEALANT WITH BACKER ROD

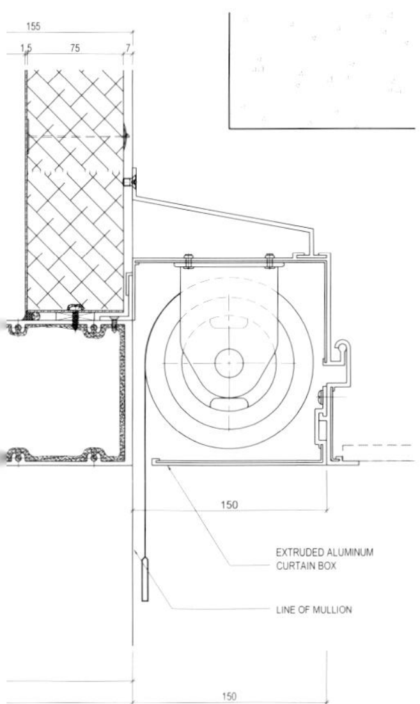
EXTRUDED ALUMINUM CURTAIN BOX
LINE OF MULLION

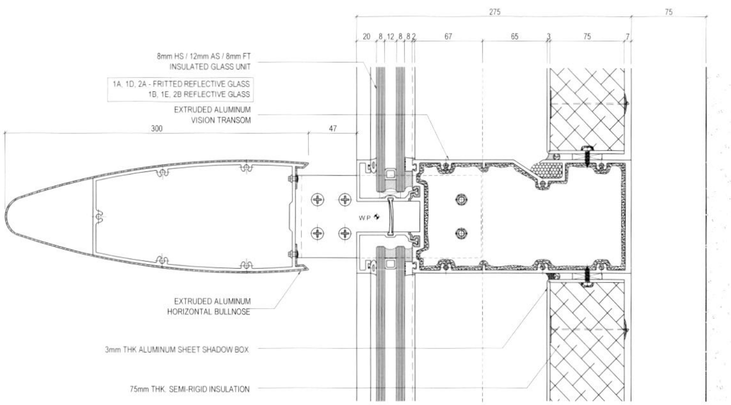
8mm HS / 12mm AS / 8mm FT INSULATED GLASS UNIT
1A, 1D, 2A - FRITTED REFLECTIVE GLASS
1B, 1E, 2B REFLECTIVE GLASS
EXTRUDED ALUMINUM VISION TRANSOM
EXTRUDED ALUMINUM HORIZONTAL BULLNOSE
3mm THK ALUMINUM SHEET SHADOW BOX
75mm THK. SEMI-RIGID INSULATION

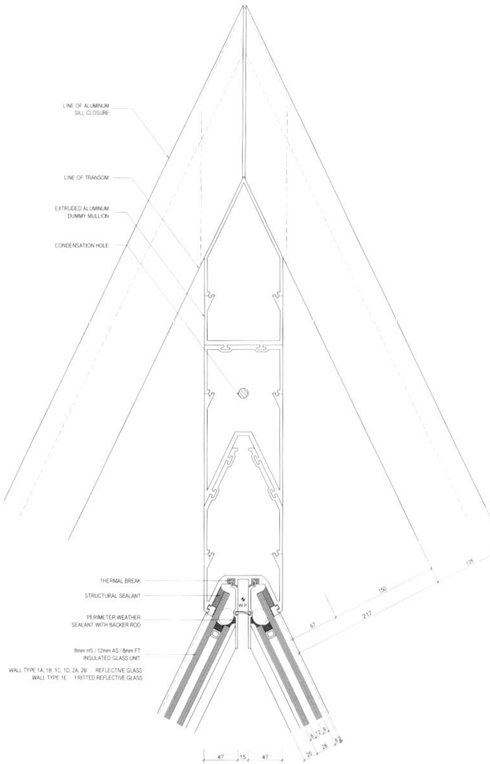
LINE OF ALUMINUM SILL CLOSURE
LINE OF TRANSOM
EXTRUDED ALUMINUM DUMMY MULLION
CONDENSATION HOLE
THERMAL BREAK
STRUCTURAL SEALANT
PERIMETER WEATHER SEALANT WITH BACKER ROD
8mm HS / 12mm AS / 8mm FT INSULATED GLASS UNIT
WALL TYPE 1A, 1B, 1C, 1D, 2A, 2B - REFLECTIVE GLASS
WALL TYPE 1E - FRITTED REFLECTIVE GLASS

arabian performance venue

arabian performance venue

opera house/mixed use
client: sama dubai llc
location: dubai, uae

site location

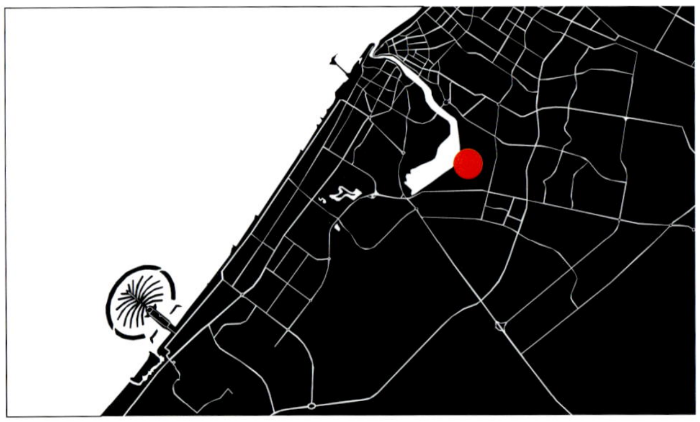

size/scale

project description

Surrounded by the desert sands and occupying its own island in the middle of a nature reserve, the Arabian Performance Venue is organically tied both to its context and through its use. The venue is experienced through an entry sequence of surprise and discovery.

The island is connected to the mainland via long span bridges for both vehicles and trains. Also approachable by boats, the entrances all cut into the mounded landscape to open into a water filled cavity. The walls, which contain the water, become the main entry foyer to the complex and a museum exhibition center. The museum rises in the center and drops on its sides, opening out and focusing on the lagoon populated with people engaging with nature and its wildlife.

Dropping down from the main foyer, the lower concourse opens up and moves underneath the water into a darkened space dappled with reflections from the water above. There are restaurants off to the side and a "black box" drama theatre near the center of the space. Inside this sedate world there are forty-four splashes of light from above. The light emitted comes from glass tubes which house forty-four elevators. Entering the elevator one rises out of the water and above the walls defining this inner space. They open up to allow for 360 degree views of the surrounding landscape and waters.

The elevators arrive at a traditional forecourt for the 2,500 seat performance venue 100 meters off the ground. It is surrounded by seven dancing figures which rise high into the sky above. This entry platform also serves as a public observation area, allowing views beyond to the migrating birds which flock to the surrounding waters.

process

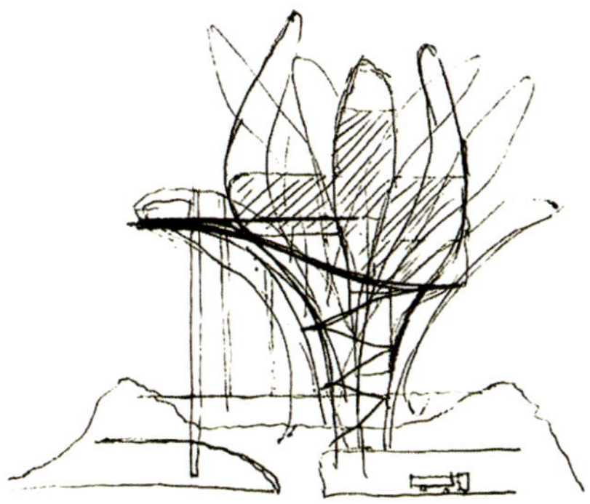

goals

To achieve a cultural complex with a civic presence and stature powerful enough to hold its own against the backdrop of Dubai's unconventional commercial buildings.

challenge

The client requested that the building become the first image one thought of when considering an "opera house"– in their minds, replacing the Sydney Opera House.

play

The foyer for the opera house, located 100 meters above the lagoon, is also an enormous public viewing platform in the middle of a bird sanctuary. Access to this platform comes through 40 glass tube elevators originating under the lagoon.

usage

residential
0 m2 0 sqf

hospitality
30287 m2 326006 sqf

office
0 m2 0 sqf

retail + f&b
16398 m2 176506 sqf

x1.5
landscape
159221 m2 1713841 sqf

theatre
98909 m2 1064648 sqf

total area: 304,815 m2
3,281,000 sqf

| = 2500 m2 / 26910 sqf

status

lagoon's master development on hold

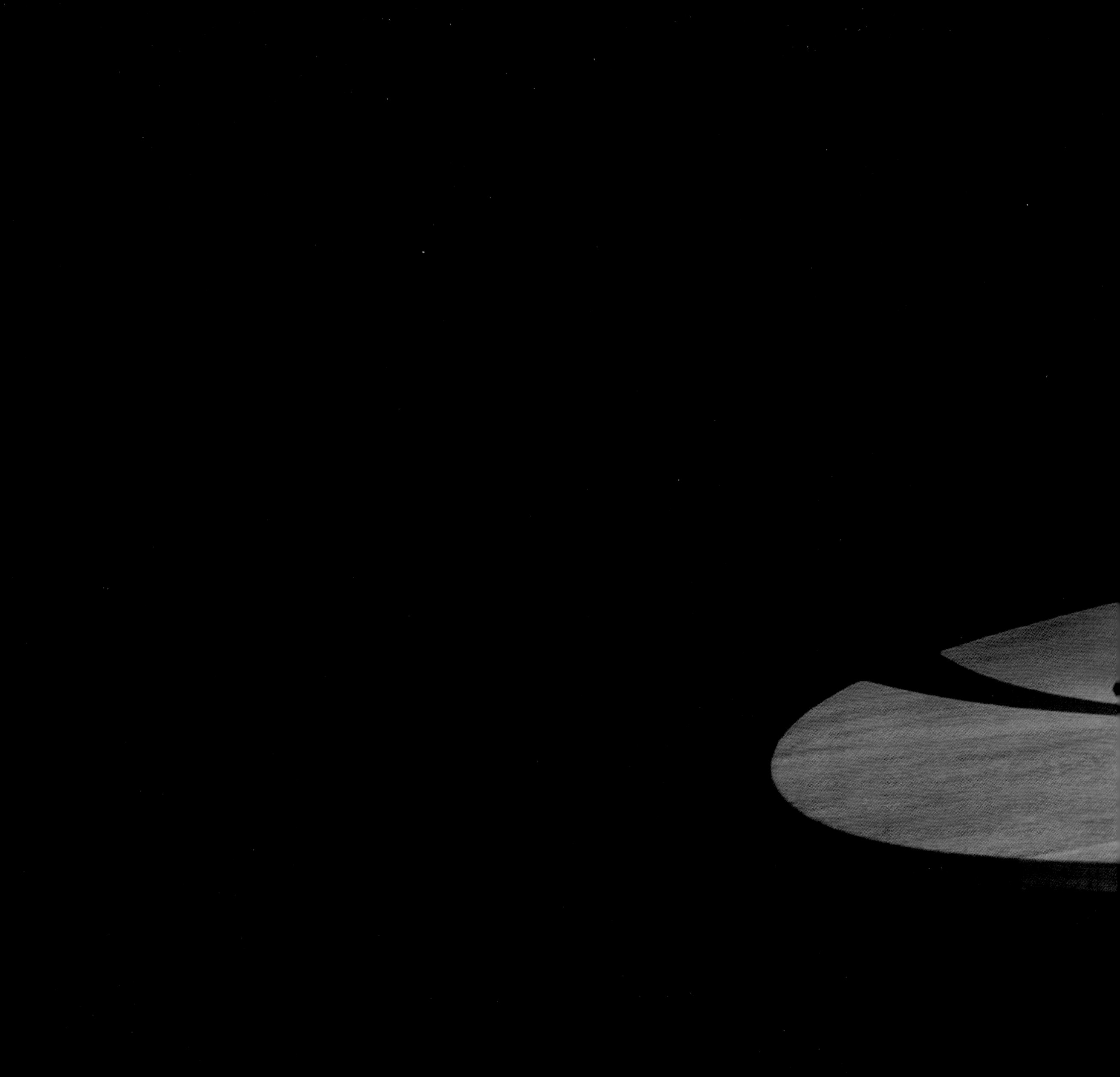

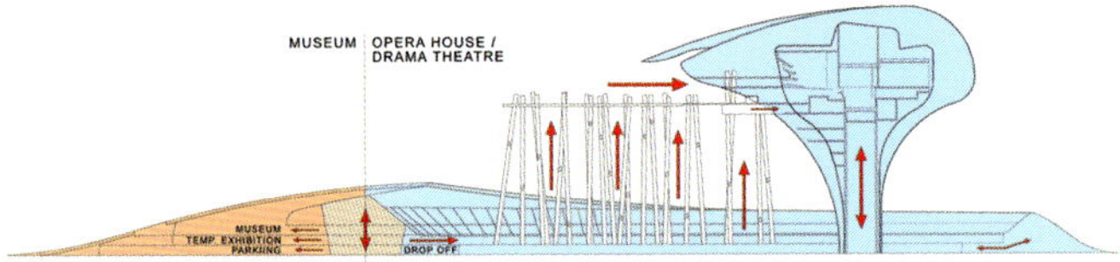

pedestrian circulation

scale comparison

1. Atrium
2. Temporary Exhibition Space
3. Museum
4. Exterior Viewing Terrace
5. Event Exhibition Hall
6. Parking
7. Valet Services
8. Passenger/Taxi Drop Off
9. Gift Shop
10. Lobby
11. Opera Platform
12. Upper Foyer
13. Opera Lift Lobby
14. Interior Opera House Lift Lobby
15. Performers Drop-Off
16. Drama Theater
17. Opera House Shipping/ Loading
18. Rehearsal Studios
19. Green Rooms
20. Truck Lift
21. Loading/Storage/Workshop
22. Management/Marketing
23. Dressing Rooms/Rehearsal Rooms
24. Stage/Fly Tower & Orchestra Pit
25. Main Auditorium
26. Staff/Performers Kitchen
27. Bridge
28. Entrance Lobby
29. Hotel Lobby

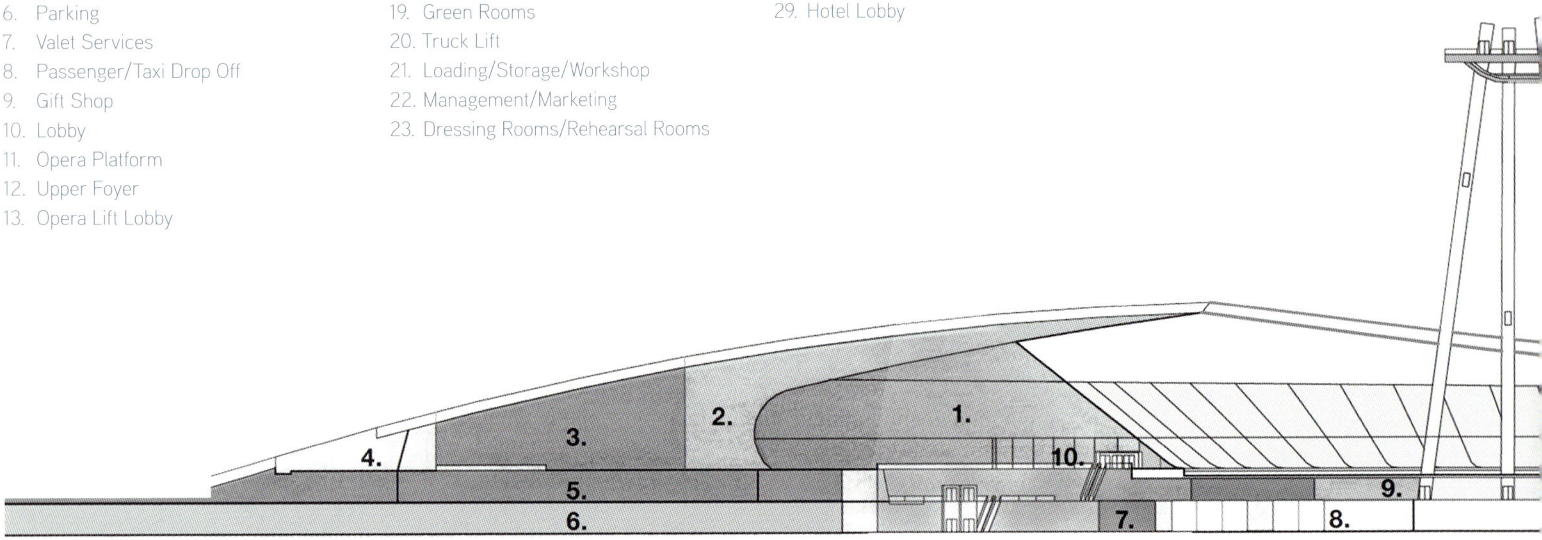

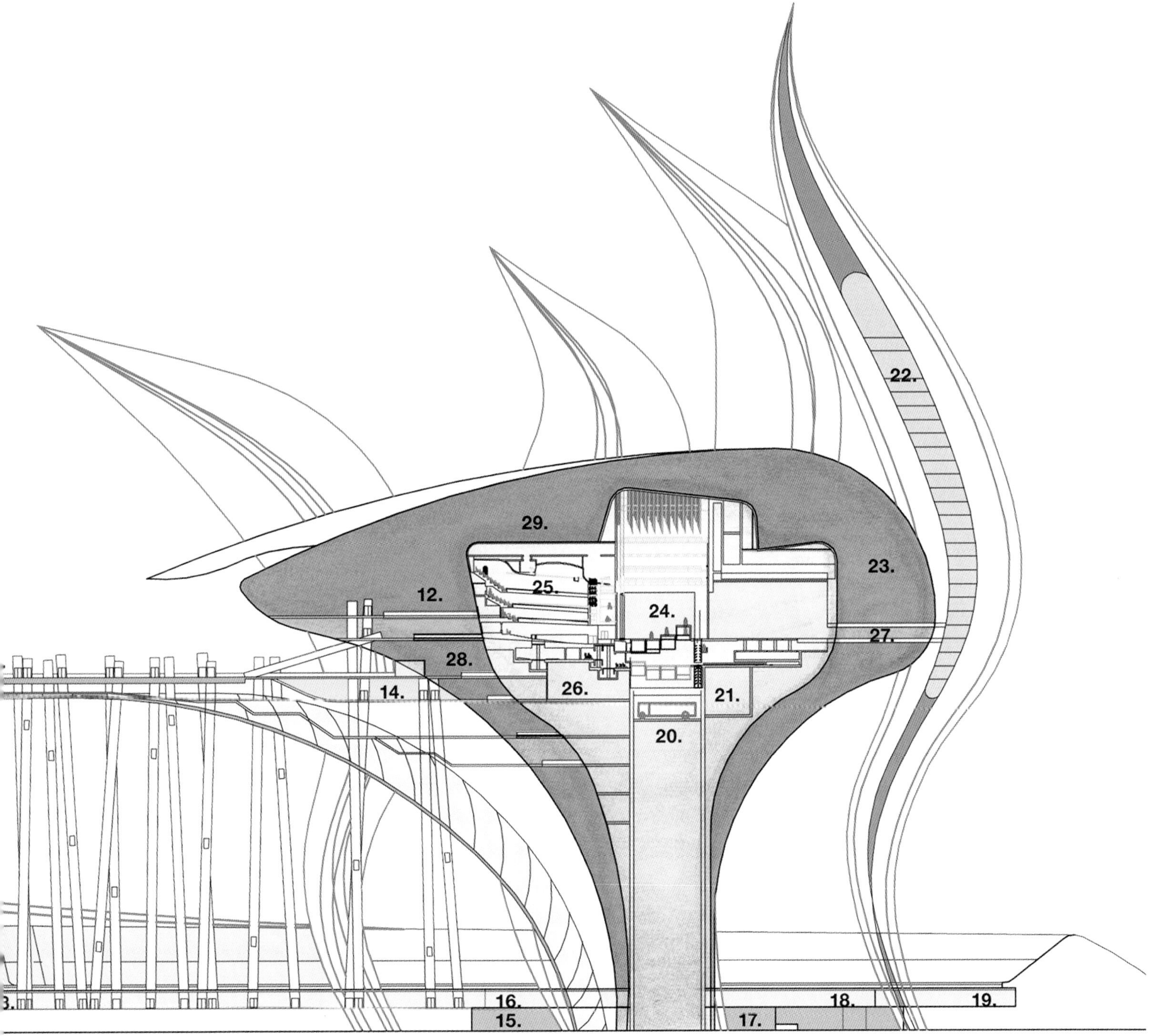
22.
29.
23.
12.
25.
24.
27.
28.
26.
14.
21.
20.
16.
18.
19.
15.
17.

At the center of these dancing figures, which are filled with different activities, is the solidity of the performance venue itself – the pearl. Entrance into the main hall exposes the volume rising from the waters below. The auditorium hall opens up above to the main lobby of the hotel sitting on top of the performance venue, which is enclosed with an outer glass shell. Reached by its own express lifts, the hotel lobby is flanked by four figures which are reached via sky-bridges. These figures house 300 hotel and service apartment rooms.

The front two figures are filled with public food and beverage outlets and provide shade to the forecourt. The back figure contains supporting facilities for the performance venue itself. These seven dancing figures or seven ruffled feathers rise into the sky with the highest one reaching 284 meters in height.

civic, cultural & retail complex

civic, cultural & retail complex

theater/mixed use

client: rock production/capitaland

location: one north, singapore

site location

size/scale

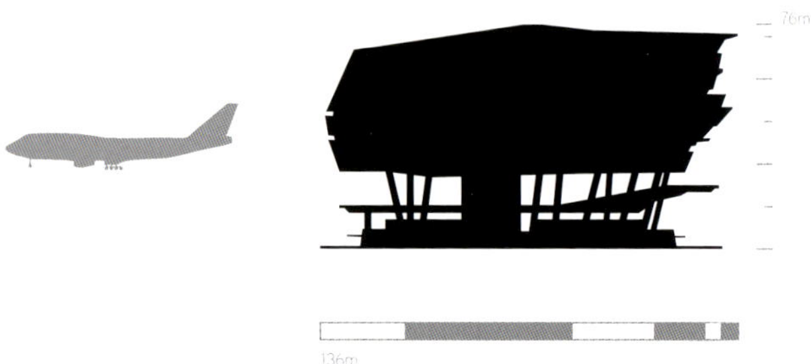

project description

The design for the Civic, Cultural & Retail Complex does not present one sole expression to describe the project. Instead it celebrates the rich and varying activities inside with a multi-faceted ephemeral and dynamic design, blurring the boundaries between the public and private realms and between the retail and cultural components. These transitions are soft and flowing, encouraging discovery and resulting in a highly public, energetic civic node within One North and beyond.

The civic and public components of the project are paramount and outwardly expressed. The south elevation is completely opened up presenting the inner workings of the facility as a section visible from and to the "Green". The mass of the theatre floating above is faceted, cut with glass fissures, and utilizes an external acid-etched glass finish Okulux cladding. All of this helps dissolve and break down the mass above, playing with a composition of positive and negative readings, in balance with the lower portion's use of solid and void.

The civic building is intended to be an organic object which is open to public discovery. One can crawl under, move through, circulate around and climb onto the complex through a series of ramps, escalators, terraces and public gardens. All circulation, movement and internal forms are soft and fluid as if the civic activities have polished the inside of the urbanely presented and strongly featured exterior.

The cultural and retail components are bound together with the volume of the 40m high, "Grand Foyer". The importance these two components have to each other is celebrated by blurring the divisions between them while maintaining functionality. This soft transition occurs vertically from the most public area of the open retail into the perceptual privacy of the theatre. This entire sequence and transition is linked visually and spatially to the "Grand Foyer" connecting the sunken retail below up through the glass floor of the theatre's main lobby and exposing its volume floating above.

process

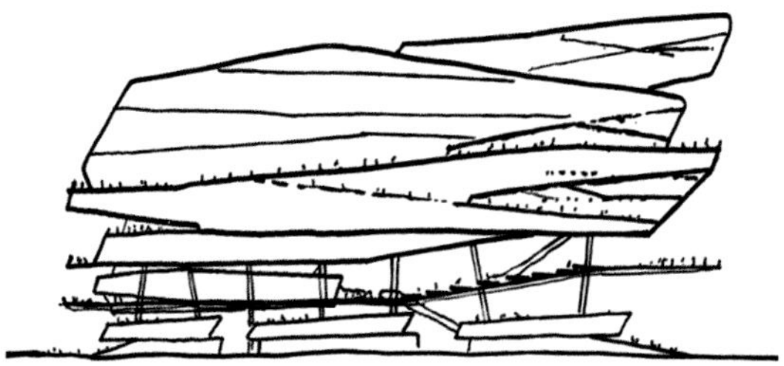

day 001

day 003

day 365

goals

The project aims to become a vibrant civic node with the cultural component of the 5,000 seat theatre and the food and beverage based retail sector working together in order to enhance each other's viability.

challenge

Floating the theatre 35 meters above the ground to allow for the appropriate outdoor terraces for the food and beverage outlets, external civic space, and 400 person outdoor theatre.

play

There is a 400 meter external loop ramp system which navigates around the entire theatre at over 50 meters above the ground below.

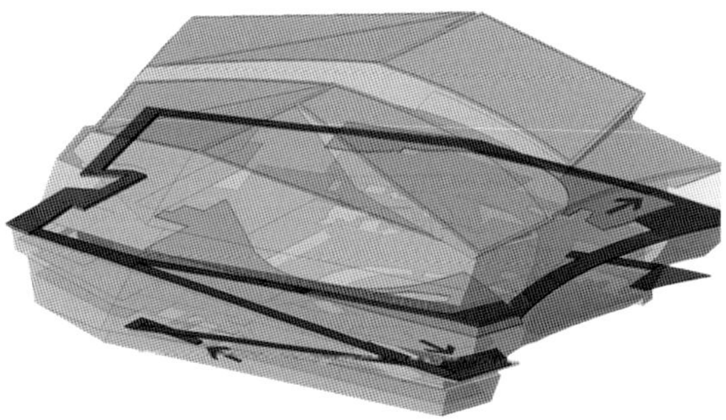

usage

residential
0 m2 0 sqf

hospitality
0 m2 0 sqf

office
0 m2 0 sqf

retail + f&b
24000 m2 258334 sqf

landscape
0 m2 0 sqf

civic & cultural
38000 m2 409028 sqf

total area: 62,000 m2
667,362 sqf

| = 2500 m2 / 26910 sqf

status

projected completion: 2012

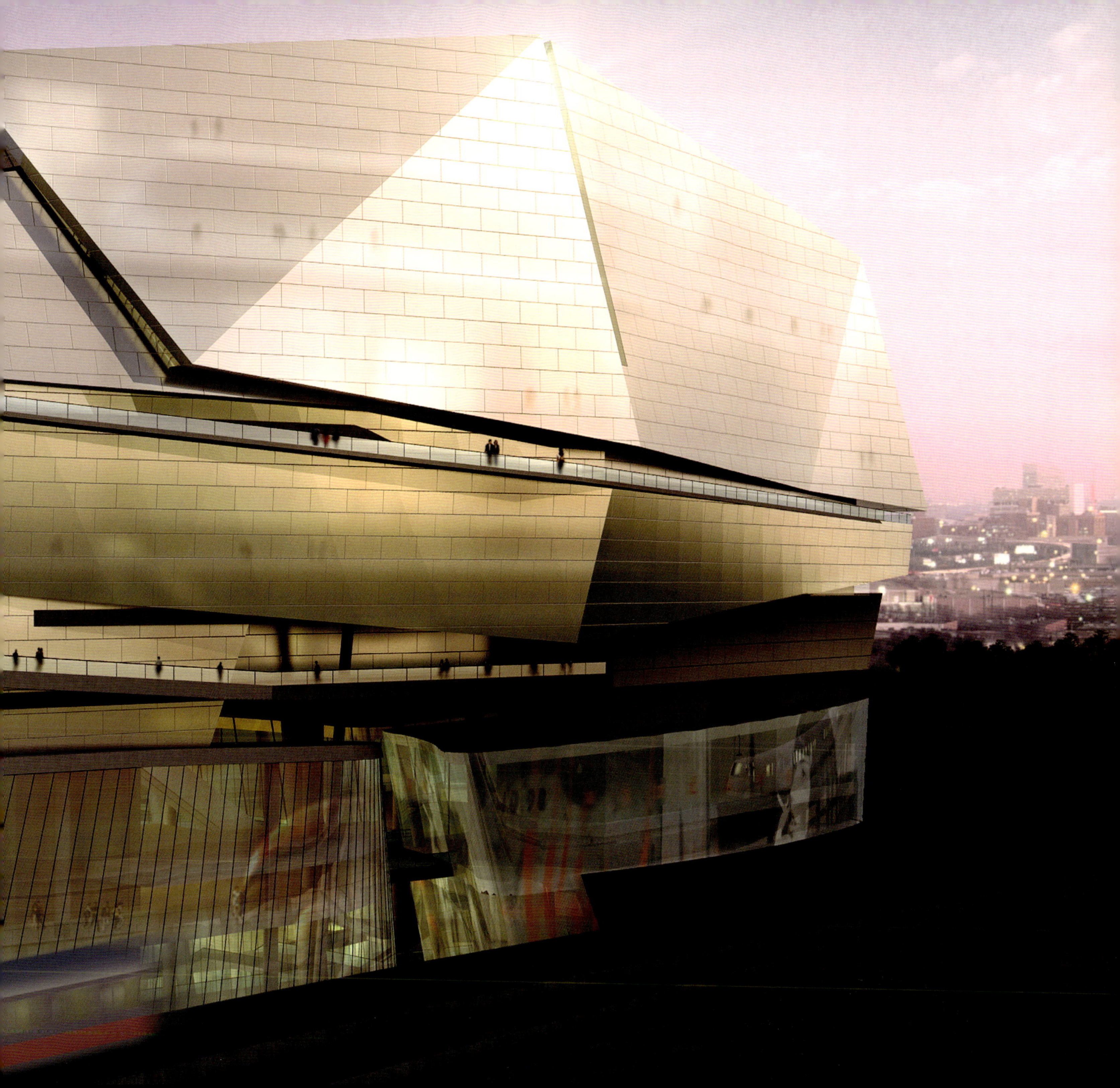

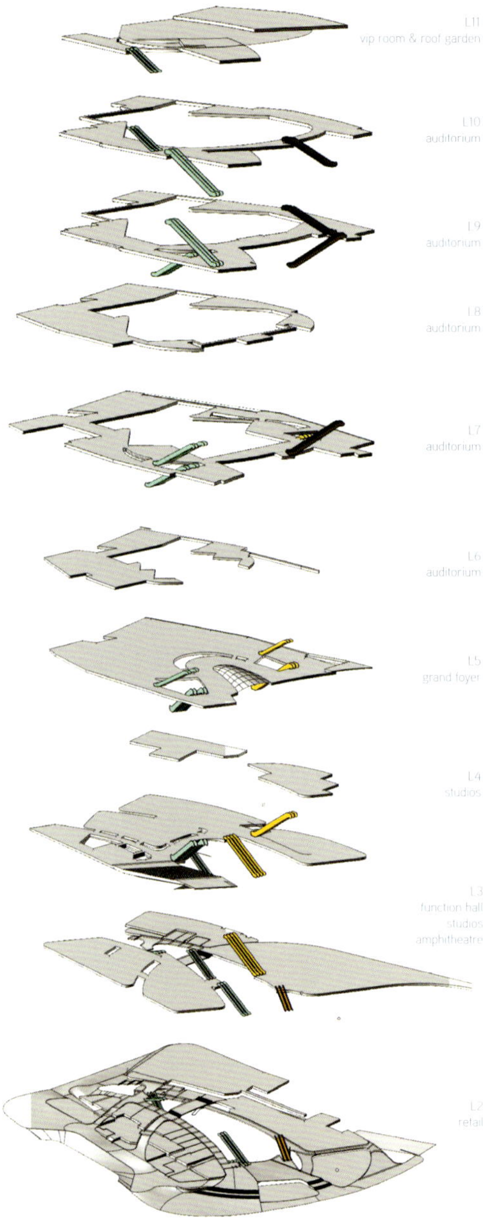

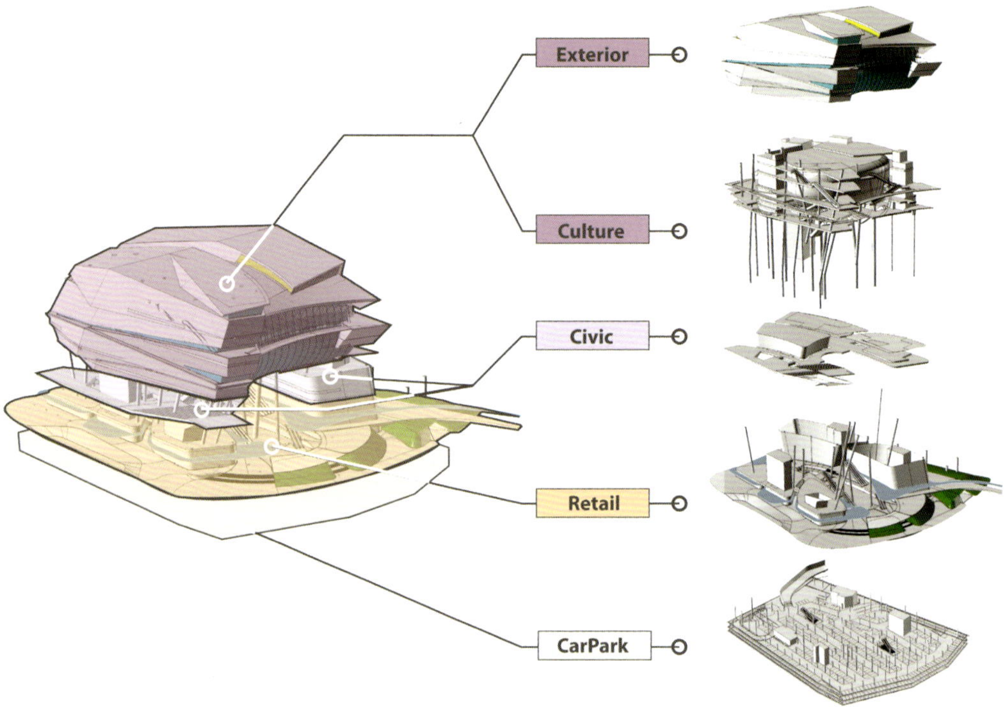

The theatre venue itself is over 60 meters in width and contains over 5,000 seats with two balconies. In order to achieve the cantilever of the balcony and preserve clear site lines to the stage, the structural steel needed to support the span was similar to that used in current stadium design. The complication comes when looking to also provide a good acoustical performance level within the facility. Sound and vibrations from the lobbies and external environment needed to be controlled. Consequently a cavity wall system for the theatre was introduced. The entire still structure thus needed to be contained.

The bowl enclosure was developed to hide the dense structure as well as to protect the venue from noise penetration and vibrations. Due to the sheer mass of the venue enclosure and the pressures of 5,000 people flowing in and out of the facility, a soft, fluid form was developed to cover structure but allow transition openings into the theatre. Similar to the external enclosure, this also helps break the mass down and reduce the perceived bulk of the object.

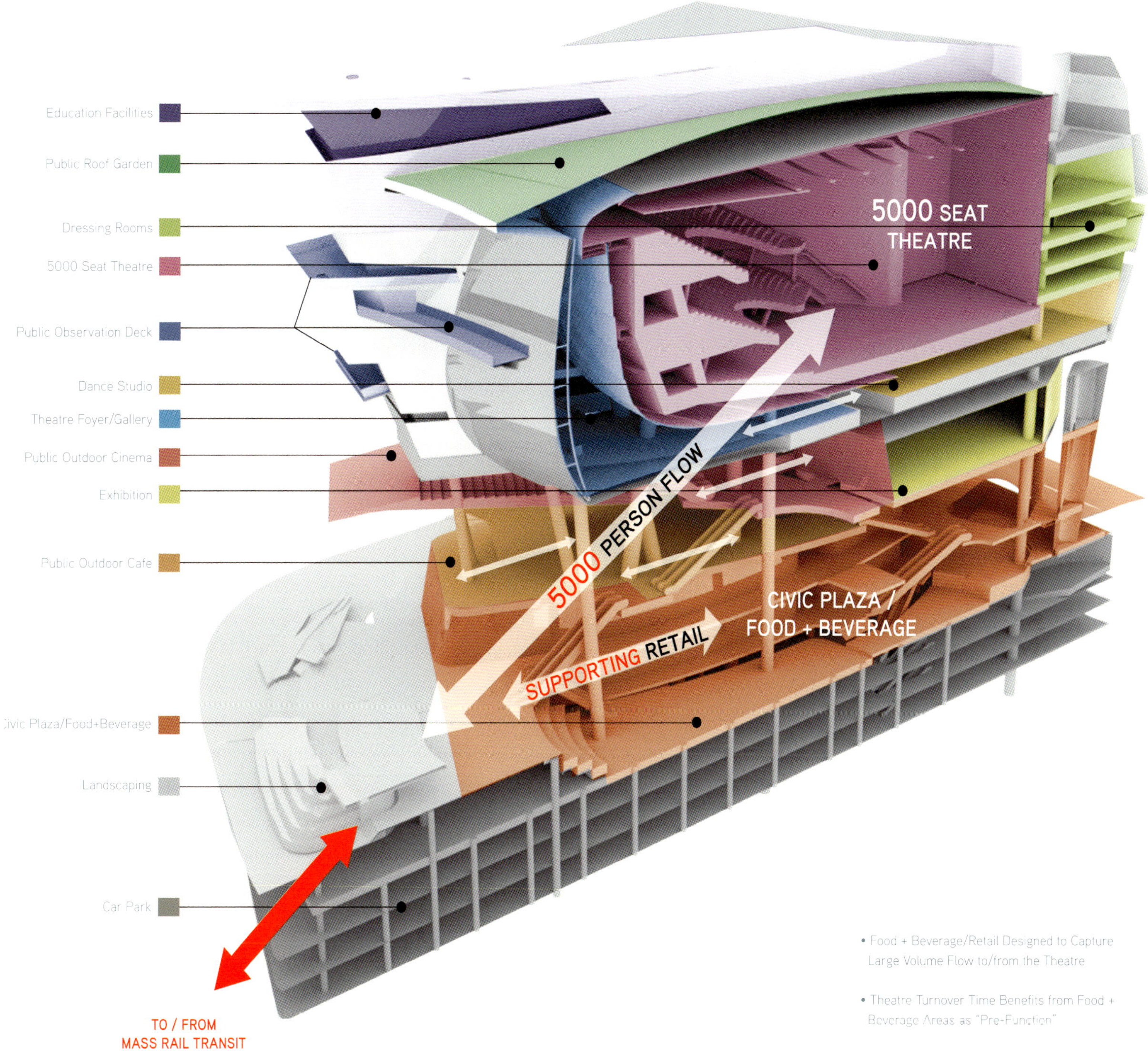

- Food + Beverage/Retail Designed to Capture Large Volume Flow to/from the Theatre
- Theatre Turnover Time Benefits from Food + Beverage Areas as "Pre-Function"

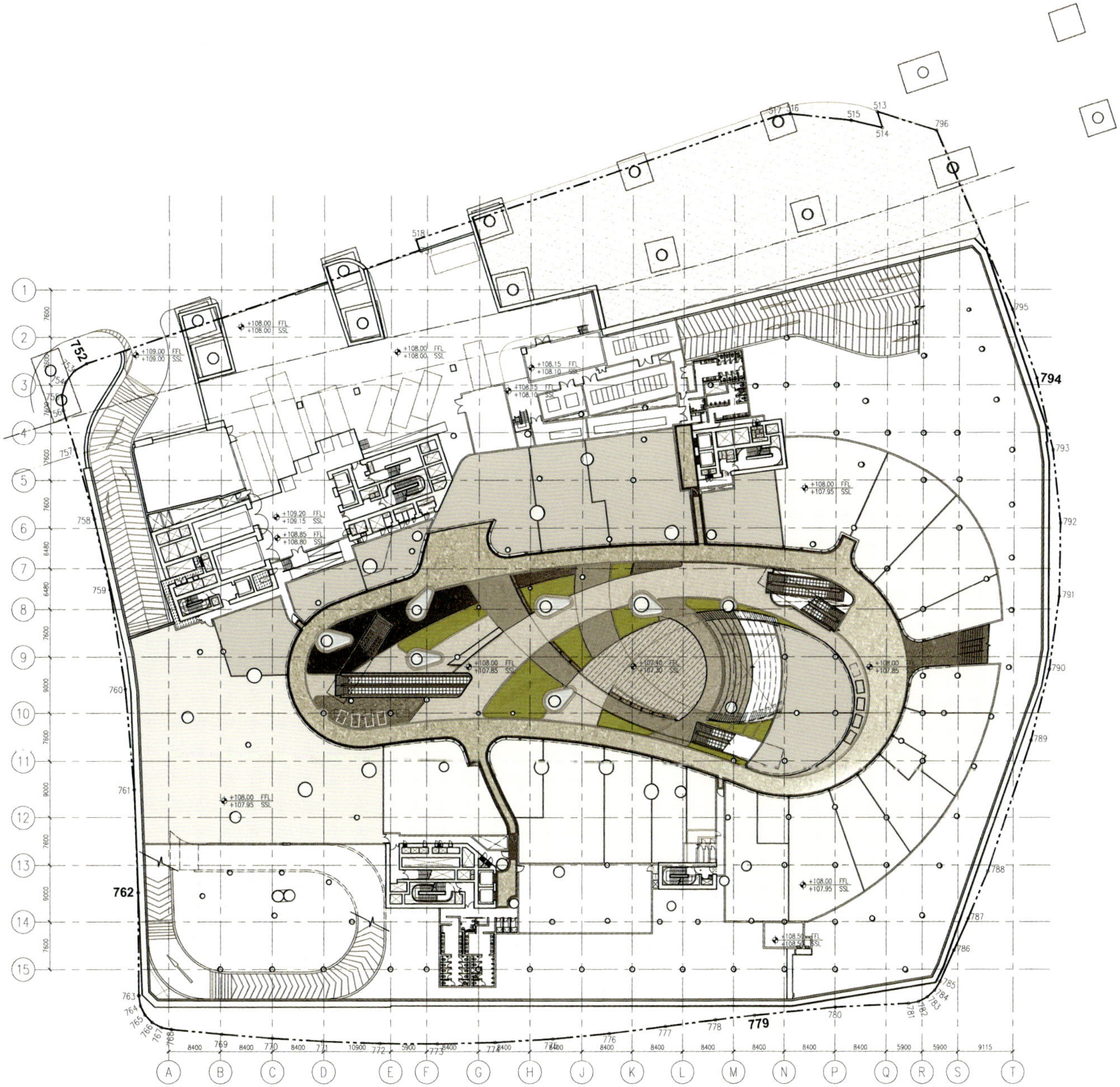

B1 plan

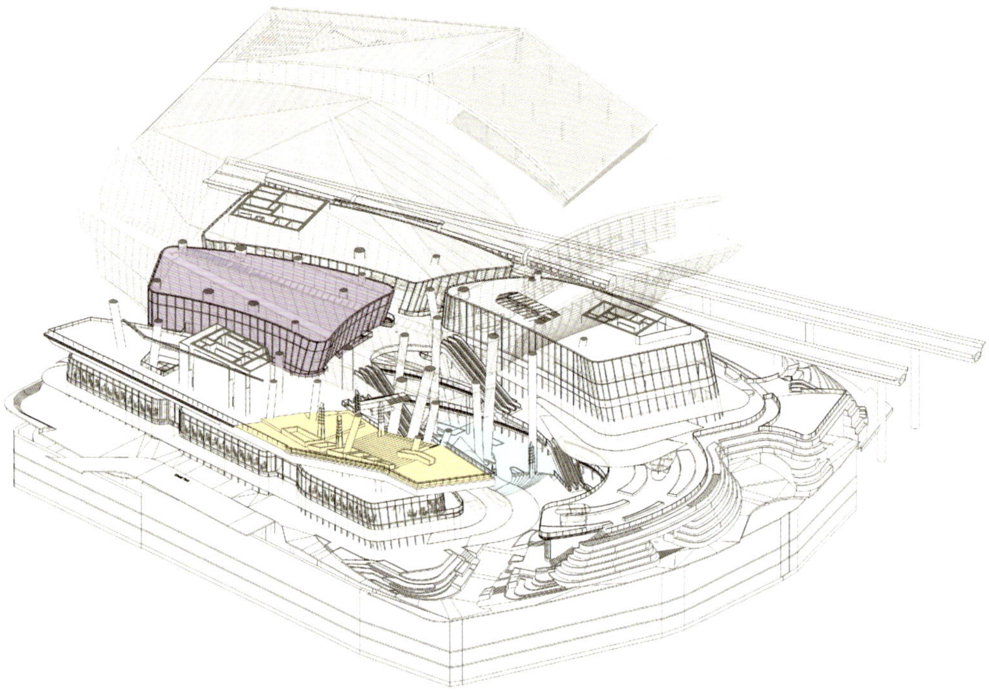

civic plaza

amphitheatre

function hall

retail

civic plaza

The theatre itself is an extension of the entire experience. The overall enclosure of the venue is faceted, utilizing punched zinc panels which are folded with a strong direction toward the stage. The main circulation aisles, balustrades and inner theatre walls in contrast, are softer and warmer as they are contained within a more fluid geometry.

The design is highly sustainable thanks to the way in which it minimizes air conditioned spaces. The retail, civic square, outdoor theatre and the pre-function areas for the banqueting and meeting room facilities are all open air, as is the "Grand Foyer".

The design has opened up all four elevations to encourage air movement through the volume. The design of these openings will explore how the heated surfaces on the southern elevation and roof can induce wind flow from the shaded, northern face through these covered outdoor spaces. This air movement can be mechanically assisted at times if necessary. The result will be an enjoyable year-round shaded environment with a cooling breeze allowing one to pass through or dwell within. Glazing on the southern face is minimized and protected by sunshading. The majority of the glass of the theatre's main lobby faces east but it also protected from the late morning sun with an external bridge that acts as a large sun shade. On top of the facility is a large roof-top garden shaded with trees and overlooking a reflecting pool. Gardens are deliberately placed throughout the facility softening the distinction between inside and outside spaces and promoting the CCRC as an eco-friendly environment.

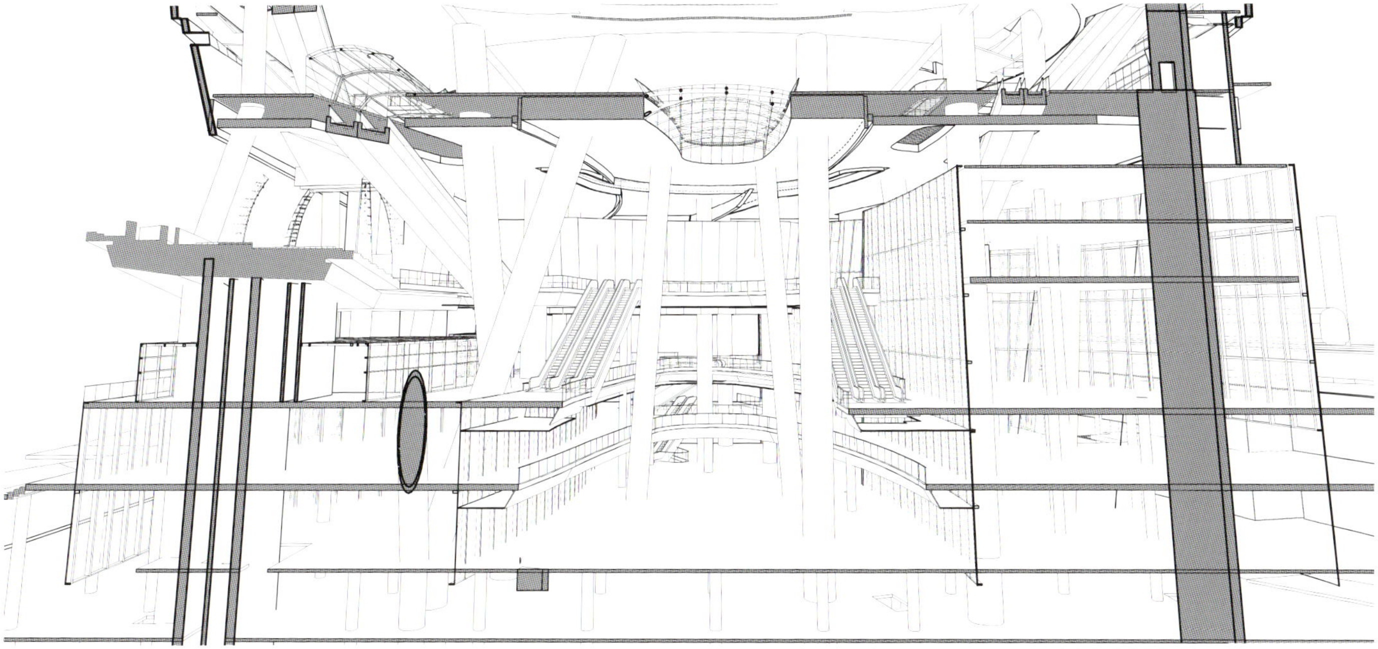

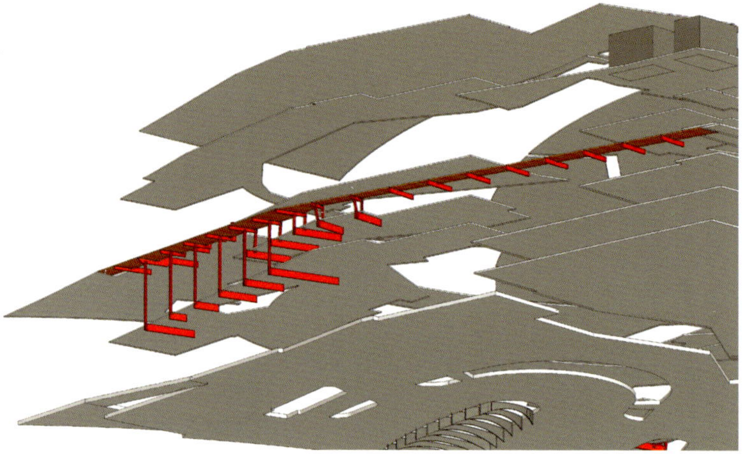

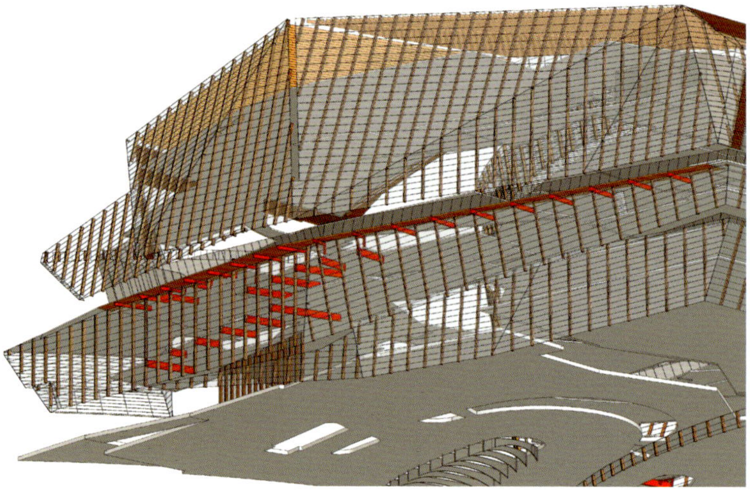

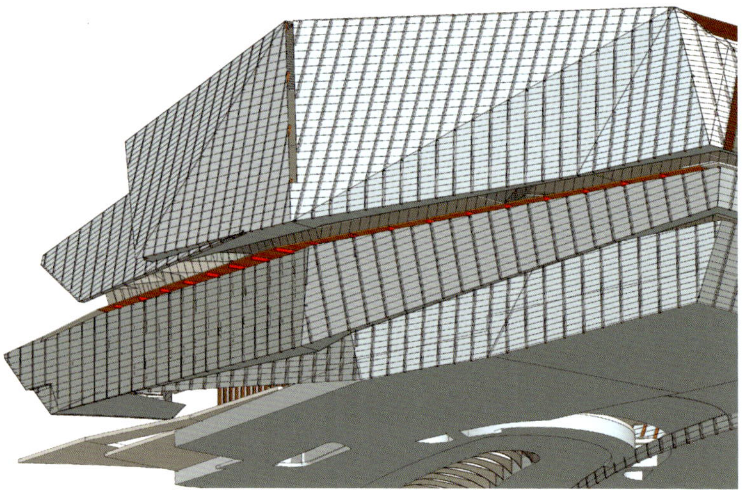

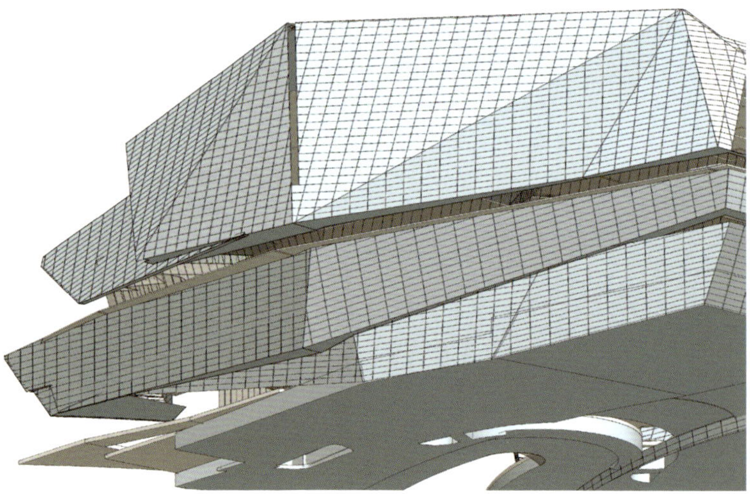

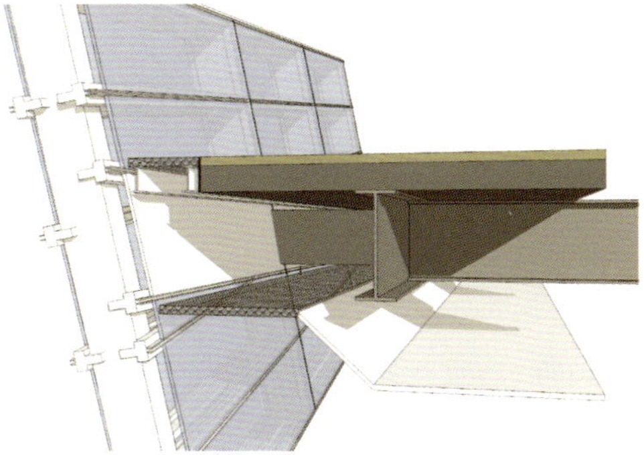

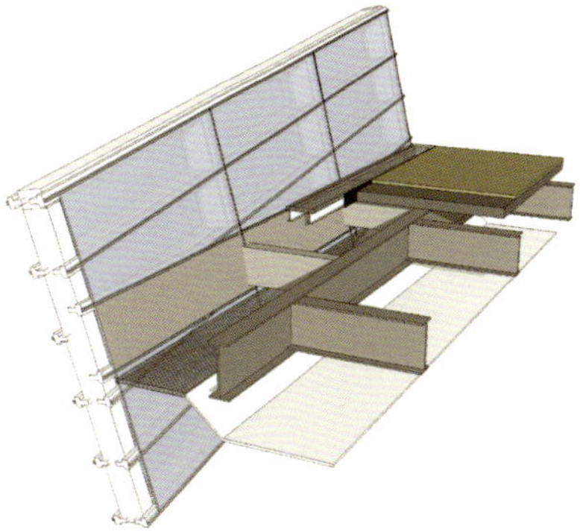

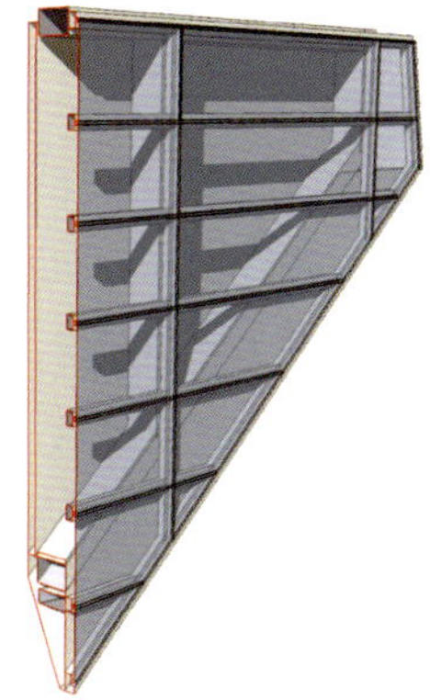

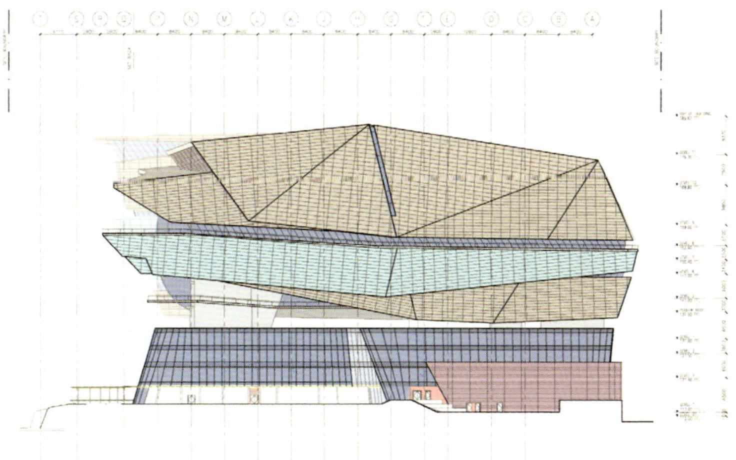

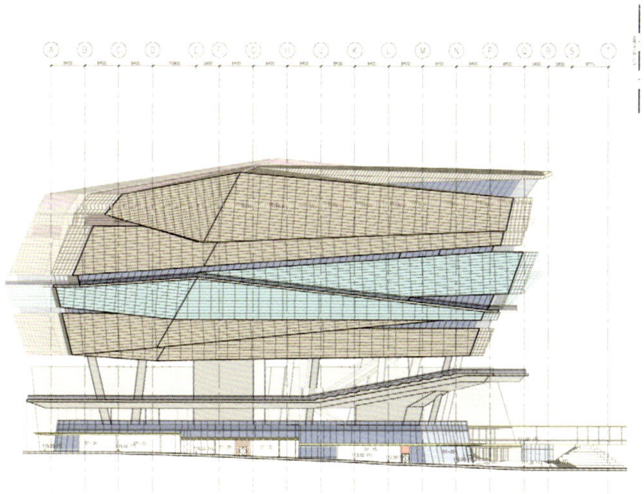

THEATRE CT-T
- double layer of light diffusing IGU : CT-T 01, 02, 03
- single layer of light diffusing IGU + solid backing : CT-T 04, 05
- clear glass : CT-T 06
- laminated glass : CT-T 07
- aluminum louvers : CT-T 08
- suspended soffit : CT-T 00
- landscaped paving

RETAIL
- clear glass: CT-R 01, 02, 03, 07 & 08
- spandrel glass: CT-R 04, 05, 06 & 09
- aluminum louvers: CT-R 10.
- micro aluminum louvers: CT-R 11.
- glazed canopy: CT-R 12.

THEATRE CT-T
- double layer of light diffusing IGU : CT-T 01, 02, 03
- single layer of light diffusing IGU + solid backing : CT-T 04, 05
- clear glass : CT-T 06
- laminated glass : CT-T 07
- aluminum louvers : CT-T 08
- suspended soffit : CT-T 09
- landscaped paving

RETAIL
- clear glass: CT-R 01, 02, 03, 07 & 08
- spandrel glass: CT-R 04, 05, 06 & 09
- aluminum louvers: CT-R 10.
- micro aluminum louvers: CT-R 11.
- glazed canopy: CT-R 12

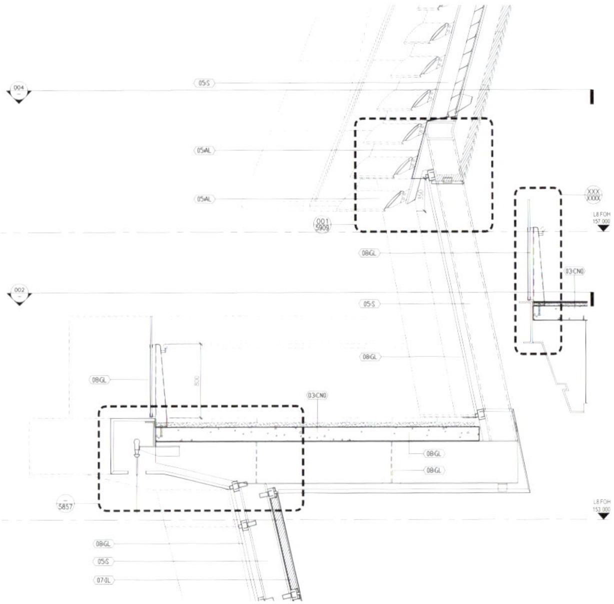

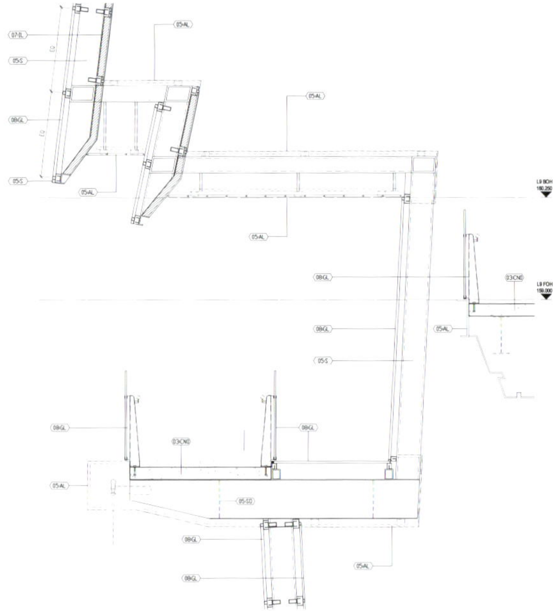

_01
public sky terrace

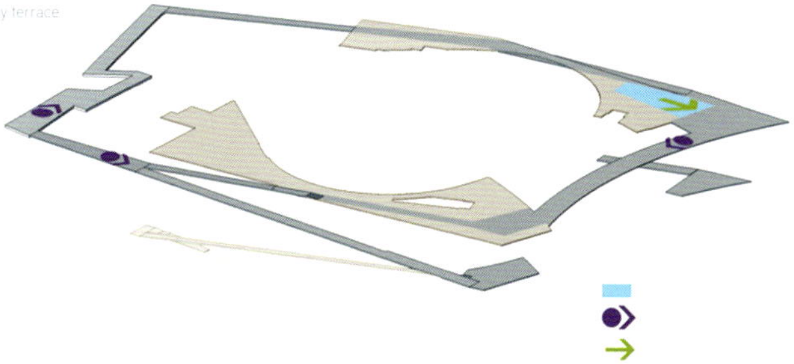

_02
public sky terrace
and floors

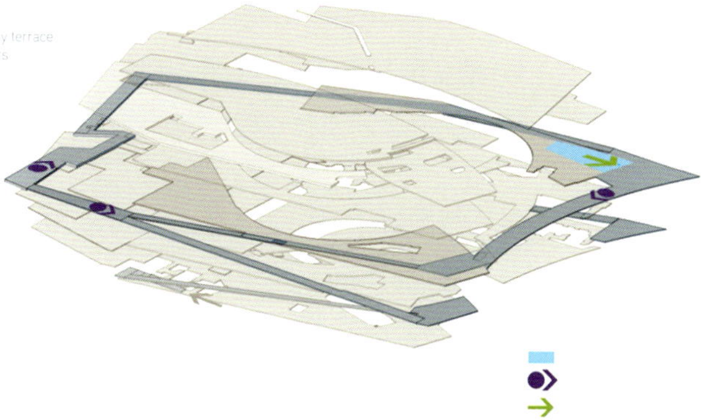

_03
public sky terrace,
floors and
external skin

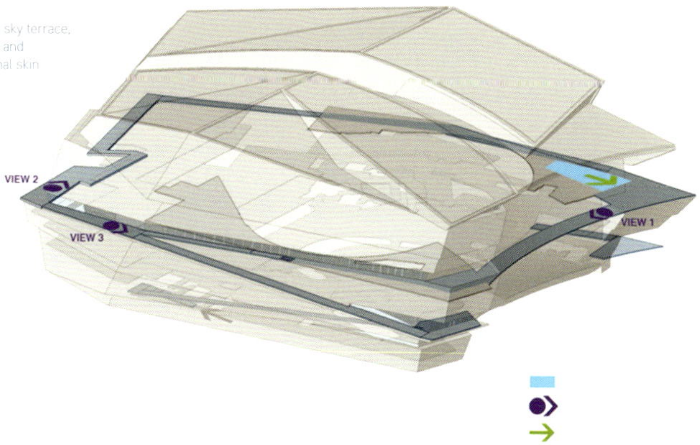

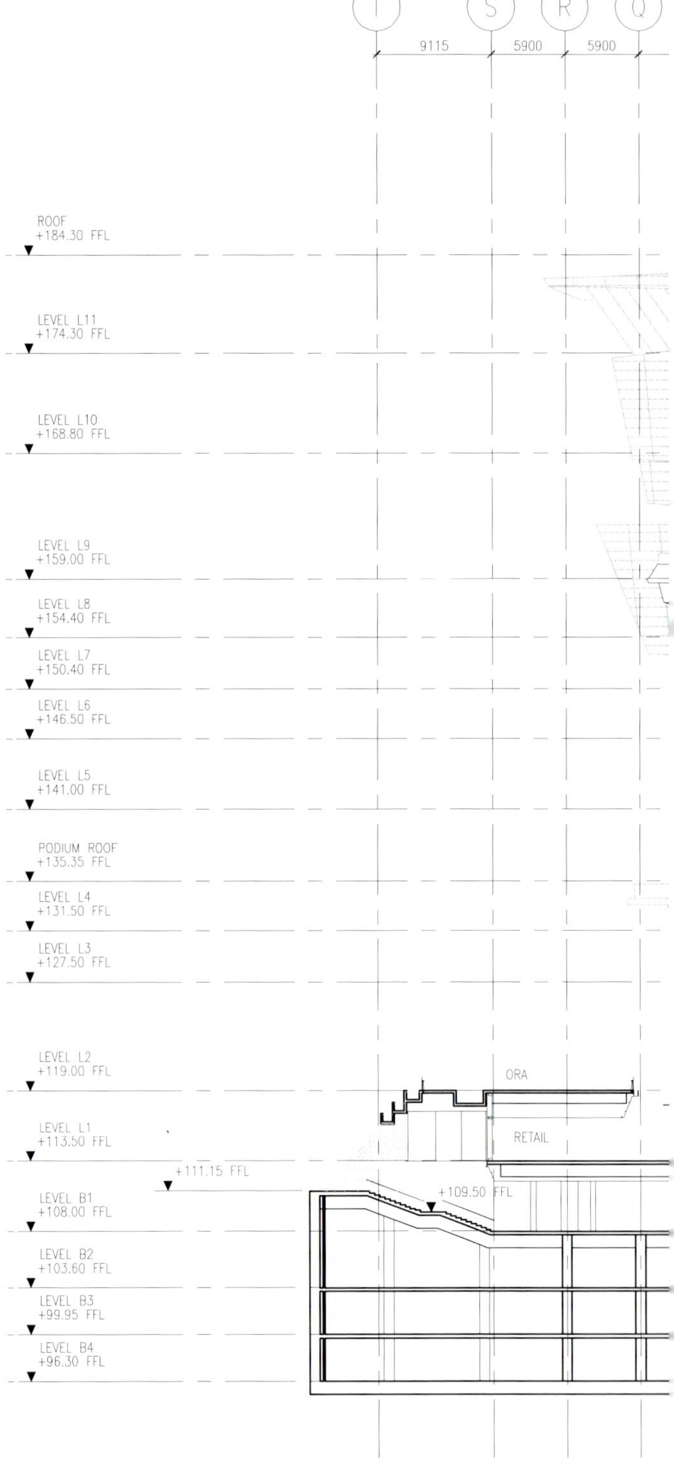
T
S
R
Q
9115
5900
5900
ROOF
+184.30 FFL
LEVEL L11
+174.30 FFL
LEVEL L10
+168.80 FFL
LEVEL L9
+159.00 FFL
LEVEL L8
+154.40 FFL
LEVEL L7
+150.40 FFL
LEVEL L6
+146.50 FFL
LEVEL L5
+141.00 FFL
PODIUM ROOF
+135.35 FFL
LEVEL L4
+131.50 FFL
LEVEL L3
+127.50 FFL
LEVEL L2
+119.00 FFL
ORA
LEVEL L1
+113.50 FFL
RETAIL
+111.15 FFL
+109.50 FFL
LEVEL B1
+108.00 FFL
LEVEL B2
+103.60 FFL
LEVEL B3
+99.95 FFL
LEVEL B4
+96.30 FFL

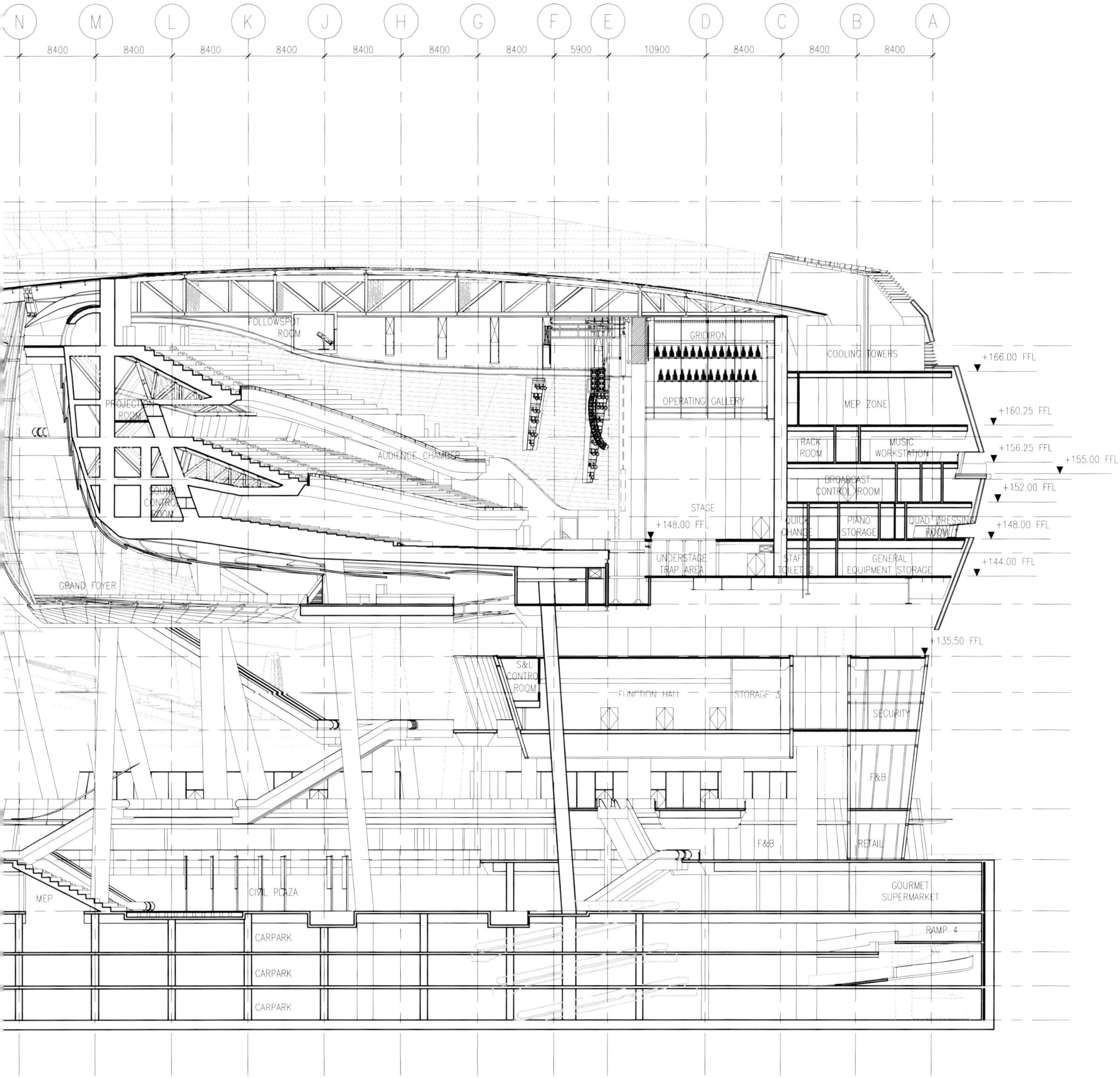
N
M
L
K
J
H
G
F
E
D
C
B
A
8400
5900
10900
FOLLOWSPOT ROOM
GRIDIRON
COOLING TOWERS
+166.00 FFL
PROJECTION ROOM
OPERATING GALLERY
MEP ZONE
+160.25 FFL
RACK ROOM
MUSIC WORKSTATION
+156.25 FFL
+155.00 FFL
AUDIENCE CHAMBER
BROADCAST CONTROL ROOM
+152.00 FFL
SOUND CONTROL ROOM
STAGE
QUICK CHANGE
PIANO STORAGE
QUAD DRESSING ROOM
+148.00 FFL
UNDERSTAGE TRAP AREA
STAFF TOILET 2
GENERAL EQUIPMENT STORAGE
+144.00 FFL
GRAND FOYER
+135.50 FFL
S&L CONTROL ROOM
FUNCTION HALL
STORAGE 3
SECURITY
F&B
RETAIL
MEP
CIVIL PLAZA
GOURMET SUPERMARKET
CARPARK
RAMP 4

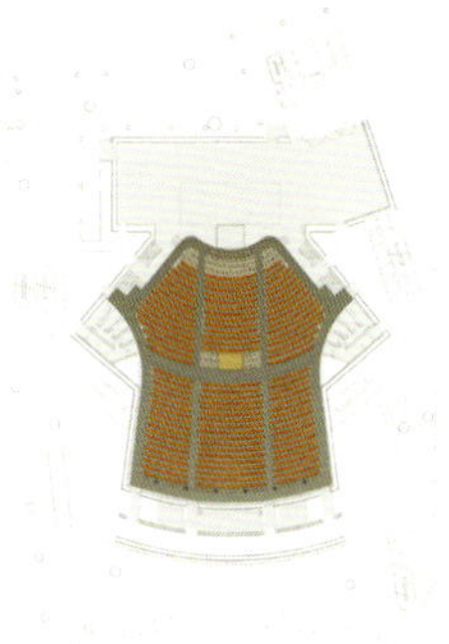

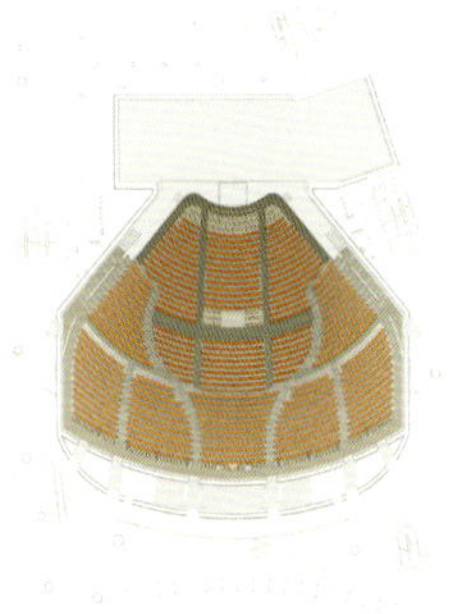

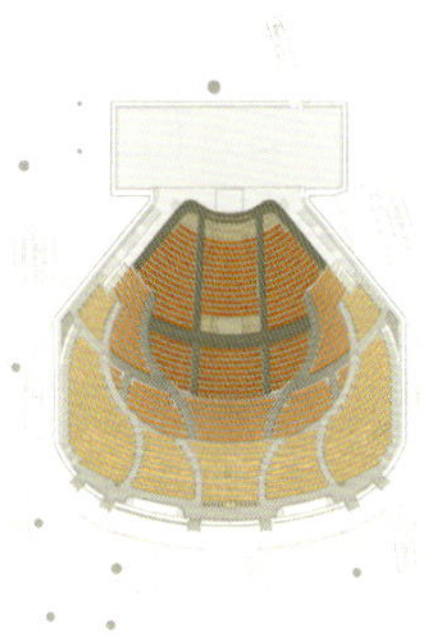

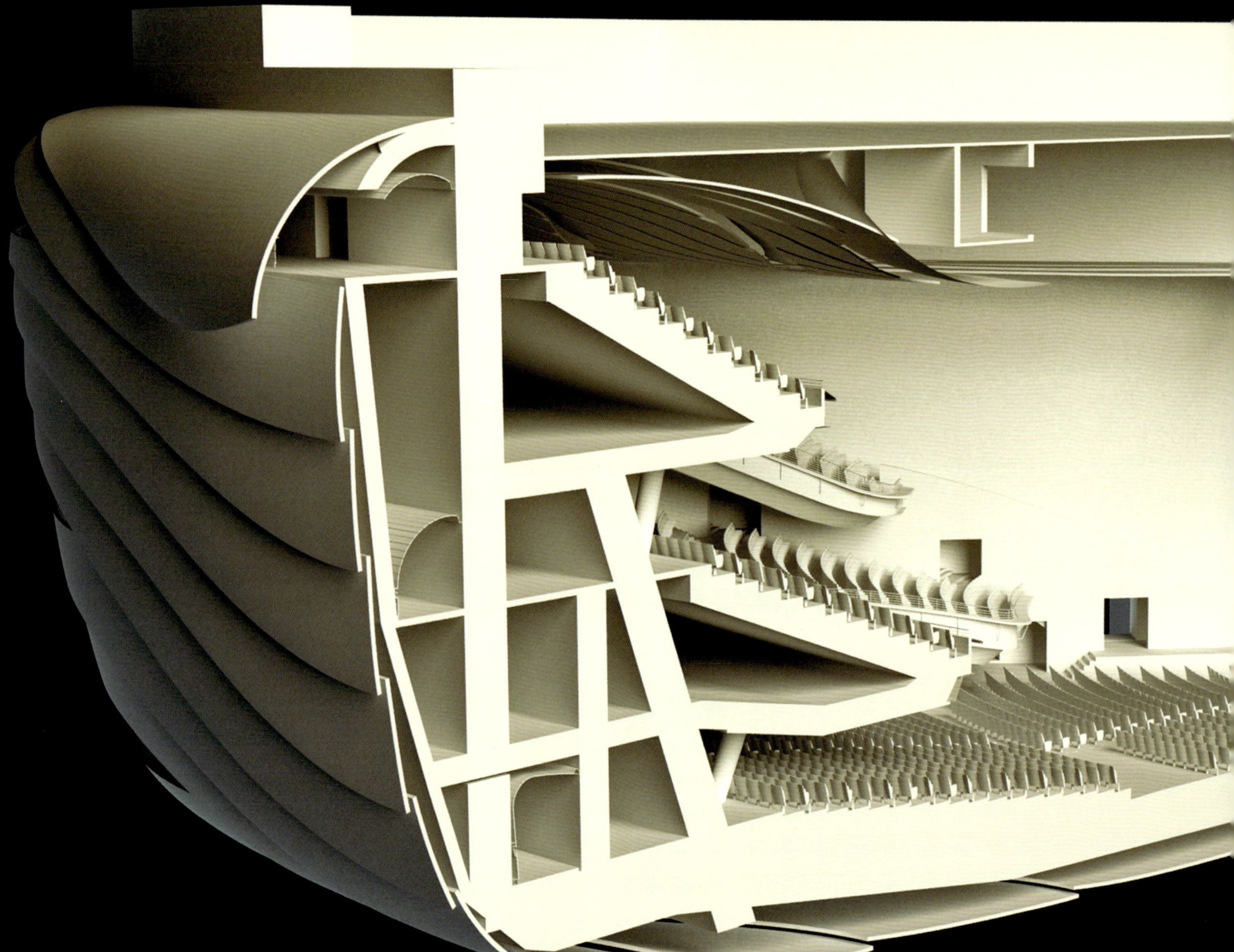

geometric evolution towards layout “bowl” enclosure over theatre structure

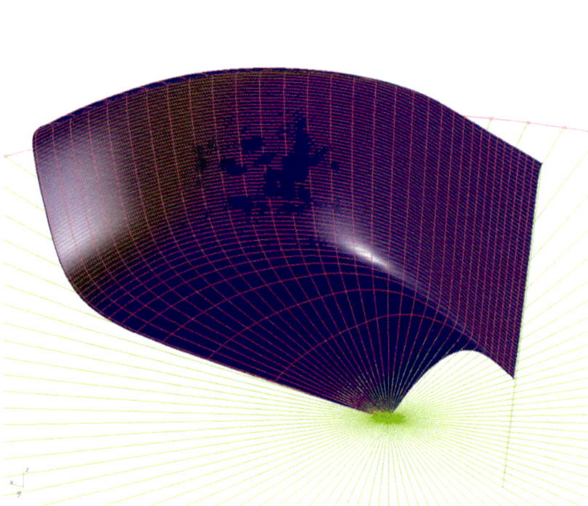

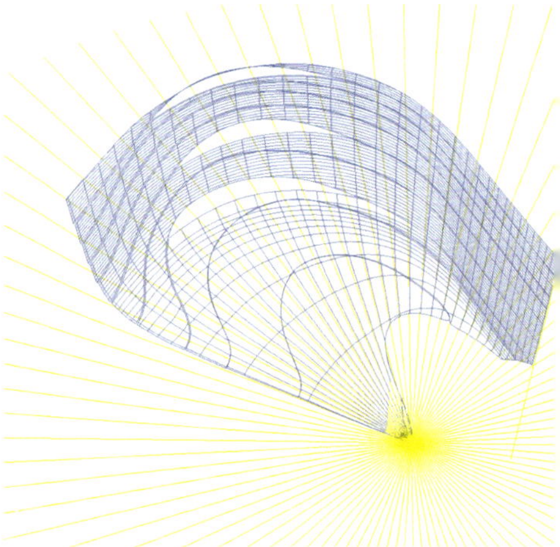

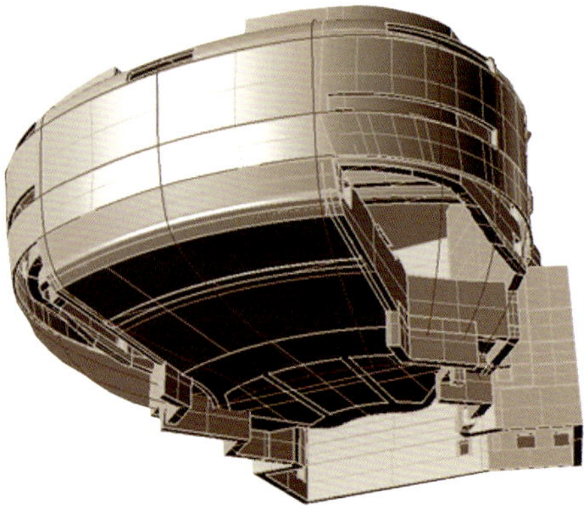

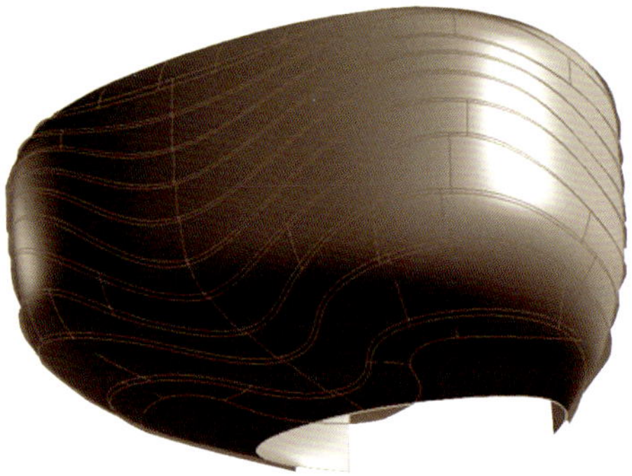

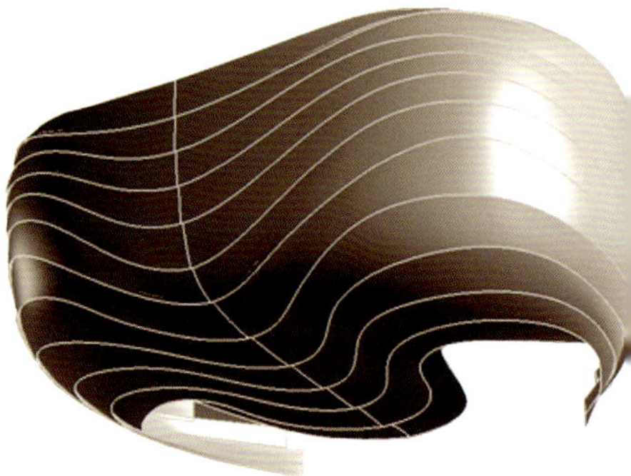

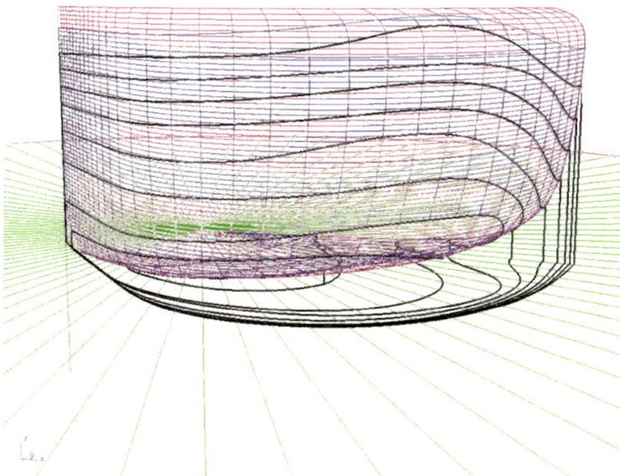

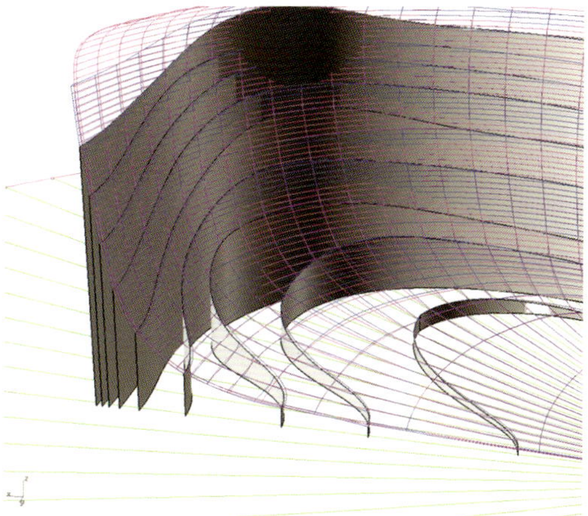

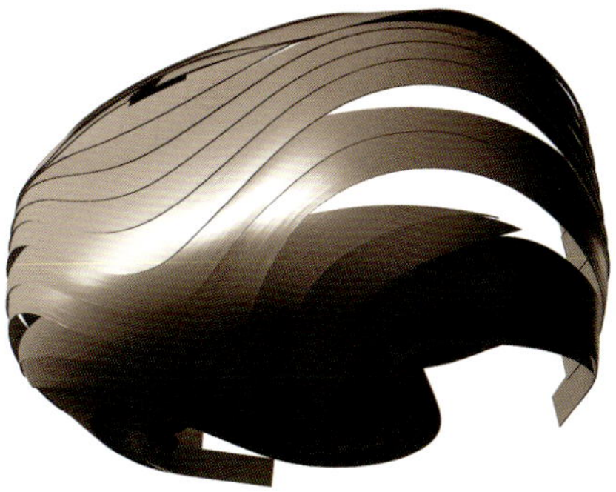

Left Side Escalator
Right Side Escalator
LEVEL 12 (+79.30)
LEVEL 11 (+72.30)
LEVEL 10 (+62.00)
LEVEL 9 (+56.90)
LEVEL 8 (+53.40)
LEVEL 7 (+50.55)
LEVEL 6 (+45.00)
LEVEL 5 (+40.50)
LEVEL 4 (+34.00)
LEVEL 3 (+27.50)
LEVEL 2 (+21.00)
LEVEL 1 (+15.50)
LEVEL b1 (+8.00)
LEVEL b2 (+2.90)
LEVEL b3 (-0.70)
LEVEL b4 (-4.30)
LEVEL b5 (-4.30)
Level 12
Level 11
Level 10
Level 8
Level 6
Level 4
Level 3
Level 2
Level 1
Base 1
Base 2
Base 3

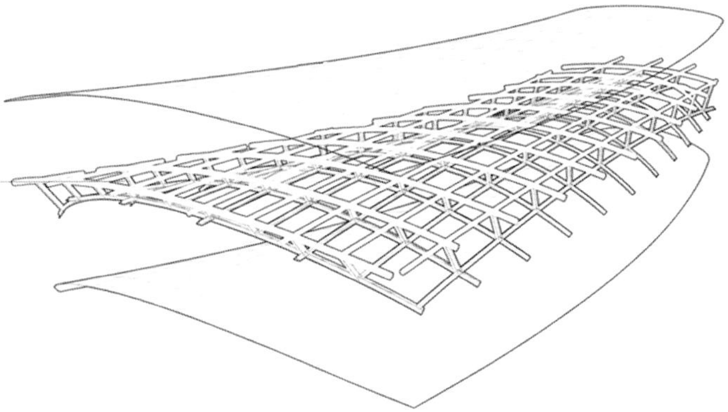

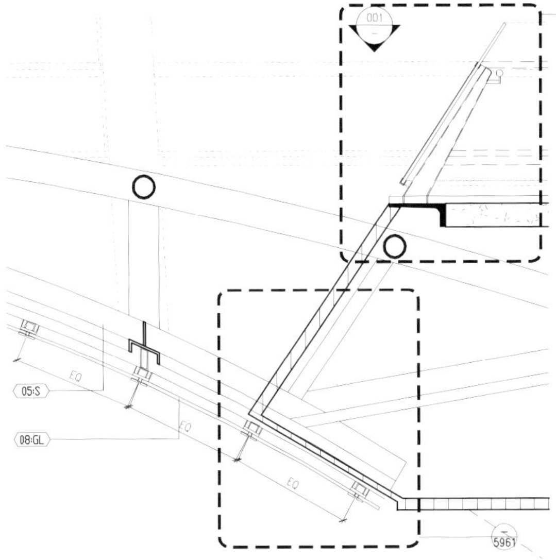
001
5960
05:S
08:GL
EQ
EQ
EQ
5961

main theatre lobby

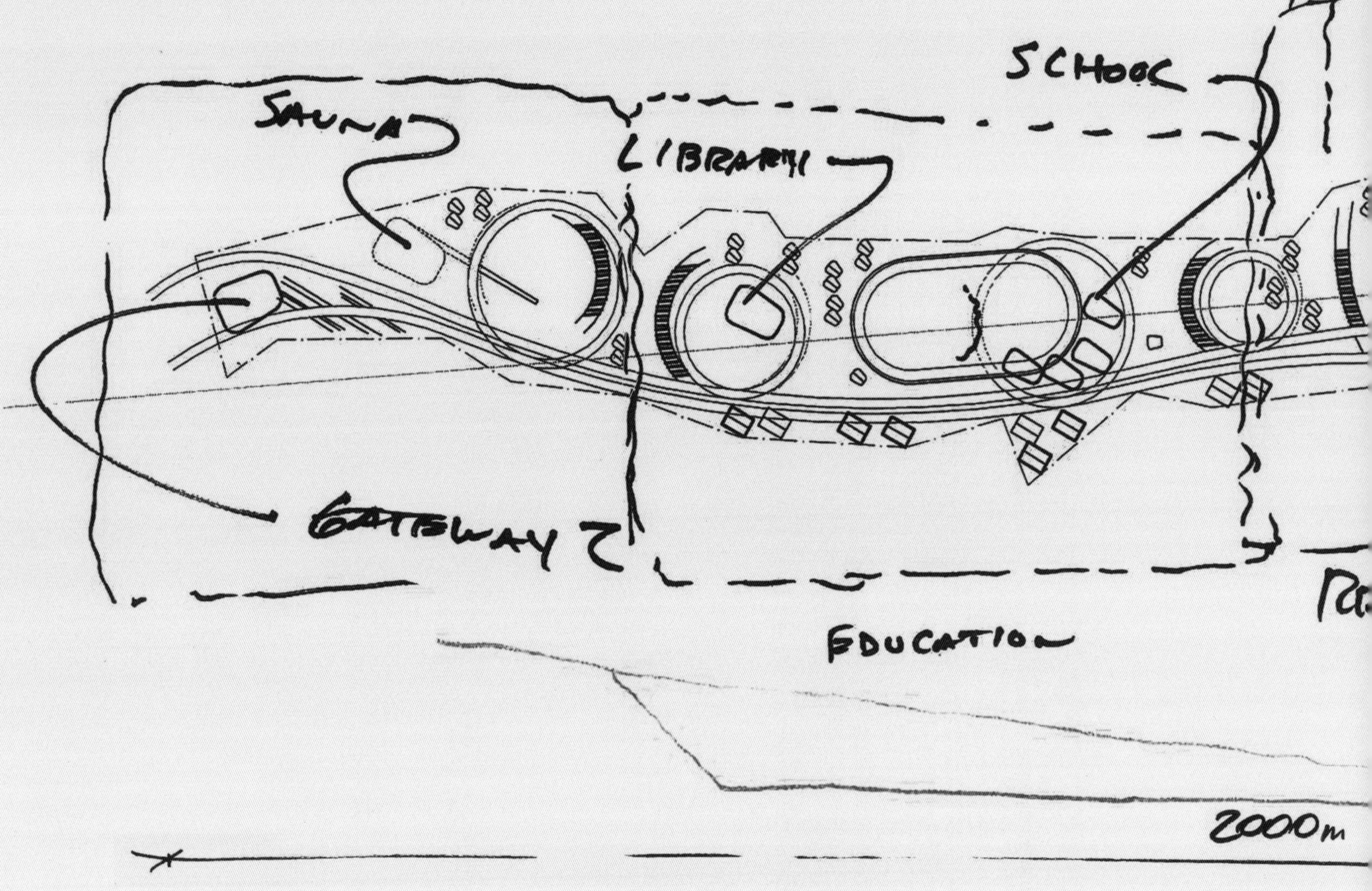
SAUNA
LIBRARY
SCHOOL
GATEWAY
EDUCATION
2000m

remizovka master plan

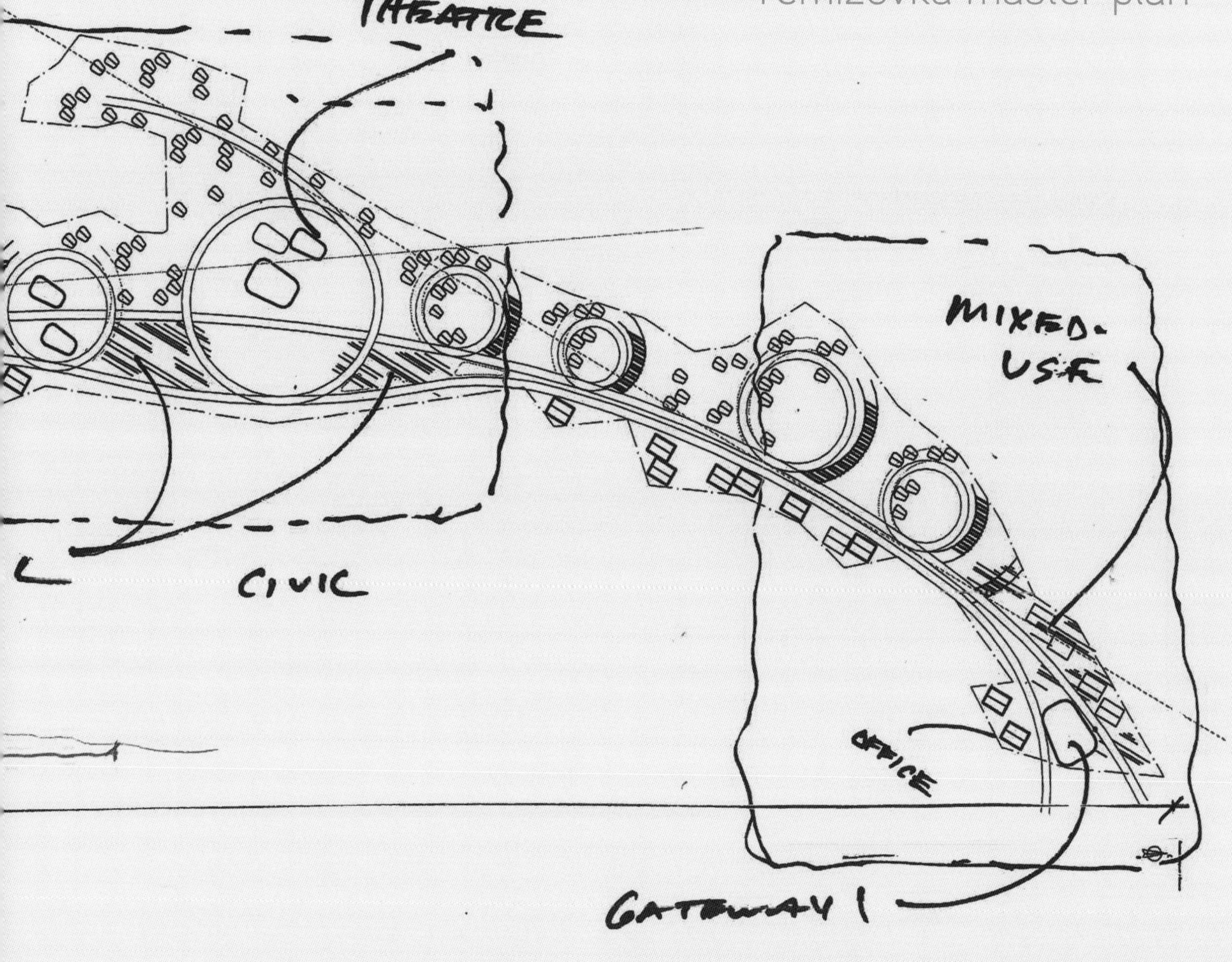

remizovka master plan

mixed use

client: sat zhoi construction lip
location: remizovka, almaty, kazakhstan

site location

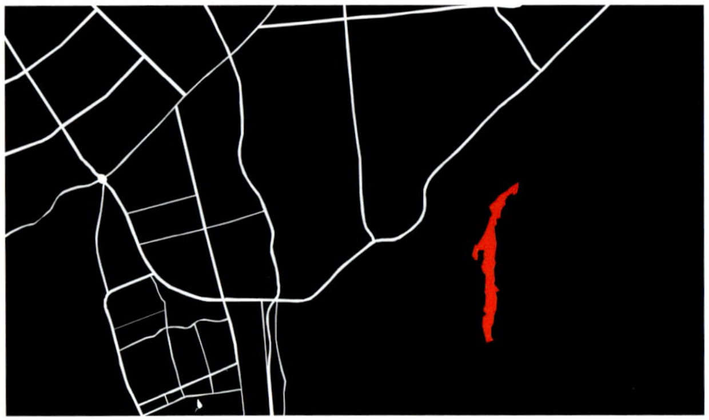

size/scale

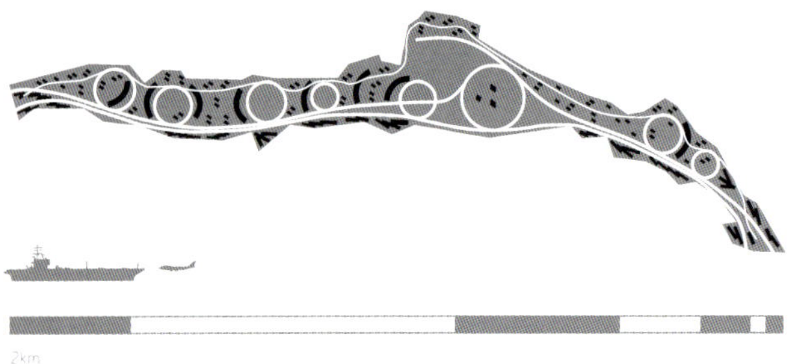

project description

Located on the western edge of Almaty, the site for the Reminovka Master Plan offered an opportunity for the city to define a portion of its sprawling urban edge. The site, which used to be a flowing river, was now dry and being used as landfill for the city's rampant urban construction and excavation program. Being 2,000 meters in length and averaging only 100 meters in width, the project offered the fantastic challenge of knitting the city with a country park in front of Almaty's 6,000 meter high mountain peak backdrop.

The diversity and program mix was developed to support a sustainable residential community but with the understanding that large commercial and retail centers would be in close proximity. With this in mind, the master plan is heavily weighted toward residential zones which make up 70% of the developable areas. Following this would be commercial offices at 20%, retail at 6% and community/educational facilities at 4% of overall available development area.

It was felt important to minimize the vehicular traffic as well as to maintain as much openness and open space as possible for the residential community. In support of this goal, all of the commercial offices were placed as controlled gateways into the site at its two narrow ends and along the eastern edge, providing a protected edge for the portion of the site adjacent to the city.

A traditional large loop road system was avoided because this would prevent the open spaces of the residential community from blending into the country park without interruption. A central artery with access fingers was also avoided because this would force a good portion of the residential area on to the "wrong side of the tracks" by divorcing it from the country park. Consequently, the major vehicular artery was also located toward the eastern edge of the site, with the majority of traffic adjacent to non-residential uses. From here a series of small "loops" off of the main artery were chosen to give appropriate access to the development but also facilitate the required traffic flows requested by the city.

process

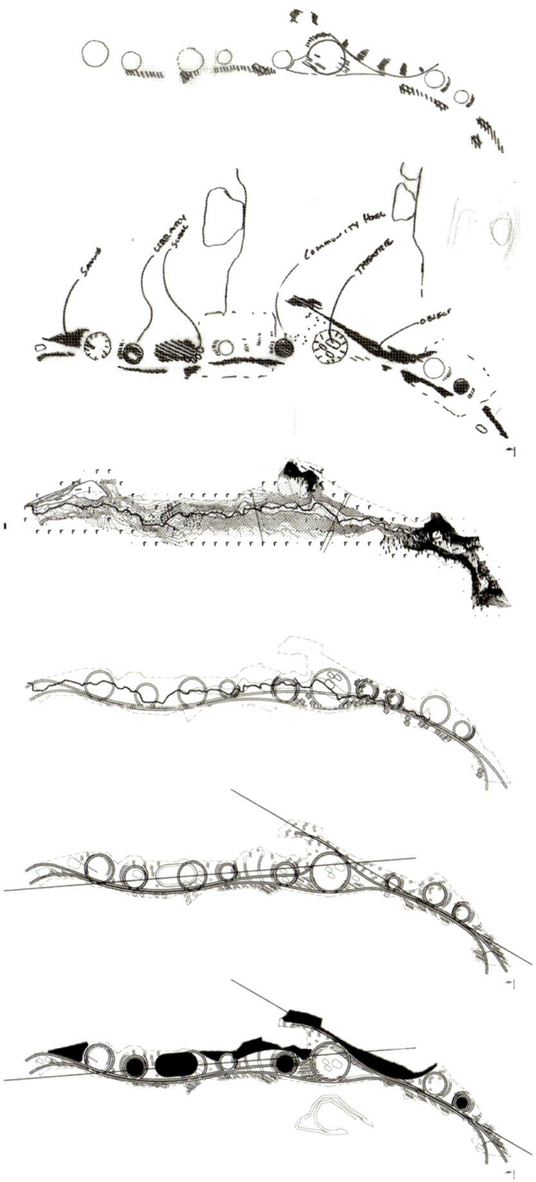

goals

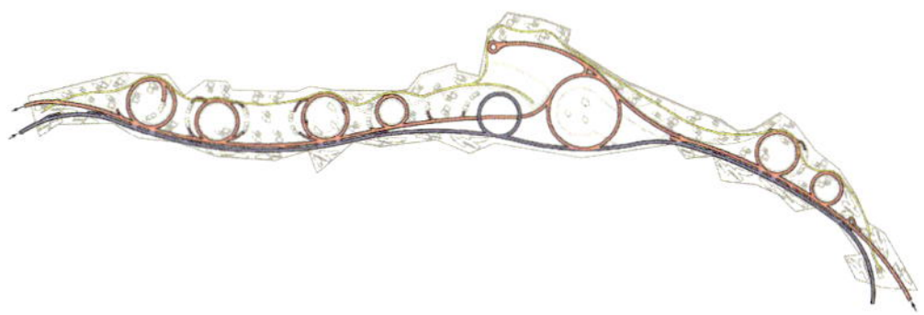

To minimize the amount of vehicular roads and enhance the quality of open space deserving of land with the spectacular backdrop of 6,000 meter high mountains.

challenge

The natural valley of this land was being "filled" with soil from other construction sites prior to design. The master plan needed to be accelerated quickly in order to guide this process.

play

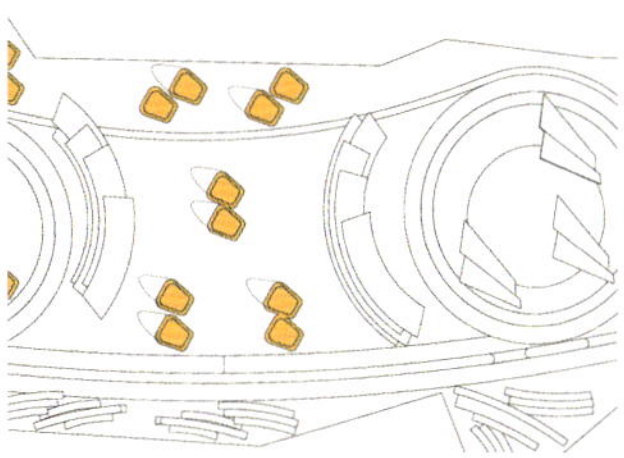

The introduction of the non-requested, small apartment block program as "boulders" left over within the majority of the site's existing dried-up riverbed.

usage

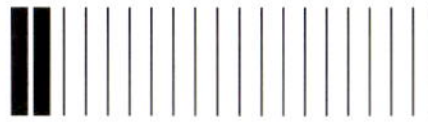

residential
102113 m2 1099135 sqf

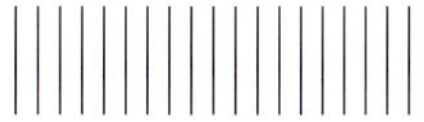

hospitality
0 m2 0 sqf

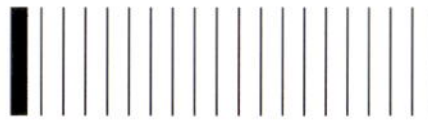

office
38061 m2 409685 sqf

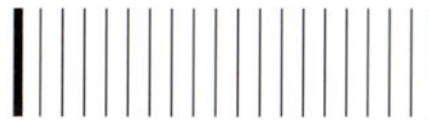

retail + f&b
25080 m2 269959 sqf

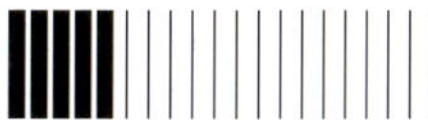

landscape
203475 m2 2190187 sqf

civic
19578 m2 210756 sqf

total area: 184,832 m2
1,989,515 sqf

= 50,000 m2 /538195sqf

status

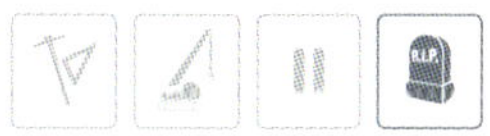

some earthwork executed

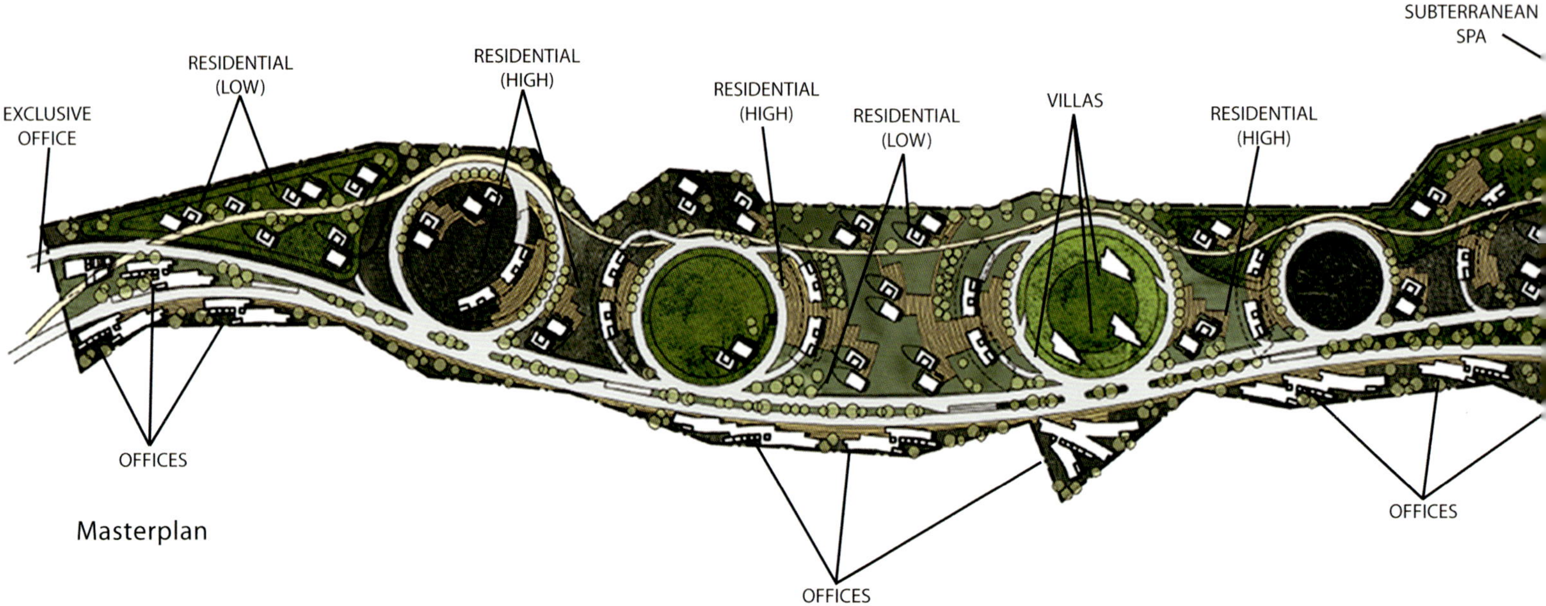

Masterplan

The educational, civic and retail cores were then located as central nodes within the medium density housing to help reinforce the "vibrancy" of a "village" community as opposed to a suburban development. Significant open spaces were placed adjacent to these uses and were knitted together by a network of pedestrian trails and bike paths flowing unimpeded into the spectacularly preserved wilderness beyond.

Dotted into this open space was the introduction of small "townhouse" residential blocks which formally recall the riverbed and the glacial movements of the past. These "boulders" become the last form of the "knit" from the urban realm of Almaty with the untamed, unspoiled wilderness of its surrounding mountains – allowing this community to reconnect to its breathtaking natural beauty which has been forgotten and lost in the frenzied development of recent years.

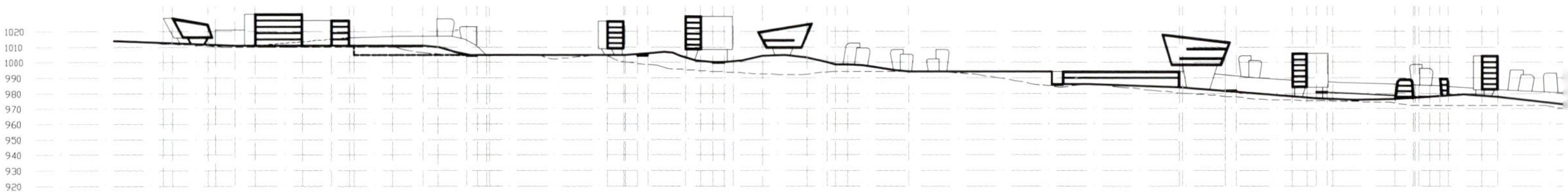

proposed topography

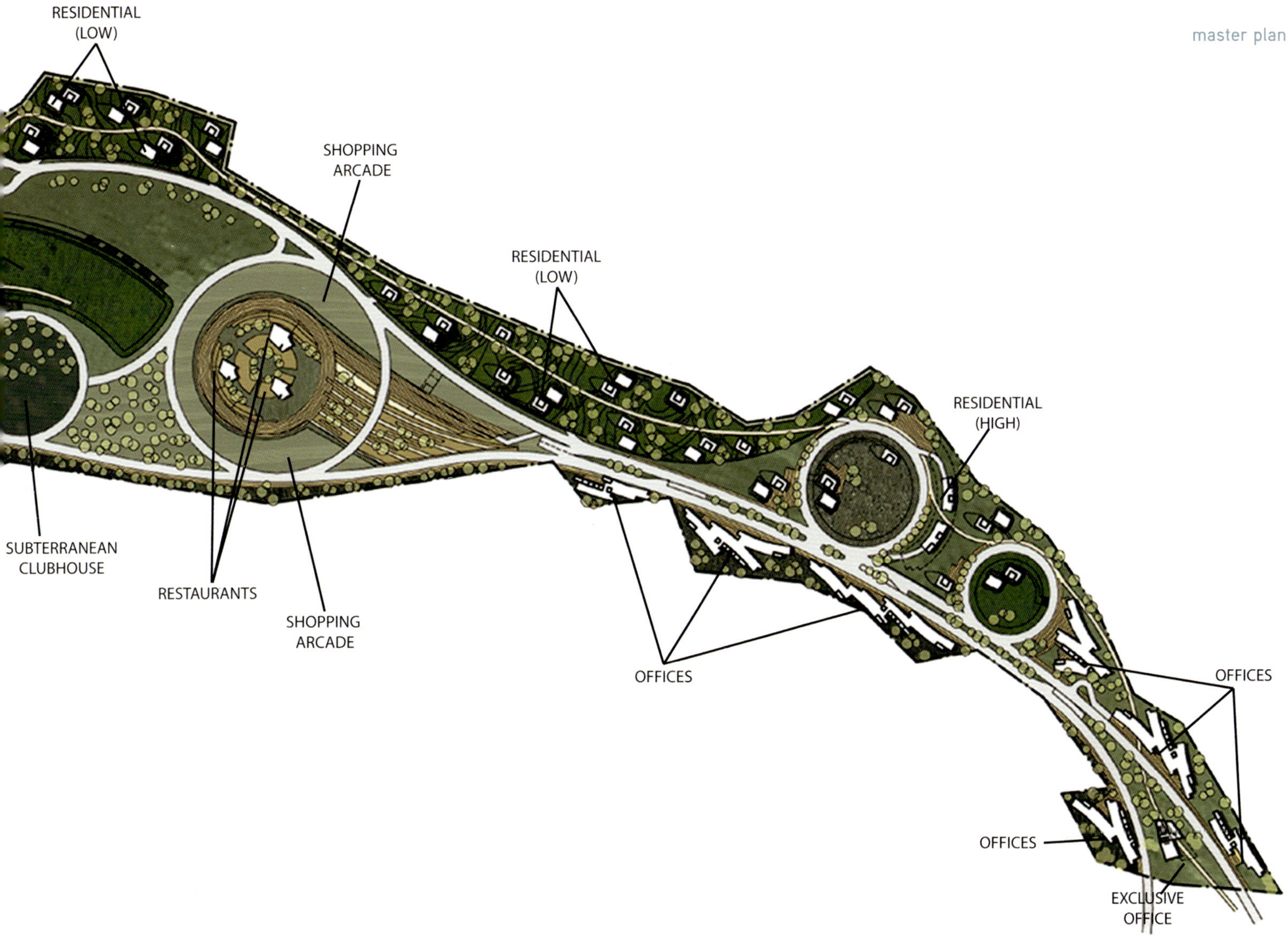
RESIDENTIAL
(LOW)
SHOPPING
ARCADE
RESIDENTIAL
(LOW)
RESIDENTIAL
(HIGH)
SUBTERRANEAN
CLUBHOUSE
RESTAURANTS
SHOPPING
ARCADE
OFFICES
OFFICES
OFFICES
EXCLUSIVE
OFFICE

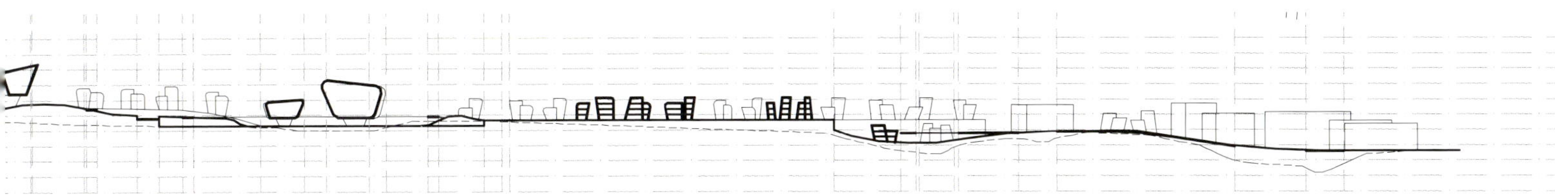

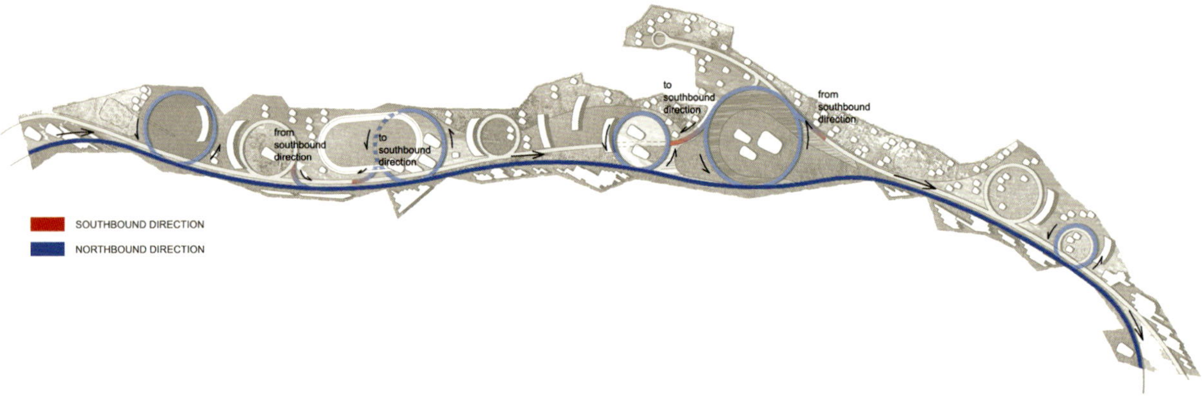

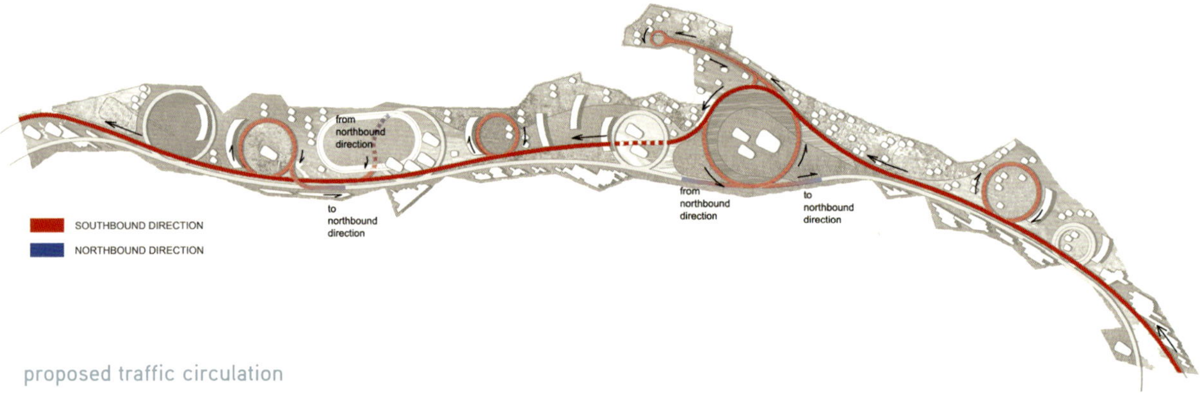

proposed traffic circulation

entertainment resort

entertainment resort

entertainment/hospitality
client: undisclosed
location: guangdong, china

site location

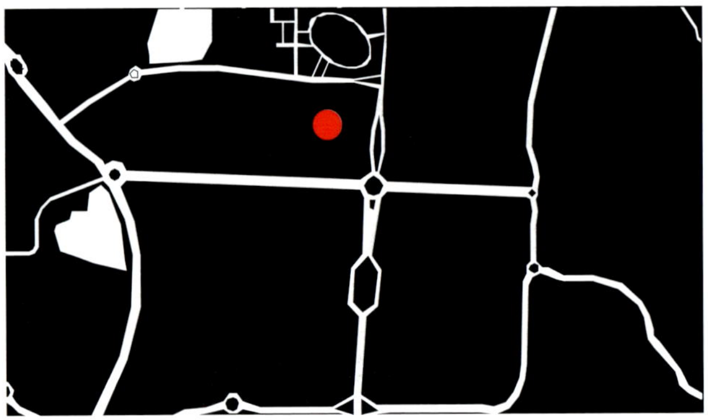

size/scale

project description

In a land of large resorts where each facility is trying to outdo the rest and the big mega resorts are now going "out of fashion", this project strove to find a design which would be both appropriate for this project type and especially timeless and meaningful on account of its location in Guangdong and its dominant Chinese tourist base.

The very dense site, containing over 600,000 square meters of entertainment mixed-use hospitality, is just one of many large projects in this region. The sizable entertainment facilities are supported by three individual hotels, a large exhibition complex, and a multi-purpose performance venue. It is considered important for its business model that each hotel maintain its own identity with its own frontage and access. Convenient access is also fundamental for the exhibition complex – which could be placed away from the primary street frontage but still required a large area.

Although the site had over 600 metres of prime frontage, the commercial demands for this edge, visible to the public, and fundamental to the success of various programs, made greater demand than availability one of the major functional challenges of this project. Large hotels often use a double loaded corridor to achieve the desired efficiency for their facilities. In this instance however, there was not enough length for the 3,000 rooms without the individual identities of the three hotels being lost. Consequently, a dense, cluster approach was looked at in both a square and triangular plan.

These objects were then shaped to allude to a specific local regional landscape, found in a portion of the Guangdong Region – the limestone silhouettes surrounding Guilin. Inspiration was taken from the way these landforms change, materialize and transform throughout the days and seasons due to varying light and atmospheric conditions. The project, through the use of large bold strokes of LED lighting as well as "fog" machines and misting devices, has developed a playful, entertaining and colorful simulation of this beauty, allowing this development to "hold its own" against the multitudes of adjacent "themed" facilities without becoming superficial.

process

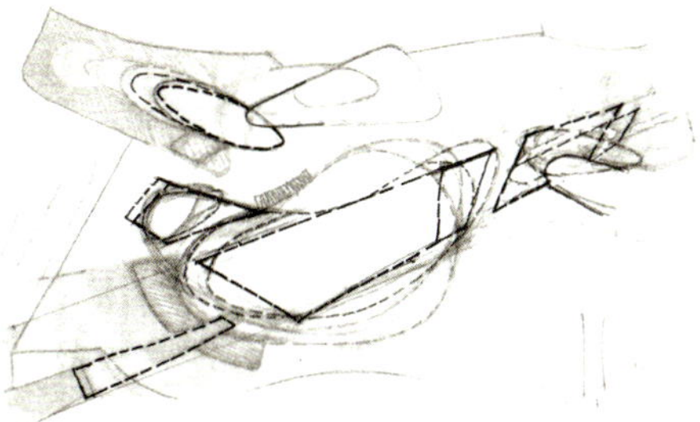

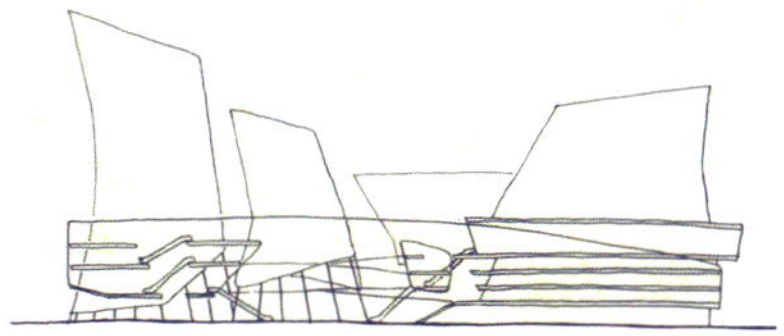

goals

To design a contemporary, timeless resort inspired by a regional landscape for Chinese patrons.

play

The transformation of the different hotels' sculptural forms through bold use of coordinated color lighting effects.

challenge

To find a fresh and meaningful response which would "hold its own" against the multitude of adjacent "themed" facilities without becoming superficial.

usage

residential
0 m2 0 sqf

x3.75
hospitality
375000 m2 4036466 sqf

office
0 m2 0 sqf

retail + f&b
48500 m2 522050 sqf

landscape
0 m2 0 sqf

entertainment
60000 m2 645824 sqf

total area: 609,500 m2
6,458,346 sqf

| = 2500 m2 / 26910 sqf

status

competition canceled

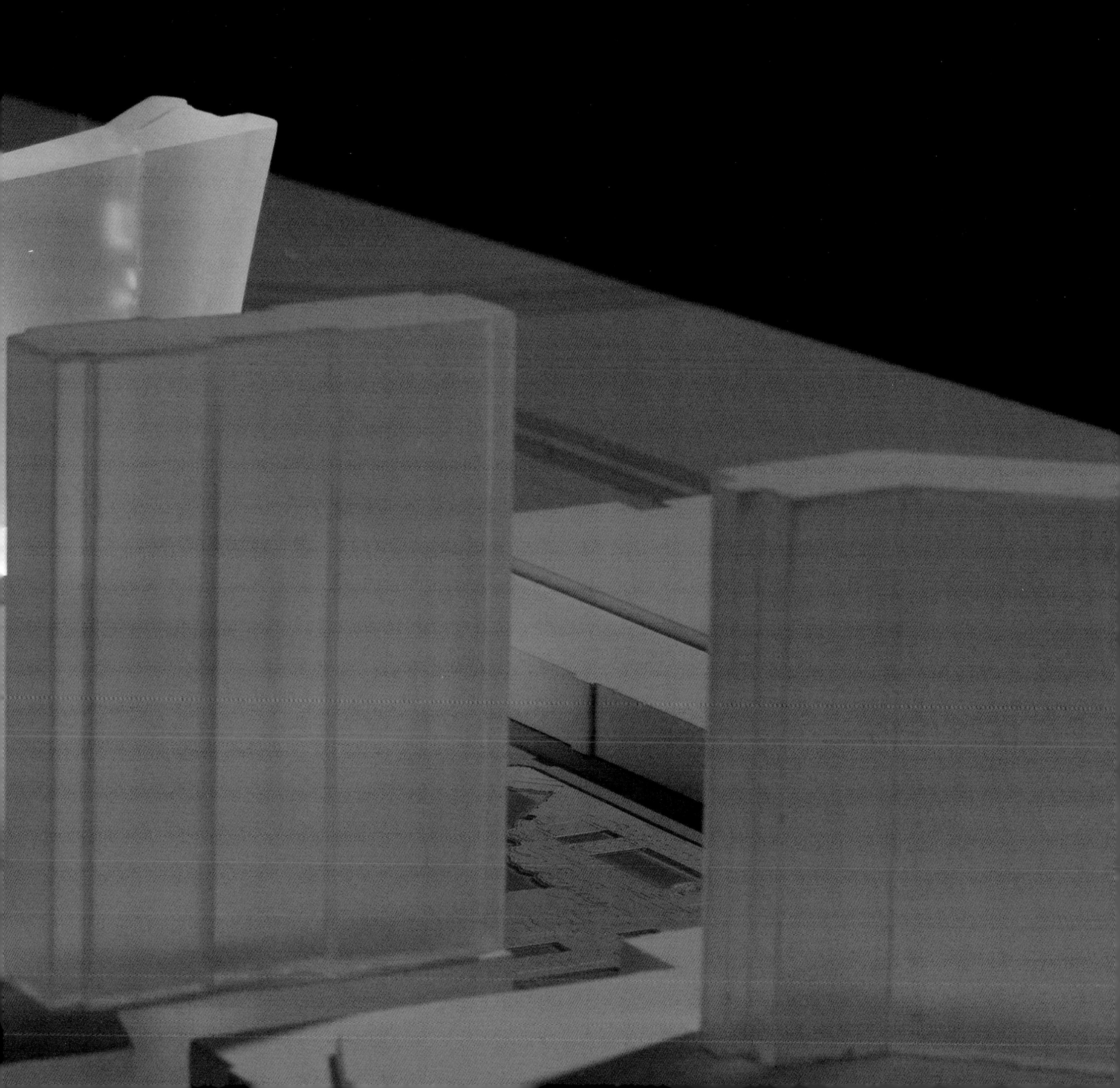

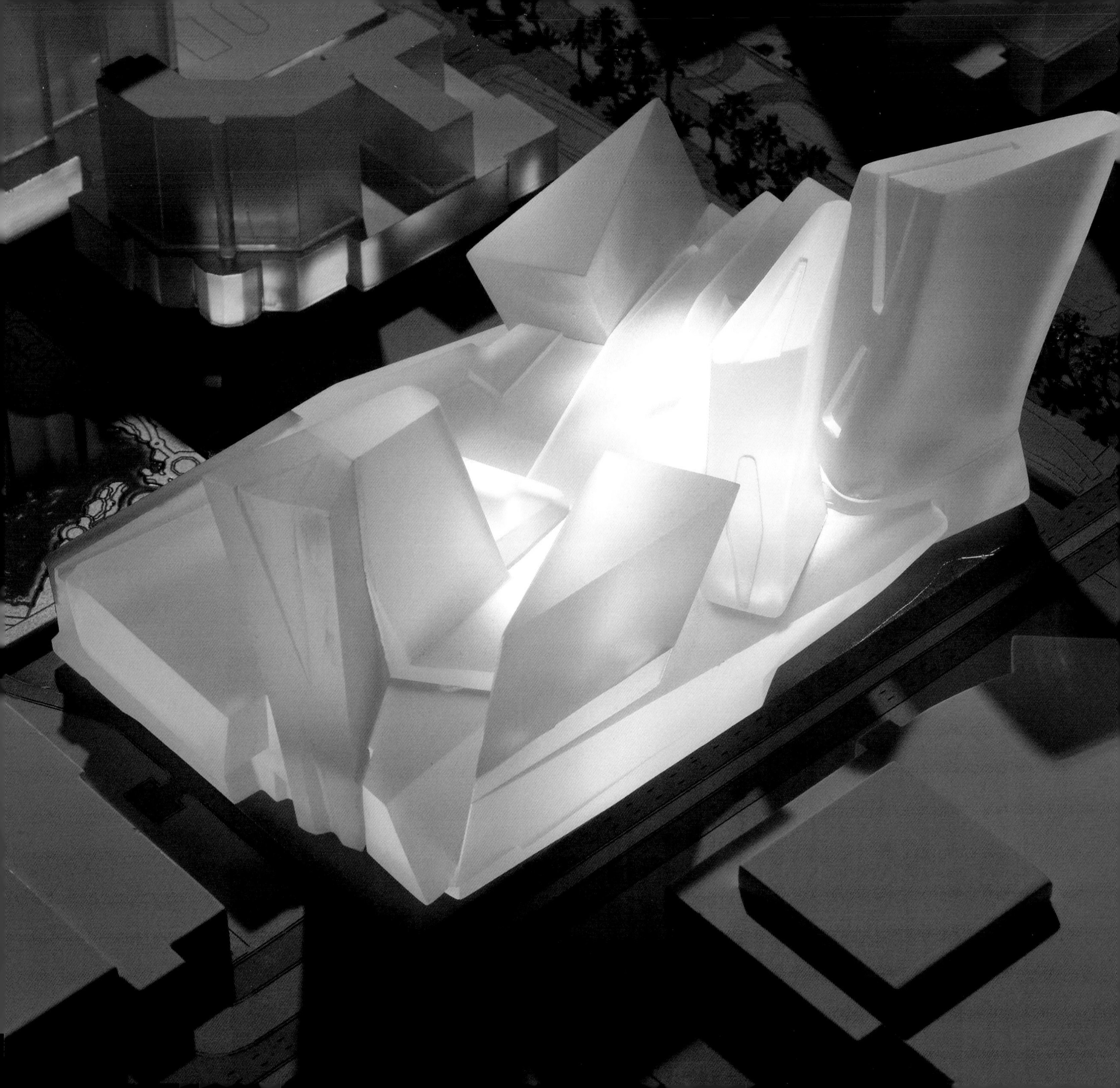

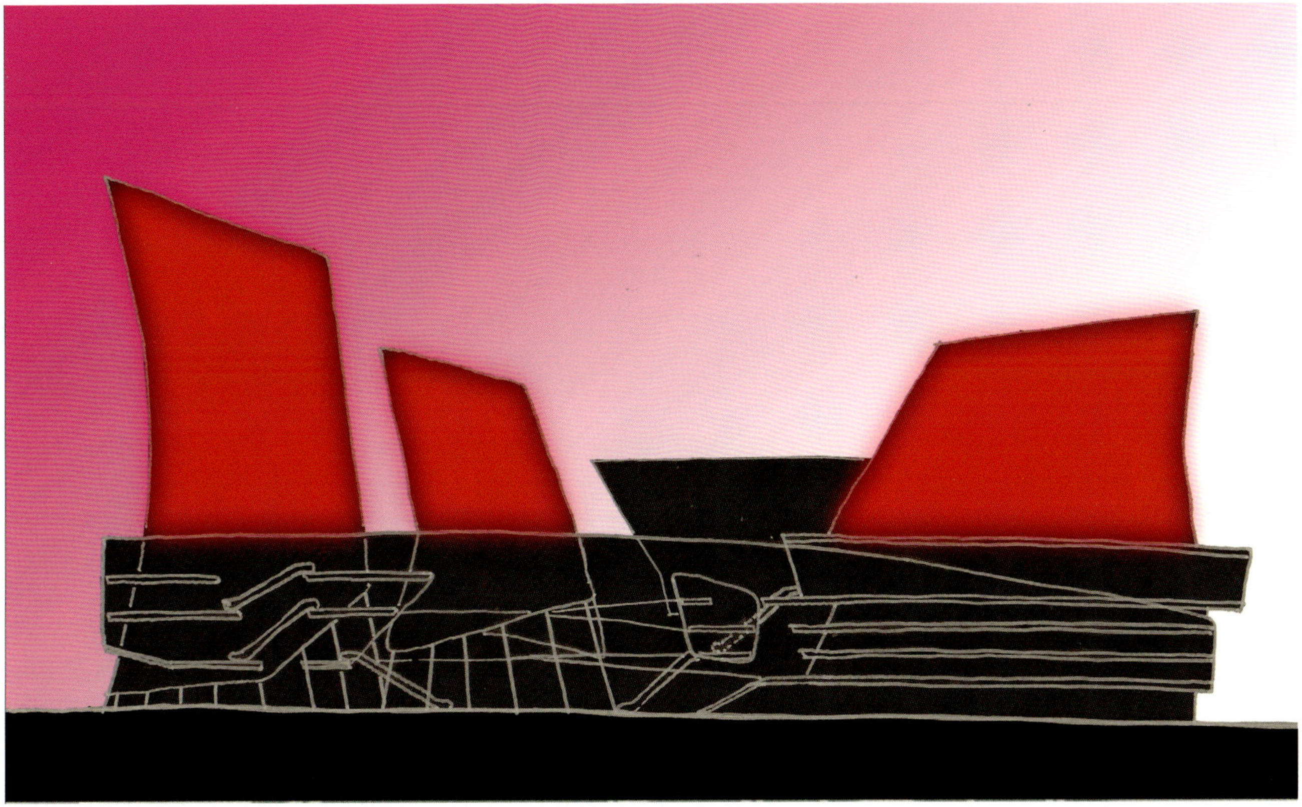

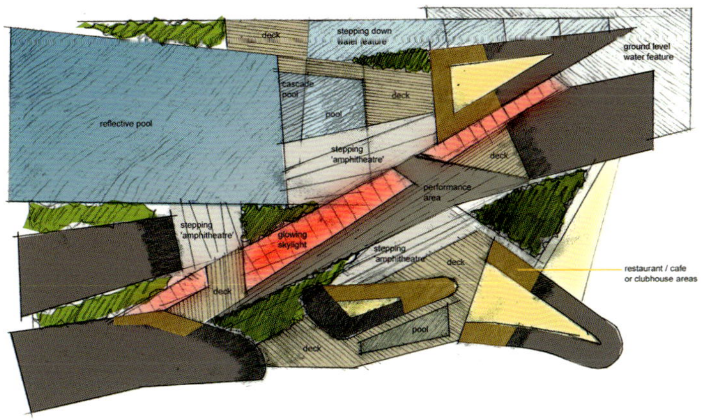
deck
stepping down
water feature
ground level
water feature
cascade
pool
deck
pool
reflective pool
stepping
'amphitheatre'
deck
performance
area
stepping
'amphitheatre'
glowing
skylight
stepping
'amphitheatre'
deck
deck
restaurant / cafe
or clubhouse areas
pool
deck

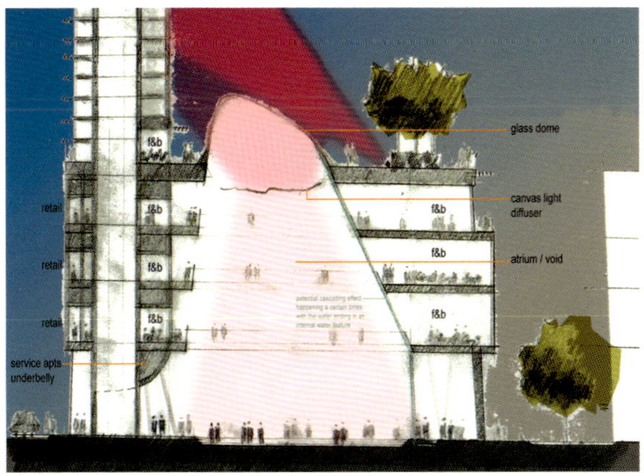
f&b
glass dome
retail
f&b
canvas light
diffuser
f&b
f&b
retail
f&b
atrium / void
retail
f&b
f&b
service apts
underbelly

pazhou exhibition complex

pazhou exhibition complex

exhibition/mixed-use
client: nan fung development
location: pazhou, guangzhou, china

site location

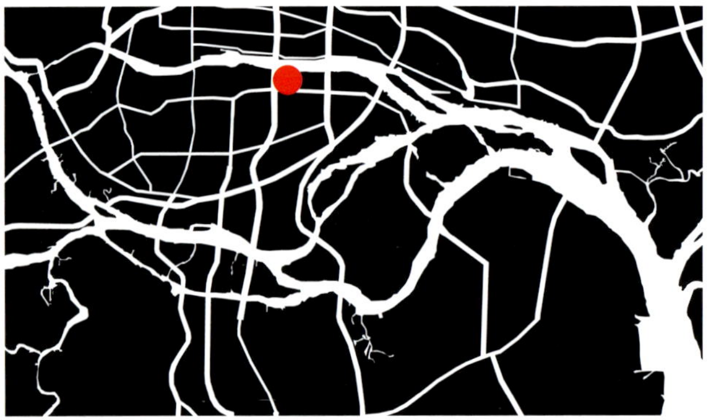

size/scale

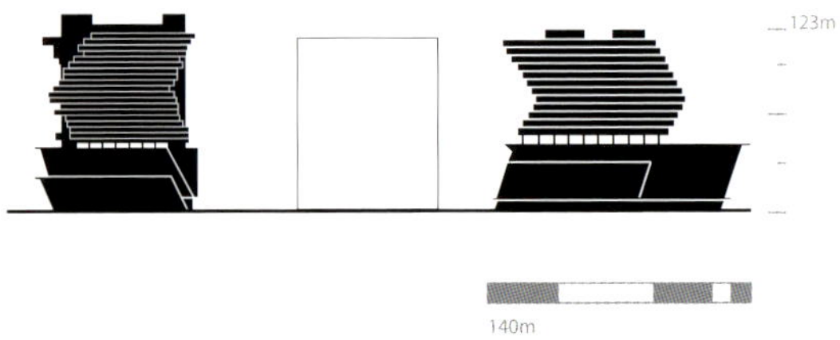

project description

Containing four distinct programmatic uses split between two different sites, the Pazhou Exhibition Complex would have already been considered a challenge. This complexity becomes even more exacerbated by the realization that the project's sites are separated 160 meters apart by another building.

Located outside of Guangzhou in China, Pazhou is an island within the Pearl River which is dedicated to exhibition related activities. The centerpiece of the development is a government funded exhibition center which currently ranks as the second largest in the world. The Pazhou Exhibition Complex is located right across the street from this facility, and needs to be competitive to ensure its success. The introduction of four primary uses helps to diversify the center and create a mixed-use vibrancy which allows the business model a stronger likelihood of success.

One site is wholly owned by a Hong Kong based developer while the other site is a joint-venture between this developer and a large international fund house. The JV site, otherwise referred to as site "1301", contains a large retail exhibition area in the podium and a large office showroom building on top. The other site, "1401", is a traditional, multi-floor exhibition center in the podium with a 500 room, 5-star hotel located above. In total, these four uses add up to around 180,000 sm of GFA.

The project design balanced the importance of "frontage" for the visibility of the center with basic functional constraints, which include pedestrian flow, traffic flow, vehicular drop-offs, and appropriate areas for load/unload zones. This was formalized into a simple functional diagram which allows very efficient area layouts to be achieved.

The primary formal drivers for the design, however, are its contextual responses to the surrounding area as well as the separation of the project's two individual sites. Contextually, the project, which initially seems large, is actually fragmented

process

day 001

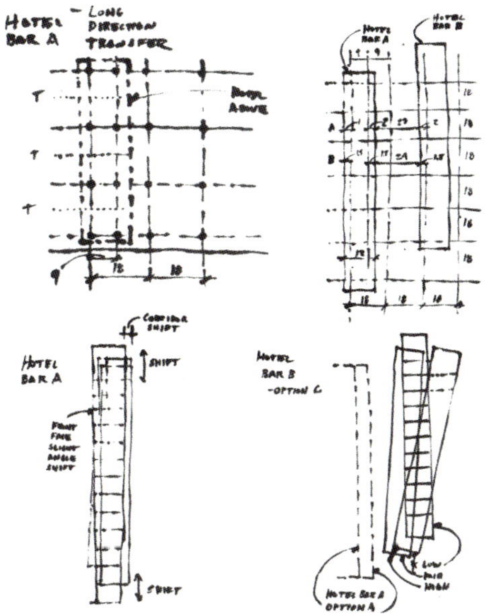

day 002

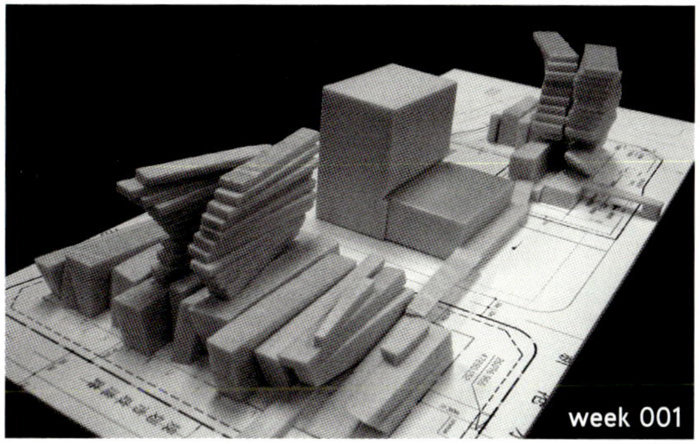

goals

To develop a cohesive mixed-use complex with a strong identity in order to stand out next to some very strong formal neighbors.

play

The "static electricity" dialogue between the buildings represented by the horizontal striations and shifts.

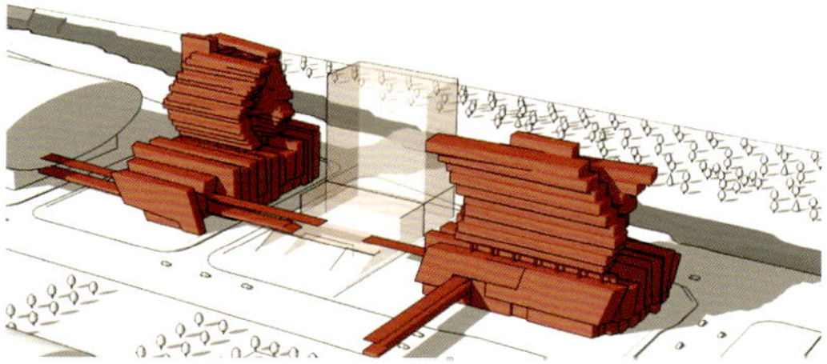

challenge

To achieve a strong dialogue between the two separate sites of the project, which are 160 meters, apart from each other and reduce the development in between to a "back-drop" for these exchanges to occur.

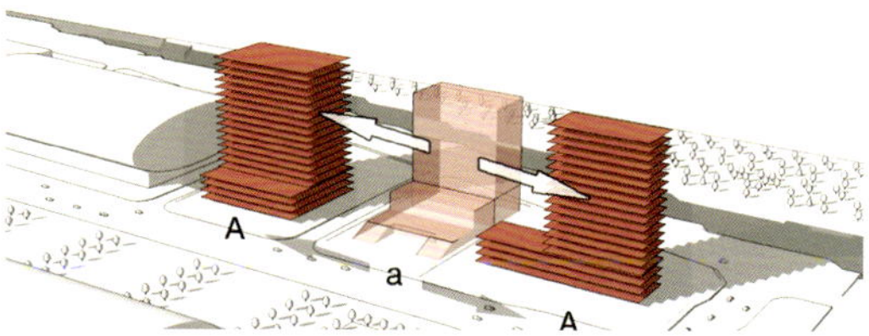

usage

residential
0 m2 0 sqf

hospitality
48935 m2 526732 sqf

office
32608 m2 350989 sqf

retail + f&b
40887 m2 440104 sqf

landscape
0 m2 0 sqf

exhibition
36490 m2 392775 sqf

total area: 159,329 m2
1,715,003 sqf

| = 2500 m2 / 26910 sqf

status

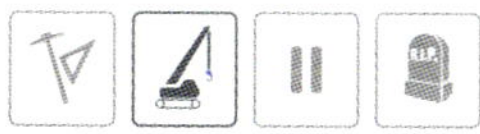

projected completion: 2012

IGNORE? 漠视?

- each site designed independently 每个项目分别独立设计

PROS 优点

- continuity in masterplan 整体规划的延续性

CONS 缺点

- relationship lacking between sites 项目之间缺乏联系
- middle neighbor as equal partner, adjacent property has equal standing 与中间建筑形成并排的局面，只能与周边的建筑物有相同的存在性

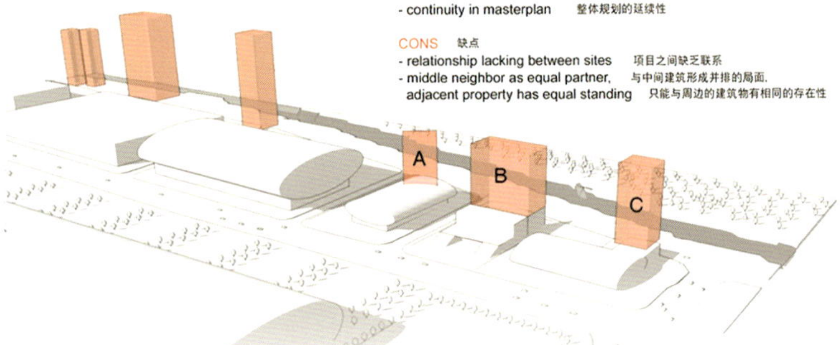

IGNORE ?

INTENSIFY- Vertical 竖向强化

- articulate our sites vs. monolithic neighbor 突出的项目设计相比平实的中间建筑
- increasing "volume" of sites while neutralizing centre building 增强项目的体积感.同时中和中间建筑

PROS 优点

- enhanced relationship between two sites 两个项目之间的关系增强了

CONS 缺点

- relationship between two sites considered "static" 两个项目的关系太静态

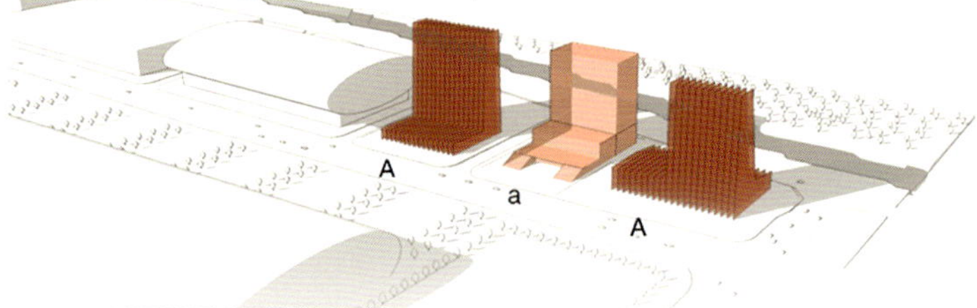

INTENSIFY VERTICAL

HIDE? 隐藏?

concealing centre building through obstruction 透过遮挡去隐藏中间建筑

CONS 缺点

- opposite result that emphasize & frame centre building 两个项目变成"书座"
- 2 sites become "book ends" 反效果而导致更突显中间建筑
- design perceived as "un-neighborly" 设计会被评为"不友善"

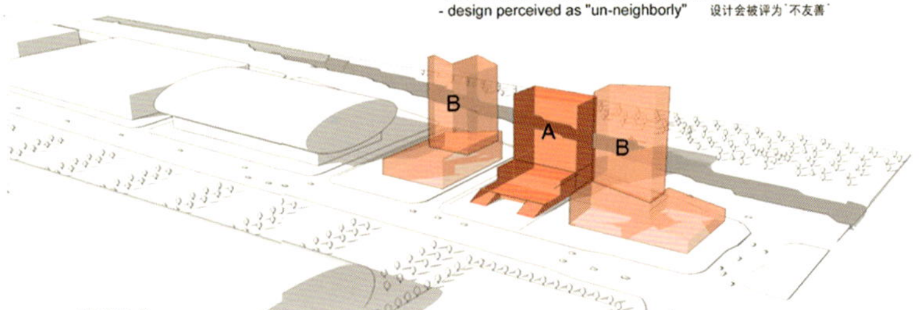

HIDE ?

INTENSIFY- Horizontal 横向强化

- articulate our sites vs. monolithic neighbor 突出的项目设计相比平实的中间建筑
- increasing "volume" of sites while neutralizing centre building 增强项目的体积感.同时中和中间建筑

PROS 优点

- horizontally articulated masses relate to context 横向的体块与环境相连
- stronger dialogue established between our sites 加强两个项目双向的关系
- centre buidling fades to become backdrop 中间建筑褪为背幕

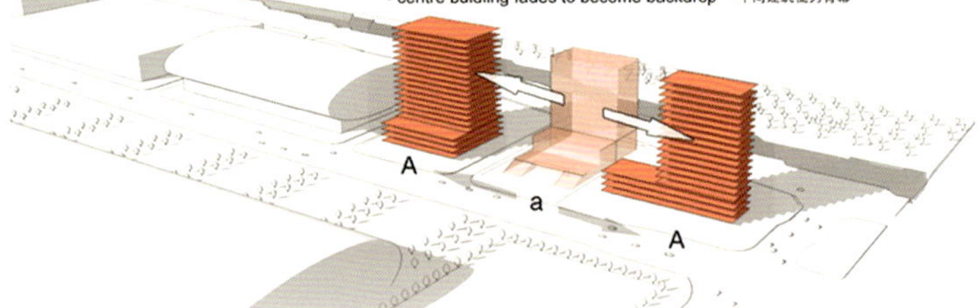

INTENSIFY HORIZONTAL

UTILIZE? 运用?

- harnessing the power of all 3 sites 利用三个工地集合一起的力量

PROS 优点

- increases perception as a complex 增强综合发展的感觉
- combined site, more competitive with surrounding neighbor in terms of power & size 在大量与发展程度上.结合发展比起周边建筑更有优势

CONS 缺点

- all 3 sites of equal "power" 三个项目只会有相同力量
- each site loses identity 个别项目不会有其特点

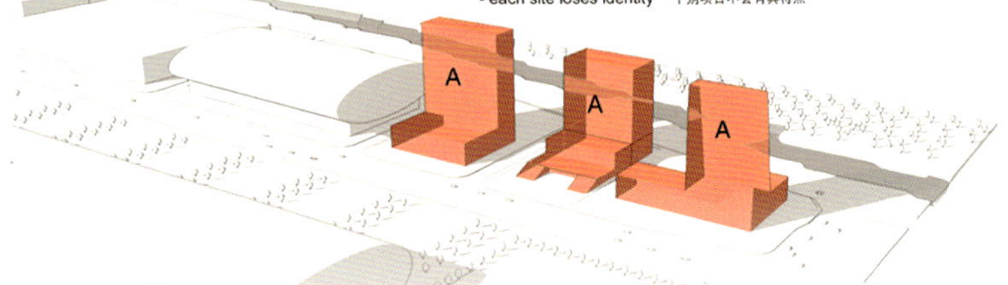

UTILIZE ?

PROPOSED STRATEGY 设计方案

- articulated horizontal movement with strong dialogue

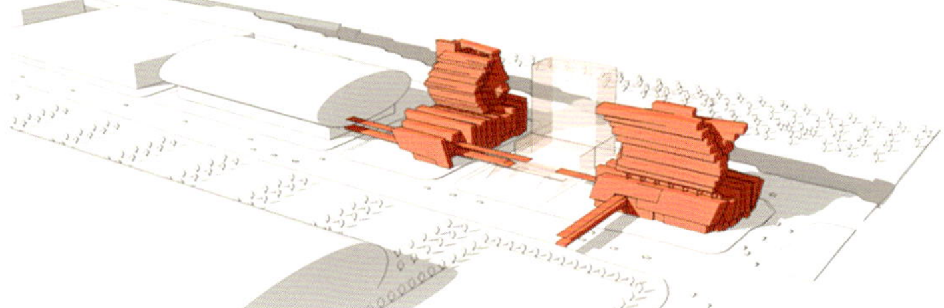

PROPOSED STRATEGY

SITE 1401
SITE 1301

foam model

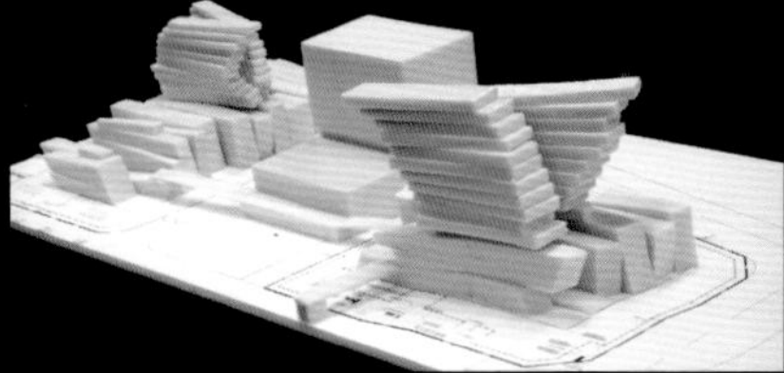

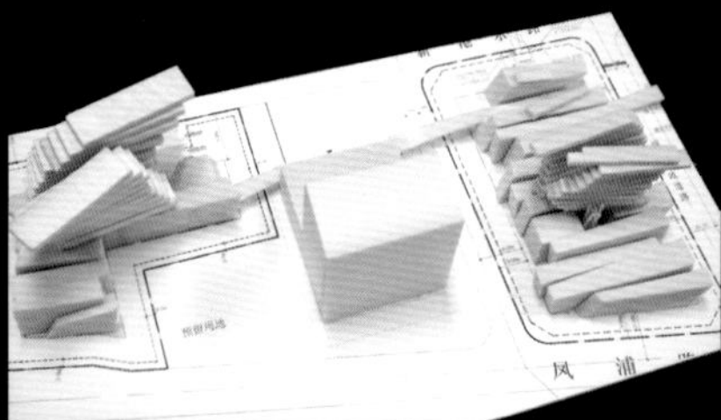

in comparison to its surrounding dominant neighbors. Consequently, urban design restrictions placed strong emphasis on the podium by requiring a simple and consistent presence on the major street wall to the north. The major entrances for the two sites were on the west side for "1301" and the east side for "1401". These faces are where more articulation and playfulness in the podium face was allowed and explored.

The 40 meter high, multi-level podium was broken down vertically toward the east and west in some very simple and bold moves. This helped to emphasize the primary entrances as well as break the mass of the volume down without diluting the monumentality of the podium height, which is equivalent to a ten story building. This is also the beginning of the dialogue between the two different sites which will clearly and visibly be of the same family, even though they are separated by 160 meters.

The office showroom building on top of "1301" was shifted as far to the north as possible to form the western terminus of an upper podium "urban room" joined with neighboring projects. The hotel of "1301" was initially positioned to align with the building tower between "1301" and "1401", also known as the "middle neighbor". This was deemed important to help emphasize the dialogue between the office showroom building to the west and the hotel to the east, as well as to de-emphasize the middle neighbor. Later the hotel was shifted further to the south due to fire regulations but it has since become apparent that the desired relationships between the three buildings are still evident.

1:300 acrylic model

1:1000 acrylic facade detail model

site 1301. retail office

How "1301", the "middle neighbor" and "1401" might relate to each other was explored in three ways. The first was to just "ignore" the relationships between all three. This may have been the simplest approach and did provide some continuity with the master plan. However, it does not have the benefit of making the two sites seem significant next to their more substantial neighbors. It also places the "middle neighbor" on an equal standing with the other sites, which did not support the client's business model.

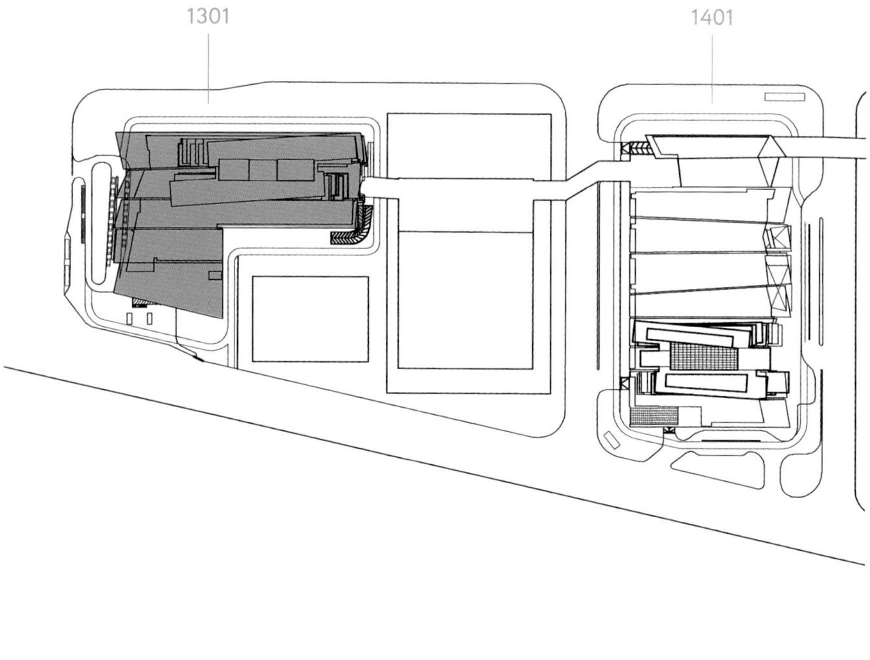

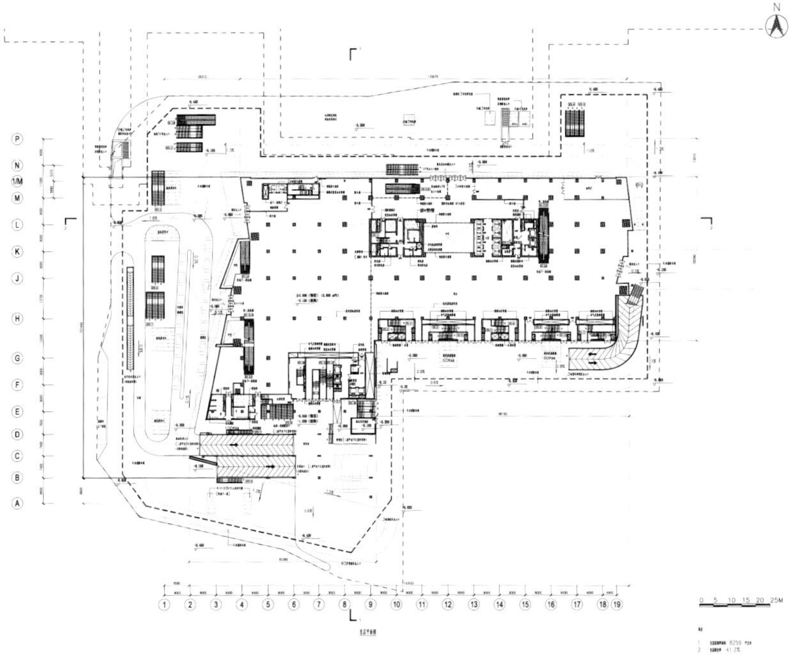

ground level

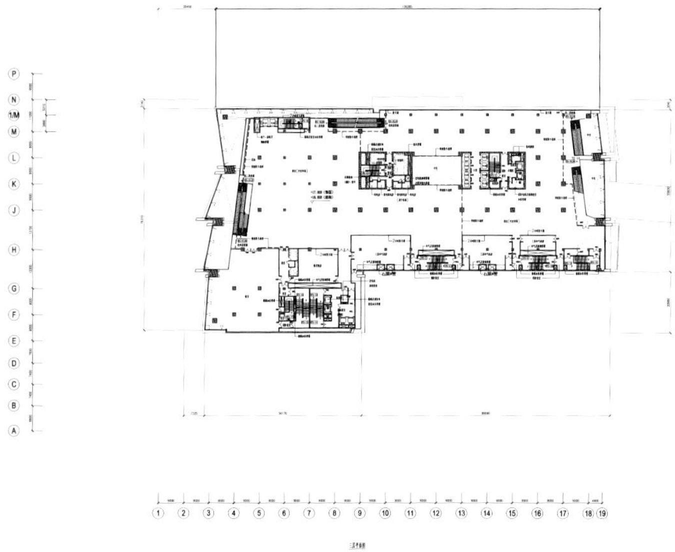

level 3

level 1

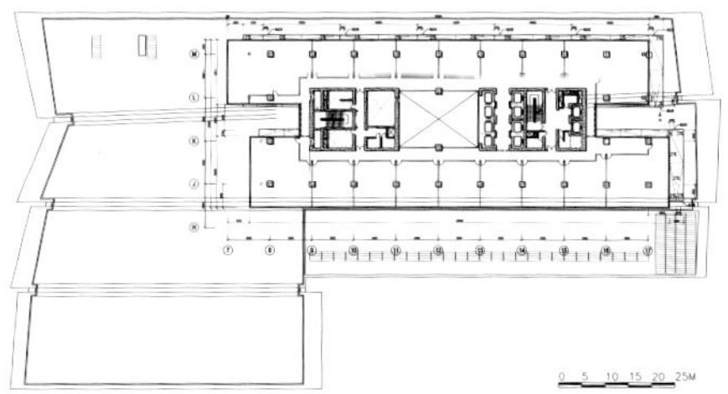

level 7

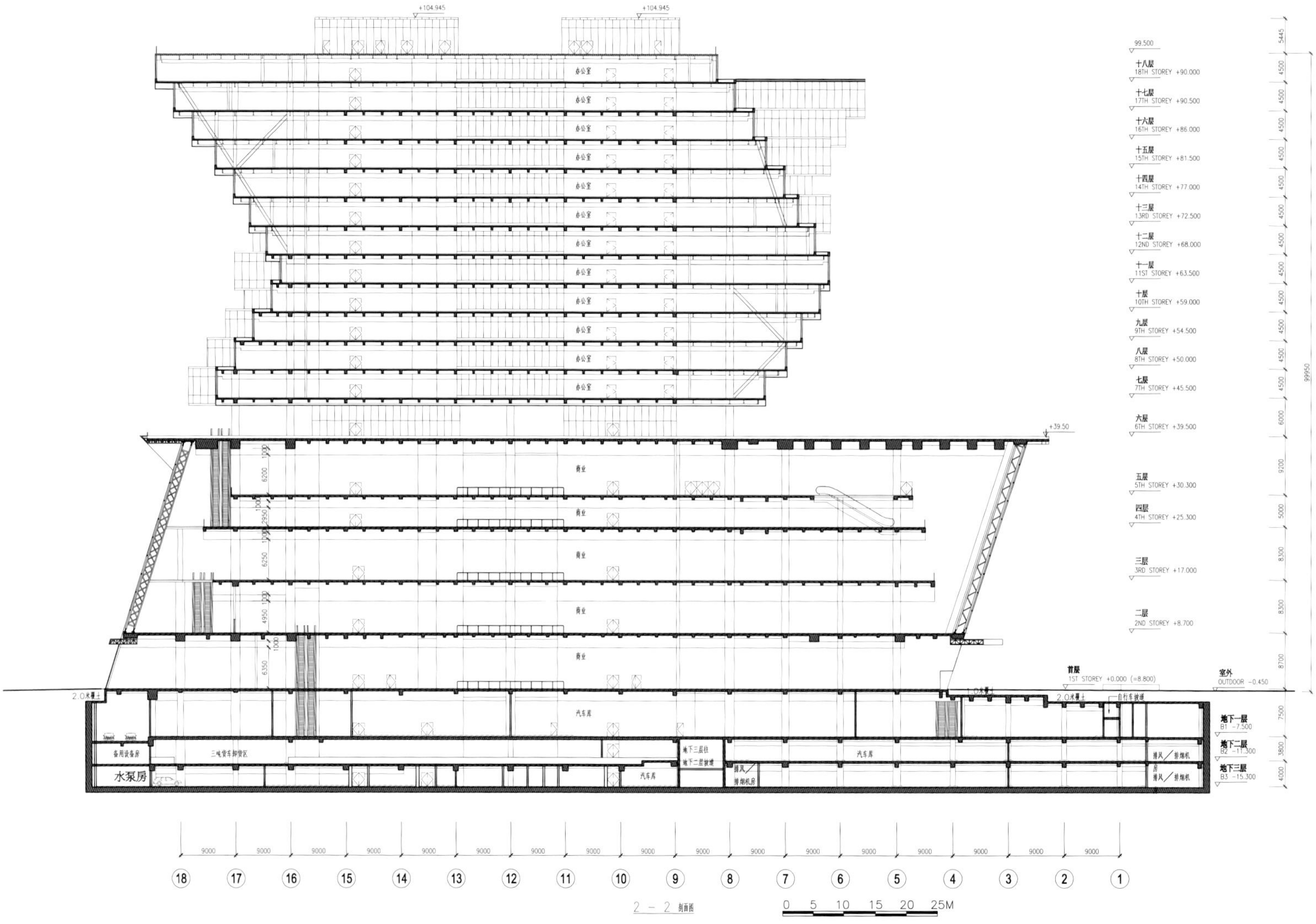

2 – 2 剖面图

The second approach was to explore positioning the towers in a manner which would conceal or "hide" the middle neighbor. Although this could have allowed the project's two sites to relate to each other better, this option was quickly rejected due to the insensitive impression which would have been communicated by being un-neighborly.

The final approach was to "utilize" the middle neighbor benefitting all parties by promoting enough critical mass to compete against the larger surrounding facilities. However, with the middle neighbor already in construction, and the realization that its formal qualities were somewhat neutral in impression, effort to create an even stronger dialogue between "1301" and "1401" was considered important.

The vertical slices of the podium were initially taken through the towers which definitely helped unify the two sites. However, the relationship still seemed static and a stronger dialogue was sought. This was immediately improved when the moves became horizontal. The middle neighbor receded appropriately into a backdrop and the moves were considered more in harmony to the "horizontality" of the surrounding context.

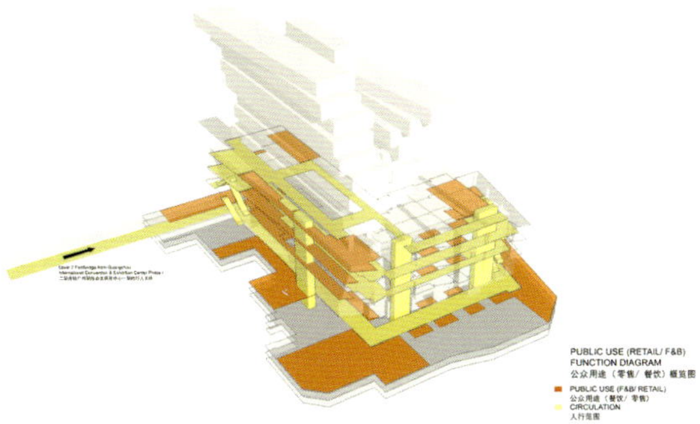

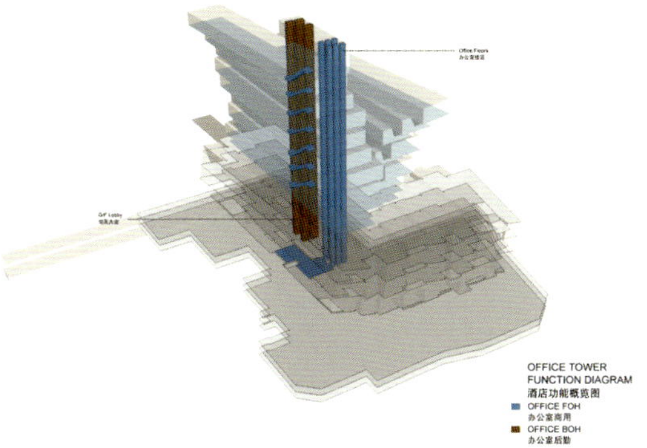

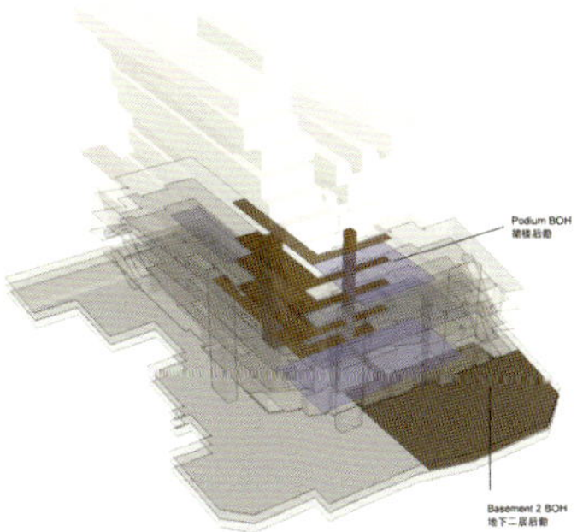

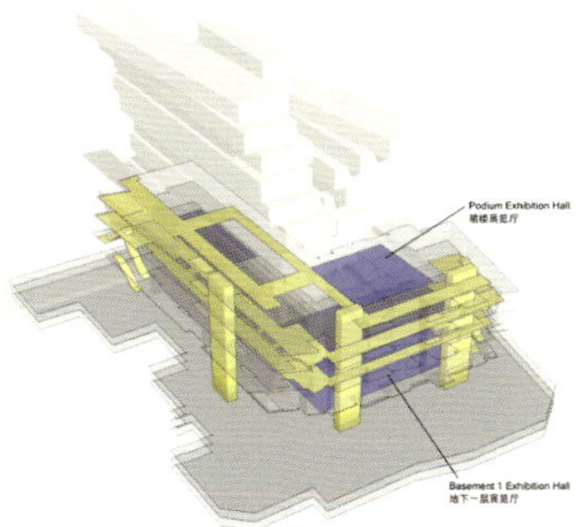

site 1401. exhibition hotel

These horizontal elements were then accentuated through shifts; both small ones in the north/south direction, and larger ones in the east/west direction which helped to animate the buildings even within construction and budget limitations.

These moves maximize a dialogue between the two sites likened to "static electricity" leaping over the middle neighbor and providing a dynamic, unified and powerful expression of this exhibition complex. This overall reading of being strongly unified is critical to the "perceived" stature of the project in Pazhou – which has a direct link to how it is marketed and, ultimately, its viability and success.

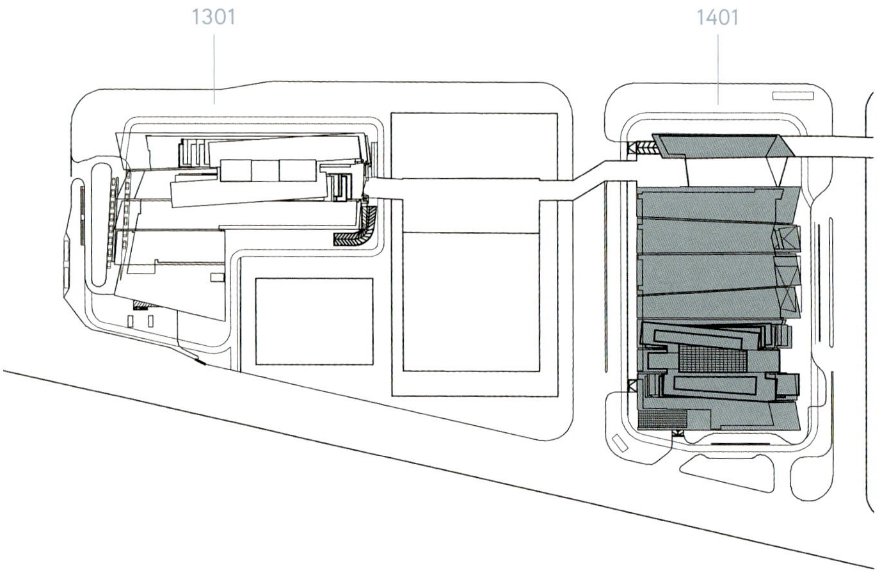

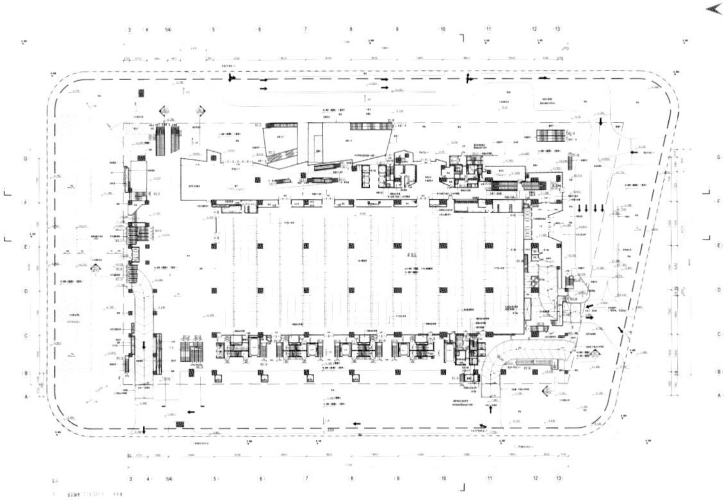

ground level

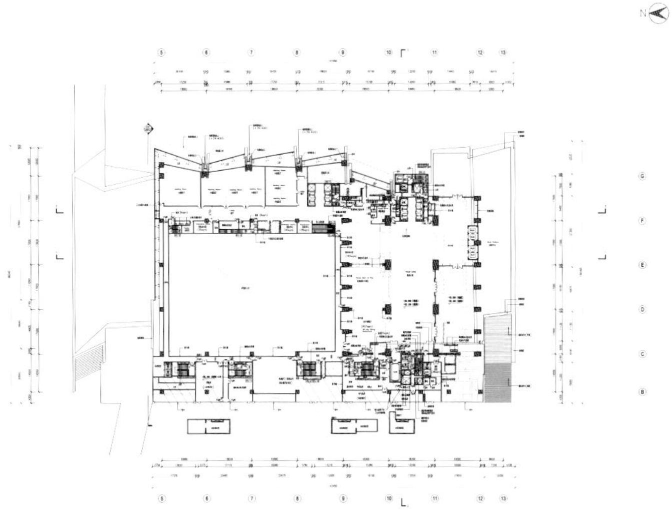

level 3

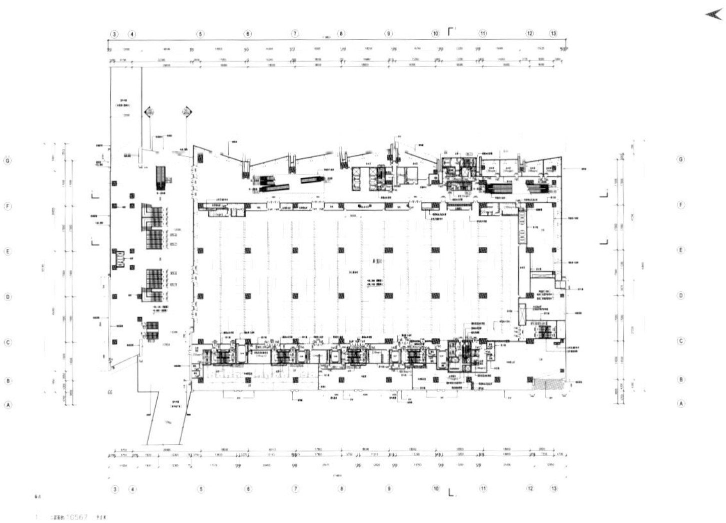

level 2

level 7

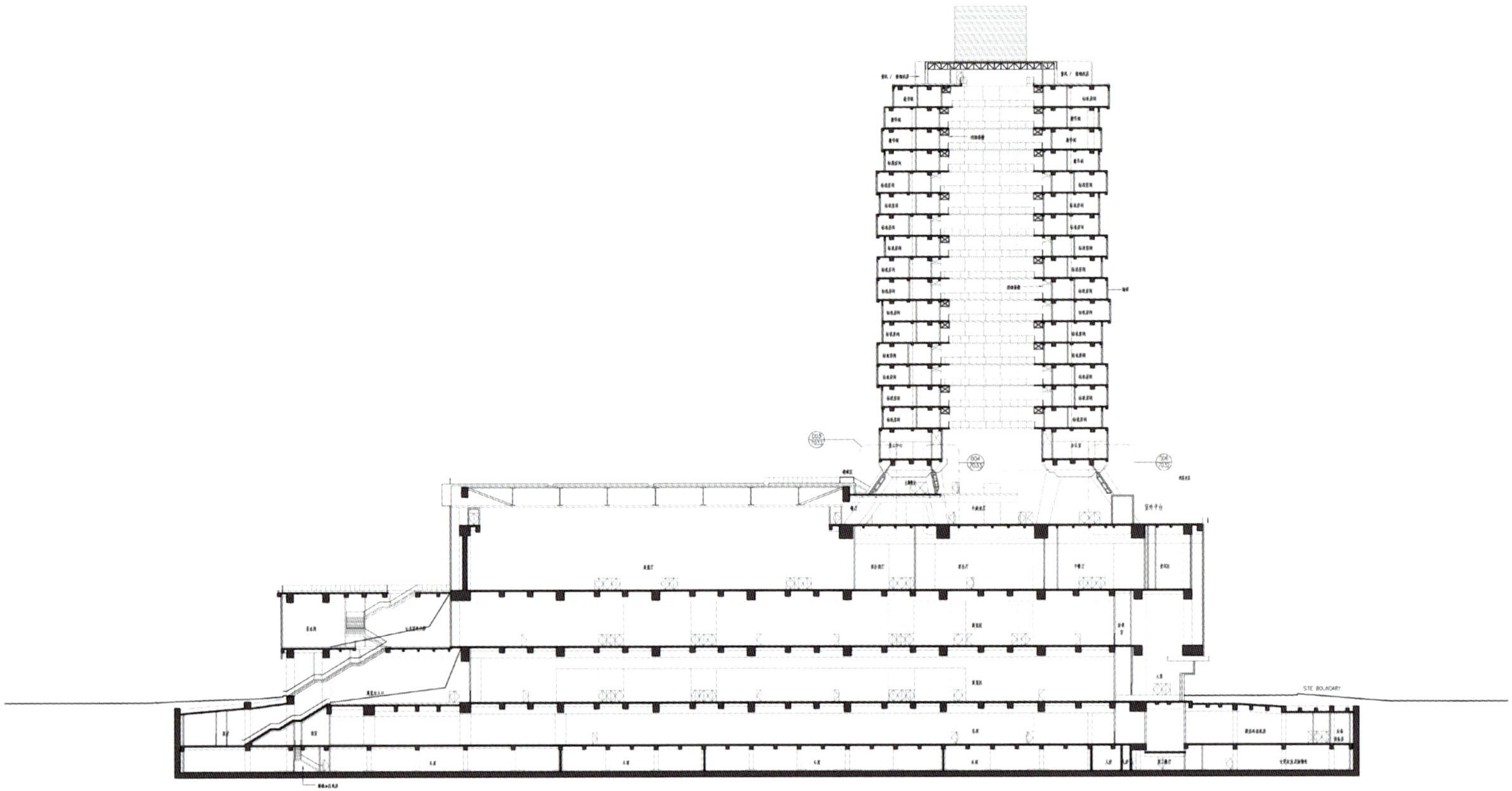

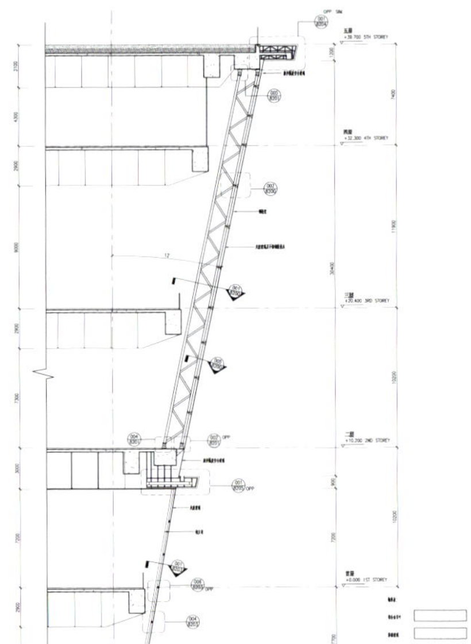

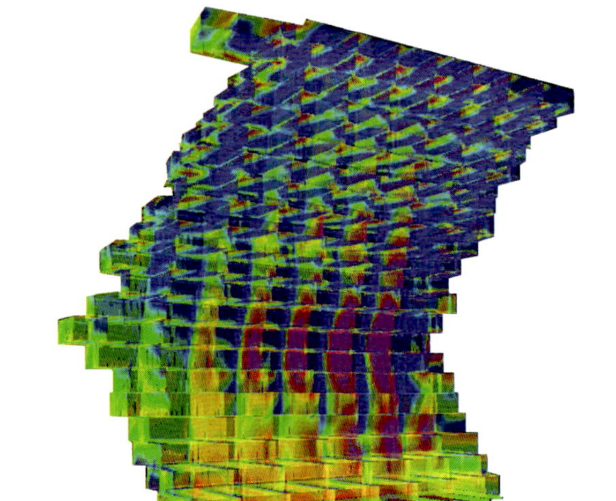

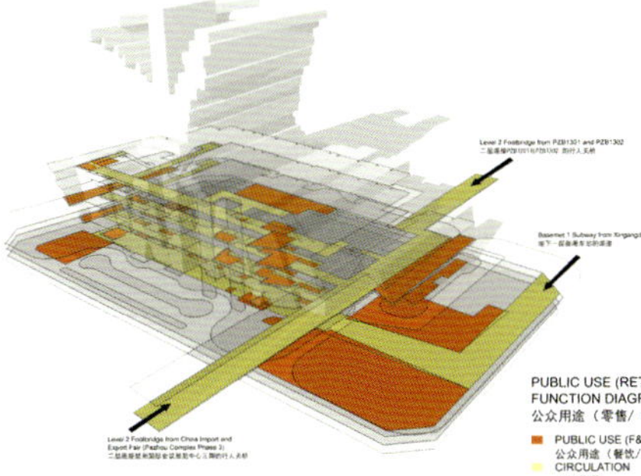

PUBLIC USE (RETAIL/ F&B) FUNCTION DIAGRAM
公众用途（零售/ 餐饮）概览图

- PUBLIC USE (F&B/ RETAIL) 公众用途（餐饮/ 零售）
- CIRCULATION 人行范围

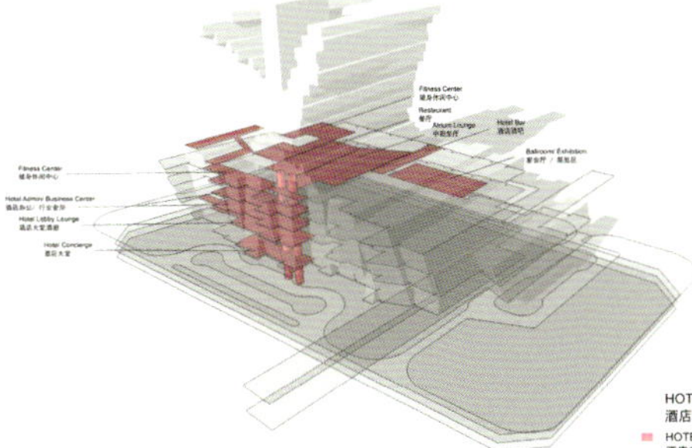

HOTEL FUNCTION DIAGRAM
酒店功能概览图

- HOTEL PROGRAMME IN PODIUM 酒店在裙楼的功能概览

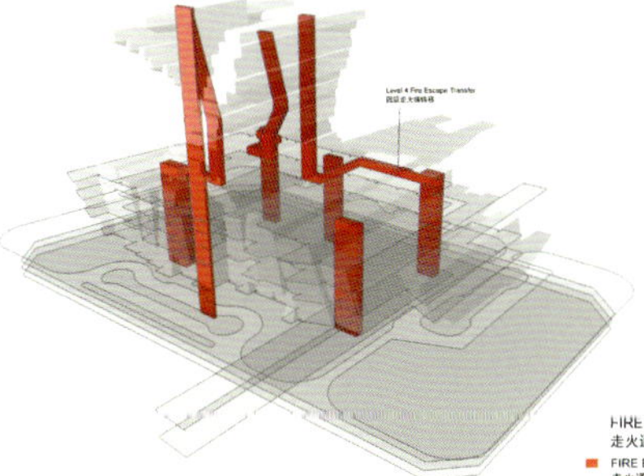

FIRE ESCAPE STRATEGY DIAGRA
走火通道示意图

- FIRE ESCAPE ROUTE 走火通道路线

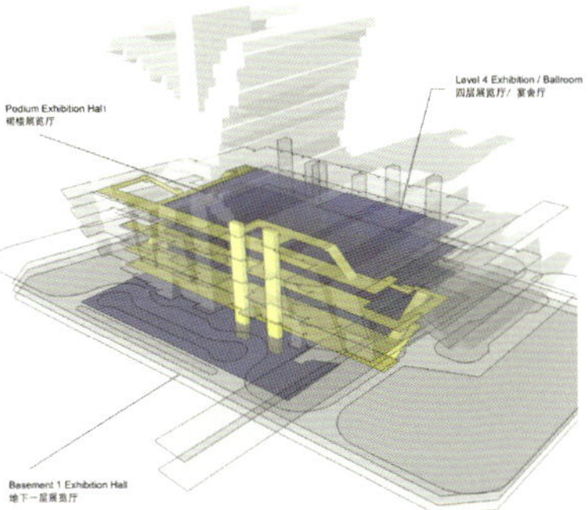

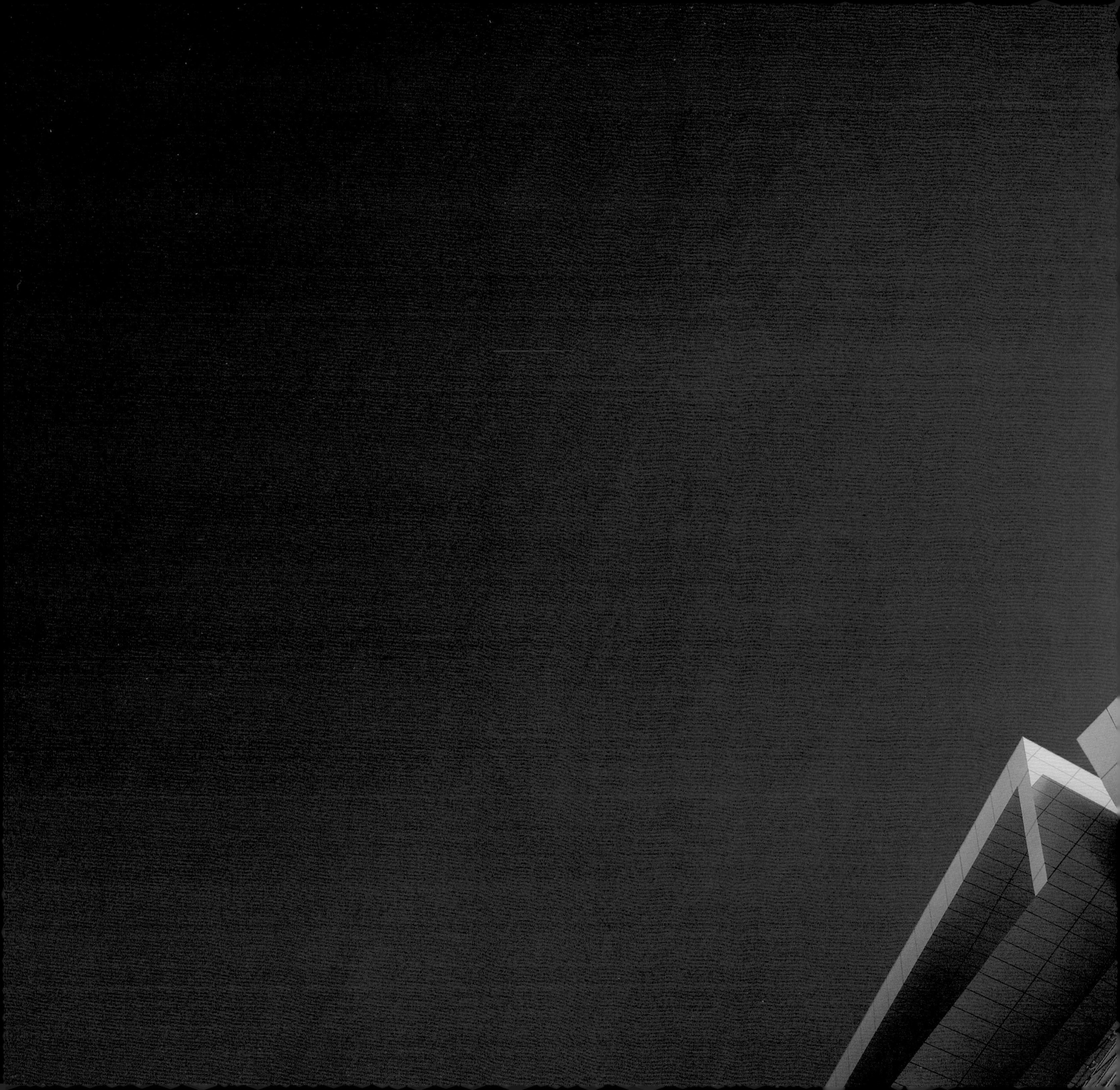

kutuzovskiy prospekt

kutuzovskiy prospekt

mixed use
client: mirax group
location: kutuzovskiy prospekt, moscow, russia.

site location

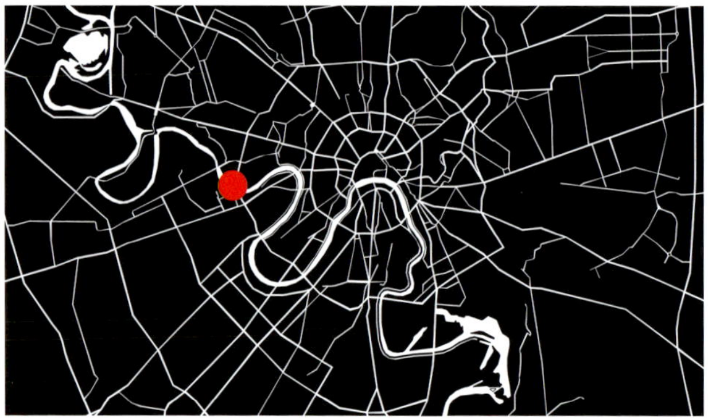

size/scale

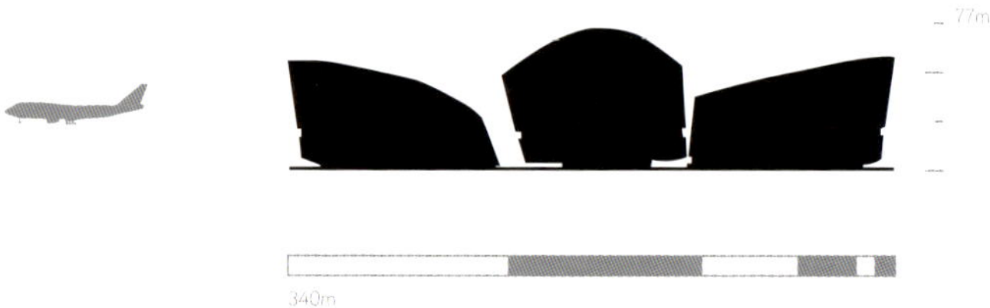

project description

It is unusual to be offered a design opportunity of this scale on a site which is fundamentally introverted. This was the exciting challenge for Kutuzovskiy Prospekt, located a few blocks away from Kutuzovskiy Avenue and a block off of the main river in Moscow.

This was a large mixed-use project that was land locked between some traditionally mandated developments and some riverside projects. Regardless of the impact of the design, it became clear that it needed to become fundamentally a destination development that if discovered, would end up being a joyful surprise. This was the opportunity of the design.

The project needed to be self-sufficient and attractive to the commercial market which was a challenge due to its non-existent vehicular frontage. An interesting balance of hospitality, service apartments, high-end residential apartments and boutique retail was agreed on to promote the "exclusiveness" of this development made possible by its "privacy" but also that it was in close proximity to the center of Moscow.

The design then took the opportunity to transform the traditional Moscow courtyard with its surrounding blocks into a modern interpretation. Kutuzovskiy is designed to maximize southern exposure to the winter sun – specifically for the residential apartments and the development's open spaces. These courtyard volumes are defined through open ended "horseshoe" masses which are lifted off of the ground at the back. This allows a sense of continuity with the defined spaces which currently exist in the surrounding urban fabric, but at the same time "liberates" the ground plane.

The quality of this topography is then optimized as a civic experience which is supported by retail activities of shopping and food and beverage outlets. These are mingled with a more passive landscape urban park experience which ultimately differentiates this project from the surrounding built densities.

process

goals

To achieve a successful development of conforming height, although the client initially requested the development of non-conforming towers, because they did not feel a good solution with the density was achievable.

challenge

A low-rise, high density, introverted site wich needed to meet day-lighting requirements for residential units.

play

An adaption of the existing Moscow open courtyard by raising the middle portion of the horseshoe shaped building – thus providing a familiar flowing landscape.

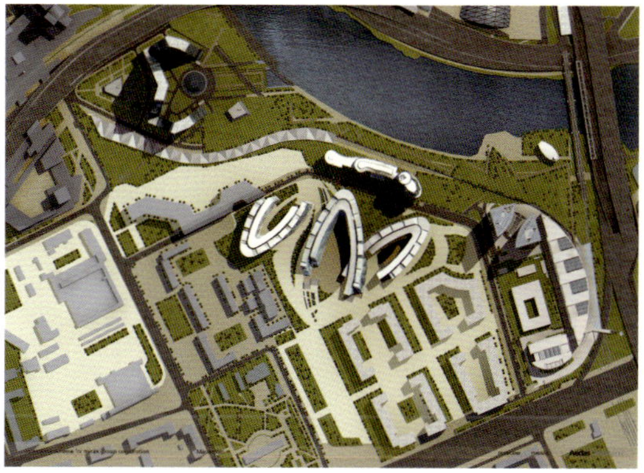

usage

residential
267651 m2 2880971 sqf

hospitality
0 m2 0 sqf

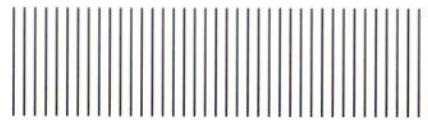

office
0 m2 0 sqf

retail + f&b
9641 m2 103775 sqf

landscape
0 m2 0 sqf

other
8261 m2 88920 sqf

total area: 378.994 m2
4.079.457 sqf

| = 2500 m2 / 26910 sqf

status

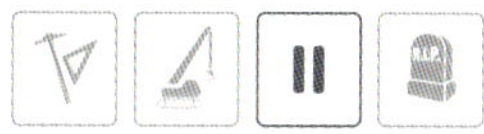

project on hold: 2009

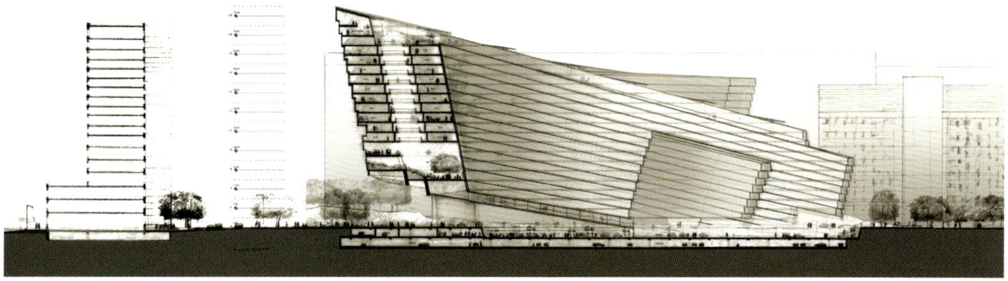

The zoning envelope for this development limited the habitable areas of the project to 70 meters in height. With almost 380,000 square meters of GFA this was a very dense proposition. A further complication to the issue was that the developments to the south were only 40 meters in height.

The project's open space became an evolution of the existing courtyards to the south. It was also considered important that the massing of the development respond sensitively to its southern neighbors. In this regard, the masses of the projects started high toward the north where the mass is lifted off of the ground, and sloped down toward the south, receding into the ground plane.

The texture of these masses is defined by two forces. The first is the emphasis of the arms toward the ground plane to the south. These become denser from north to south. The collapsing of the horizontal plane is then countered through the knitting of this move with the actual horizontal floors. The collisions of these forces are then expressed through usable balconies and sky gardens presented outwardly as reconciliation.

These arms were then located at the end of all the view corridors from the south, appearing as crystal ice forms which provided a visual interest and counterpoint to the surrounding urban fabric of heavy earth-borne rectilinear masses. As one moves into this new topography, the surrounding restrictions are not removed – but liberated. The result is a project with reasonable density and contextual response to be sensitive to its neighbors, exclusive enough to be viable as an introverted development, but still fresh and intriguing enough to make the chance discovery of the development uplifting and memorable.

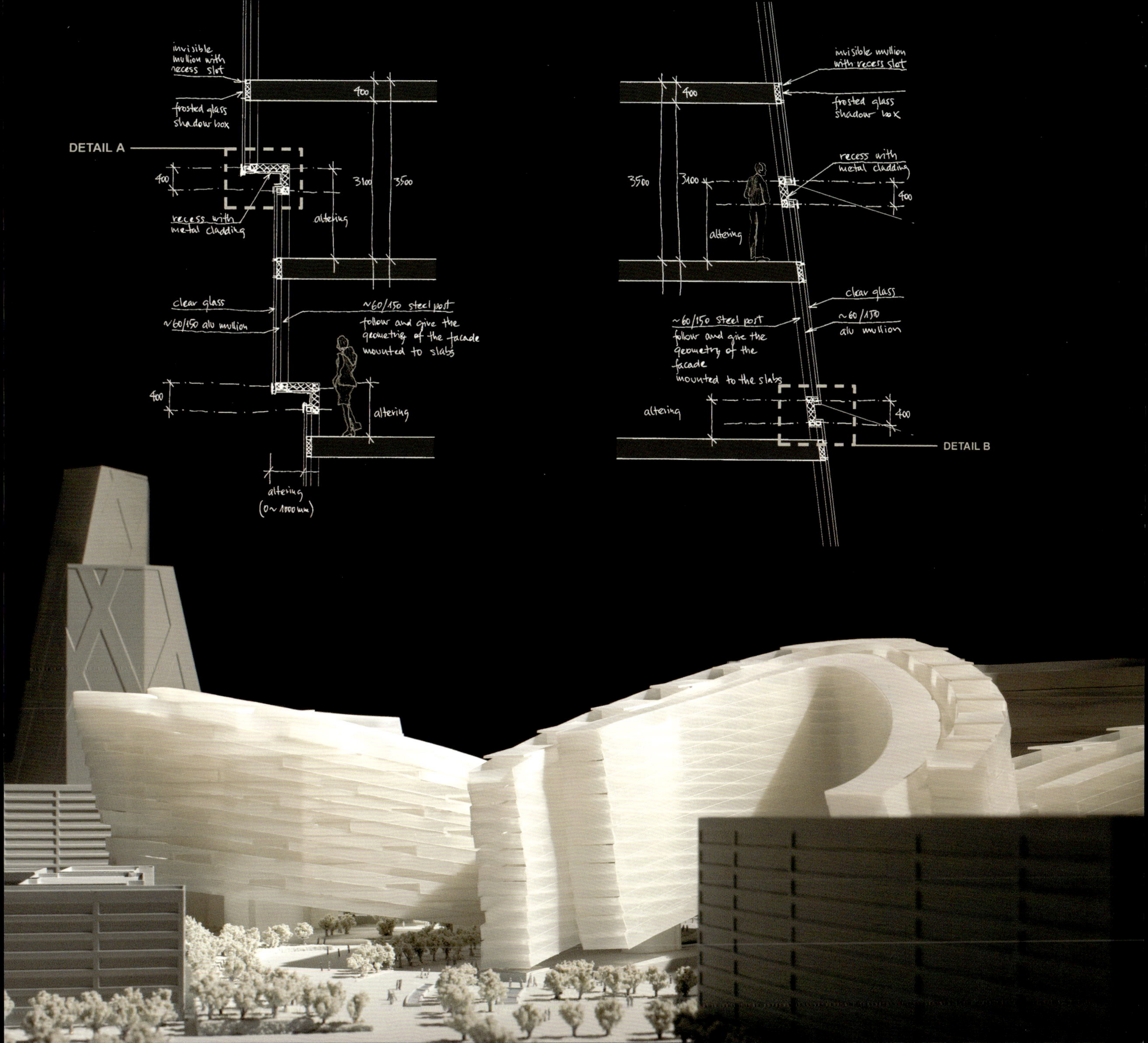
invisible mullion with recess slot
frosted glass shadow box
DETAIL A
400
3100
3500
recess with metal cladding
altering
clear glass
~60/150 steel post
follow and give the geometry of the facade mounted to slabs
~60/150 alu mullion
400
altering
altering (0~1000mm)
invisible mullion with recess slot
400
frosted glass shadow box
recess with metal cladding
3500
3100
400
altering
clear glass
~60/150 steel post
follow and give the geometry of the facade mounted to the slabs
~60/150 alu mullion
altering
400
DETAIL B

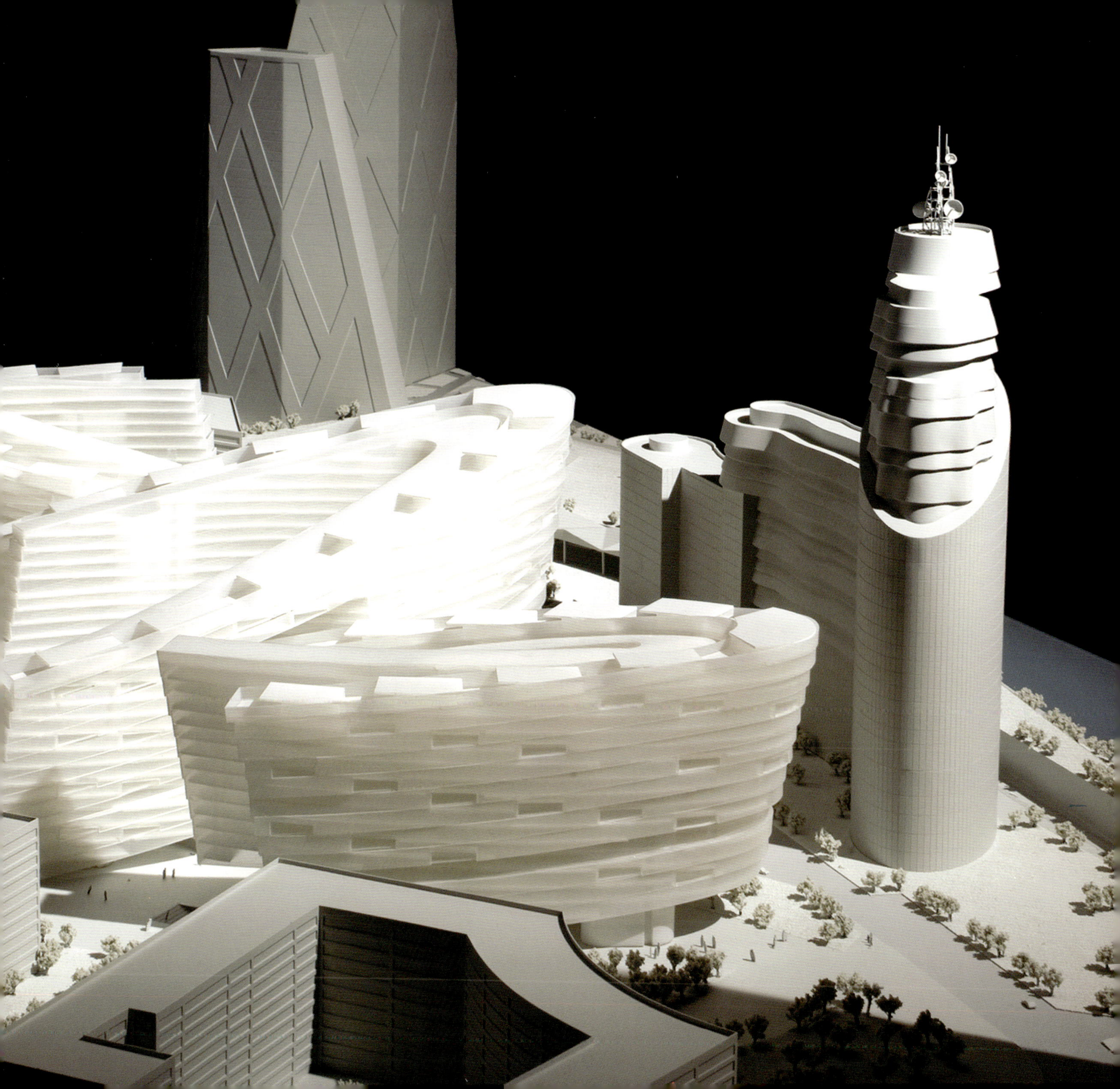

khor dubai

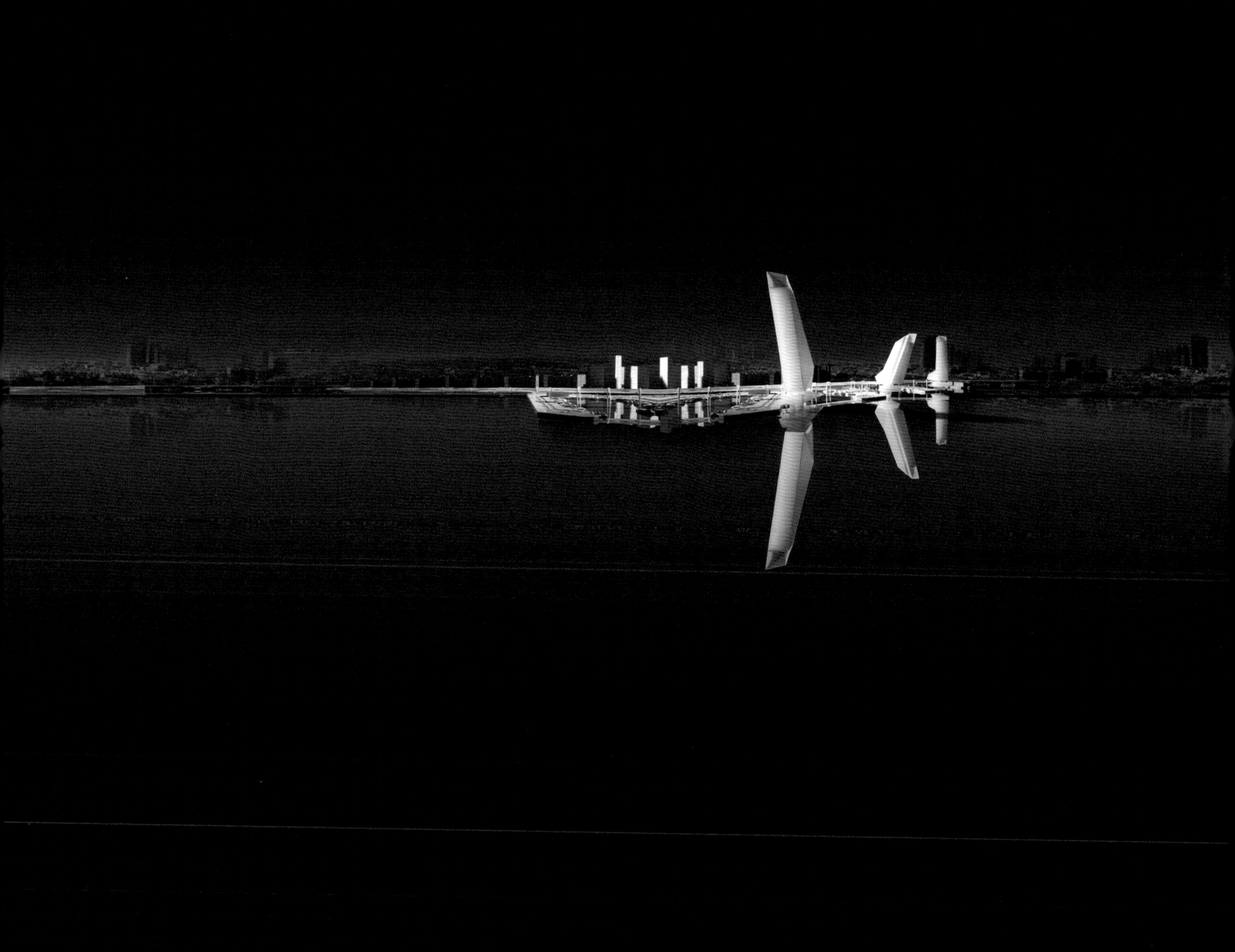

khor dubai

mixed use

client: mizin
location: dubai creek, dubai, uae

site location

size/scale

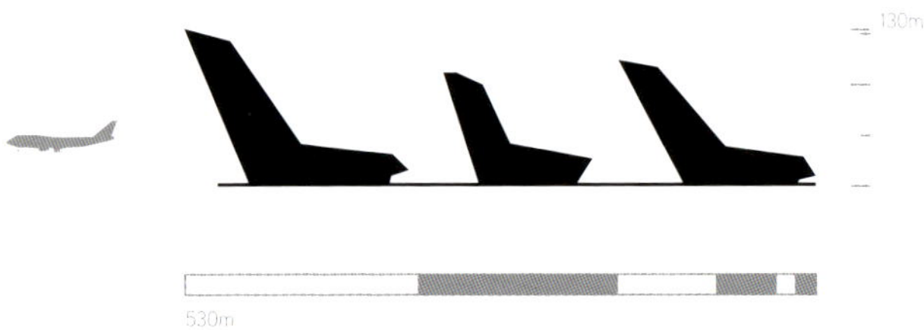

project description

Three Amphibians

Three figures float softly off of the edge of three fingers of active wharfs within Dubai Creek.

Surrounding these wharfs is the continuous trading activity which is rooted deep in the region's history.

This is evident from the number of boats and barges bringing the commerce into the Souks of Deira.

Two of these figures contain commercial office space while the third is a hotel.

The location for this project is not urban – as opposed to Dubai's old center of Deira looming behind.

The location is not nautical – as opposed to the boats which arrive and depart to the open sea.

The project is a built manifestation of a morphing between these two worlds.

The three figures are buildings and they are also aquatic.

Their identities, striving to belong to their context, echo the movement of harbor cranes, blending them appropriately into the activity of the wharfs to which they are paired.

The placement of these figures was deliberately not in the designated site within the actual wharf but rather off to the side, in the water.

This was chosen to minimize disturbance and disruption of wharf activities during and after construction.

The figures bend and rotate individual view corridors up and down the creek.

process

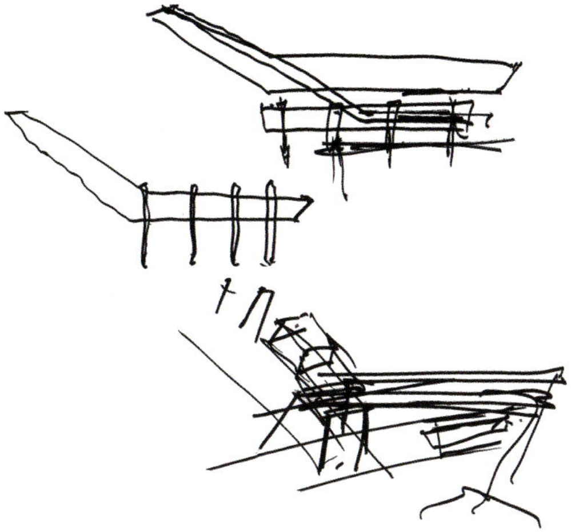

goals

To develop buildings belonging equally to both land and sea as the site is an actual wharf.

play

A perceptual play and transformation of form common to existing wharfs into habitable "amphibians".

challenge

The existing activity on the functioning wharf could not be interrupted, both in the final design as well as during the construction.

usage

residential
0 m2 0 sqf`

hospitality
20219 m2 217635 sqf`

office
29192 m2 314220 sqf`

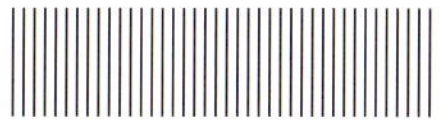

retail + f&b
0 m2 0 sqf`

landscape
0 m2 0 sqf`

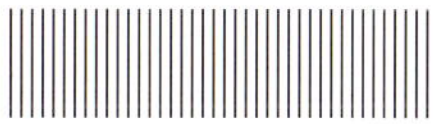

other
0 m2 0 sqf`

total area: 49.411 m2
531.856 sqf

| = 2500 m2 / 26910 sqf

status

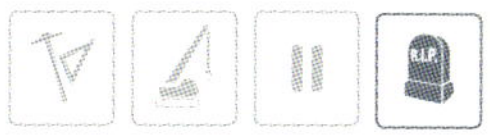

all competition entrants disqualified

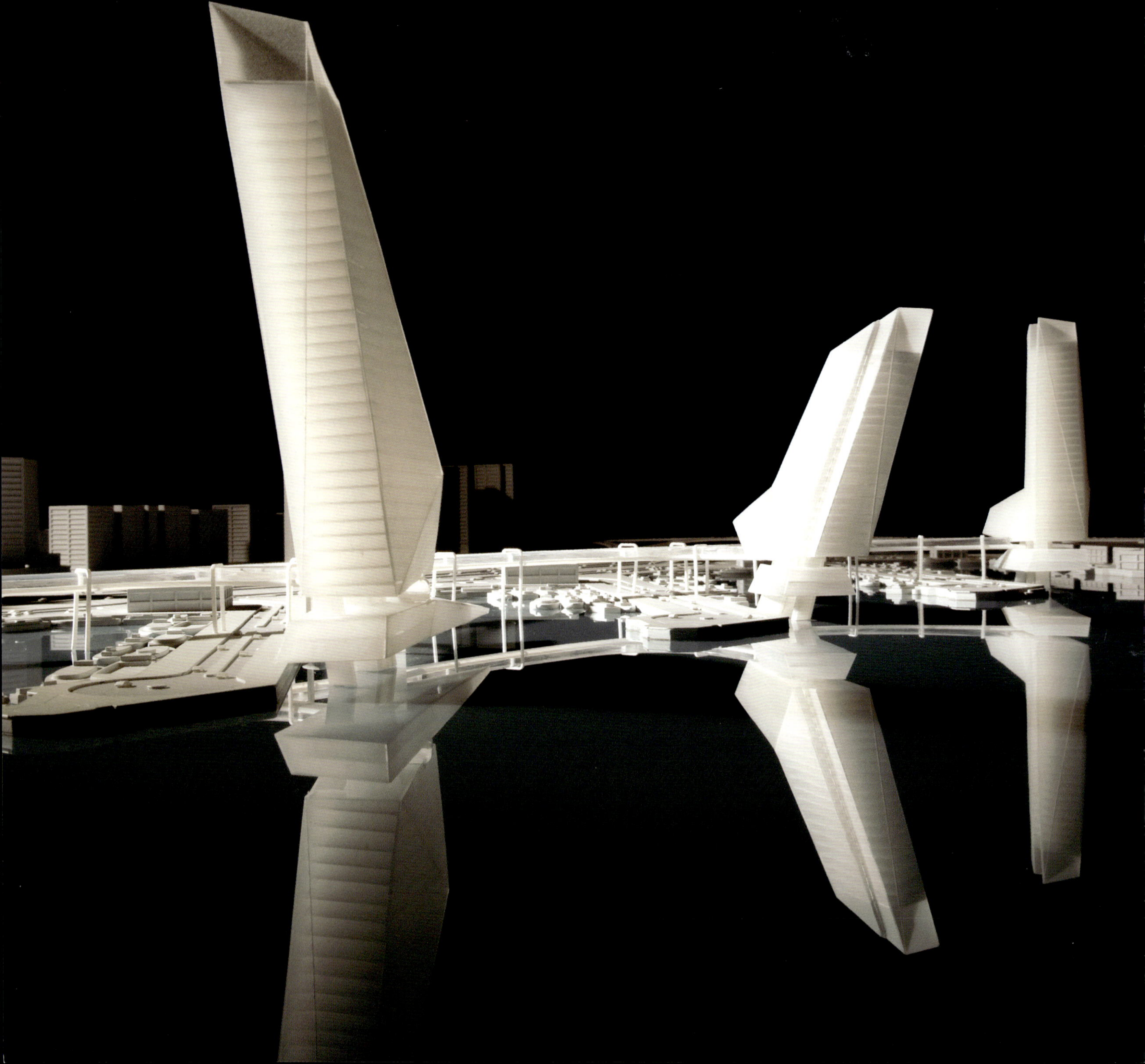

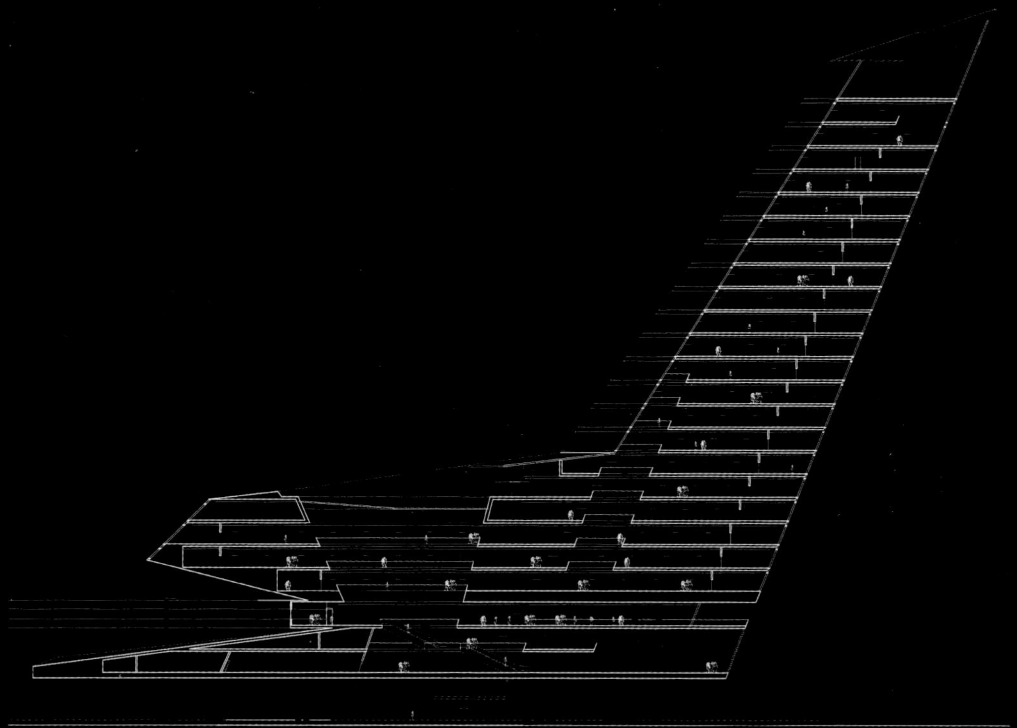

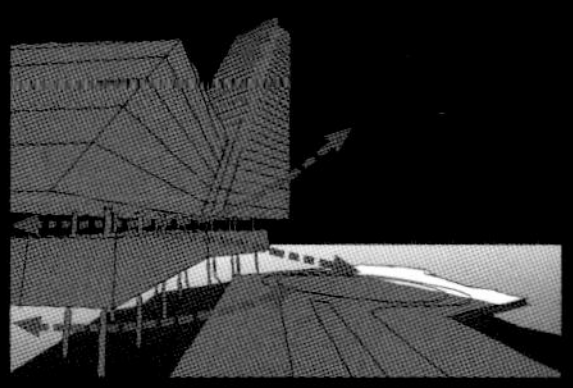

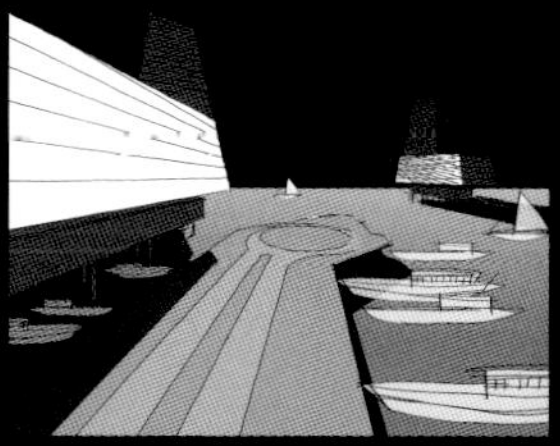

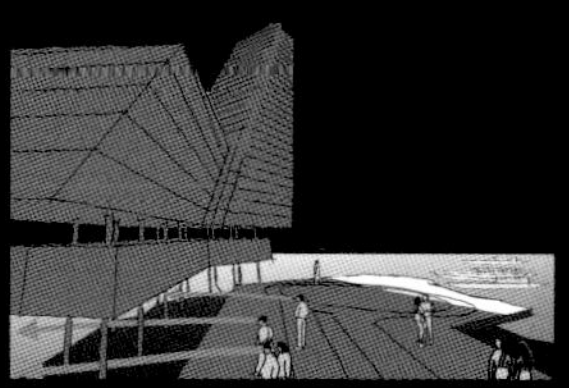

The faceted facade allows for the varying surrounding activities to be perceived by passing audiences.

Simultaneous reflections are mirrored off of the glass allowing for the richness of these built forms to be as much about their own formal qualities as they are about the creek, the wharfs, the surrounding cities and the changing sky above.

Three Amphibians, belonging to both sea and land, rise up sculpturally. They powerfully proclaim the importance of the wharfs they co-habit symbolizing Dubai's importance as a leading center of commerce – historically, currently and most definitely in the future.

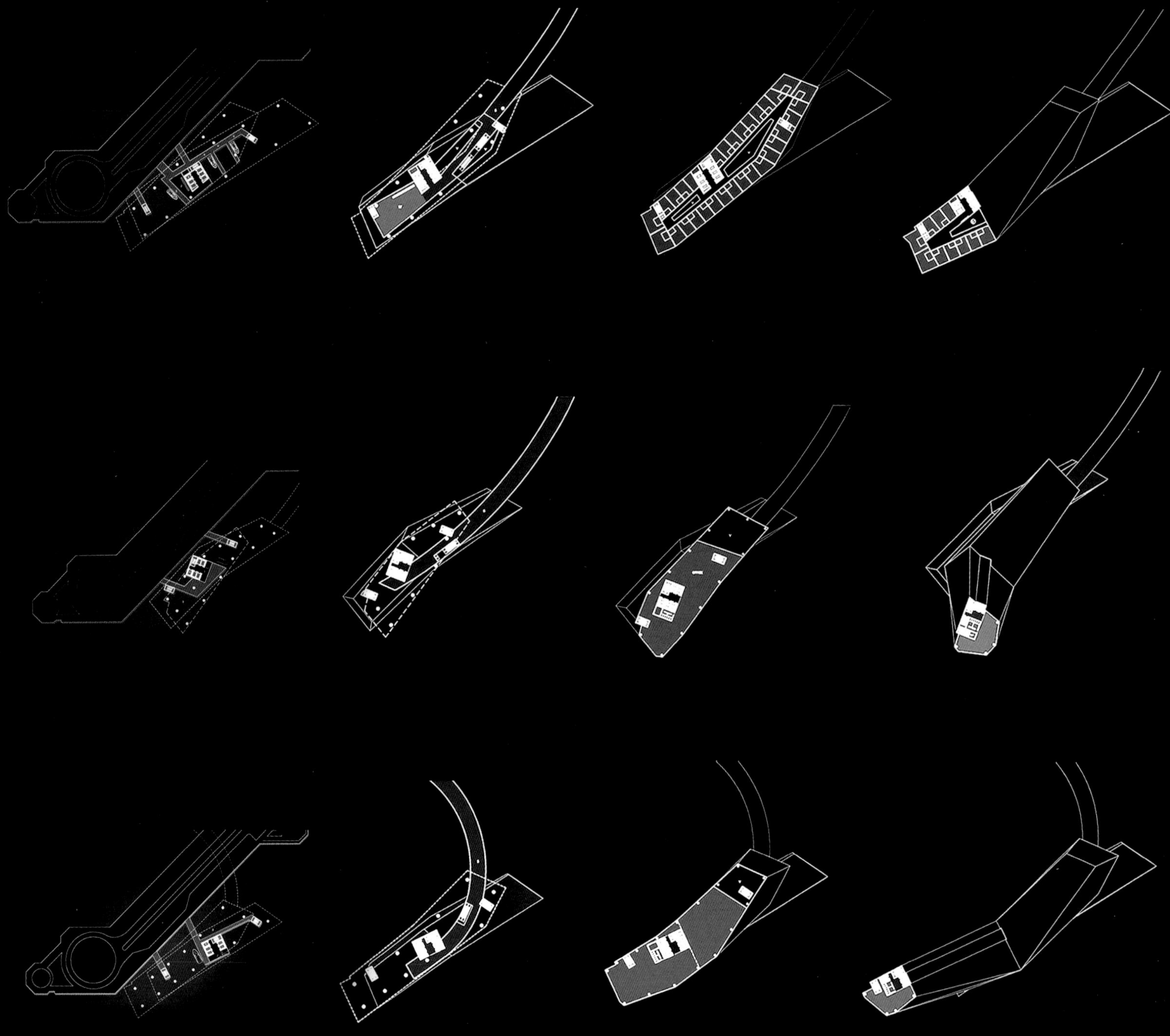

aerovokzal

aerovokzal

mixed use

client: city property group sa

location: leningradskiy prospekt, moscow, russia

site location

size/scale

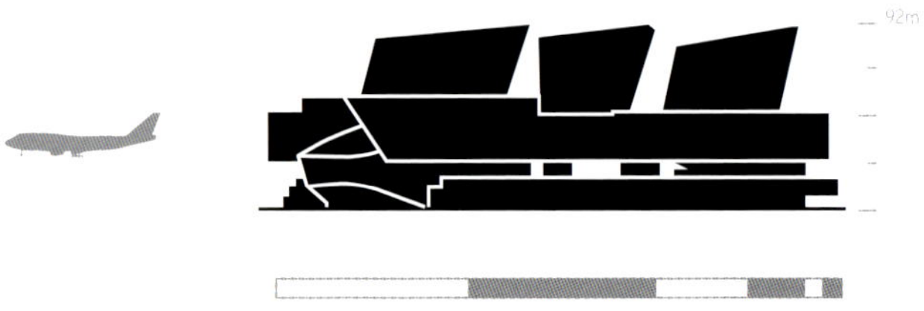

project description

Located close to the center of Moscow, adjacent to an abandoned military airport, a MiG factory and across the street from the historic Peter's Traveling Palace, the Leningradskiy Development is surrounded by a diverse and exciting context. The client labeling the development as "Aerostar", requested that the project have some relationship to the aeronautical history of the surrounding land. Inspiration was derived from the rhythm of MiG-29 tailfins on the land's historical tarmac.

With a floor area ratio of 5.5 and a height limit below 90 meters, the project is an extremely dense development. However, this major challenge was amplified when considering the mix of development programs. The primary uses include office and hotel functions. The viability of these two uses is dependent on minimizing overlooking and maximizing views. Due to the density restrictions, - this became the governing constraint in the development of the scheme.

In addition to the primary uses, the project contains 80,000 square meters of retail development as well as a 10,000 person arena. After these two items are programmed to be as functional as possible, the available remaining height is now reduced to 70 meters. The available site area is also significantly reduced by the arena as construction costs dictated that any load placed on top of its long span trusses should be avoided.

For the retail to be viable, a mall interlaced with the arena needed to occupy almost three full floors of the site, making it extremely difficult to access the office components above without interruption. Consequently, the new programmatic element of an elevated, café filled concourse was introduced between the retail below and the commercial above. This indoor/outdoor interstitial zone is a functional lifeline which facilitates the success of all components and provides a new urban space unique to the city. All this evolved solely out of the constraints of the project.

process

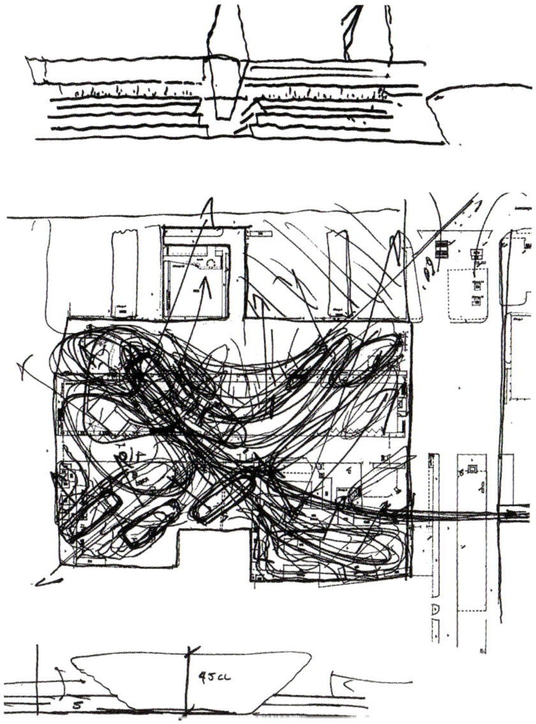

goals

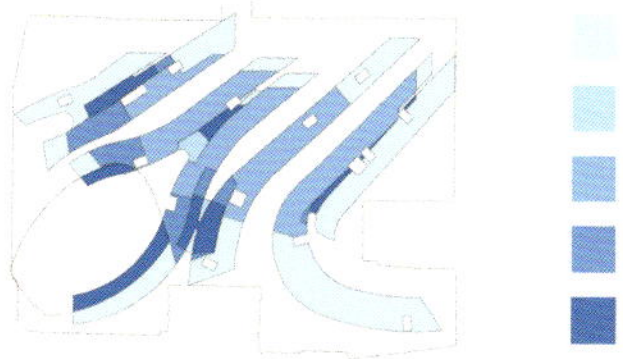

The project strives to minimize overlooking and maximize views/frontage for both the office and retail components.

challenge

Extremely high density with a height limit of 90 meters and an area of 360,000 sm.

play

An indoor/outdoor interstitial zone which is semi-public in character and knits the retail located below with the office spaces located above.

usage

residential
0 m2 0 sqf

hospitality
30294 m2 326082 sqf

office
209806 m2 2258333 sqf

retail + f&b
80395 m2 865365 sqf

landscape
0 m2 0 sqf

arena
40089 m2 431514 sqf

total area: 566,228 m2
6,094,827 sqf

| = 2500 m2 / 26910 sqf

status

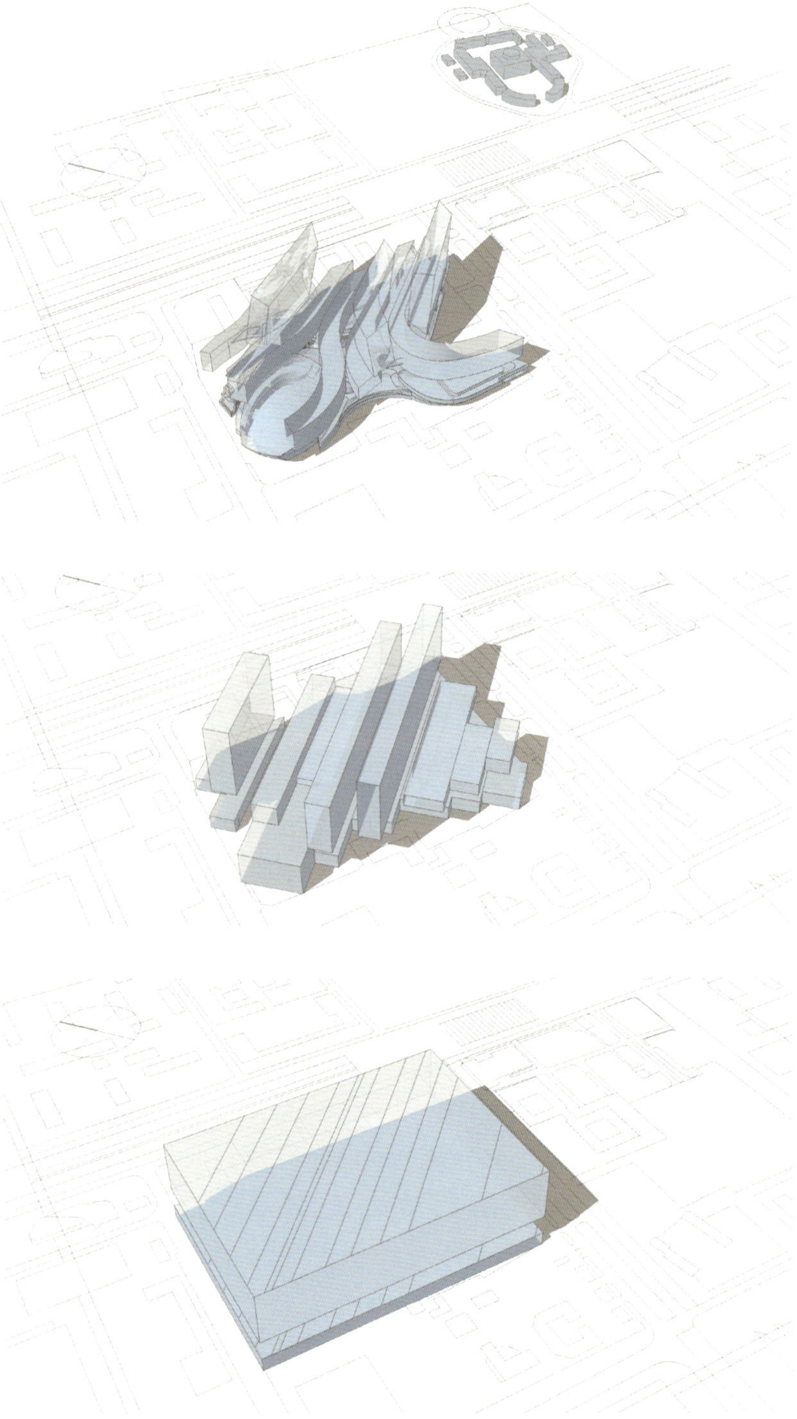

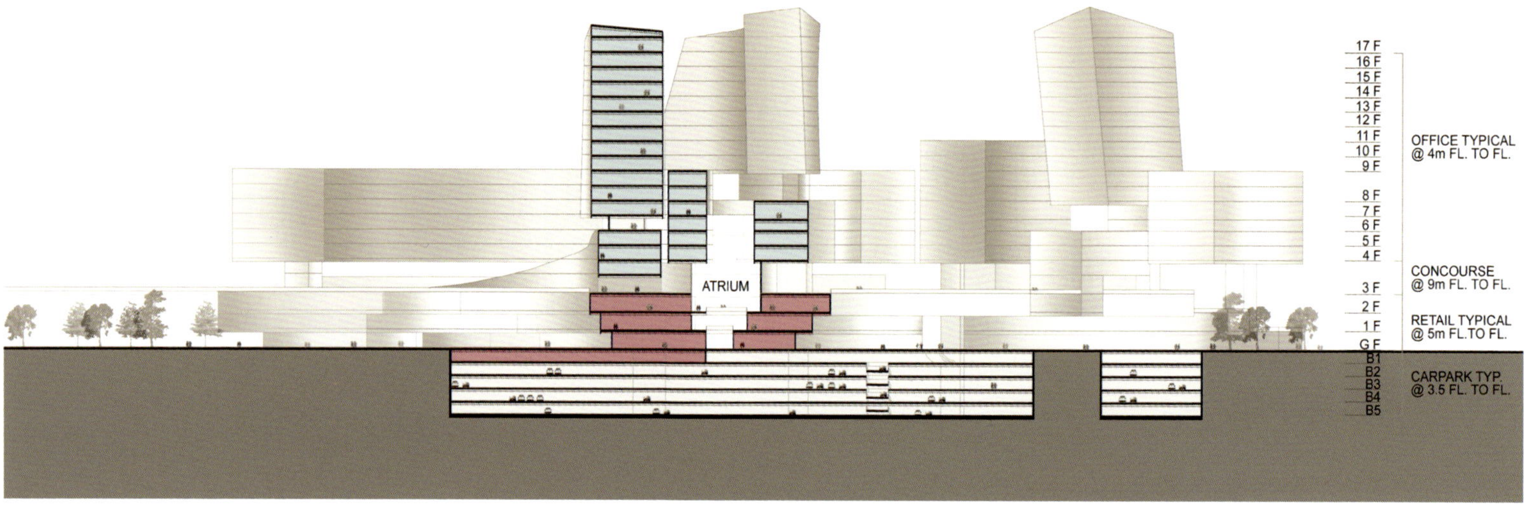
ATRIUM
17 F
16 F
15 F
14 F
13 F
12 F
11 F
10 F
9 F
8 F
7 F
6 F
5 F
4 F
3 F
2 F
1 F
G F
B1
B2
B3
B4
B5
OFFICE TYPICAL
@ 4m FL. TO FL.
CONCOURSE
@ 9m FL. TO FL.
RETAIL TYPICAL
@ 5m FL.TO FL.
CARPARK TYP.
@ 3.5 FL. TO FL.

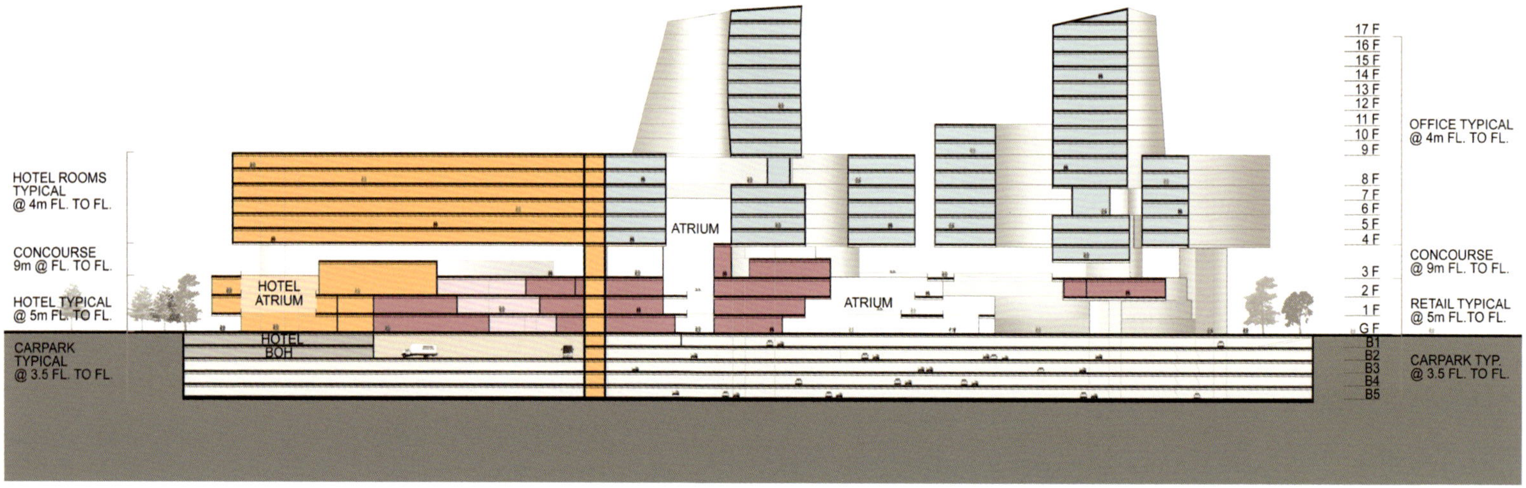
HOTEL ROOMS
TYPICAL
@ 4m FL. TO FL.
CONCOURSE
9m @ FL. TO FL.
HOTEL TYPICAL
@ 5m FL. TO FL.
CARPARK
TYPICAL
@ 3.5 FL. TO FL.
HOTEL
ATRIUM
HOTEL
BOH
ATRIUM
ATRIUM
17 F
16 F
15 F
14 F
13 F
12 F
11 F
10 F
9 F
8 F
7 F
6 F
5 F
4 F
3 F
2 F
1 F
G F
B1
B2
B3
B4
B5
OFFICE TYPICAL
@ 4m FL. TO FL.
CONCOURSE
@ 9m FL. TO FL.
RETAIL TYPICAL
@ 5m FL.TO FL.
CARPARK TYP.
@ 3.5 FL. TO FL.

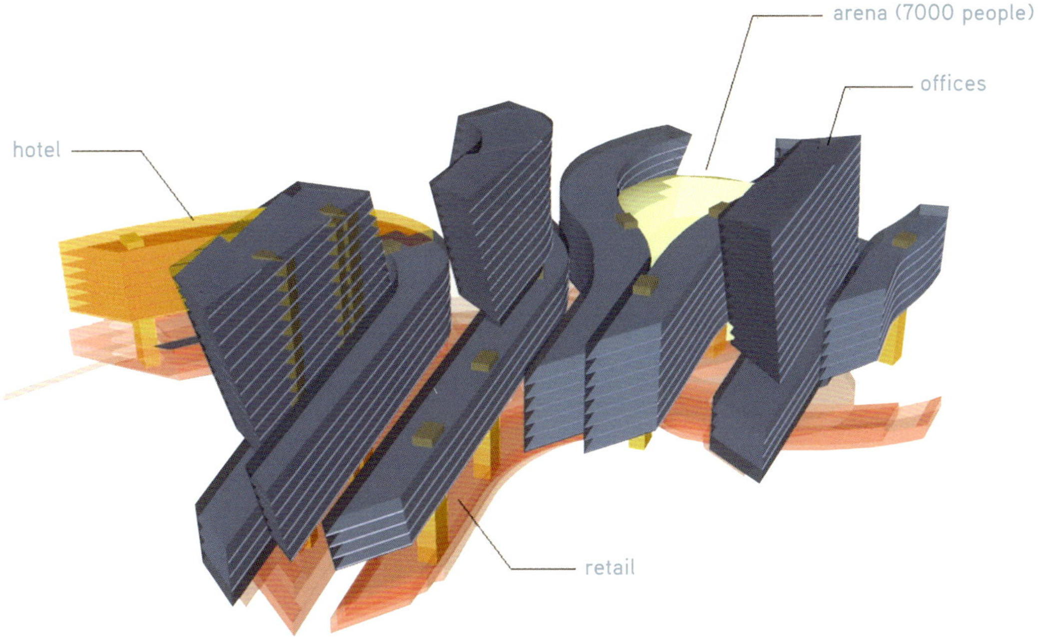

functions

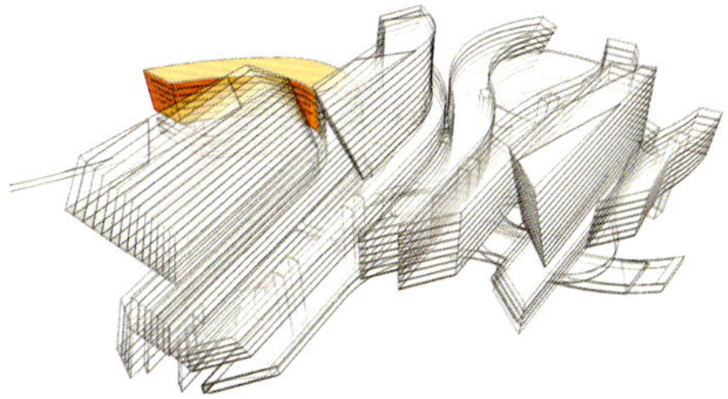

hotel

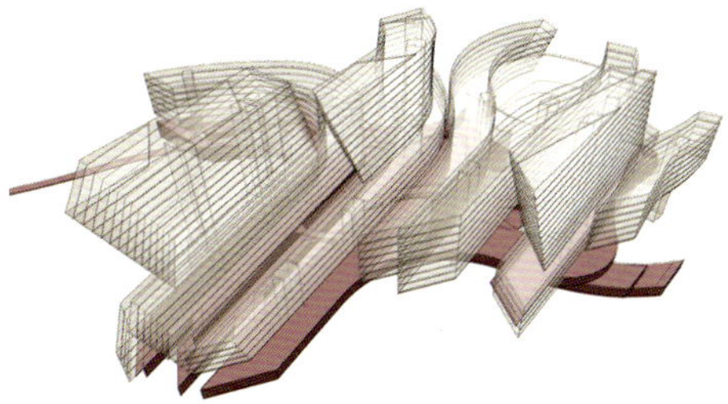

retail

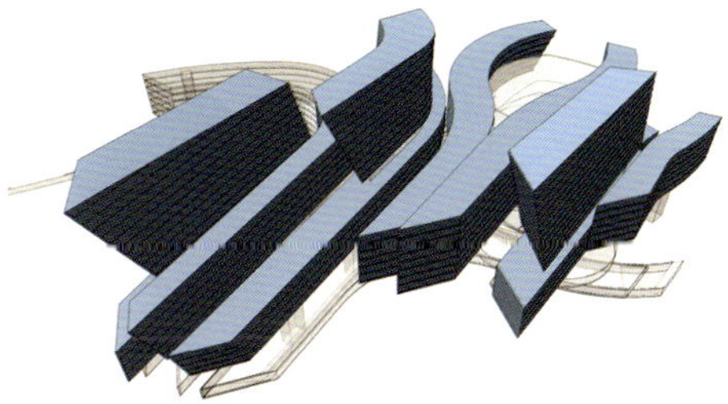

office

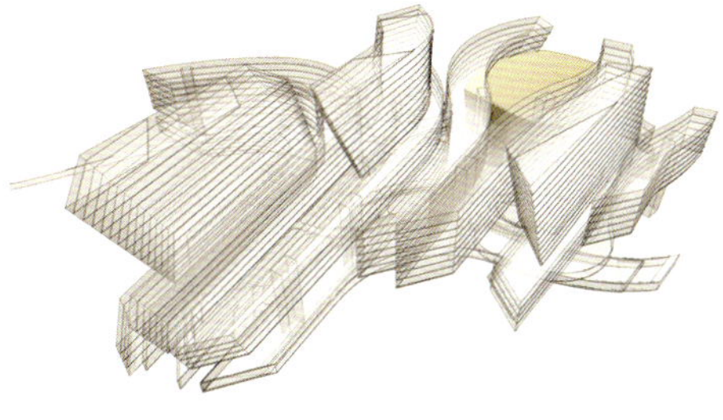

arena (7000 people)

In order to increase office frontage and thereby reduce the amount of overlooking, diagonal alleys were utilized running across the rectilinear site. This also allows the buildings to strongly address the corner of the site. The mass of the office was placed in three angular towers reflecting the tailfins of the MiGs. The remaining area was used to reinforce the alleys in a similar height to width proportion as existing Moscow commercial streets. In this approach almost 70% of the office areas have an open view with another 20% having views similar to what is currently found in Moscow's urban streetscapes – between 10 to 25 meters in distance.

The alleys were internally focused on Peter's Traveling Palace beyond Leningradskiy Prospekt and twist around the arena on the opposite ends. The retail spaces flow up into these alleys and the concourse and office lobby functions drop into it along with some of the hotel functions which inhabit the space. The result becomes an extremely active mix of 24 hour activity in which all of the programmatic elements are benefited and celebrated.

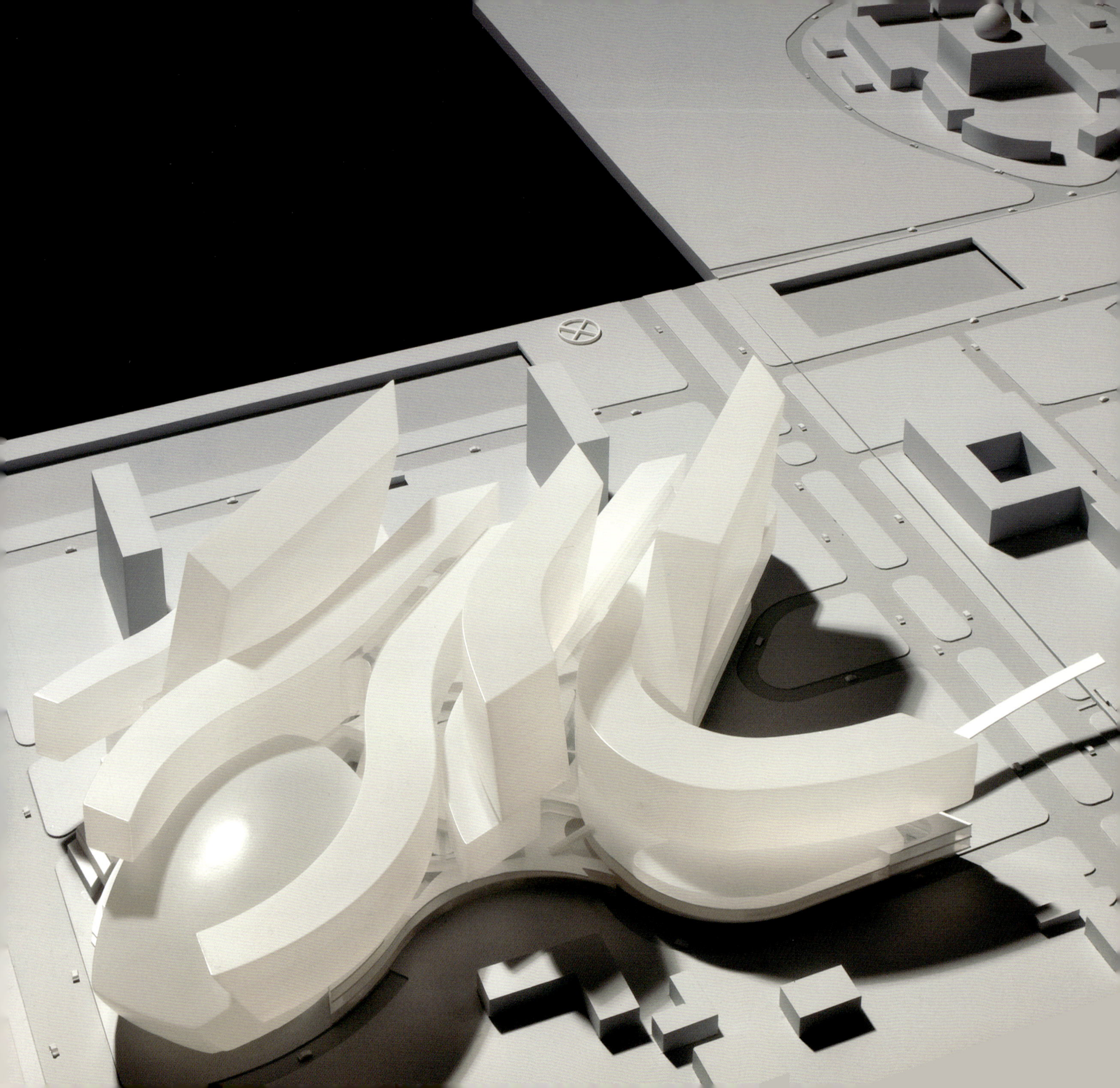

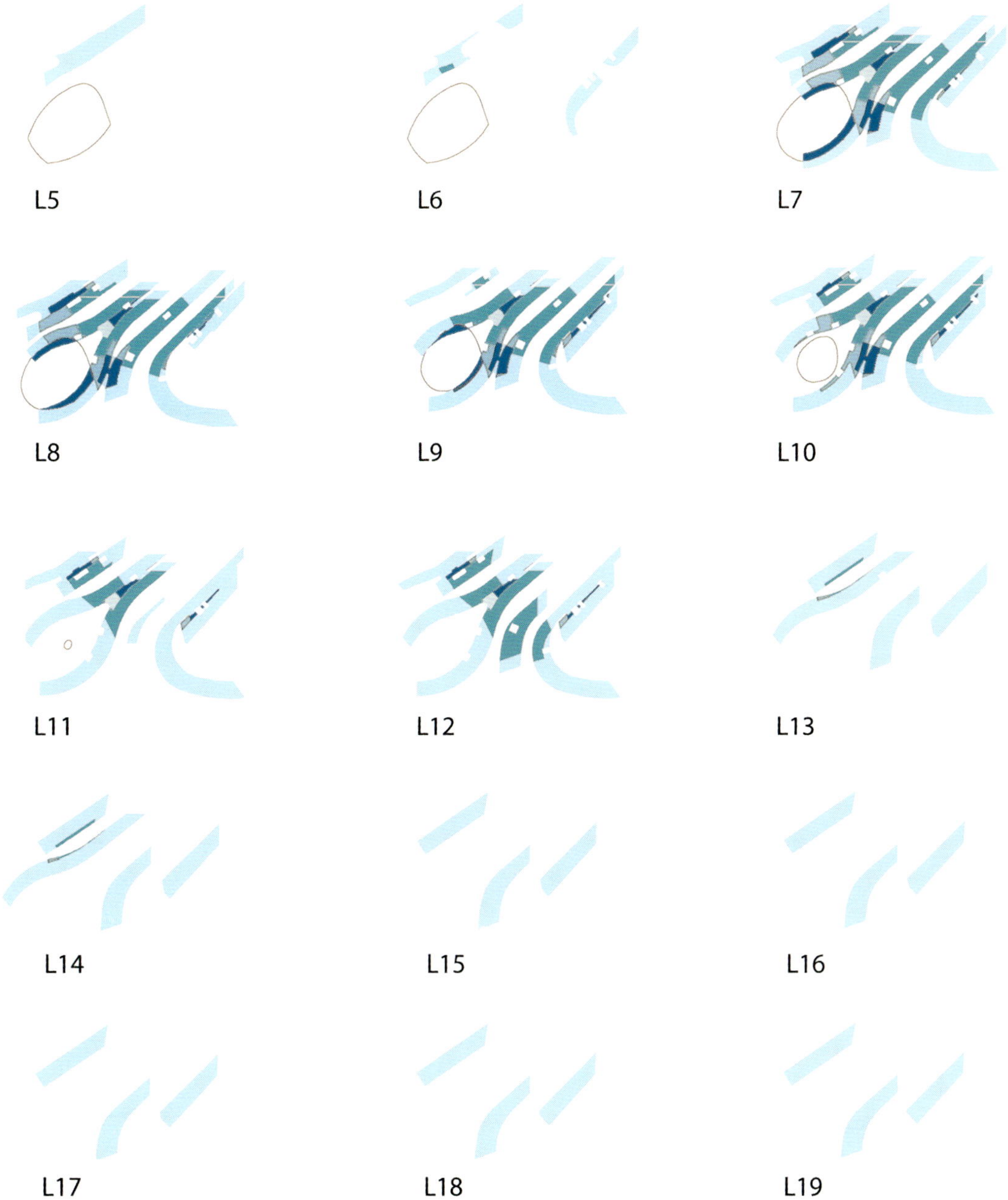

view quality diagrams

EXCELLENT VIEW /100% OPEN/	68%
VERY GOOD VIEW / >25m /	1%
GOOD VIEW /10m - 25m /	21%
ACCEPTABLE VIEW /5m - 10m /	5%
LIMITED VIEW / <5m /	6%

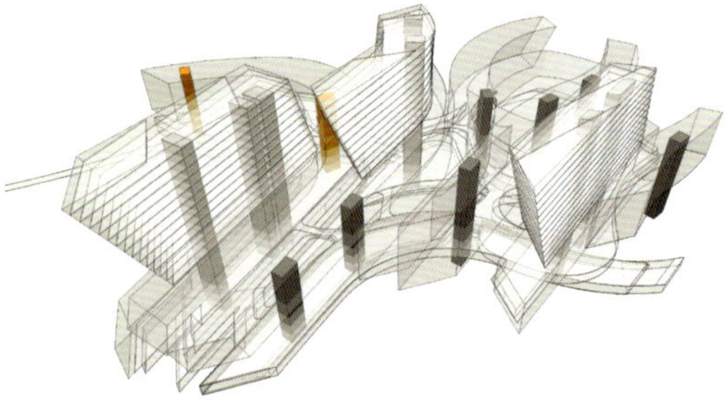

hotel cores

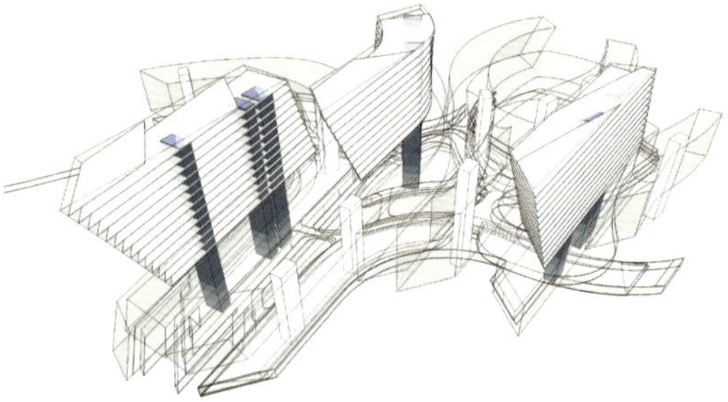

tower cores

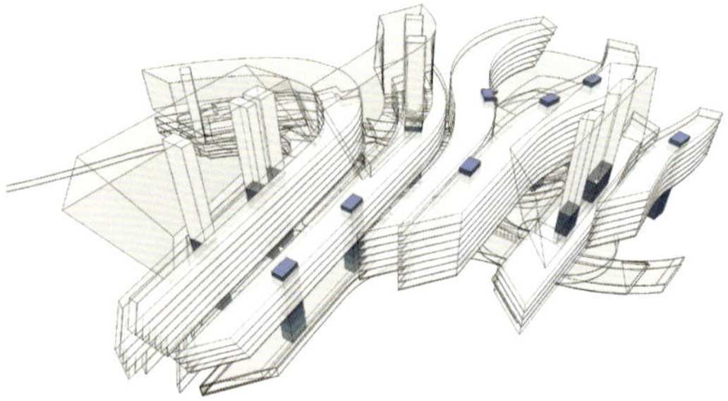

office cores

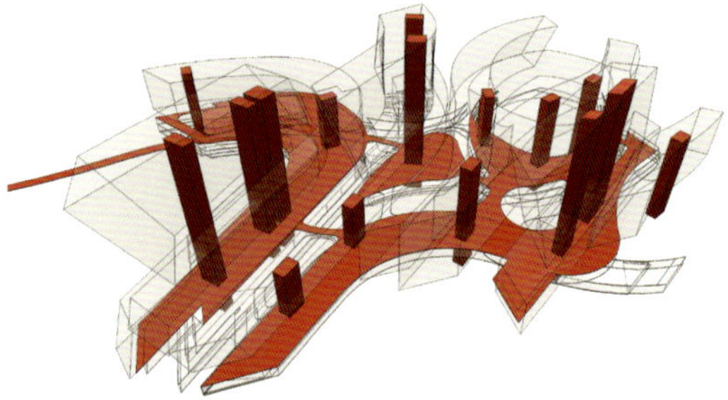

concourse and cores

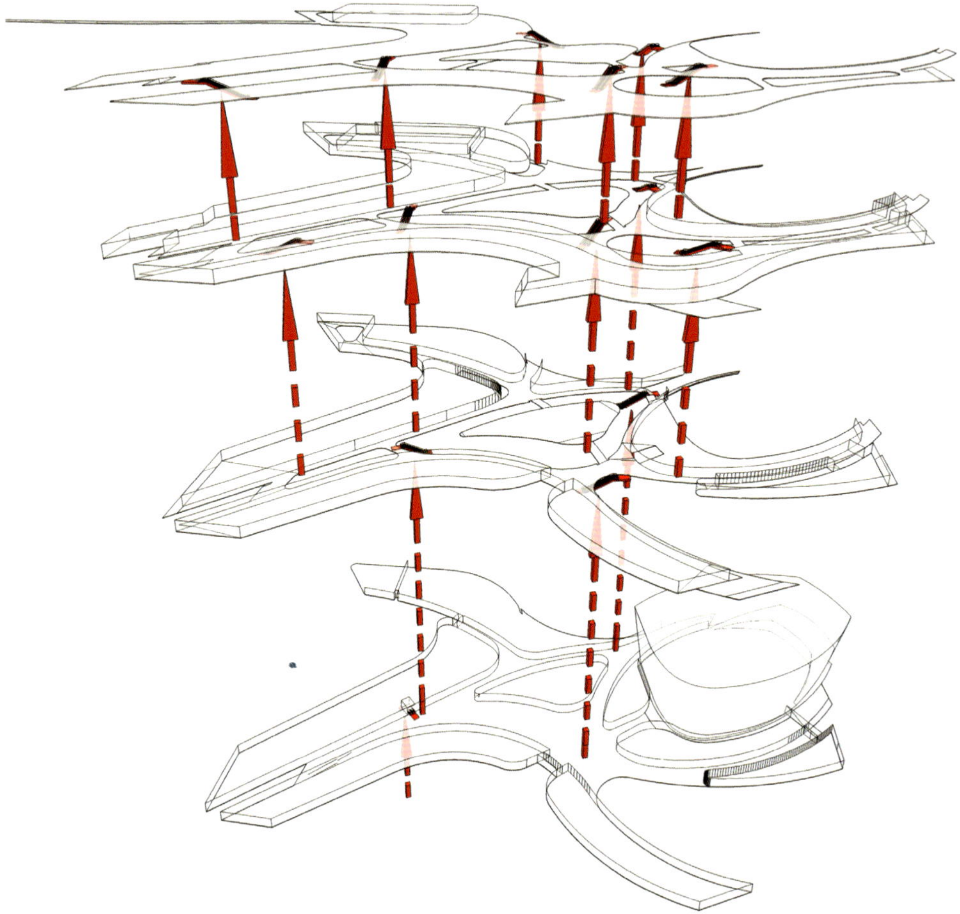

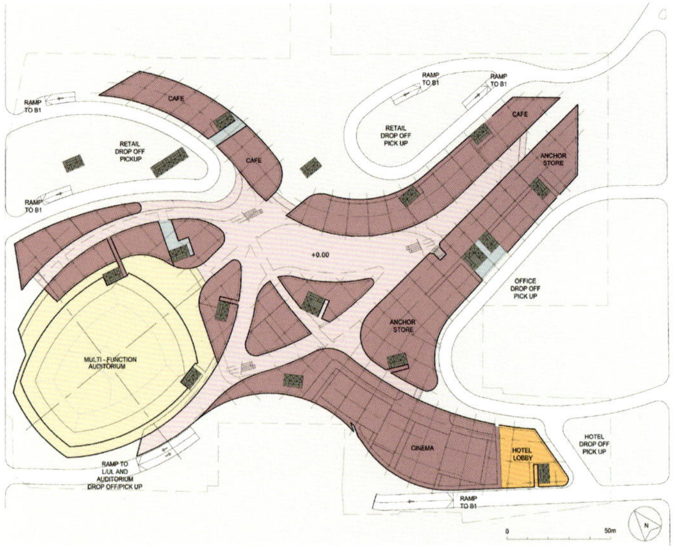

ground

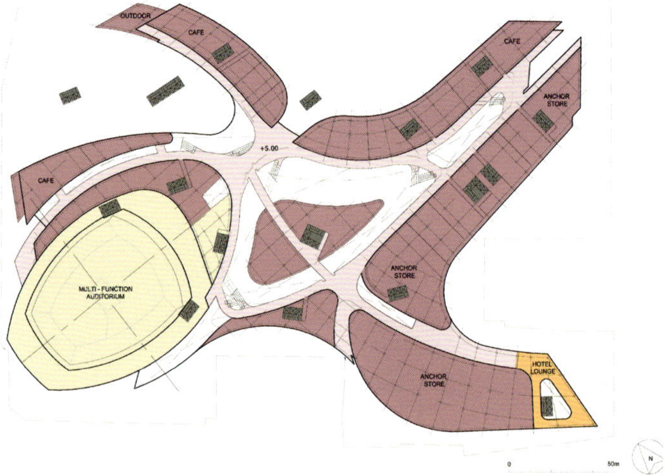

L1

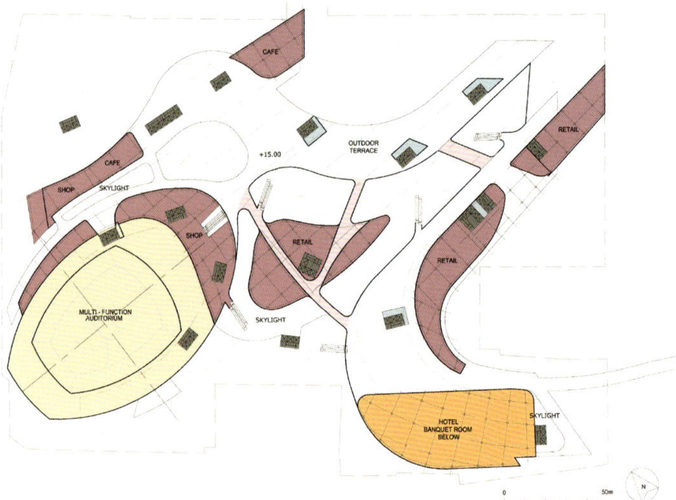

concourse

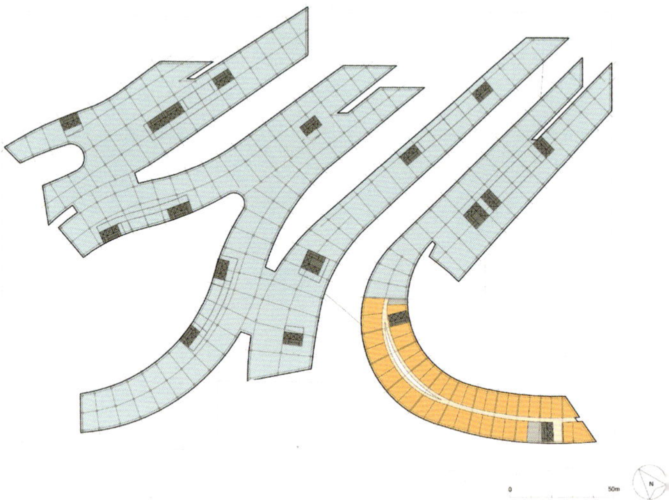

L-office/hotel-low

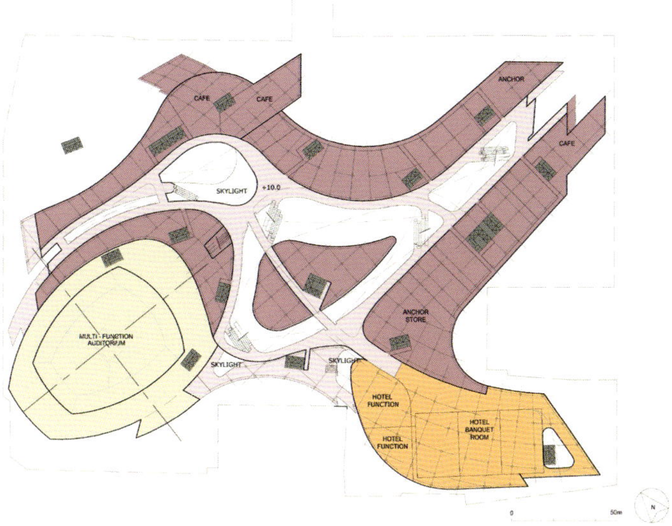

L2

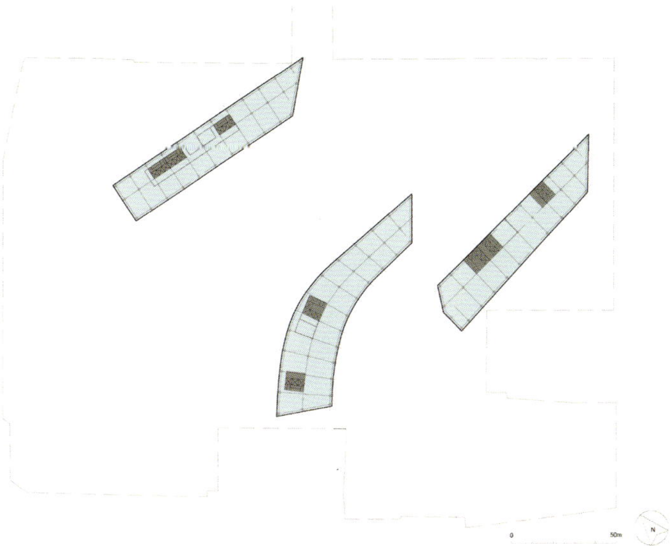

L-office-high

towers of arabia

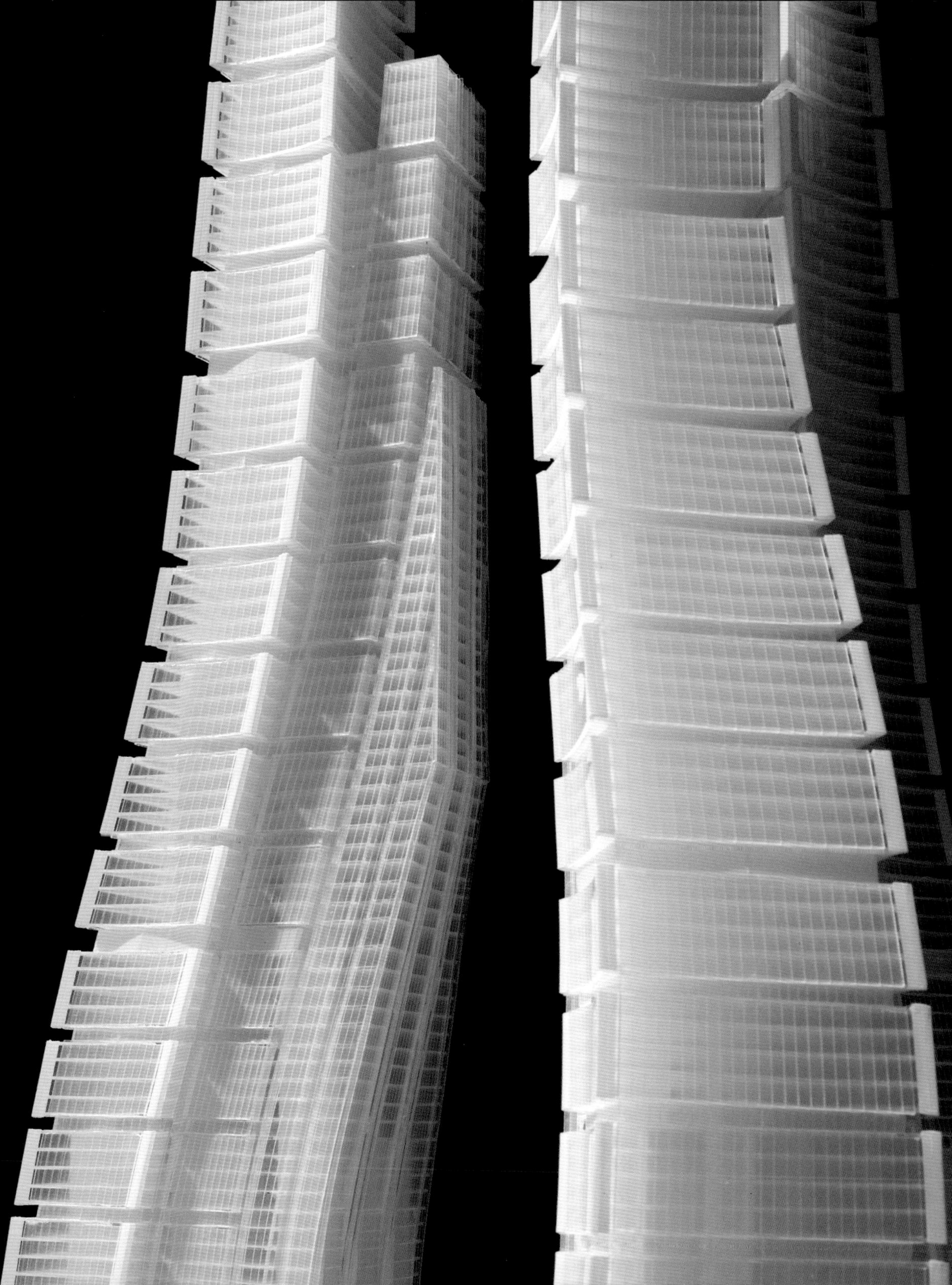

towers of arabia

mixed use

client: undisclosed
location: middle east

site location

size/scale

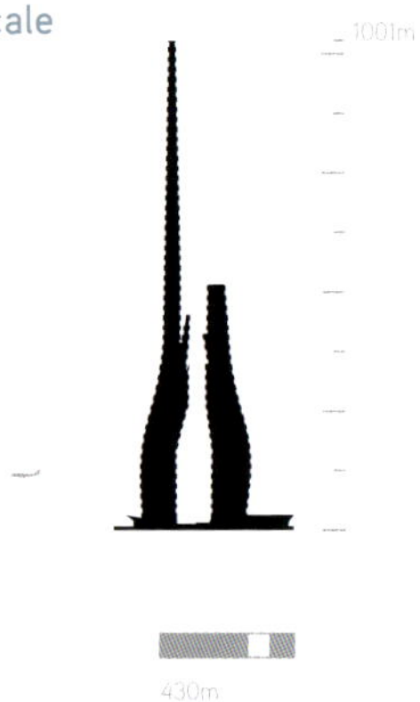

project description

The three slender Towers of Light play off of each other to define a large civic square as the civic centerpiece of a commercial master plan. Located within a Middle East city of influence, the project strives to not only give importance to the development in which it resides but aspires to become a future symbol for its country and even potentially the Islamic World.

The mixed-used development, if built today, would achieve three of the five tallest towers in the world including the tallest. The three towers step down in height and are focused toward each other like the legs of a tripod. They are positioned evenly around the civic plaza and slowly arch toward each other, almost touching, but independent. The "almost touching" portion allows them to infer the shape of an Islamic arch from any vantage point. The "independent" portion allows them to be built individually to minimize up-front capital.

The design does however, consider a scenario in which the whole project could be built at the same time and interconnect, which would significantly reduce overall construction cost. Further constructability was carefully considered with regards to a simple structural solution that would also be sensitive to the forces of the wind. Every fifth floor was recessed to create a texture up the sides of these buildings, "breaking" the frequency of the wind. This greatly helps in reducing the stress on the structure. In addition, these five story modules helped provide a perceptual scale to the towers – felt to be important due to the lack of a "frame of reference" around them.

The "civic plaza" is also an element taken straight out of both religious and vernacular Islamic architecture – where the social space or place of prayer, is defined by its surrounding architecture, which is arguably in a supporting role.

process

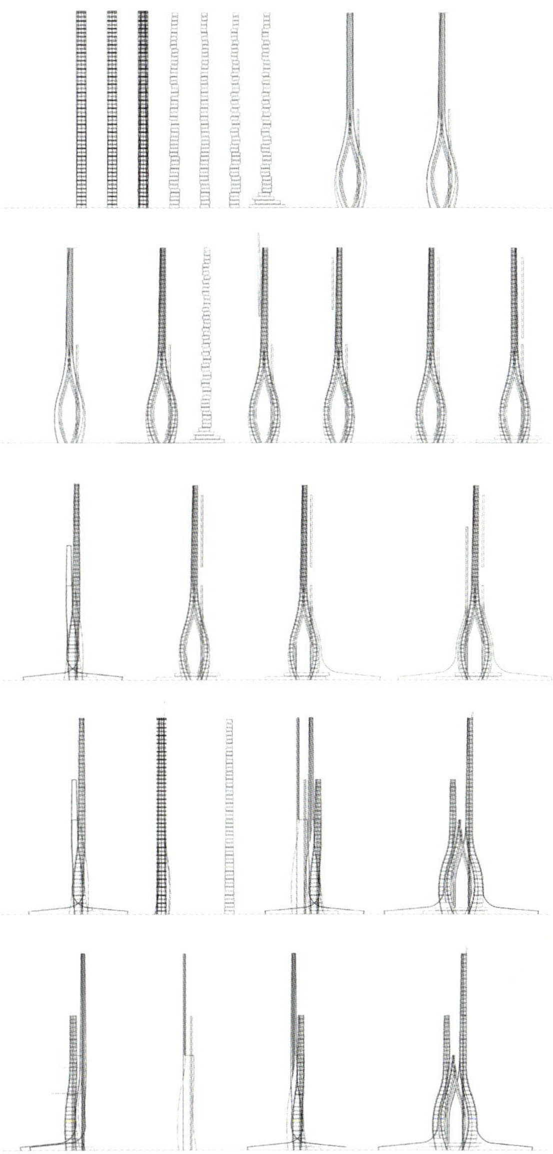

goals

To design a complex with aspirations of becoming a symbol of a country and a faith.

challenge

To balance the vision with realities of extreme structural and wind constraints exerted on super-tall towers.

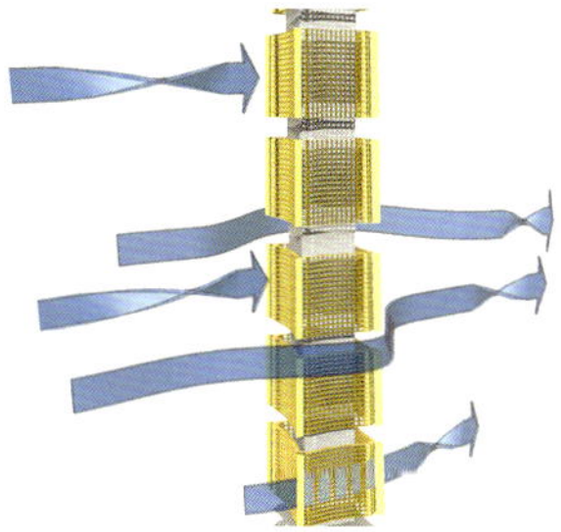

play

The introduction of the civic square and the monumentality of its volume.

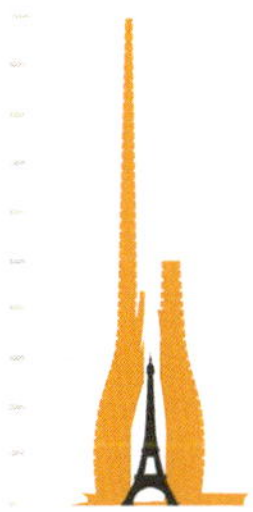

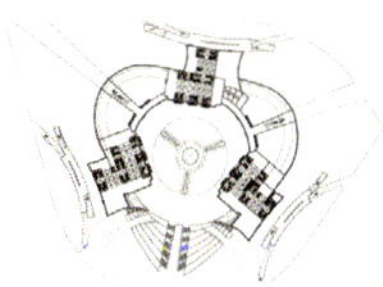

usage

residential
174491 m2 1878205 sqf

hospitality
75249 m2 809973 sqf

office
30491 m2 328202 sqf

retail + f&b
13264 m2 142772 sqf

landscape
0 m2 0 sqf

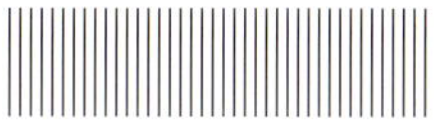

other
0 m2 0 sqf

total area: 293495 m2
3159154 sqf

| = 2500 m2 / 26910 sqf

status

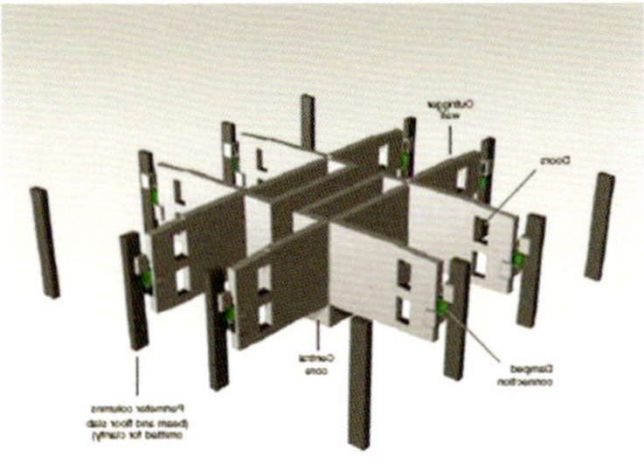

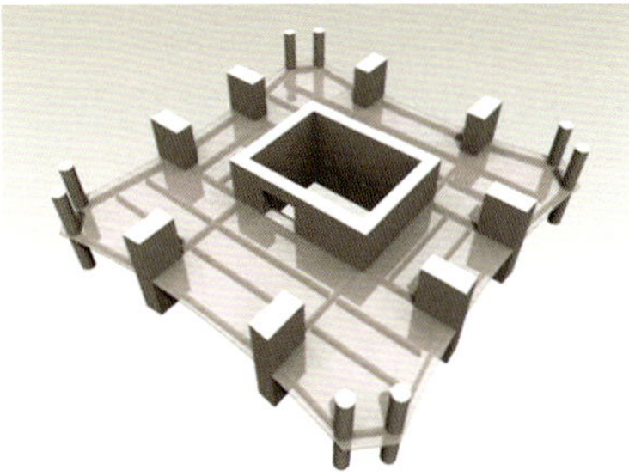

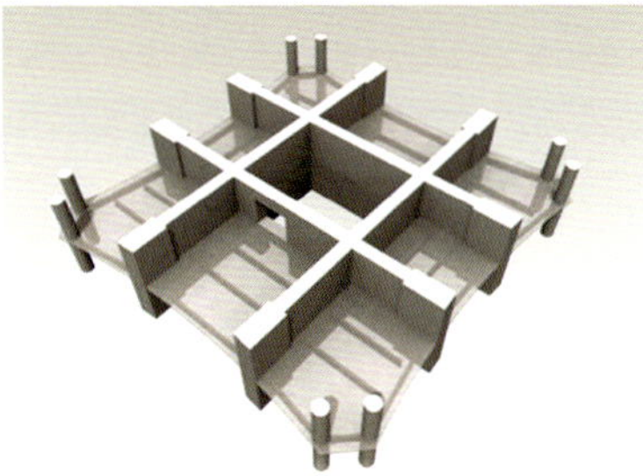

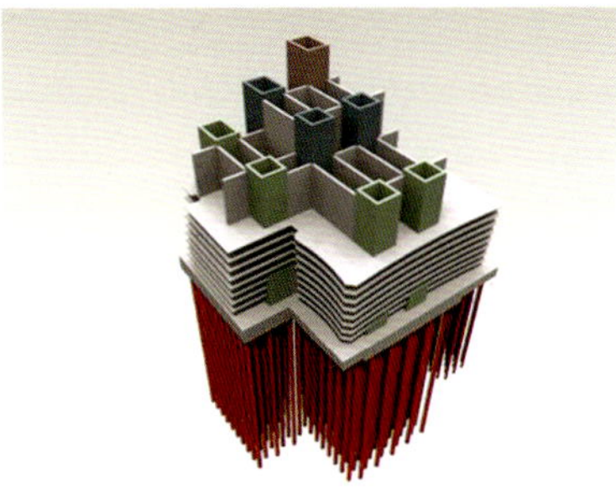

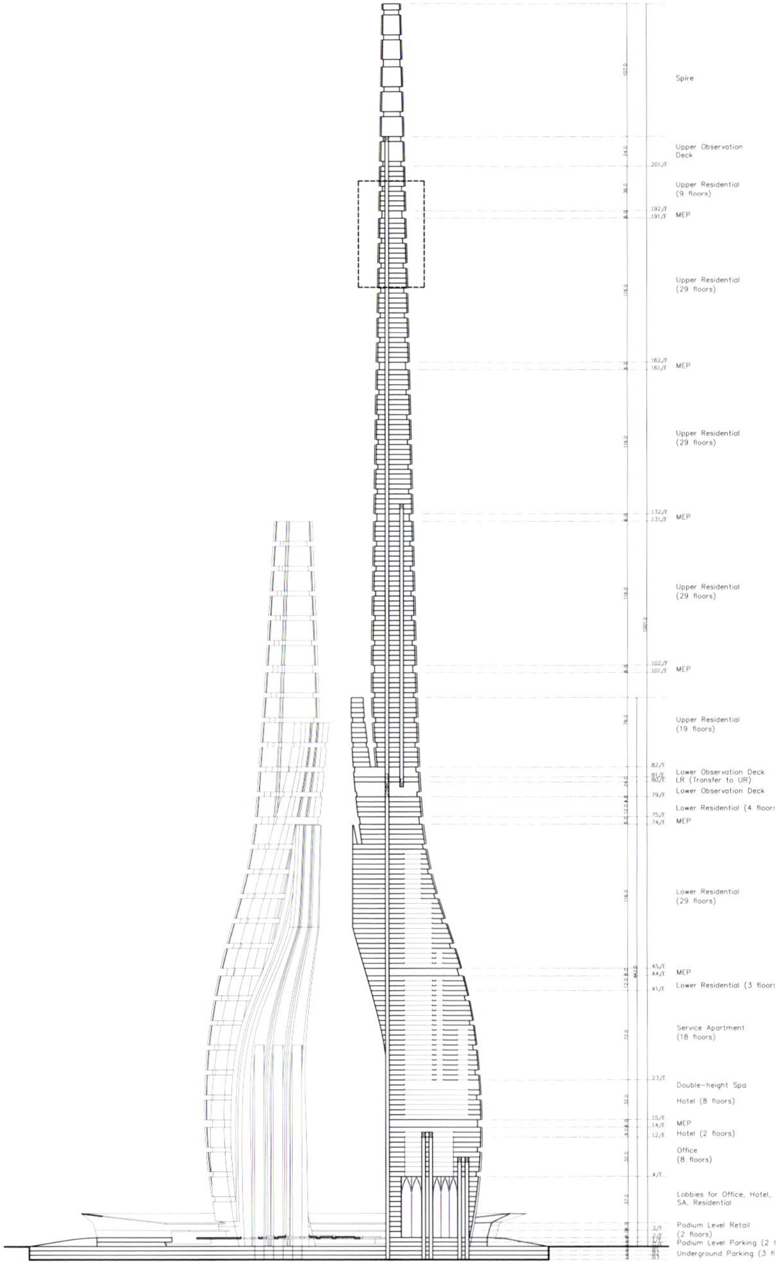
Spire
Upper Observation Deck
Upper Residential (9 floors)
MEP
Upper Residential (29 floors)
MEP
Upper Residential (29 floors)
MEP
Upper Residential (29 floors)
MEP
Upper Residential (19 floors)
Lower Observation Deck
LR (Transfer to UR)
Lower Observation Deck
Lower Residential (4 floors
MEP
Lower Residential (29 floors)
MEP
Lower Residential (3 floors
Service Apartment (18 floors)
Double-height Spa
Hotel (8 floors)
MEP
Hotel (2 floors)
Office (8 floors)
Lobbies for Office, Hotel, SA, Residential
Podium Level Retail (2 floors)
Podium Level Parking (2 f
Underground Parking (3 f

The Towers of Light are no exception to this idea. The Civic Plaza, and its volumetrically defining arches bending above, defines a space which could easily contain the Empire State Building. The Eiffel Tower would behave as an element of sculpture in the center of the plaza. The space may be undersold if just labeled "monumental".

With the towers looming high over the monumentality of the Civic Plaza the scale of the project is unprecedented. Hopefully it will meet the ambitions of the client, reflect the importance of this country in the world, and appropriately and sensitively represent the influence of the Islamic faith.

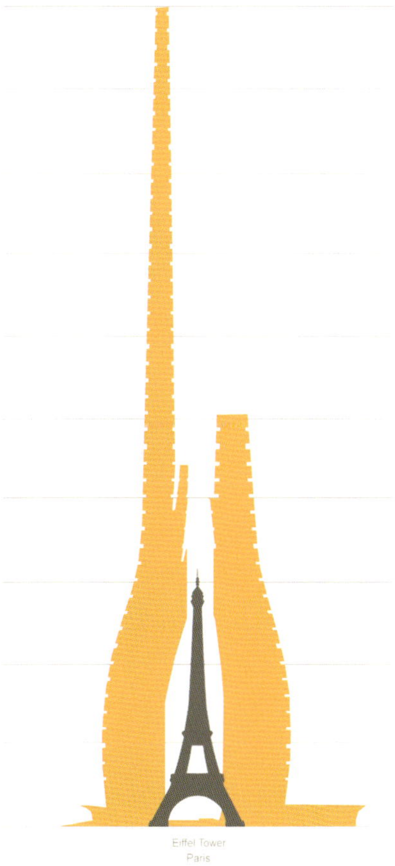
Eiffel Tower
Paris

CX-2-1

CX-2-1

commercial
client: undisclosed
location: one north, singapore

site location

size/scale

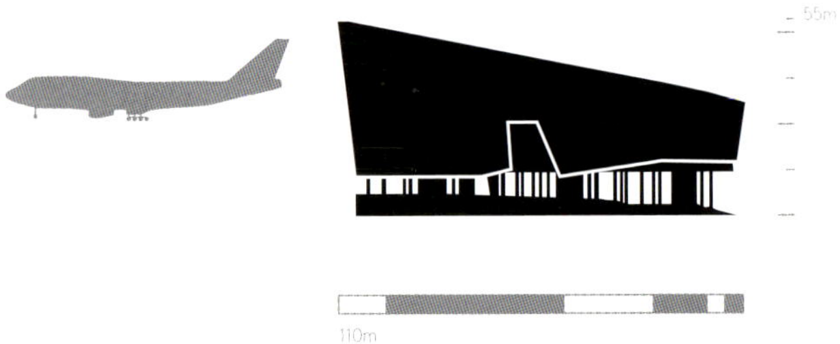

project description

CX-2-1 is both a regional headquarters, for a major entertainment company, and a revenue generating office building. Combining this with a strong civic intent within the One North master plan in Singapore, the design for this project not only enjoys this ambiguity but also seeks a solution which celebrates its diversity.

The master planning guidelines for this project are highly defined, dictating height envelope and setbacks. What is unusual about the controls is that they stipulate that the building needs to be a certain height and follow a specific sloping topography. The guidelines also regulate the minimum amount of mass on all faces of the enclosure. The design approaches these guidelines deliberately to fulfill the viability requirements of the revenue earning office space but also with strong civic quality as a statement for the local headquarters.

The width of the floor plates was kept at an average of 19 meters in depth for reasonable day-lighting within a double aspect office space. These floor plates were "maxed" out as they related to the three faces. On the one face which did not have any minimum requirements, the floor plate was kept open. The result was a tapering "horseshoe" plan. This achieves a floor plate with an average net to gross area efficiency of over 82% – exceeding the client's brief. From this point, floors were reduced from the bottom up until the correct allowable GFA was reached but also maintaining the minimum stipulated surface area per face.

The result is a building floating up to 13 meters above the ground below. This plane was then bent up from the open side of the horseshoe to cover the main lobby on the opposite side. The open space is highly landscaped in a natural, overgrown manner. It has been proposed that the pedestrian space may provide public connection visibly past the main lobby and down into the MRT subway below.

process

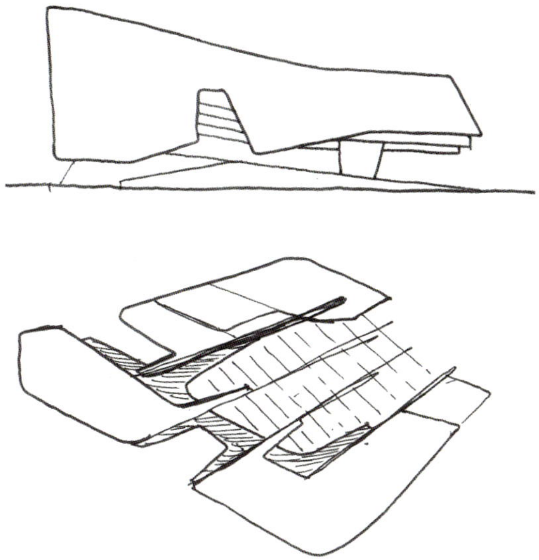

day 001

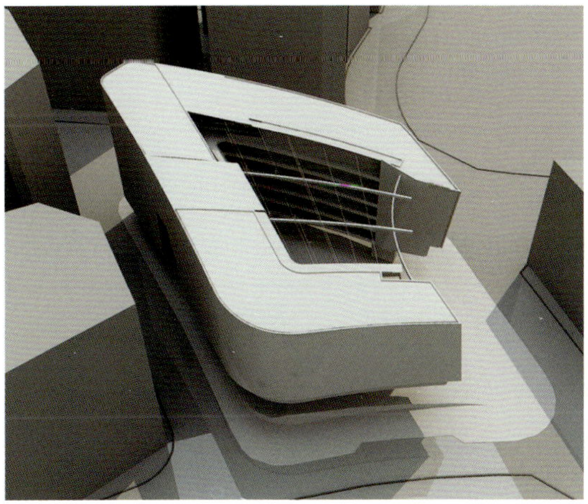

week 001

goals

To achieve a building which was balanced between being a highly efficient, flexible commercial solution, but also introducing public, semi-public and semi-private programs to allow a more "civic" presence.

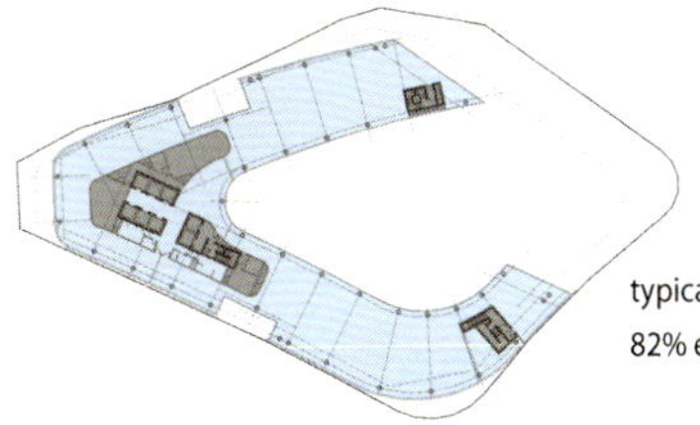

typical plan
82% efficient

challenge

The ambiguity of a building that was intended for both commercial development and as the local headquarters for a strongly branded end-user who is also the owner and primary tenant.

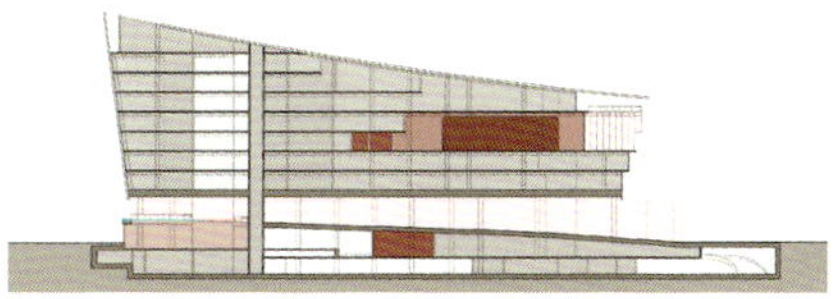

play

The introduction of the un-programmed open space components: both public and semi-private.

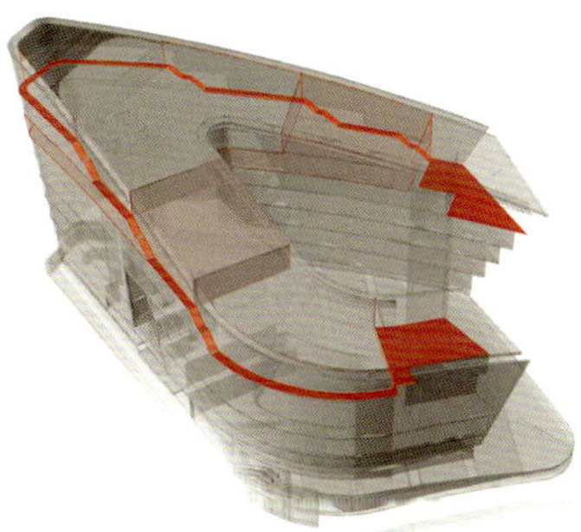

usage

residential
o m2 o sqf

hospitality
o m2 o sqf

office
15100 m2 162535 sqf

retail + f&b
231 m2 2486 sqf

landscape
5810 m2 62538 sqf

theatre
215 m2 2315 sqf

total area: 21,468 m2
231,080 sqf

| = 2500 m2 / 26910 sqf

status

projected completion: 2012

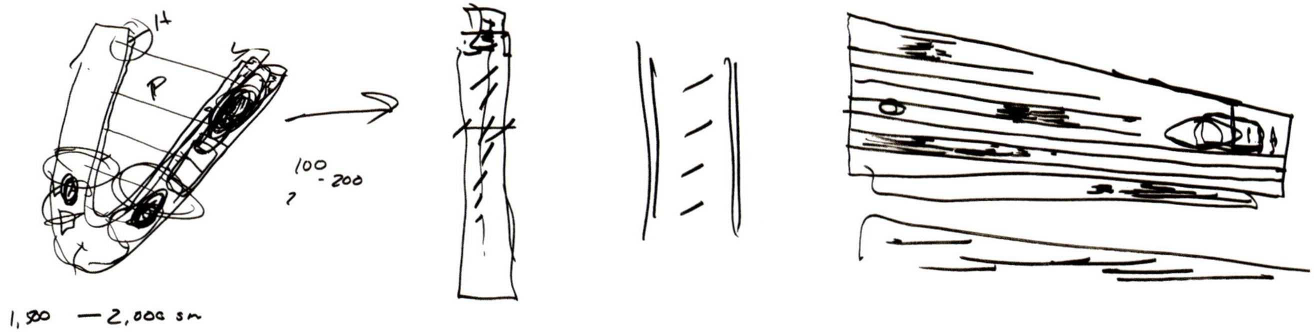

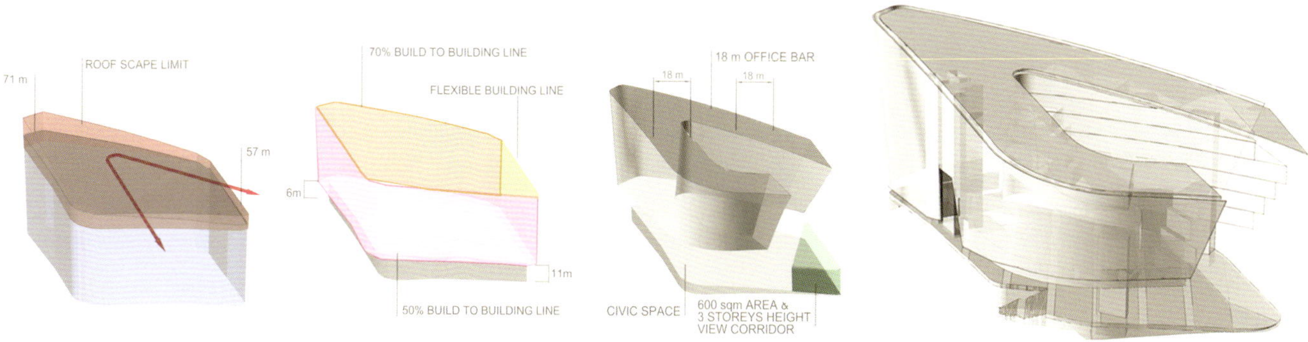

The facade addresses different audiences and contexts. The "taut" external metallic glass skin allows for good solar protection and privacy on the more exposed faces as well as presenting a more aerodynamic appearance of the vessel. The skin is cut away on the lower edges and uses a low-iron clear glass which relates more to the pedestrian level of the street. This highly transparent glass is utilized in the end faces of the wings, the courtyard elevations and wraps under the vessel's soffit.

In addition, the floor slabs off the wing walls and courtyard, slowly step out from the lower floors to the upper ones. This helps maximize the "perceived" volume within the landscape deck but also reduces the aperture moving up to reduce solar gain in both the office floors and the deck below. On the exposed wing faces, planting and green terraces were added which hang down in front of the glass, further protecting these zones from solar gain but also tying the vessel into the untamed landscape it is floating above. A taut glass canopy over the courtyard is then introduced in the plane of the louvered roof, to provide even more environmental protection to the public spaces below.

grand floor

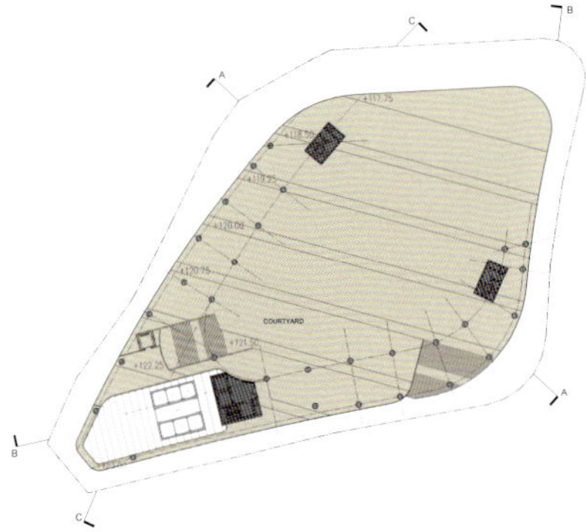

roof landscape-plaza

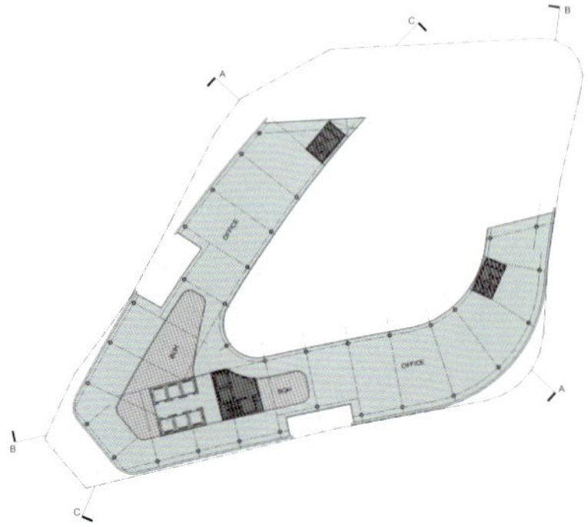

typical office floor

theatre floor

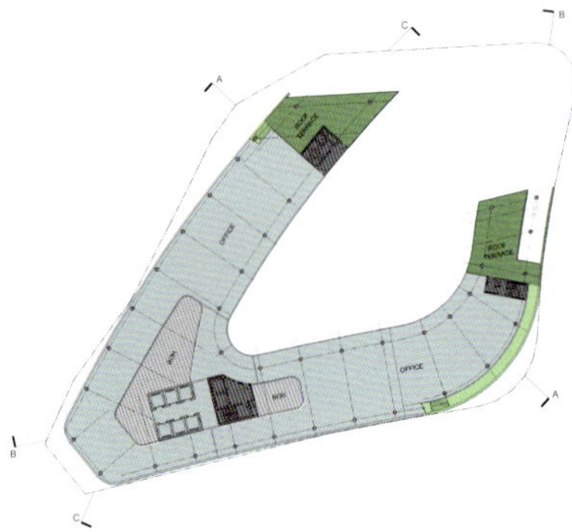

open space floor

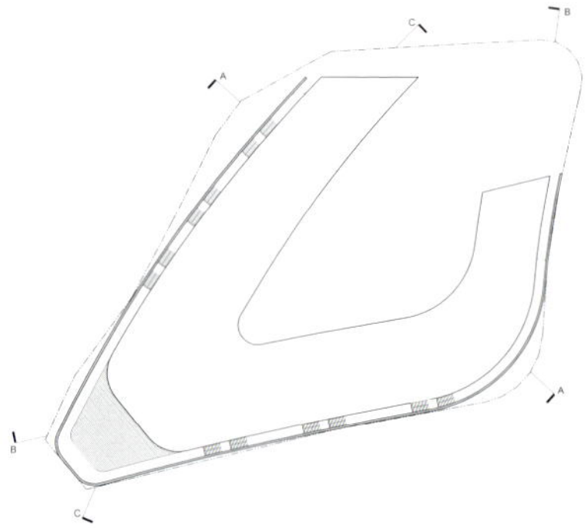

roof plan

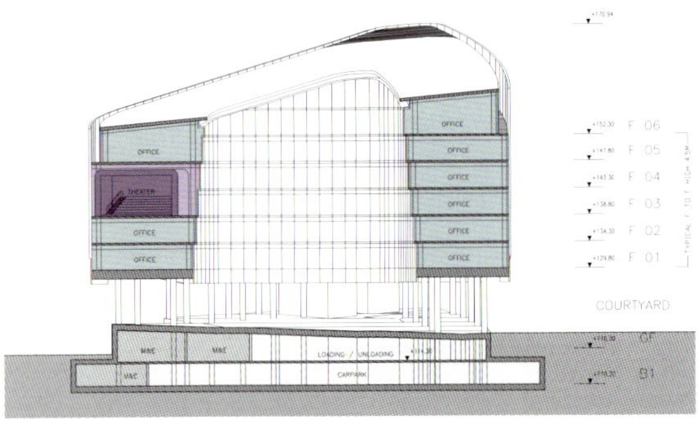

section AA

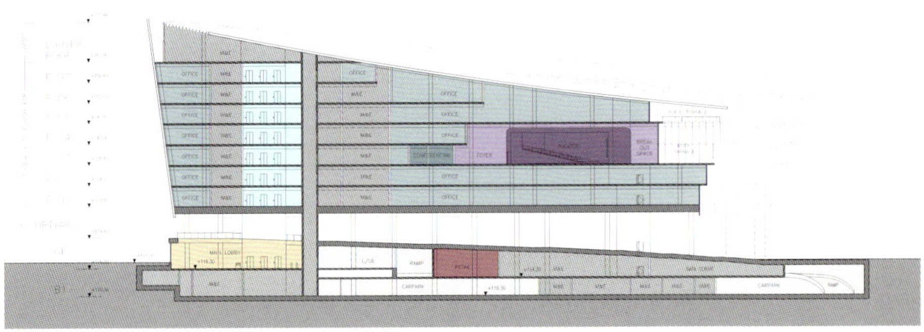

section BB

AIDC

Lastly, a state of the art one hundred person movie theatre was requested by the client. This facility would relate directly to the end user tenant of the entertainment company but also could be leased out for revenue to the commercial tenants in the building. It was determined that locating the facility in the middle of the vessel was most convenient. The facility needed a double high zone and was placed on the upper levels of the lower end user zone, immediately below the leased tenant spaces. Conferencing facilities, a gallery, pre-function facilities and an external patio were also located in the same zone. Slightly visible through the metallic skin to the outside and openly visible to the courtyard, this feature further differentiates this building from being considered purely a speculative office building but rather a vessel which invites speculation.

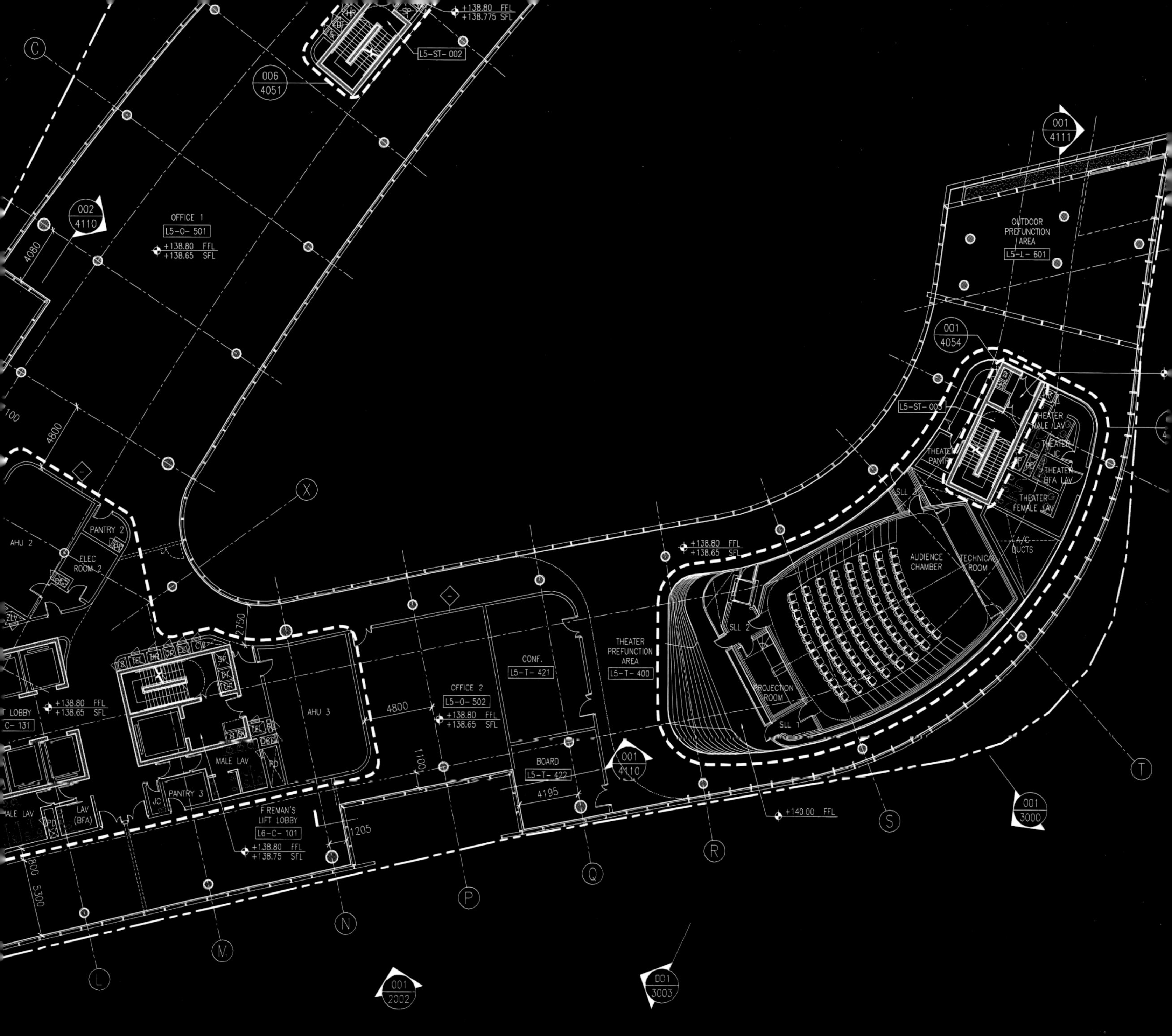

OFFICE 1
L5-O-501
+138.80 FFL
+138.65 SFL
OUTDOOR PREFUNCTION AREA
L5-L-601
L5-ST-002
L5-ST-003
THEATER MALE LAV
THEATER JC
THEATER BFA LAV
THEATER FEMALE LAV
THEATER PANTRY
AUDIENCE CHAMBER
TECHNICAL ROOM
A/C DUCTS
PROJECTION ROOM
THEATER PREFUNCTION AREA
L5-T-400
CONF.
L5-T-421
BOARD
L5-T-422
OFFICE 2
L5-O-502
AHU 3
AHU 2
PANTRY 2
ELEC ROOM 2
LOBBY
C-131
MALE LAV
PANTRY 3
LAV (BFA)
FIREMAN'S LIFT LOBBY
L6-C-101
+138.80 FFL
+138.75 SFL
+140.00 FFL

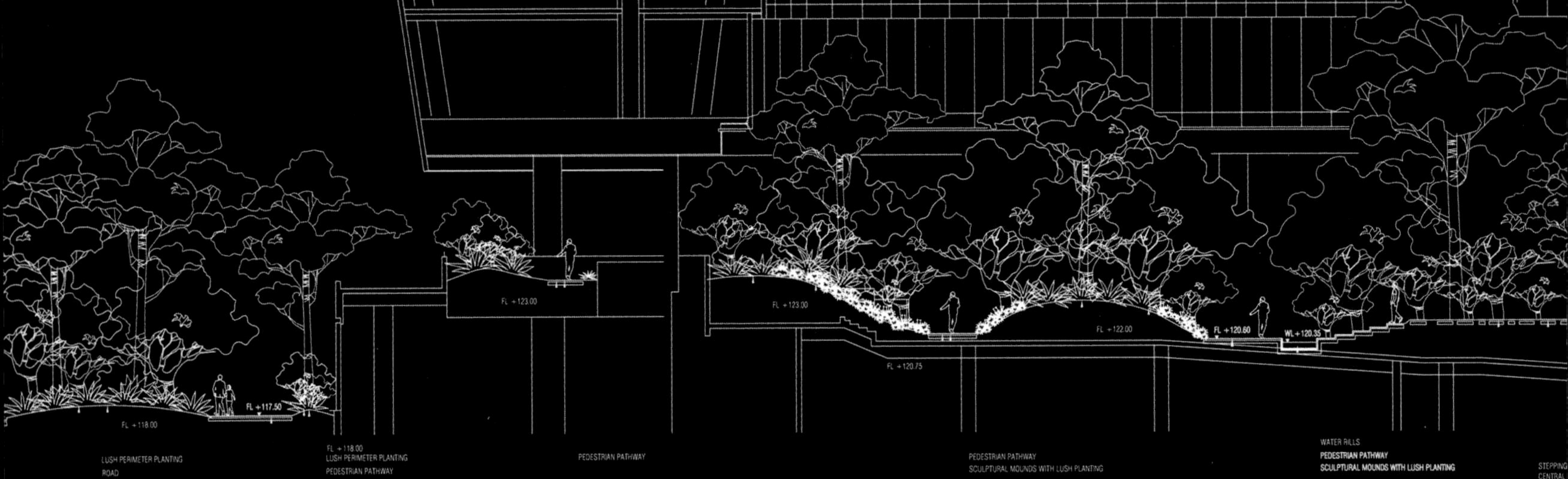

A LANDSCAPE SECTION A - A
SCALE 1: 100@A1 / 1: 200@A3

B LANDSCAPE SECTION A - A
SCALE 1: 100@A1 / 1: 200@A3

NOTE:
THIS DRAWING IS TO BE READ IN CONJUNCTION WIT
ARCHITECTURAL, STRUCTURAL AND BUILDING SER

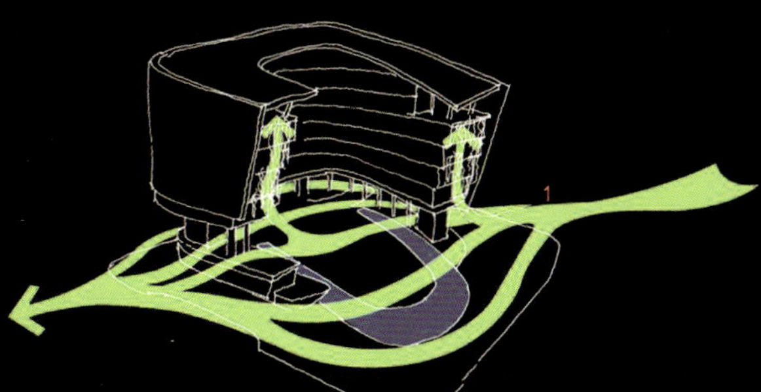

1. Visual green corridor from "NEPAL HILL" to park creating heart of forest within the central courtyard.
2. Water to form base of architecture.

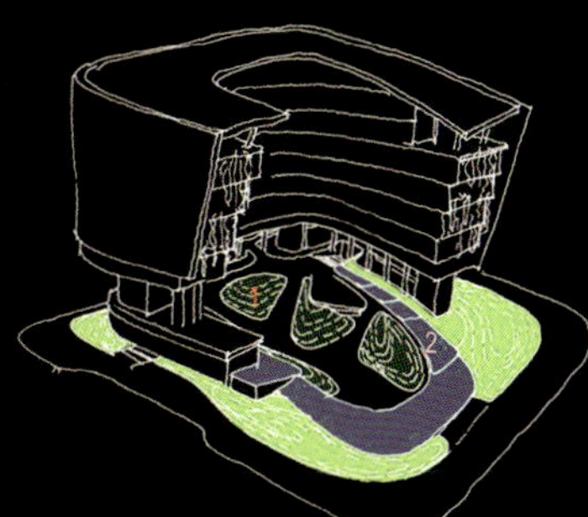

1. Sculptural mounding formed to create horizontal planes to central courtyard.
2. Rill reinforces level change.

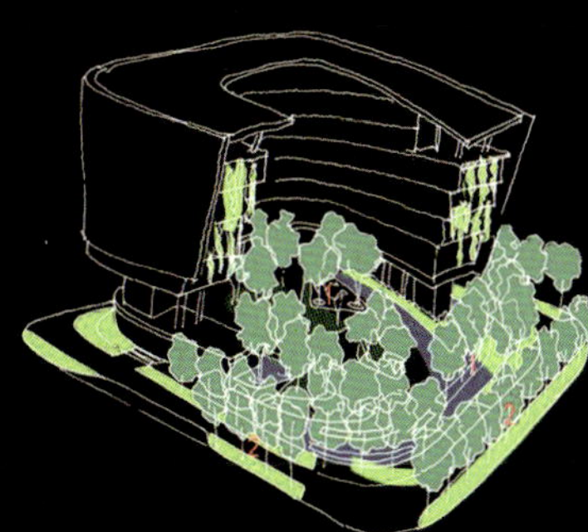

1. Sculptural trees to mounding.
2. Rows of large trees to perimeter to reinforce vertical green & create enclosure to the site.

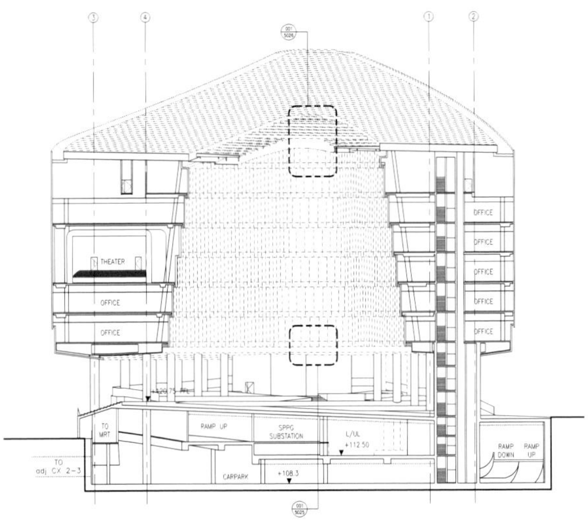

short section through courtyard

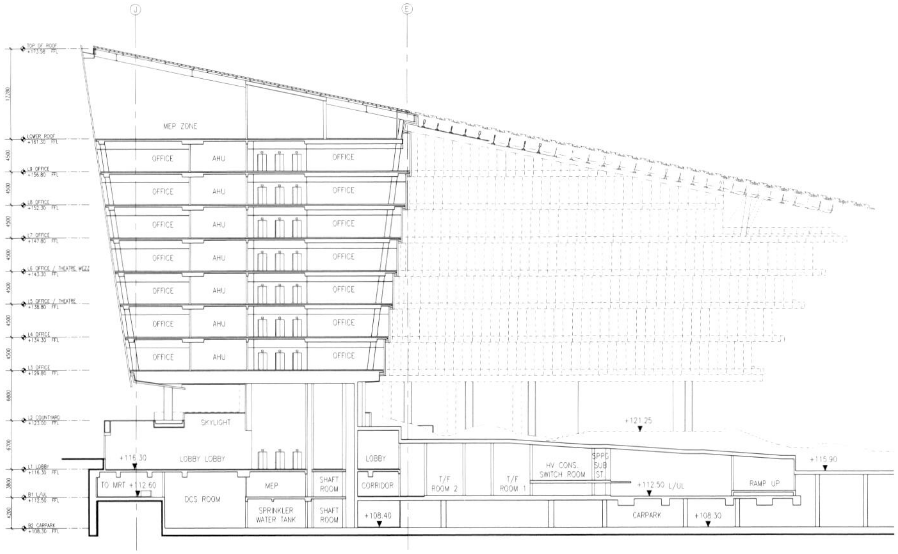

short section through courtyard

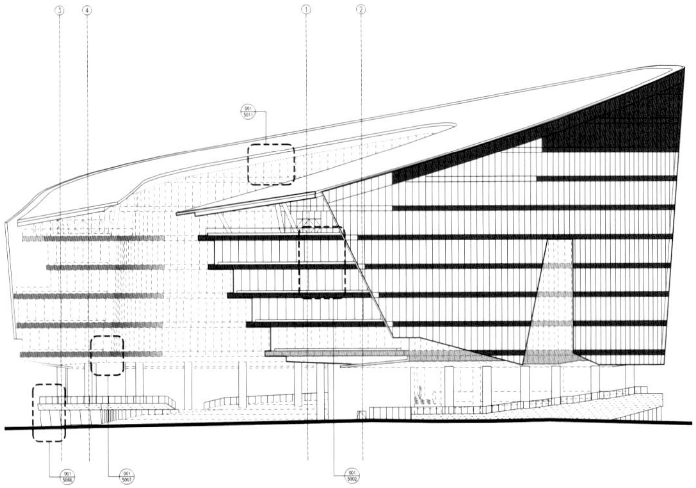

north elevation

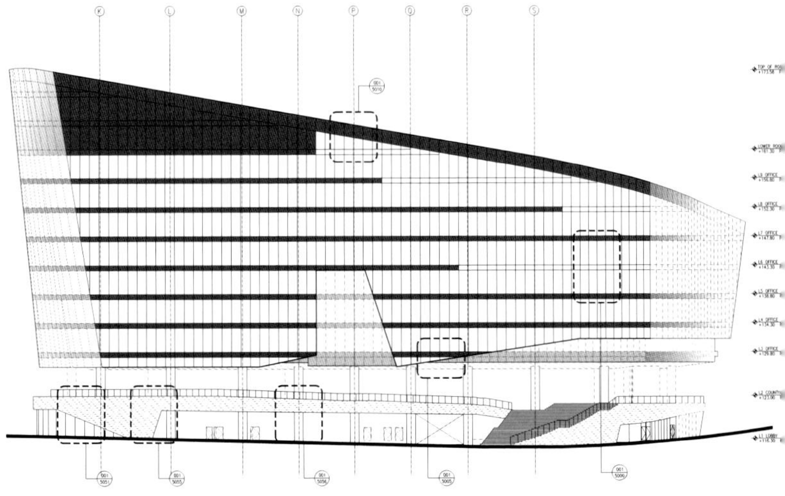

south elevation

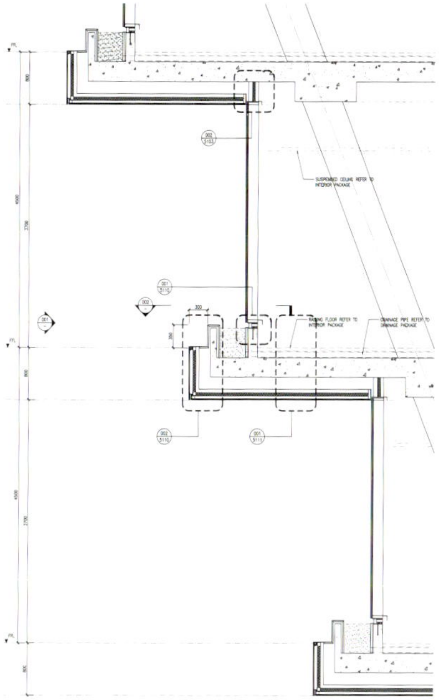

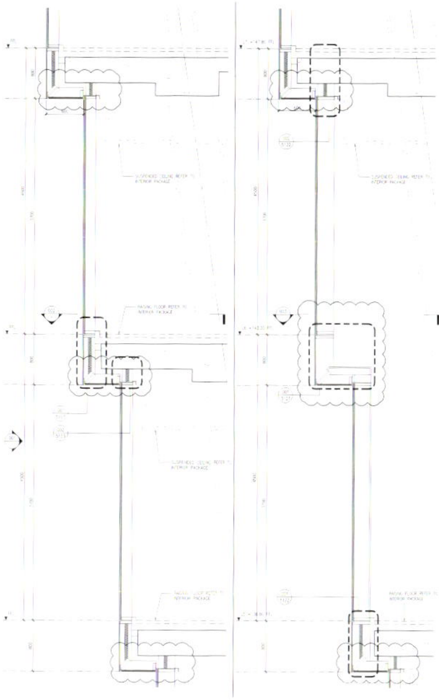

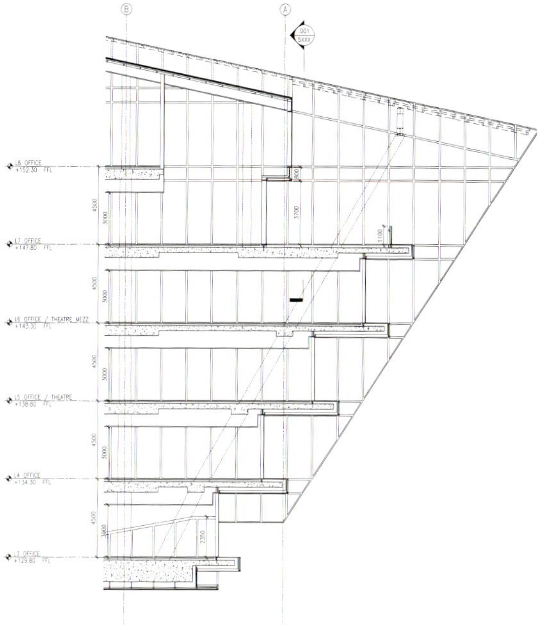
L8 OFFICE
+152.30 FFL
L7 OFFICE
+147.80 FFL
L6 OFFICE / THEATRE MEZZ
+143.30 FFL
L5 OFFICE / THEATRE
+138.80 FFL
L4 OFFICE
+134.30 FFL
L3 OFFICE
+129.80 FFL
4500
3000

west kowloon terminus

west kowloon terminus

civic

client: mtr corporation ltd.
location: west kowloon, hong kong, china

site location

size/scale

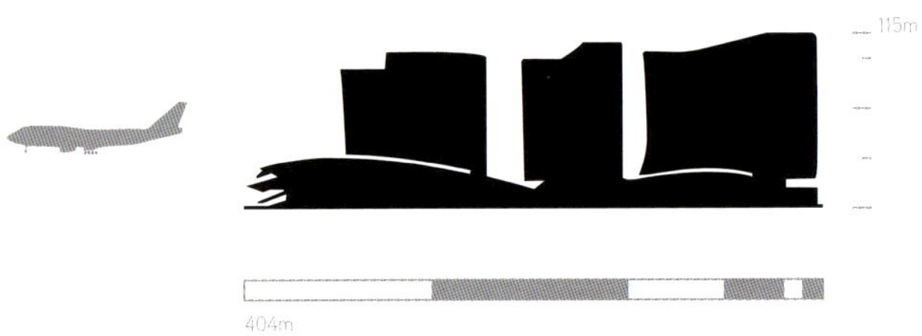

project description

The West Kowloon Terminus is a strong symbol and functional representation of the improvement in relations between Hong Kong and mainland China in recent years. The high-speed rail terminus station will connect Hong Kong to Beijing with the largest rail network in history. Located centrally in Hong Kong within the city's existing urban realm, the 430,000 square meter, fifteen track facility will be the largest underground terminus station in the world.

WKT will function more like an international airport than a rail station as the Hong Kong Special Administrative Region maintains economic and political autonomy from the P.R.C. Consequently, the facility needs to have both customs and immigration controls for departing and arriving passengers. What is highly unusual in this facility is that West Kowloon Terminus will have immigration domains for both Hong Kong and China in the same facility as opposed to the way immigration normally works in a typical international airport, where it is solely the domain of the host country.

It became apparent that the WKT facility needed to function as a built ambassador for the city of Hong Kong as the gateway to both Hong Kong and China. The site's prominence immediately adjacent to the future West Kowloon Cultural District and next to Victoria Harbor required a design completely motivated by civic demand. Enriching the challenge was the fact that there would be 400,000 square meters of commercial development on top of the station which would be auctioned off to a developer at a later date.

At the time of the competition, a one-year feasibility study was conducted with the client by another architect. This scheme became the "baseline" by which all other schemes were evaluated and if proven to be the most viable, would have maintained itself as the chosen scheme moving forward. Our first concern with the scheme was that it had allocated future commercial facilities in both front corners of the site with the above ground entrance building of the station sandwiched in between. With no control over the commercial facilities and the limitation of station frontage,

process

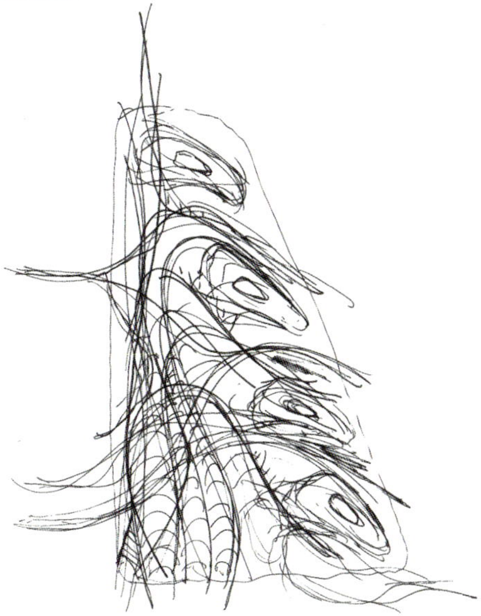

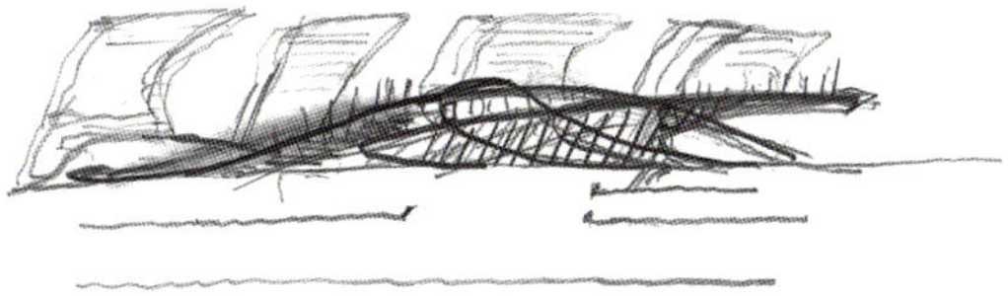

goals

To design an underground, high speed rail terminus, that will not feel "below ground" to create immediate awareness of arrival into Hong Kong.

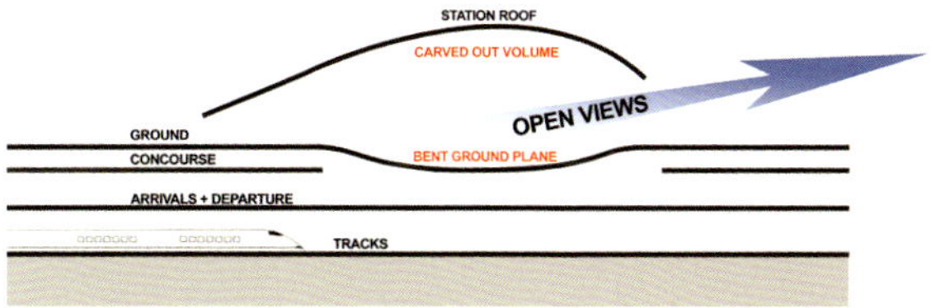

challenge

To contain and control the top-side development, situated above the station, which will go out to auction for future development.

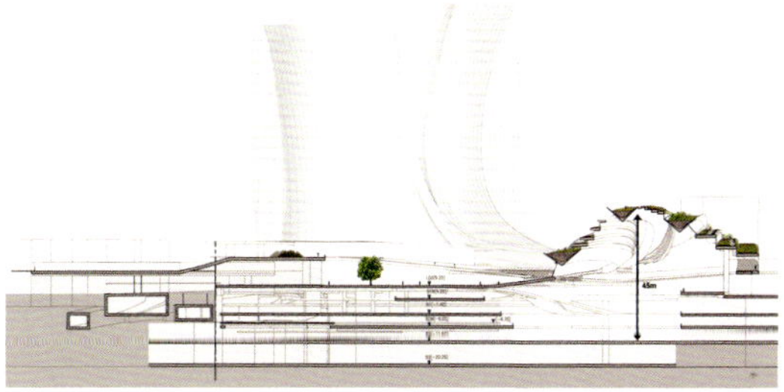

play

A 20,000sm planted park on top of the station roof, with public access, overlooking the harbor.

usage

residential
0 m2 0 sqf

hospitality
0 m2 0 sqf

office
264600m2 2848131 sqf

retail + f&b
29400 m2 316459 sqf

landscape
58800 m2 632918 sqf

rail station
380000 m2 4090286 sqf

total area: 732,800 m2
7,887,815 sqf

| = 2500 m2 / 26910 sqf

status

piling commenced late 2009

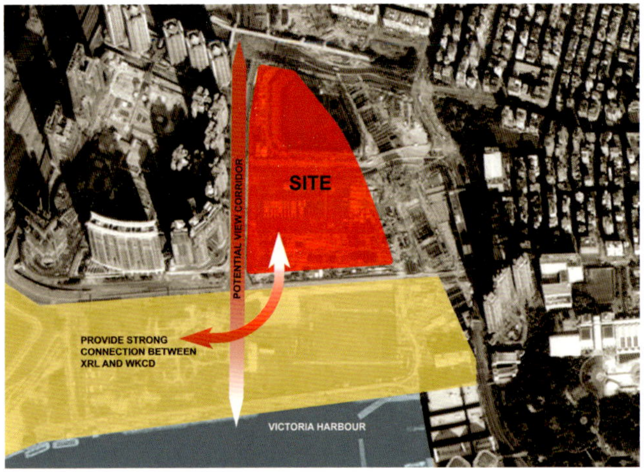

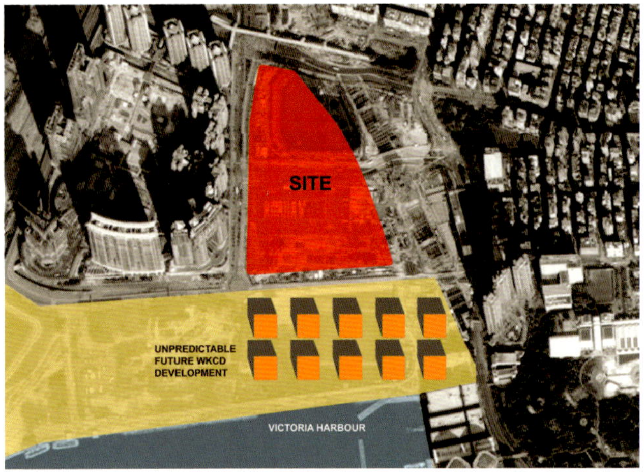

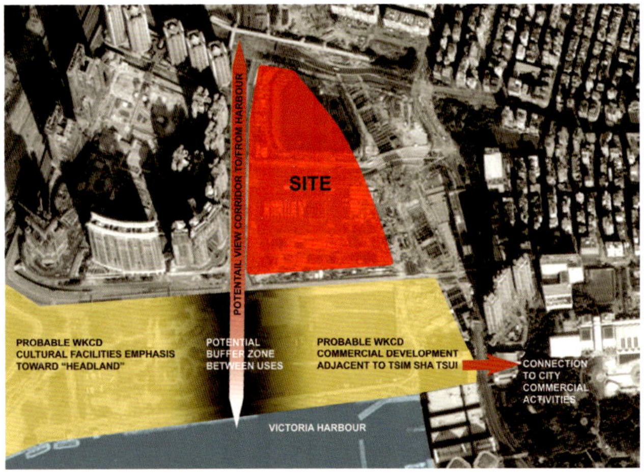

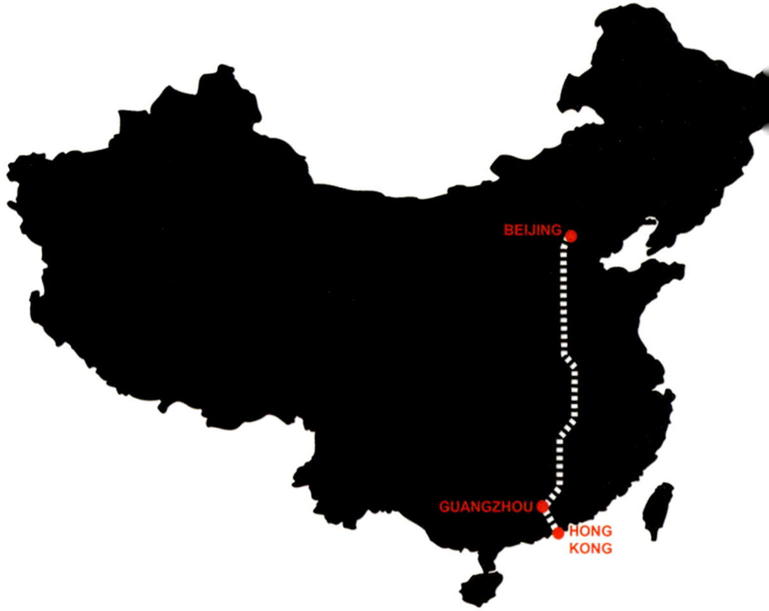

we were concerned that the project would be perceived as a commercial development which had a station below it as opposed to being a civic "gateway" into Hong Kong with supporting commercial activity.

For the competition, the designers explored two main options for the location of the station component; at either front corner of the site. It was felt to be a fundamental move which gave the station an address and a presence appropriate to its role in the city. From an urban design point of view, having the station entrance building in the southwest corner gave more frontage to the commercial activities which was beneficial to both views of the harbor and access.

Within the station itself, there was one underlying goal to the scheme. As the "gateway" to Hong Kong, it was considered vital to connect the station with the surrounding urban context and make one aware that whether arriving or departing: "You are in Hong Kong". In order to do this, the design compacted all of

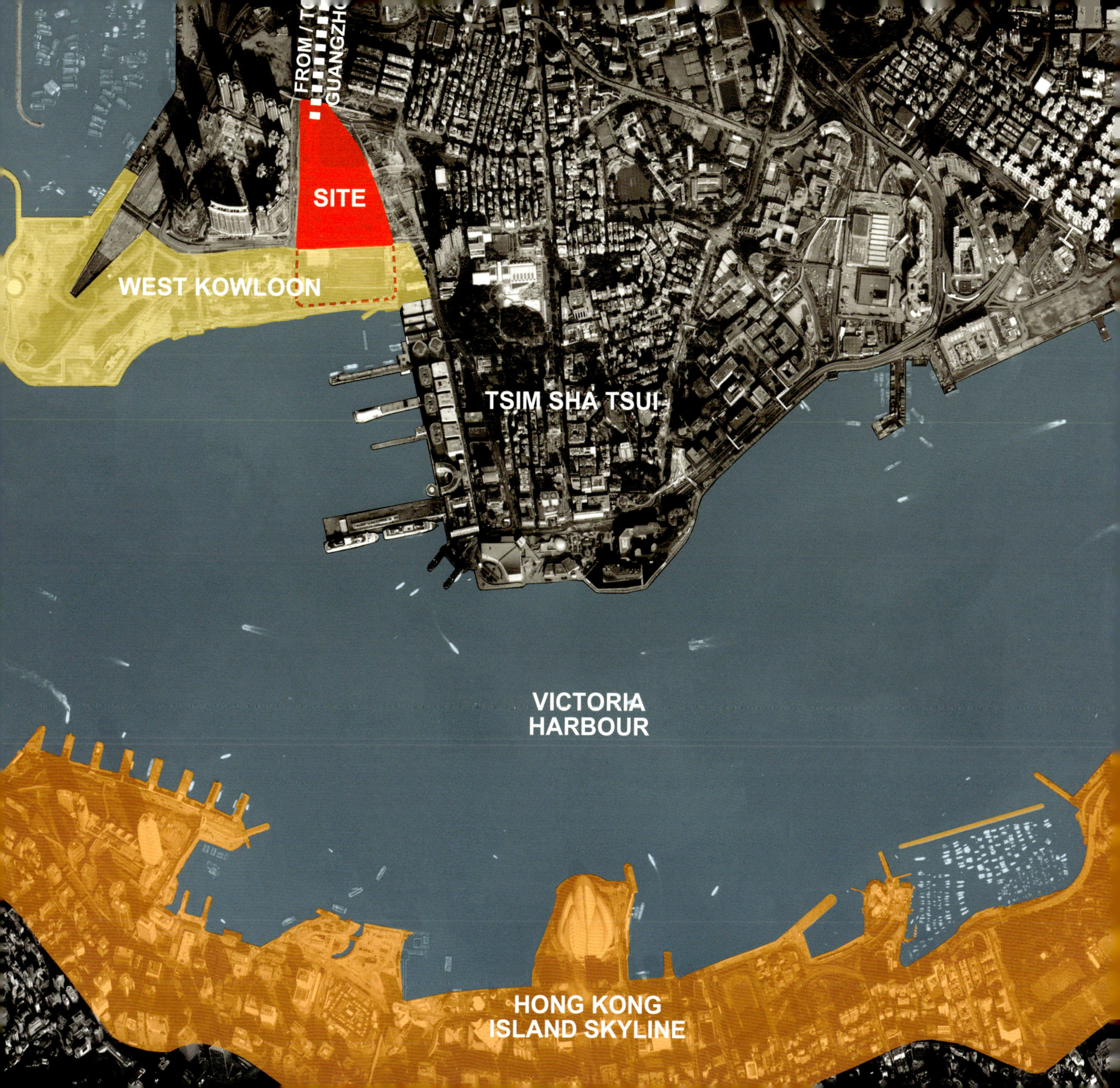
SITE
WEST KOWLOON
TSIM SHA TSUI
VICTORIA
HARBOUR
HONG KONG
ISLAND SKYLINE

scheme a

- conforming to the commercial no build zone
- conforming to the height limit
- conforming to the plot ratio of 5.0 (4.5 commercial and 0.5 retail)

scheme b

- proposed new commercial no build zone (same size)
- conforming to the height limit
- conforming to the plot ratio of 5.0 (4.5 commercial and 0.5 retail)

scheme c

- proposed new commercial no build zone (same size)
- beyond height limit west of Langham Place
- conforming to the plot ratio of 5.0 (4.5 commercial and 0.5 retail)

scheme a

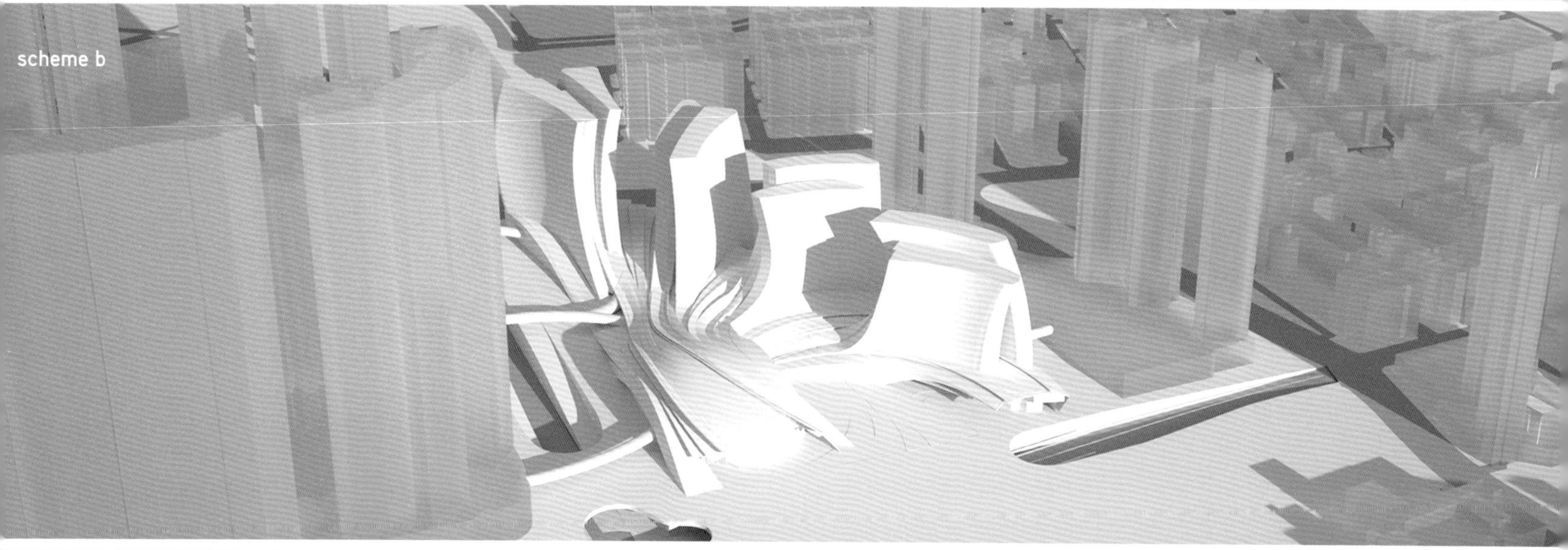
scheme b

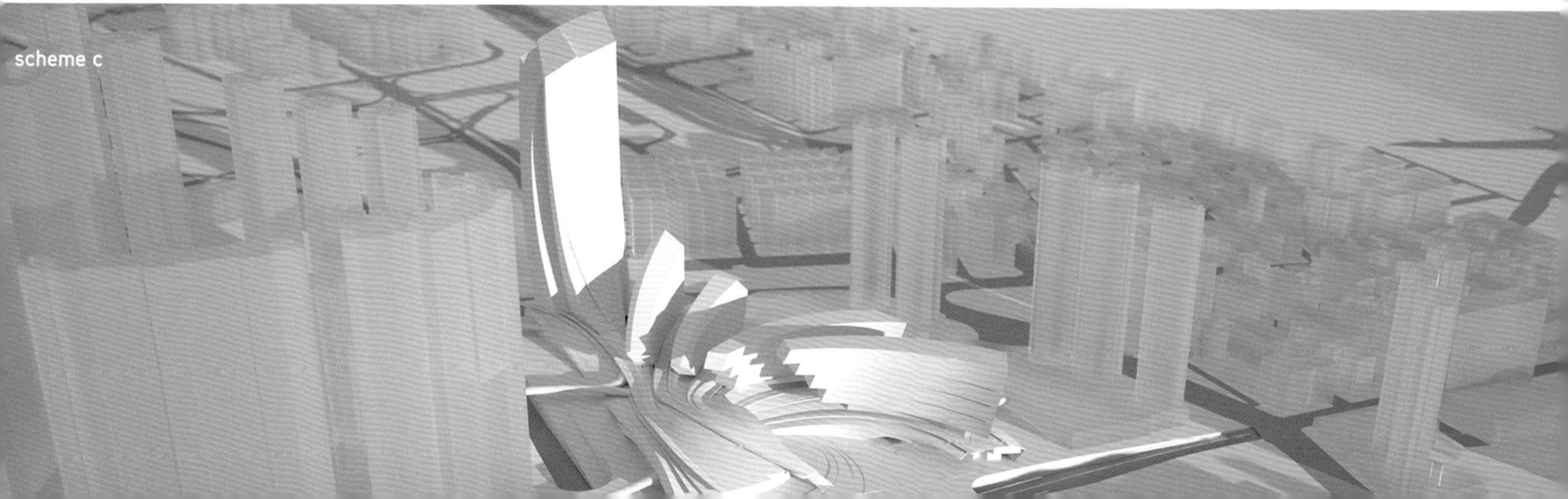
scheme c

key data	track level (mPD)	(-21.5)
	excavation volume (m^3)	3,876,912
	foot-print (m^2)	124,260
	major void space (m^2)	41,470
	perimeter of diaphragm wall (m)	1,574
CFA *excluding topside property	total CFA	432,547
	property car park (m^2)	41,503
	total station CFA	391,044
	above ground station CFA (m^2)	8,851
	below ground station CFA (m^2)	382,193
	extra area to WKCD (m^2)	21,581
	total station CFA if including extra area to WKCD	412,625
	total CFA if including extra area to WKCD	454,128
open space	total open space (required $8900m^2$)	40,624
	ground floor open space (m^2)	8,924
	elevated open space (m^2)	31,700
	greenery (required 20% of site area)	11,760
public area	total public circulation (m^2)	125,779
	paid circulation (m^2)	104,946
	un-paid circulation (m^2)	20,833
	public area over station CFA (%)	39%
	non-public area over station CFA (%)	61%
retail area	STA (required 7700m2 - 8800m2)	10,604
	duty free (required: 2200m2 - 3300m2)	3,974 / 3,055 / 919
	bonded good store (required 50% of shop area)	1,987
travel distance	average arrival travel (m)	693
	average departure travel (m)	508
	from centre of arrival/departure gates to AUS (m)	228 / 123
	from centre of arrival/departure gates to PTI (m)	430 / 431
	from centre of arrival/departure gates to KOW (m)	384 / 468
	from taxi drop-off to centre of departure gates (m)	115
	from centre of arrival gates to taxi pick-up (m)	49
	from centre of arrival/departure gates to short-stay car park (m)	363 / 259
	from centre of arrival/departure gates to WKCD (m)	363 / 259
	from AUS station to KOW station (m)	566
short haul	arrival (from transfer level to unpaid concourse)	
	number of 90 degree turns	6
	number of 180 degree turns	-
	departure (from unpaid concourse to transfer level)	
	number of 90 degree turns	6
	number of 180 degree turns	1
	secured delivery route to short haul	365
	secured refuse route to short haul	354
	trolley route (from unpaid area to short haul)	677
	trolley route (from station car park to short haul)	518
long haul	arrival (from transfer level to unpaid concourse)	
	number of 90 degree turns	6
	number of 180 degree turns	-
	departure (from unpaid concourse to transfer level)	
	number of 90 degree turns	4
	number of 180 degree turns	1
	secured delivery route to long haul	108
	secured refuse route to long haul	111
	trolley route (from unpaid area to long haul)	237
	trolley route (from station car park to long haul)	696

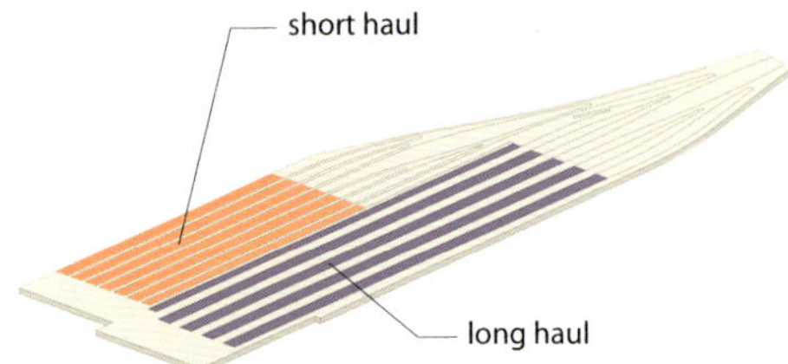

track level (-21.50mPD)
platform level (-20.50mPD)

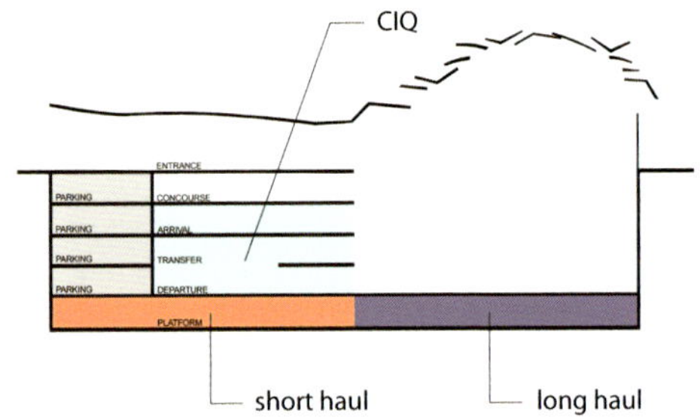

track and CIQ arrangement

- location of short haul is fixed
- 80% of pedestrian flow goes to short haul
- short haul travel distances are 40% less in scheme a than scheme b and c
- customs immigration quarter (CIQ) is placed on top of short haul to reduce travel distance and travel time.

scheme A was chosen as the final design

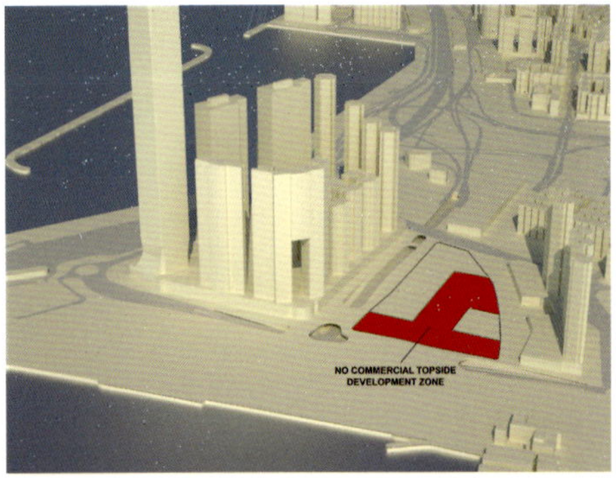

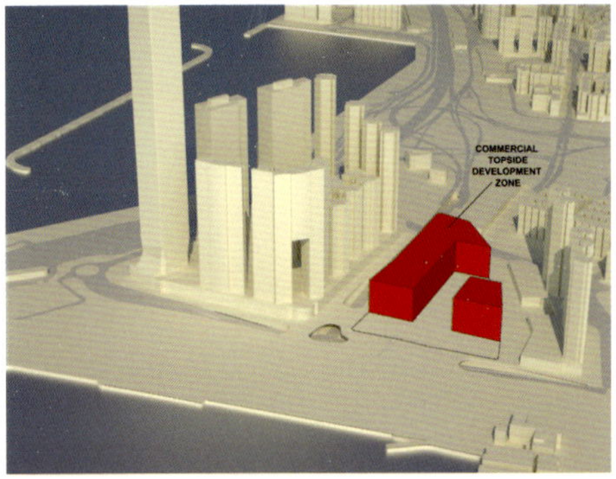

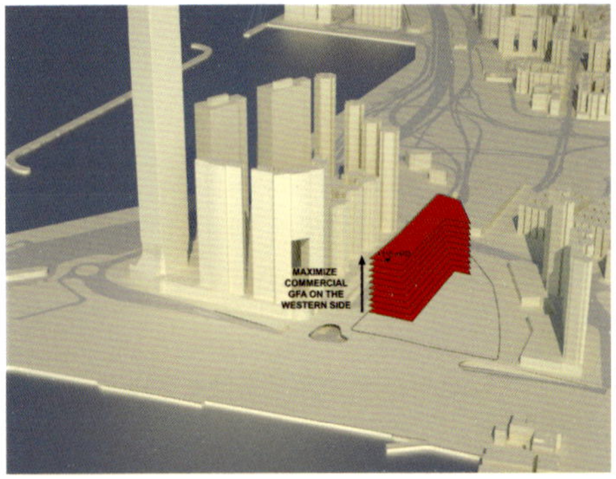

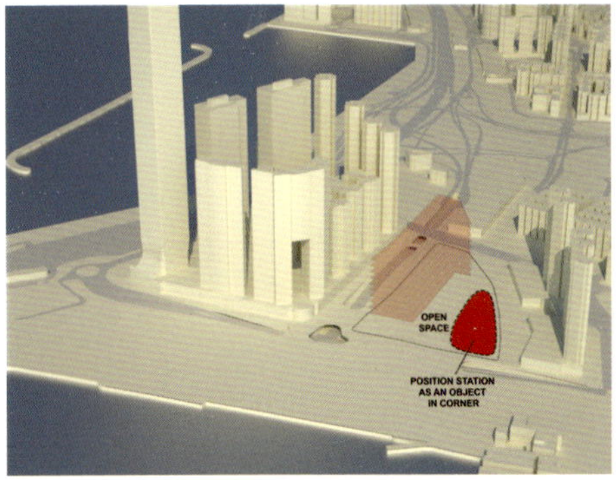

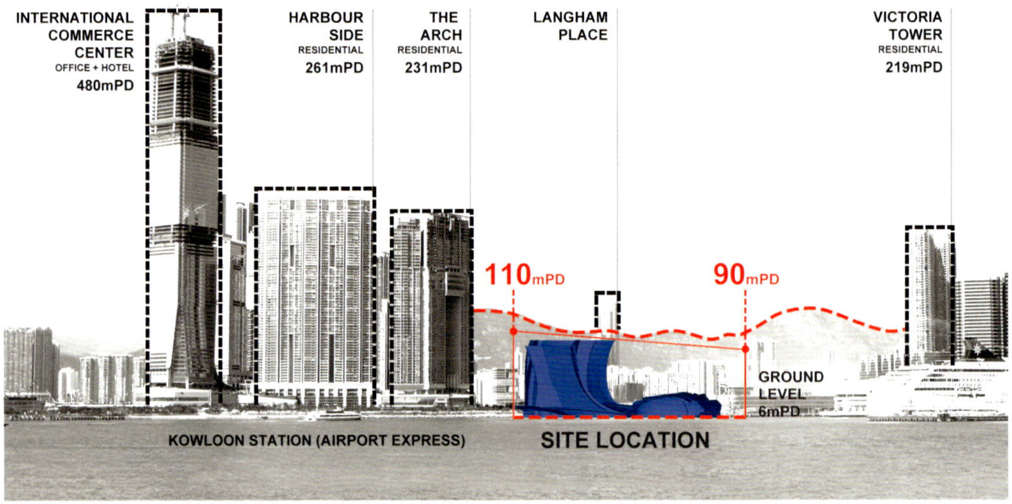

the supporting spaces more efficiently to allow for a very large void down into the departure hall below as well as apertures down to the track platforms. The outside ground plane is bent down to the hall and the roof structure above gestures toward the harbor. The result is a 45 meter high volume which focuses all attention through the south facade toward views of the Hong Kong Central skyline and Victoria Peak beyond.

In order to achieve this volume, the inner workings of both Hong Kong and China immigration facilities were explored. The "baseline" scheme had segregated immigration by operation. All of HK immigration was on one floor and the PRC immigration was on another. This seemed to make sense from a territorial point of view but it caused great inefficiencies within the planning diagram. Our scheme actually stacked territories so that all immigration facilities for arrivals are on one floor and all departure facilities are on another. By relating jurisdictions on top of each other, so that both arrival and departure facilities are stacked and connected, the inner workings were made easier and consequently more efficient.

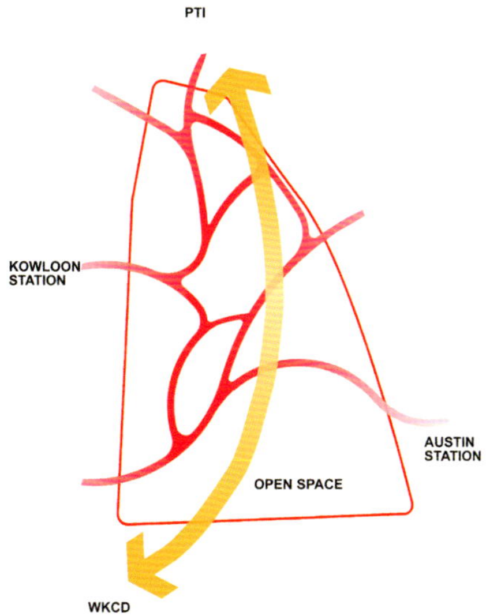

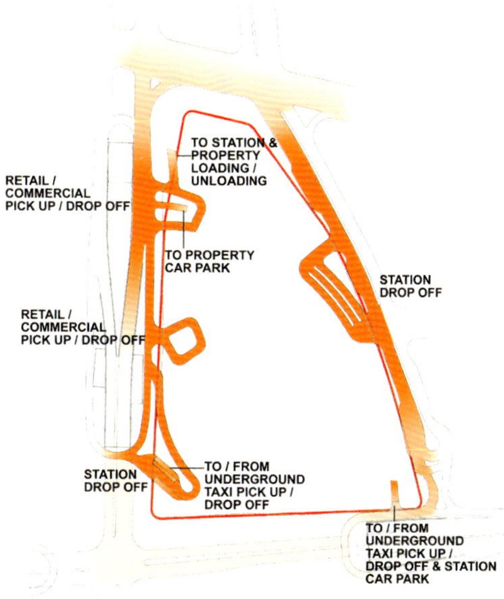

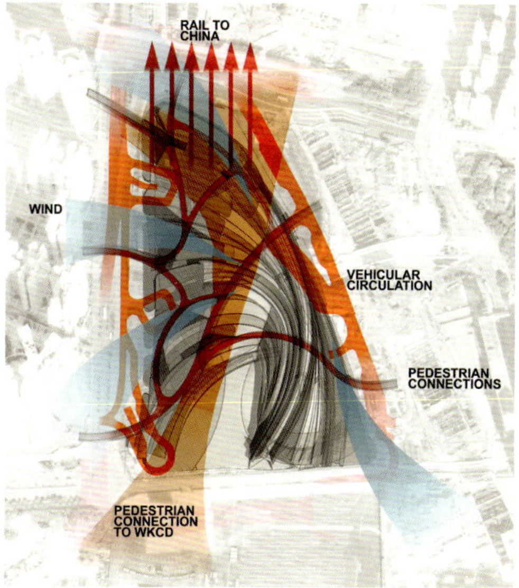

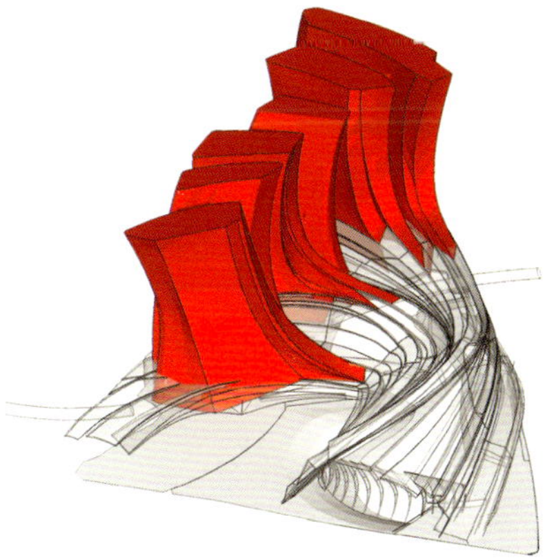

commercial - office

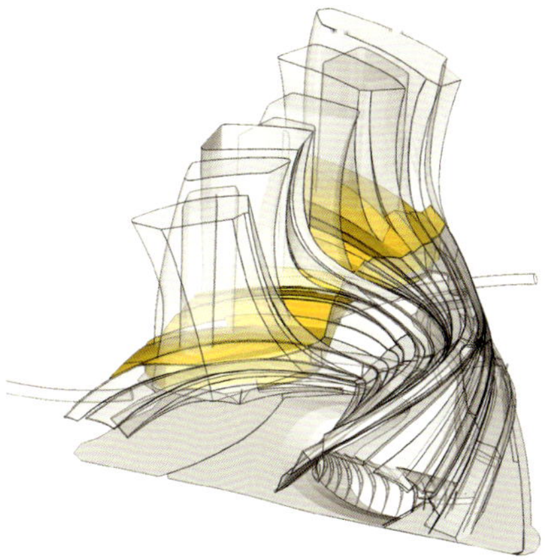

commercial - retail

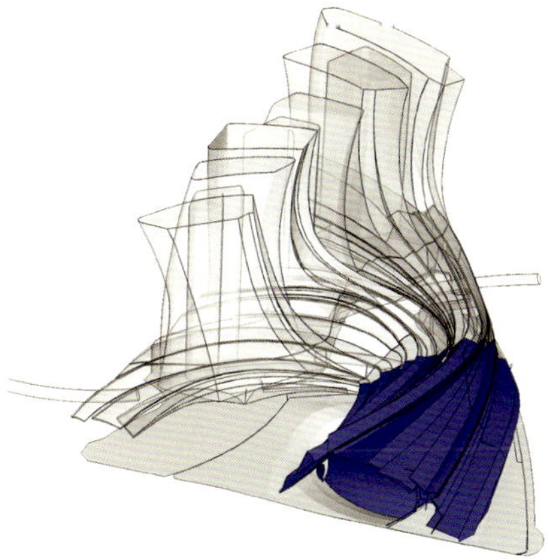

above ground station

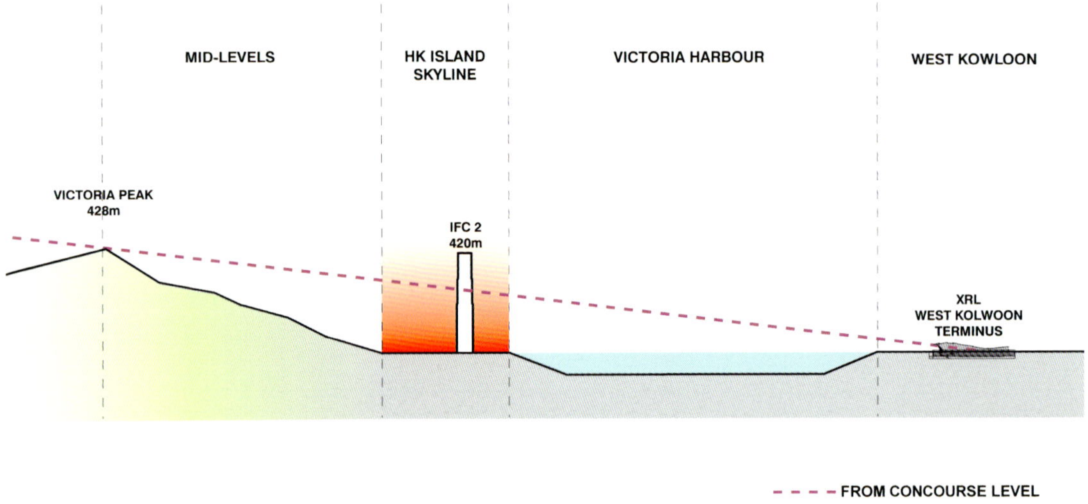

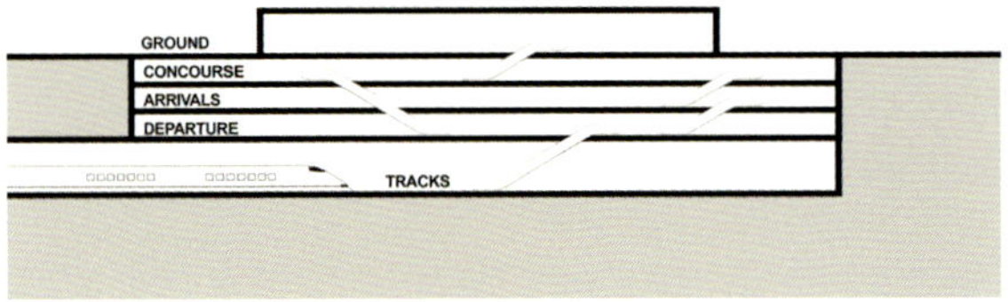

It was not until after winning the competition and beginning a more rigorous two month exercise to bring the scheme up to a similar level of development as the "baseline" scheme that it was confirmed that placing the entrance building in the southeast corner was far superior from the point of view of the station's functions. The analytical data supporting this conclusion is derived directly from track layout and disposition.

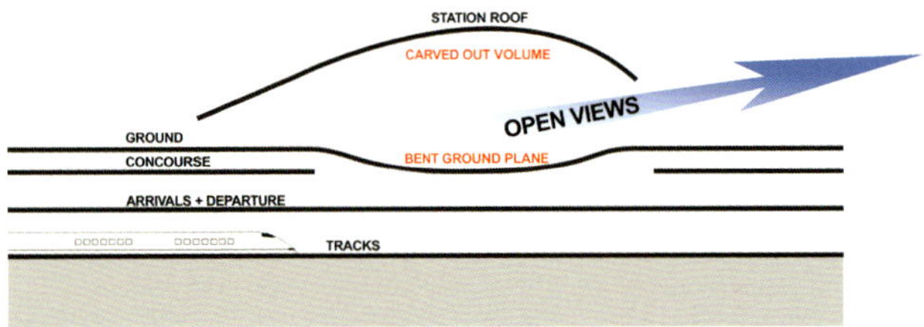

Departures

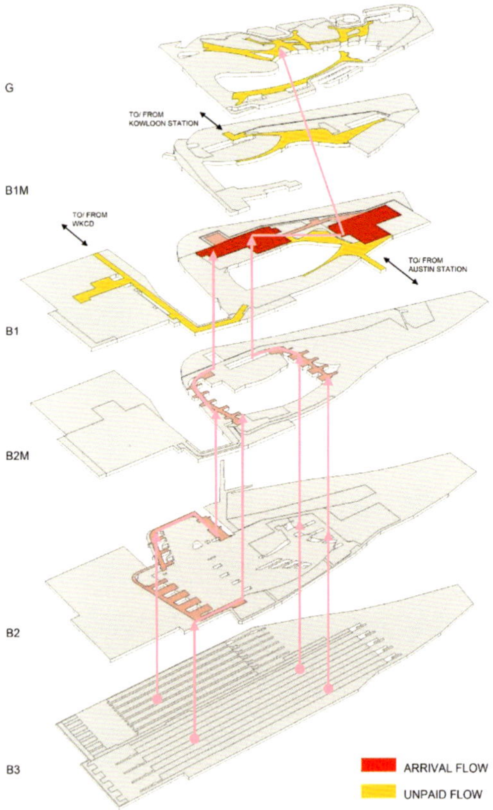

arrival experience

The terminus station has two target destinations: for regional commuter trains and long-haul high speed trains. The commuter trains go across Hong Kong territory to Shenzhen, a booming China border city, and further north to Guangzhou, the capital of Canton. At the time the project was awarded, years of research had already been performed on the civil engineering side which came to the conclusion, based on urban make-up and internal site restrictions that the short haul tracks needed to be placed on the western side of the site with the long-haul ones located to the eastern side. The locations of these tracks were/are fixed. In addition, there is the fact that 80% of the station users are short-haul commuters. Consequently, reducing travel times for these passengers is a priority.

departure experience

Locating the immigration facilities over the short-haul tracks significantly reduced station travel times for short-haul passengers. The immigration facilities are quite dense formalized spaces with both front-of-house and back-of-house uses. They can function quite well within a column grid environment. Their location beneath the density of the future commercial spaces also optimizes the openness of the void and entrance building on the opposite side of the site. As the short-haul tracks are located on the west side of the site, the immigration facilities are also located to the west, along with the commercial facilities. This leaves the entrance building of the station located on the eastern edge of the site.

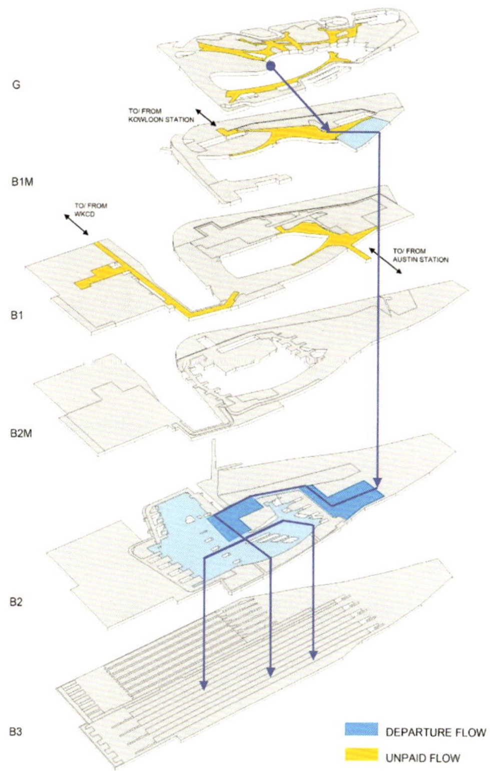

plans at time of 2nd VE

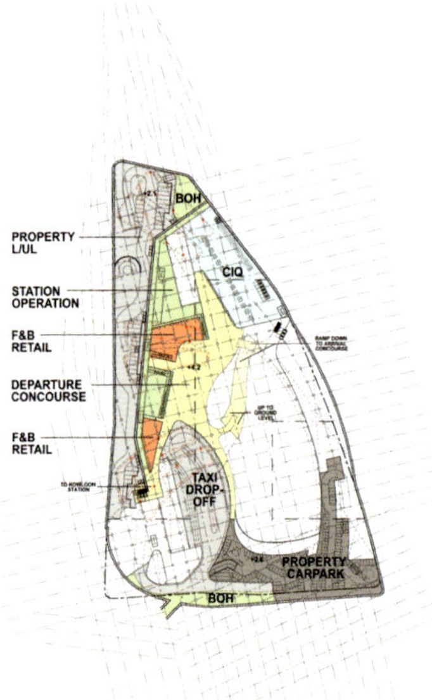

concourse level

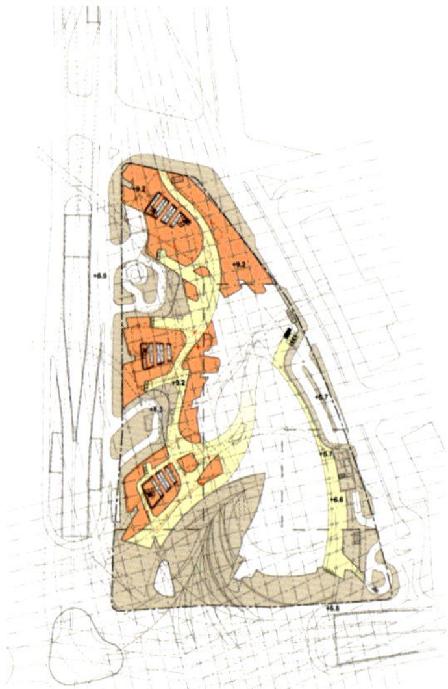

ground level

bridge level

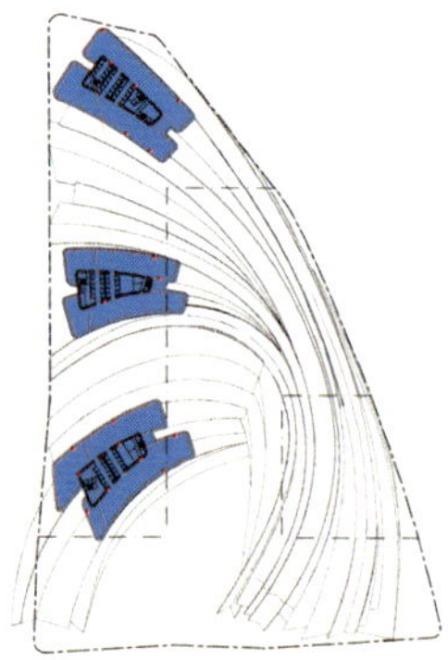

tower plan

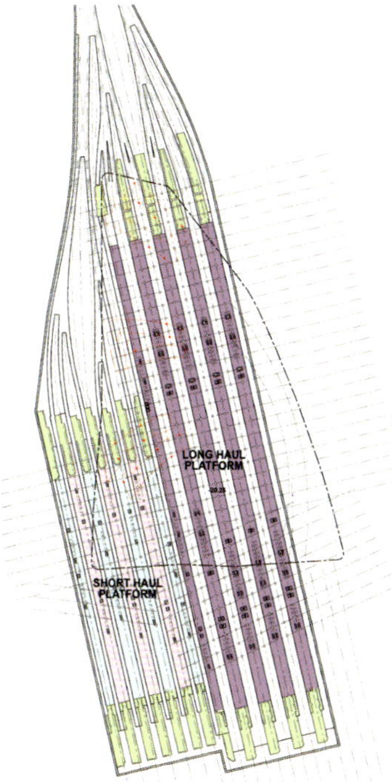

platform/track level

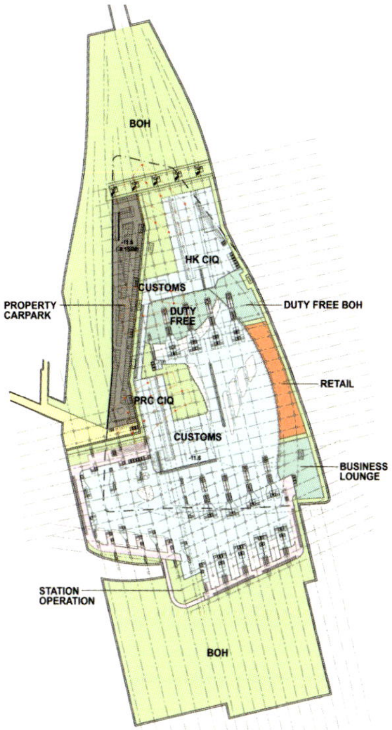

departure CIQ level

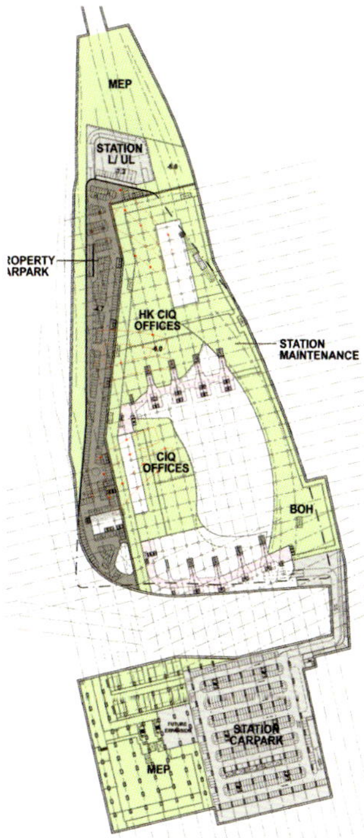

arrival transfer level

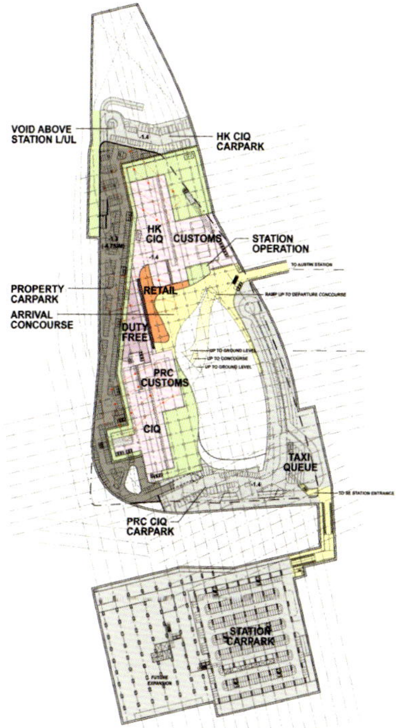

arrival CIQ level

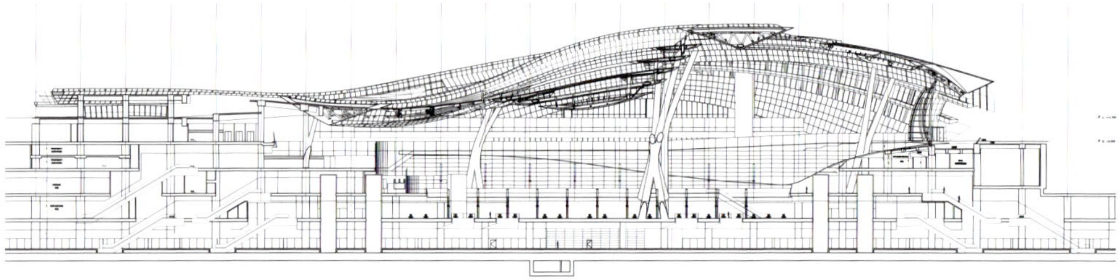

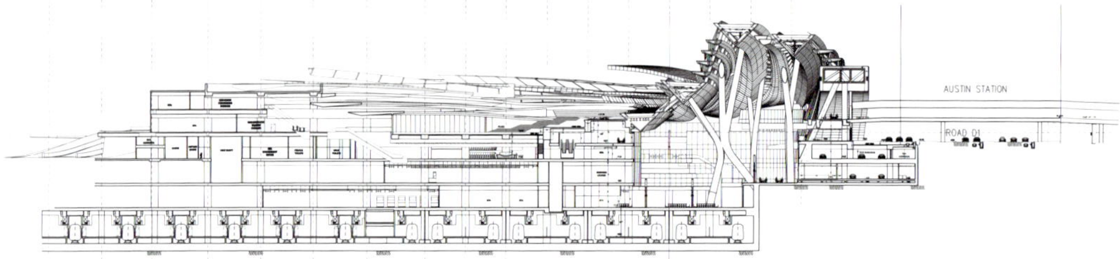

The scheme was then analytically compared to the "baseline" scheme in over 60 major items of criteria. On a scale of 1000, voted on by more than 200 political and technical leaders in Hong Kong, this scheme strongly outperformed the "baseline" scheme with 875 points compared to 540 points and was adopted as the chosen scheme to be moved forward to implementation.

The organization of the design was inspired by converging forces all oriented toward Hong Kong – likened to the converging tracks coming into the terminus station itself. The project maximizes civic gestures both internally and externally. The station is sculpted out of the energy of these moves and strongly defines its motive to open up and focus toward Victoria Harbor and the Hong Kong skyline. The cultural district of WKCD is invited into the site. A large "Civic Square" opens up toward the cultural district and is defined on the other side with its own outdoor performance amphitheatre.

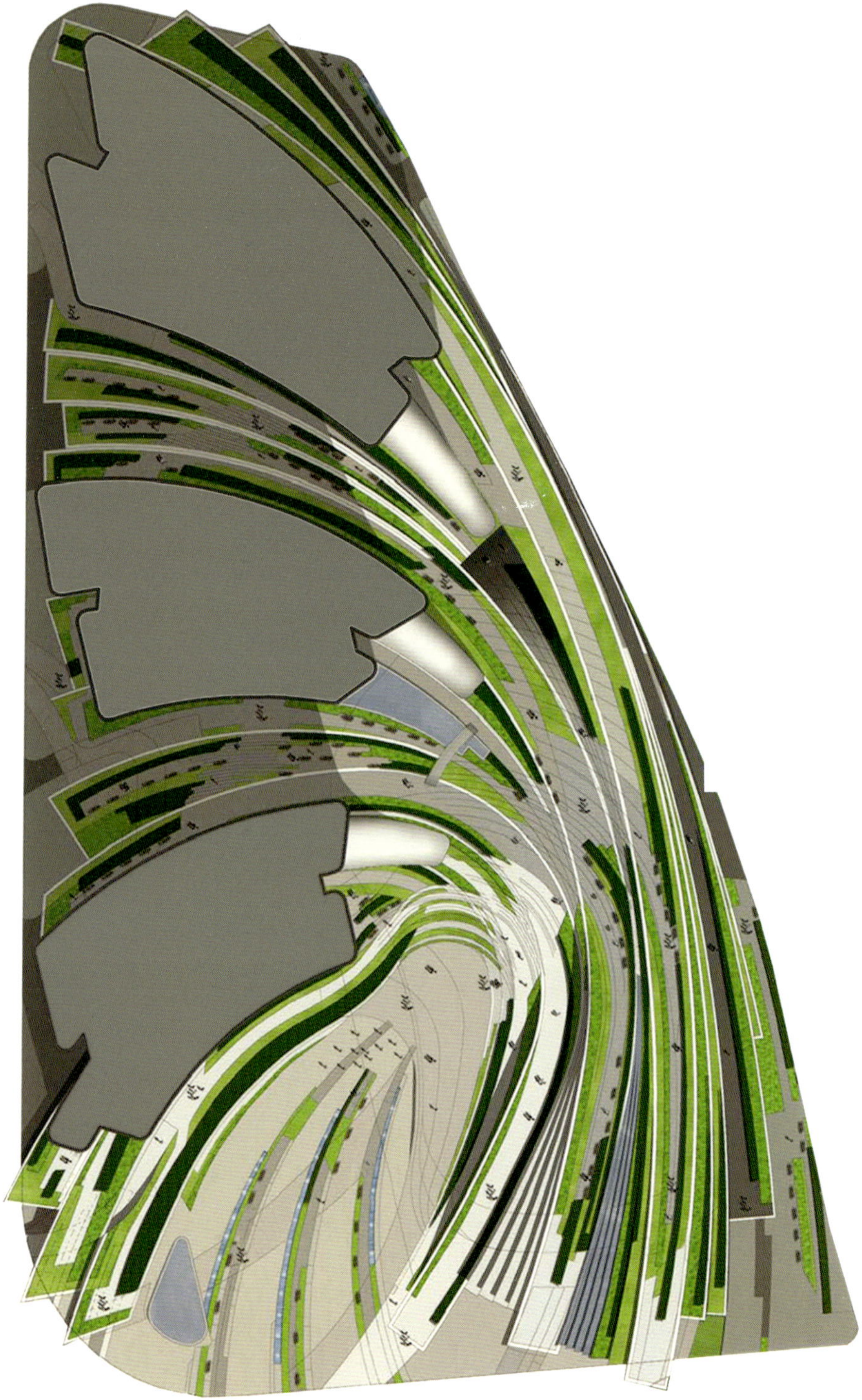

roof structure sustainable design integration

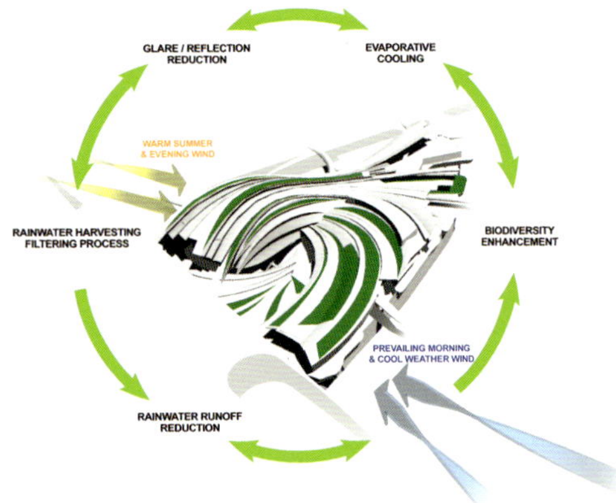

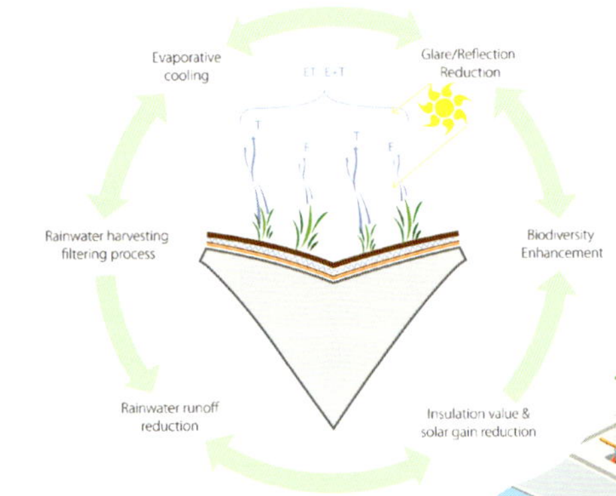

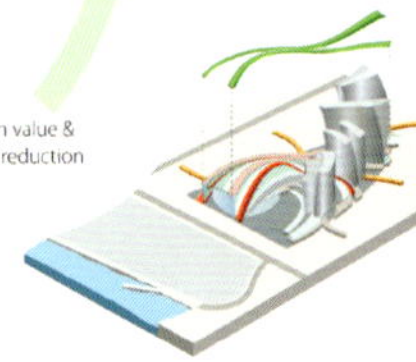

environment

The pedestrian flow into this amphitheatre continues upwards, accessing almost the entire rooftop of the station itself in a densely planted sculpture garden and landscaped extension of the green below. The resultant open space has an area almost five times greater than an already ambitious mandate in the master plan. The green space provides links flowing through the site to a Public Transport Interchange to the North, the Austin Station subway station to the East, the Kowloon Station Development and Elements Mall to the West as well as internal connections into the WKT station itself and its future commercial development.

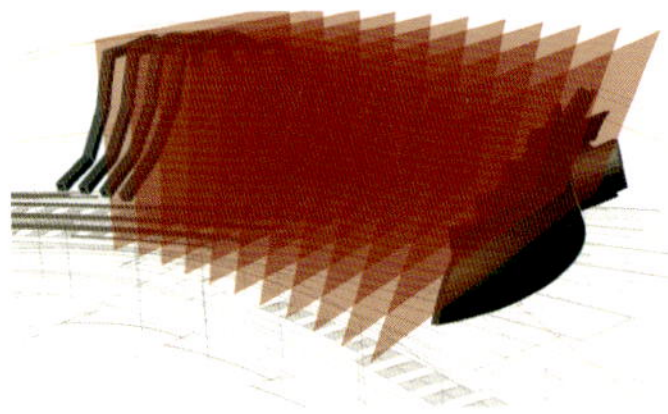

structure with structural planes

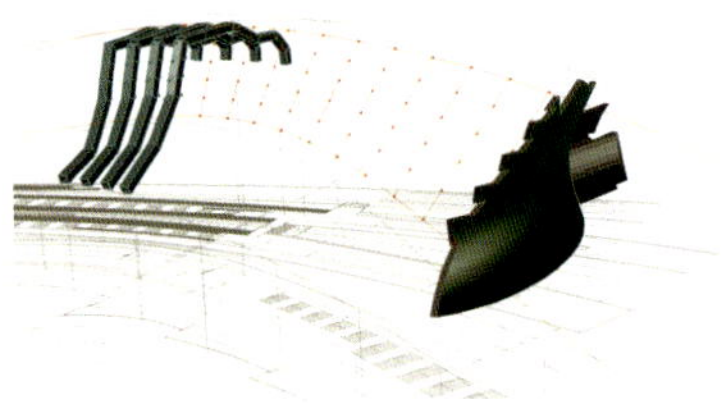

dividing the structure lines into five

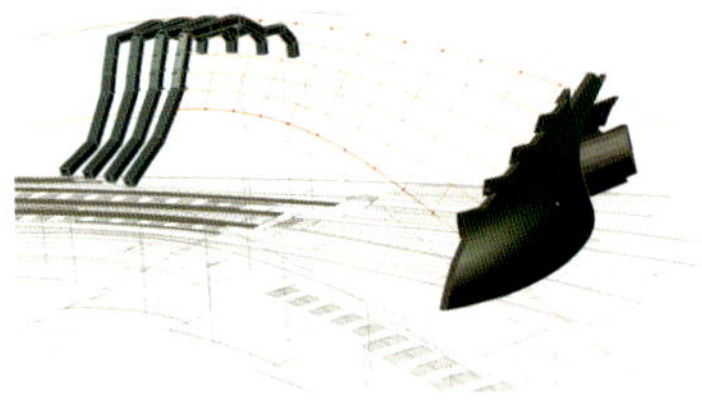

forming the curves

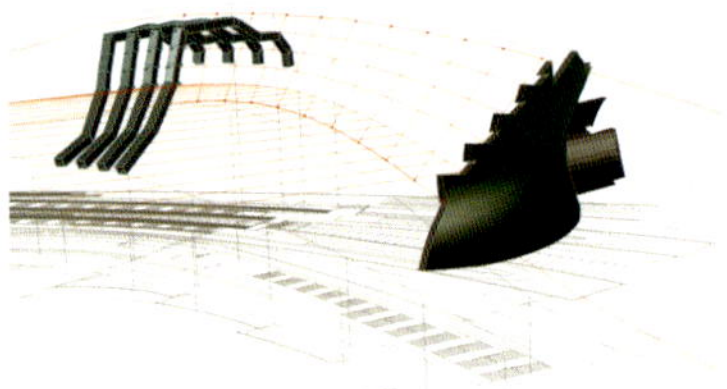

orientate a line to the horizontal frame

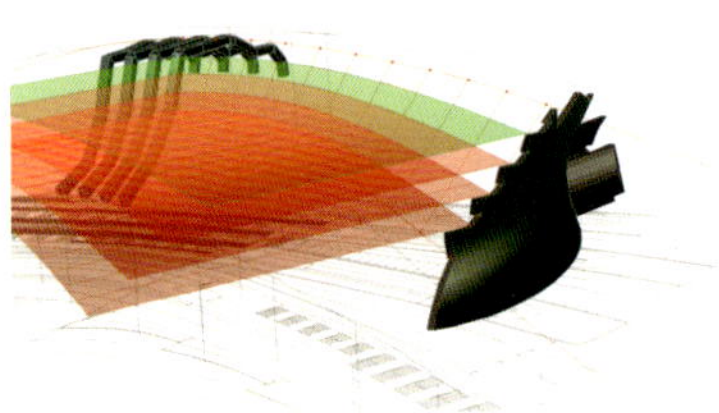

fin profile from intersections

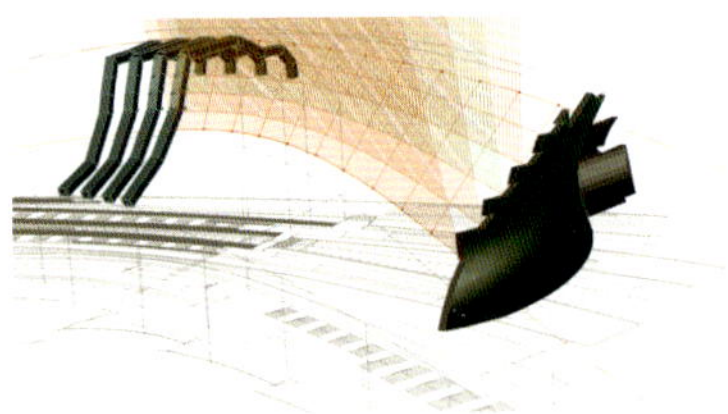

fin angles parametric control

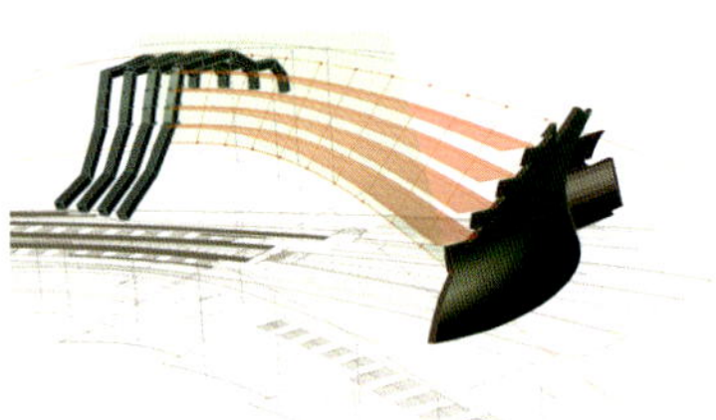

fin surfaces

outer and inner curve for fins

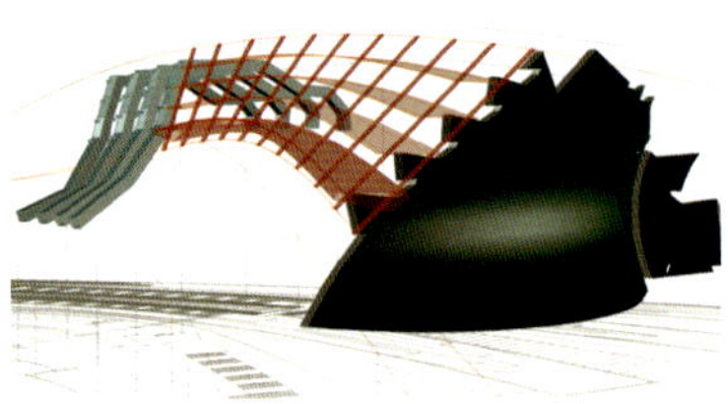

outer and inner curve for fins

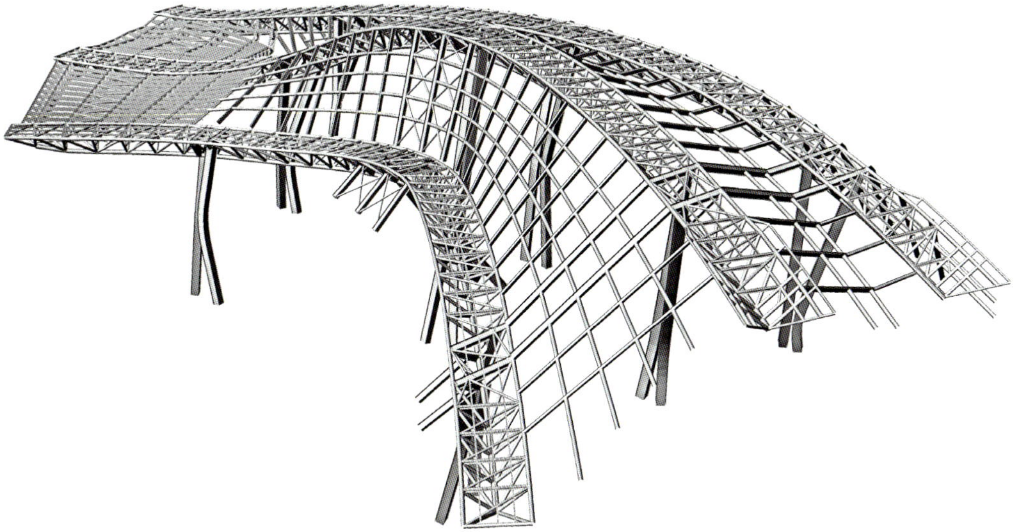

structure

The hope is that this commercial development will eventually be seamlessly knitted into the overall flow of the project and so was developed to a point where it would demonstrate viability. Fortunately however, the success of the development is not dependent on this integration. The image of the station will be preserved in the southeast corner of the site. The Civic Square will be defined by station entrances and station facilities on the east and west sides as well as adjacent, accessible paths moving up on top into the green "roofscape".

At the culmination of these moves one finds oneself at an observation deck on top of the crest of the entrance building – twenty-five meters above the Civic Square and forty-five meters above the Departure Hall below. At the top there is the perfect overlook as an extension of the journey into Hong Kong – into and beyond the West Kowloon Cultural District; into and beyond Victoria Harbor and into and beyond the tower-filled alleyways of Hong Kong. The station may be visible below as a reminder of where one came from – but the future paths of discovery present themselves invitingly beyond...

Trains au départ

asia retrospective

Perhaps the biggest building boom in the history of mankind has taken place over the last decade from the Middle to the Far East, and Andrew Bromberg is at its epicenter, practicing. The unprecedented scale of the boom and the unprecedented scale of the commissions have presented Bromberg a set of design problems and opportunities different from those posed by projects at more usual times and in more traditional cities. The scale of projects in the Middle and Far East has exploded by orders of magnitude, becoming astonishingly large and complex, and Bromberg has had to make humanistic sense of commissions where conventional architectural responses are inadequate or inappropriate.

For the last eight years, running a boutique architectural office in Hong Kong, nested within the much larger corporate office, Aedas, Bromberg has found himself positioned to interpret architecturally the explosion of scale within the explosion of work. Trained in the United States, where he worked in the Nbbj offices, among others, he helped in the design of several large-scale projects, including the South Terminal project in Seattle, the Denver International Airport in Colorado and the Reebok World Headquarters in Massachusetts. He has practiced as an expat for the last eight years, fielding large projects with great alacrity. With 38 offices and a staff of 2500, Aedas has provided the infrastructure to support Bromberg as a designer specializing in cutting-edge design for marquee projects. Despite the fact that most of these are commercial rather than institutional, Bromberg has sustained work of a remarkably high conceptual caliber.

The location of Bromberg's projects ranges widely, from Abu Dhabi and Moscow to Singapore, Hong Kong and the great cities of China—Beijing, Guangzhou and Xian. Unlike more traditional European cities that still maintain the idealism and after-image of a pedestrian-based urbanism, most of these new world cities have exceeded the scale of pedestrian environments, and are dependent on wide boulevards serving neighborhoods distant from their putative centers. Even those served, and well served, by new subway systems, sprawl. Beijing may have the most acute case of vastness. Building on the imperial scale of the ancient regime, the Chinese further extended the city and scale in the context of Communism's expansionist ambitions. The Chinese urban project was aided and assisted by Stalinist city planning inherited from Russians who had scaled Moscow beyond the bourgeois and aristocratic city, to the size of a state that idealized and empowered the collective power of the masses.

China, like Russia, was built for "the people," and the population of China is more than a billion strong. Its recent prosperity is fueling unprecedented interior growth. All the major Chinese cities, and most of the emerging Middle Eastern capitals, are characterized by plans that strain and even exceed urban coherence, displacing the emphasis from the street as the binding urban factor to the building itself, which has emerged as a self-contained city. This paradigm has shifted to an as yet uncodified dynamic between city and building. Urbanism has invaded the building while the building no longer shapes the street. The paradigm is not only true of Asia and the Middle East, but in cities as diverse as the new quarters of Istanbul or the new developments in Las Vegas. Even the entertainment complexes on 42nd Street in New York, have left the street in favor of unseen multi-story icebergs of program inside.

The new Asian and Middle Eastern sprawl reiterates the sprawl of automobile-based cities like Los Angeles and Dallas, and the classic architectural dilemma of suburban sprawl is that few buildings make a strong impact on the city. Landscape, not architecture, is the binder. The building no longer shapes urban space. Instead space gobbles up and marginalizes the architecture. The same is true of the new Asian megalopolises, characterized by high-rise buildings: the expanses of space swallow and even trivialize large buildings. In Beijing, the width of boulevards ten and twelve lanes wide, compounded by the speed or congestion of the traffic, separates one side of the street from the other, dousing whatever urbanism the density might spark.

As a Western architect, Bromberg cannot import the nostalgia of European urbanism to a context predicated on a different urban organization. Faced with the fait accompli of size generated by an unprecedented momentum of growth, Bromberg has had to strategize design differently to build in these expanding urban universes. Although his division within Aedas might be a boutique operation, it is really a think tank experimenting in real time with a new set of conditions in a new context with international consequences. His practice may be the future.

Bromberg accepts the new scale. Take his new hotel and office complex now under construction in Guangzhou, a building that is a kilometer long. The site is next to a vast, even larger convention center scaled not to the nation but to the world. If China has a trade show for toys in Guangzhou, it is not just for internal consumption. At this point in time, China manufactures toys for all of humanity, and the world comes to the convention center, across the Pearl River from what might be called the city center. Wide, high-speed roads with few cross streets surround the convention center, next to which Bromberg has designed two large complexes, each on either side of an existing multi-story building.

The convention center, with an airfoil profile, is an iconic building of which the city is proud and protective. Its iconic quality gives value to this rather remote site both as a symbol of a progressive city, and as a destination. Bromberg understands the value of large icons in this context, because they act as radiant forces exercising a gravitational pull on spaces too large to be affected by architecture trying to shape life on the street.

In this commission for a hotel and office building, Bromberg has designed a talismanic structure that complements the convention center, while creating a zone of its own. In each of the two complexes, a base of retail space several stories tall supports a stack of what appear to be randomly dislocated rectangles, each a floor in the 12 to 17 story buildings. The buildings are efficiently organized inside around elevator cores, and the structure is a rational grid. But from the outside, the expression appears accidental—as though the result of a capricious earthquake that dislocated an otherwise well-ordered building. "There's always a contextual response to the site, either apparent or overt," he says. "This was a horizontal response to try to link the two different sites across the building in between. The horizontal striations generate a kind of static electricity between the two buildings. The crackling connects them."

The floors cantilever beyond each other, creating outdoor decks and overhangs. Bromberg has responded to vastness with presence, and presence of an imposing scale. "The moves are specifically responding to the context in which the building is sitting," he says.

The imposing mass is broken down so that it is no longer a mass. But he does not simply break down the mass into graphic striations, but does so dynamically, so that the parts imply movement: "I do like a sense of motion in a building," he says.

"Human movement for me is sensual and soft and dynamic, and I try to harness a natural flow through space, instead of controlling it."

The building is not simply extruded from a single floor plan, even though all floors may be essentially identical. The building is efficient without efficiency being the subject.

But the gestures that will make the building a question mark in the skyline are not simply formalist. Bromberg's complexes are indeed that—complex—and he pursues a variety of ambitions in any one project. Some are simply rudimentary: "The moves deliberately explain what's going on, how the architectural expression reinforces the particular hierarchies that exist in a building. The design gives layers of information that reinforce the big ideas," he says.

For Bromberg, vast size need not intimidate or alienate. He compares huge buildings to the scale of nature, which has its own ways of breaking itself into negotiable parts. "I'm never afraid of large scale because big buildings are mountains and hills, made of boulders and rocks and ravines and spurs that make them accessible. I break the mass down in different ways."

Characteristically he breaks large scale buildings into visual manageability. In Guangzhou, simply by breaking up what could have been a monolith into its constituent floors, Bromberg is individuating the parts, making the whole approachable and understandable. The decks create outdoor spaces that Bromberg intends to use as spas, restaurants, event spaces, gardens—"Anything to introduce human activity," he says. "Human activity produces human scale." Bromberg is creating an occupied facade that is ipso facto "humanist," because the figures that will occupy its terraces are human beings pursuing everyday activities in unexpected places.

He pursues the humanist ideal inside. As in many of his buildings, he has developed a multi-level shopping mall that, despite its commercial basis, gives the building a civic space that pools the occupants of the building. Mixed-use buildings are more the rule rather than the exception in Bromberg's projects, and he now designs projects like Guangzhou as self-contained cities, where a resident audience (occupying a hotel on one side, and an office "slab" on the other) convene in multi-story public spaces. If there is no immediate urbanism to respond to outside on the street—no sidewalks, no cafés, no pedestrian life—he acknowledges the possibility of an internalized urbanism fed by hundreds if not thousands of people. He shapes the urbanism inside into a multi-story piazza.

In the United States, clients of such multi-story commercial spaces would require architects specialized in malls, but Bromberg is really a director, and the mall is merely one component, albeit a significant component, of the larger whole he is orchestrating. "For sure, there's an approach to the vastness. There's a challenge to bring a level of humanism and enjoyment to the project that's universal on some level," he says.

Bromberg stores many different arrows in his architectural quiver, all of which he uses to cultivate an interior life in his buildings. "I really like civic, public qualities of buildings; to try to bring some of these aspects into a building. I'm cognizant of trying to take the public realm into a building."

In Hong Kong, Bromberg won a prestigious competition to design the station that will be the terminus for the high-speed train from Beijing, a project of great symbolic importance to both China and Hong Kong. Formally, the building expresses the dynamism of the high-speed enterprise. Bromberg constructs the shell of the structure in striations of streaming ribs that vault the space. Originally the ribs turned vertically at their ends and climbed into the facades of office towers that would be integrated into the mixed-use project. The towers will instead be built by developers, so now only the station will benefit from the original idea.

The commission is for what is possibly one of the most urban and urbane projects in the world, at a strategic point in Hong Kong along the harbor, at the receiving end of thousands of travelers arriving from Beijing. The high-speed train is itself a potent symbol of China's increasingly powerful presence in the world, and the station is, effectively, a national and nationalist stage. The Chinese were ready for a building that mirrors their sense of arrival. Hong Kong itself needed the equivalent of Beijing's Bird's Nest.

Bromberg, who hails from Colorado and still hikes, thinks of this very prominent and aesthetically conspicuous structure as a natural land form. "I hike every week, and rather than going deeply into the country parks, leaving the city, I try to find the edge between city and nature. I trace paths through parks where the nature is tangential to shopping and markets. The trails are interesting hybrids of nature and retail. I'm

hiking but I can grab a juice. This whole blurring of nature and the built environment is what I try to do between the public and private realms within a building."

Metaphorically, Bromberg thinks of the station—a huge mixed-use building on a site the size of a nine-hole golf course—as a natural land form within the dense city. "The urban realm flows up and over the building," he says. "You sell the building to the client on the basis of a business model that increases population inside. You cultivate the commercial aspects to make the civic part work."

Bromberg applies the analogy of a natural land form to another huge, mixed-use project in Singapore, the Civic and Cultural Complex.

Consciously and unconsciously analogies to nature help drive this and other projects. In Singapore, he designed the 5-story podium beneath the 5000 seat theater as a mixed-use, multi-story canyon of shopping terraces that visitors climb and explore.

Bromberg's goal is basically to orchestrate an implicit public-private partnership in which successful commercial activities breed public spaces that have the civic role of collecting large numbers of people commingling in the same space. The key to making these large public spaces commercially viable is to tap into public transportation and parking so that within a building, people flow in from public transport or well up from parking. The shopping mall inside acts as a social condensor.

The Singapore building has both public transportation and parking. A rail node is adjacent to the site, and Bromberg builds a bridge from the station to the second story of the five-story shopping canyon.

Below the base are several vast floors of parking. Singapore is one of the rare cities with both well-developed, well-integrated rail and subway systems and a successful network of roads. Those who drive to this suburban location—within a high-tech zone master-planned by Zaha Hadid—park in the base, and filter through a series of lushly landscaped passages up to the shopping terraces. The destination of many will be the auditorium at the top, designed for rock and other kinds of large-scale concerts, and for Sunday church services. A congregation headed by a charismatic minister is effectively the anchor tenant in the project. The terraced shopping plazas are necessarily traversed by anyone parking below or arriving by train, guaranteeing the stores an active client base. Bromberg designs and deploys the infrastructure to activate the pedestrian life of the interior. "I'm always cognizant of trying to create a public realm within a building, but in a completely commercial, single-use building, that goal becomes more elusive and frustrating".

Treating the building as "a human landscape" where layers of activity are visible, often in section, breaks down the scale of the massive 62,000 square meter building, which risked overwhelming the neighborhood.

The podium—basically an outdoor shopping mall and food court, densely landscaped with thriving tropical vegetation—supports the carapace surrounding a huge 5000 seat theater. The shell of the theater would be massively imposing on the neighborhood had Bromberg not taken great care to break down its scale. He fragments the volume by faceting exterior walls, changing materials and employing lyrical asymmetries.

He slants and leans shapes to dynamize the parts into a whole charged with visual movement. Cantilevered decks further splinter the mass. He has designed an iconic structure that engages on-lookers by piquing their curiosity. What would otherwise be a bland and predictable building and environment instead becomes enticing.

Shoppers flock to malls in Singapore, partially because of their cultural proclivities, but also because malls are air conditioned and protected from the sun. Bromberg, however, proposes a different paradigm, the outdoor mall, shaded by upper floors, open to cross ventilation and lavishly planted with tropical specimens. For a garden metropolis, he is proposing an environmentally responsible garden mall. A few other architects practicing in Southeast Asia have opened buildings that would normally be closed like canisters because of air-conditioning. But Bromberg does this at a scale well beyond that of the few boutique projects that have gone green. The podium of shopping is porous horizontally and vertically, rising with palm trees planted in the sub-basement up to the higher stories of the open atrium. The floor of the theater's foyer is even glazed to allow views to the shopping arena below.

Shopping is all about the promenade, and Bromberg reifies the act of strolling and window shopping by designing corridors with a fluidity that starts where pedestrians enter the building from the rail terminus. Curving terraces and corridors flow through each floor, between the shops and the central atrium, in a plan that is not extruded from the ground. Each floor follows its own curvilinear logic, and the stack of differently flowing terraces, curves seen against counter curves, forms a spatially baroque composite. Bromberg has simply diagrammed in plan the natural desire lines of shoppers navigating the space. The plans seem, at a glance, radical, but are in fact well suited to their function. The curves move people through the space.

Outside the carapace, among its cliffs of acid etched glass with okulux, Bromberg creates a promenade that circumambulates the shell like a hiking trail. The human activity he cultivates inside breaks through the shell and activates and humanizes an exterior that might otherwise be dauntingly large. It also extroverts a composite of building types—the shopping mall and the auditorium—which are usually closed and introverted. The fragmented facades and the hiking trail make an inviting gesture to the city. "Introducing this walking circuit nearly a half kilometer long, floating it 55 meters in the air, enables you to gaze down into a shopping center that looks like a vertical urban park," says Bromberg. "It's one of the pieces of project that could have gone away at several points, but I felt that if you lost that one significant un-programmed element, you would lose the opportunity of adding a human dimension to the facade, and you'd lose part of its experiential quality."

Shopping malls are a fact of life that the scale and size of Asian cities necessitate, and in mixed-use buildings programmed for shopping, Bromberg welcomes them not only as a necessity, but also as an opportunity to socialize the building.

In Beijing, North Star, a large apartment and office complex centered on a five-story shopping center, is perhaps more typical of complexes in climates that are not as benign as Singapore's, climates in which bouts of extreme cold prevent open-air shopping. Still, the design principles that Bromberg demonstrates in Singapore remain, especially his use of the building section to help foster a sense of community. In both, he uses shopping as what the Russian Constructivists called "social condensors." The agenda of shopping here is to work as a condensor activating public space.

As in many shopping centers in Asia, North Star is surrounded and fed by the high-rise offices, apartments and hotels of a multi-use complex, and these tall structures, visible through its space-framed glass roof, have striated floor sections stacked like pancakes. Other than the lobbies of these buildings and the elevator cabs, the buildings offer little opportunity for a building to cultivate a sense of community beyond the individual offices and floors they serve.
Communication is confined to a horizontal not vertical dimension.

As in many shopping complexes in high-density buildings, North Star occupies several floors (five), and Bromberg makes every effort to oxygenate the mall with people. He prefers, for example, escalators to elevators, and deploys them in the most public, visible places. By feeding the shopping mall with equal-opportunity elevator stops from the towers above and the parking levels below, he gives equal value to all floors, not simply to the first. As in the Civic and Cultural Center in Singapore, he harnesses the flow of people from the nearby train stop with a bridge, "To make the journey to the towers exciting," he says. Bromberg designs curving corridors and terraces that reify flow, allowing overlooks and views of other landings and terraces. He inscribes the floors with lava-like patterns, a short hand of his intentions as well as a calligraphic signature.

As in the drum of Frank Lloyd's Guggenheim, to which the North Star shopping center is related formally and spatially, the feeling of contact with people across the atrium helps breed a sense of community, along with the feeling that something is happening when only shopping is happening. Counterintuitively, rather than leaving the atrium as a hole in the doughnut, he occupies the hole with a stack of stores shaped into a prow cutting through space, which tenses a large, open space that would otherwise feel lax. Richard Sera plays his sculpture off against walls that he intentionally keeps close, and Bromberg does the same with the stores of his program. The shape of the space contains and perhaps magnifies a collective human energy totally absent from the major streets in Beijing, where the density and speed of the traffic severs contact between the two sides of the roadway.

Here shoppers and people passing by on their way to work or who live in the towers see themselves and the building from different vantage points. "The different ways of moving through the space, the bridges, the horizontal and vertical circulation make things connect and happen," says Bromberg. "We're not making a space so obvious that it no longer entices you to explore and discover it. I'm passionate about the psychology of perception, about movement through space you discover. Often my projects are not form-driven but space-driven, encouraging a sense of movement and exploration."

If the two shopping malls, the one in Singapore and the other in Beijing, share spatial similarities and design strategies, they are hardly formulaic. Bromberg's

buildings are indisputably modernist— abstract, sculptural, rational, clearly structured—but they are also contextual and culturally sensitive. He adapts his language. The Singapore project was built with a softer, more open and responsive attitude to the natural environment, featuring air flow, vegetation, and a more relaxed atmosphere. Although the Singapore center does have cross paths through it, it is conceived and planned more as a destination, with spaces of repose, where citizens can linger in an environment without feeling they are passing through. The Beijing project, on the other hand, makes a strong connection between the nearby above-ground rail station and the office and apartment towers, and the shopping center is situated and designed to capture and handle the through-flow of pedestrians. "The space is about making an exciting event around the journey, as opposed to making it a destination in itself," says Bromberg.

The silhouettes and postures of Bromberg's buildings are so striking that Bromberg is sometimes considered a formalist, much to his chagrin. He does not design, however, from the outside in, but like a modernist evolves the building from the plan, which is the generator.

But his plans are not squares but energy fields. He does not work in Platonic geometries conceived within Cartesian grids, but moves and shapes pieces in response to pressures and attractions felt on sites that he senses like ouija boards. The forces push and pull in what might be called distortional ways, and the forms, inside and out, are results of the pressure systems.

One possible response to the accusations of formalism is that Bromberg is an architect for whom space is the medium. It is certainly true that rather than designing form, he conceives buildings in terms of spatial flow and sectional diversity. The outside of the Singapore project may be sculptural, but the sculpture is the result of breaking down what could have been a monolithic mass, and then weaving in a trail that leads people on hikes on and through the facades. The people walking in these facades, or in the Guangzhou towers, or any number of Bromberg buildings with exterior spaces, are not representations of human beings. Unlike the ancient marble figures sculpted for the pediments of classical Greek temples, it is people who populate, animate and in some sense, complete the building.

Calling Bromberg an architect of space, however, is only half the story, because architectural space is always defined by form, whether it be a box or a lozenge or a sphere. There is in architecture history a category of architect for whom space is the ying of a formal yang.

R.M. Schindler, the Viennese architect who practiced in Los Angeles during the first half of the 20th century, considered space and form, at least as he conceived them, integral and reciprocal: he called the concept "space/form." In his work, form modeled space, and space pushed form. Paul Rudolph, who practiced in Southeast Asia during the latter part of his career in some of the same vicinities as Bromberg is working, is also an architect of "space/form." His forms move and shape space, which is in turn vectorial: Rudolph would draw schools of arrows, like fish, swimming through space he conceived as a liquid. Sometimes his forms were fluid too but the space always flowed.

Bromberg falls squarely—or rather fluidly—in this rarefied tradition.

In the Singapore project, he stirs and activates space into a medium of its own with the flowing curves of the terraces, railings and storefronts. Form moves space, and space moves form. Both move people, and in pockets of rest, they form eddies. Along the way, he sometimes posits objects, what he calls "events", along the journeys.

Bromberg further activates space structurally. The columns supporting the shopping decks in Singapore lean. This is not a formalist gesture but a structural idea. He inclines columns to receive point loads from the floors above, to distribute the loads to receptor points below. Structure for Bromberg is not simply a matter of statics. Where the budget permits, he uses structure to shape and inflect space.

"I'm always in a quandary," says Bromberg, who admits to being an intuitive designer. "Some of my designs have fluidity, and others are angular. I tend to make softer flows where there is human interaction".

Circulation spaces tend to be more flowing and soft. Events along the journey are more angular or faceted.

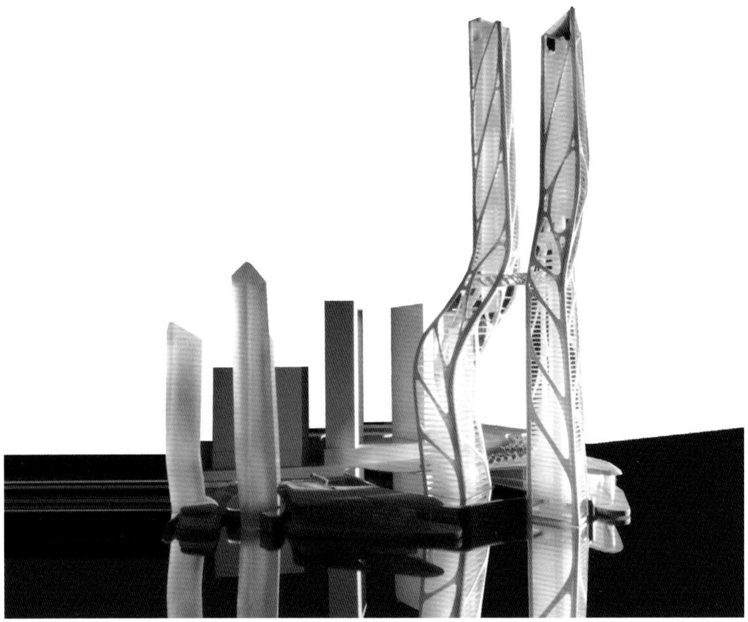

In North Star in Beijing, the opposition between curvilinearity and angularity is quite strong. With all its promenades, the shopping center curves as the site of public interaction with the building. But the high-rise volumes that house the offices and apartments form angled prows with cuts in their surfaces on the outside. Large volumes are fragmented. The formal moves are not forms shaped for the sake of form. Bromberg designs the buildings in response to interior demands—multiplying corners; capturing views, increasing the ratio of surface to volume—and to the exterior context. He's working with a three dimensional understanding of the site conditions, a panoptical view that's omni-directional rather than planimetric. "If the form moves, I'm responding to something in the surrounding context. Or I'm adapting the form to emphasize or focus something," he says.

"Buildings are always going somewhere else, toward an attractor. In Beijing, I lean one of the prows to try to point and bring you around the corner, to indicate there's something important there—the entry. The tall wall of the apartment leans, to reinforce the corner and refocus the building, which seemed important to the overall poise of the building. If the two towers appear to be pulling away from each other because of their respective attractions, the shopping center tethers them together. The composition is not static. It's held together in dynamic tension. And there is always a motive to the dynamism. I don't like to do fussy things. I don't like to do more than I need to."

Asia has presented Bromberg with multi-use typologies that allow him to cultivate the interior life of buildings. But in a single-use commercial building type—an apartment or office tower, for example, which is more typical of his Middle Eastern commissions—Bromberg has had to find other urban opportunities. As the Gulf States re-center the Arab world, and emirates like Abu Dhabi, Dubai and Qatar emerge as city states, financial centers and international ports of call, they have presented Bromberg with different kinds of building opportunities.

Not least is the poetic imperative of creating visual equivalents of Sydney's Opera House for countries without the symbolic stature of iconic buildings. For an island in one Arab country, in the Arabian Performance Venue, he proposed an opera house and museum complex that can only be described with metaphorical evocations. Centered on a mushroom-shaped building housing the theaters and museum, tall twisting abstract forms evoke the profiles of standing cobras, licking flames and spiraling antlers. Built, the phantasmagoric complex would have been one of the new wonders of the modern world. Perhaps the clients did not think it practical.

Less fantastical were The Legs, a twinned pair of towers containing a hotel, apartments and offices. The towers twist and turn mid-height at their knees in different directions. Both projects are evidence of the smoothing effects of the computer on the work. Rather than the boxes projecting helter skelter, as in earlier work, the architect differentiates facades in gradual rather than sudden increments of change. Bromberg may be designing principally for the Asian and

Middle Eastern contexts, but he is also operating within a professional context that has been deeply affected by the logarithmic persuasions of the computer.

Unlike the Chinese complexes, which are composed of different building types, the projects in the Middle East are largely predicated on the point tower, a more restrictive building type. "The commercial buildings tend to be shaped to maximize views to areas of interest, so that defines the shapes," he says. The urban potential for towers confined to the tighter Middle Eastern sites is largely consigned to a charismatic presence that defines a neighborhood or serves as a symbol.

The facades of Bromberg's Dancing Towers in Abu Dhabi torque in compound curves that result in corners and facades that lean and bend. The towers respond to each other in an intimate tango of moves and responses. A retail complex at the base is almost perfunctory compared to the Chinese shopping malls. But the twisting forms make the tower exceptional in the skyline, giving it a signature, and the shifting geometry angles virtually all the units in different directions that dial varying views.

In another tower, the Pentominium, now under construction, the views completely shaped its form. Because of a tall, nearby tower that compromised one view, the architect decided to dedicate 65% of the square footage to the side with a panorama. Bromberg took the extra square footage from the "back" side, where he carved out sky gardens on every fifth floor. That side of the building acquired a serrated edge, and proved more popular than the front. Wind tunnel tests confirmed what Bromberg intuitively designed, that asymmetries in the form, including striated seams, broke down the force of winds on the 122 story tower, making it more efficient structurally. Wind has a stronger cumulative impact on monolithic towers. Behaving as two towers, the structure emerged with forms and plans that were highly differentiated from front to back, top to bottom.

It is a central tenet of chaos theory that simple systems, once compounded, can breed complexity. The complexity of Bromberg's buildings is not necessarily intentional; he does not start a design with Venturi's images of complexity and contradiction in his mind's eye. But the sum total of so many rational decisions over large projects, within an elastic conceptual framework that tolerates differentiation, yields very rich, highly varied forms, spaces and environments. Bromberg intentionally spares no arrows in his quiver when he designs. He is not a minimalist. But by breaking down his large projects into constituent parts, and articulating parts within the parts, he allows designs to evolve bottom up rather than designer down. Buildings under his guidance tend to become what they want to become. He claims to make the fewest number of moves required for the required level of performance. He's a pragmatic functionalist.

He respects the business plans of his clients.

All those considerations are part of a larger, inclusive design strategy that allows multiple, sometimes conflicting requirements to compete for their own space and expression. Bromberg mediates. He smoothes. Then he makes it all move.

The shapes are dynamic, and this is what gives his buildings their universal appeal. He speaks an Esperanto of design that everyone, regardless of age or nationality, understands. The body understands what is level and straight, but, as Emily Dickinson once admonished, he makes it slant. His designs speak to the inner ear by which everyone sees. The designs thrill the body through the eye.

Fundamentally, they are studies that push perception. This is why at their best, they inspire awe.

---

joseph giovannini has written on architecture and design for three decades for such publications as the *New York Times, Architectural Record, Art in America, Art Forum* and *Architecture Magazine*. He has also served as the architecture critic for *New York Magazine* and the *Los Angeles Herald Examiner* and is currently a contributor to numerous publications including *Architectural Digest*. Mr. Giovannini heads his own design firm, Giovannini Associates, and he is currently working on several apartments in New York and lofts in Los Angeles. Published projects have appeared in *Architectural Digest*, the *Los Angeles Times Magazine, A + U, Domus, House and Garden, GA Houses, Architekur und Wohnen, Sites,* and *Interior Design*.

chronology

Chinese University College of Technolog

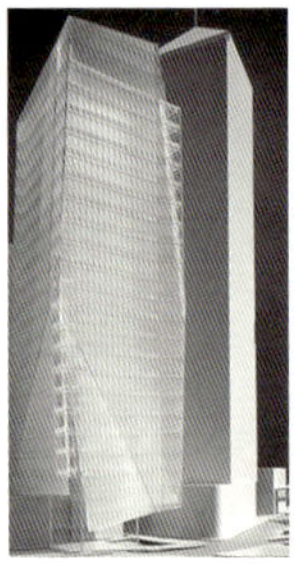

01
The Landmark
2002
Hong Kong, PRC
Program - Commercial
Site Area - 1500sqm
Floor Area - 32,000sqm
Building Height - 115m

02
Beijing International Plaza
2002
Beijing, PRC
Program - Retail
Site Area - 150,000sqm
Floor Area - 300,000sqm
Building Height - 50m

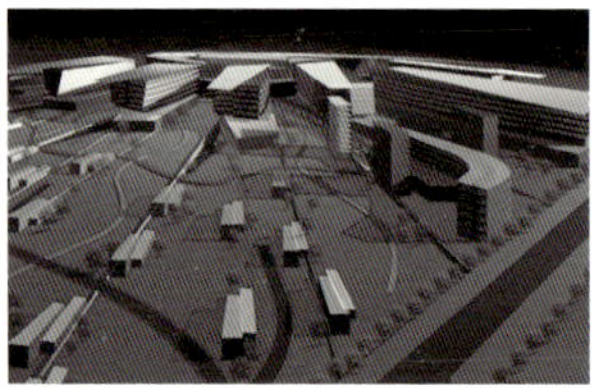

03
Oriental Silicon Valley Master Planning
2002
Beijing, PRC
Program - Mixed Use
Site Area - 80,000sqm
Floor Area - 100,000sqm
Building Height - 35m

04
Chinese University College of Technology Chapel
2002
Hong Kong, PRC
Program - Religious
Site Area - 2,000sqm
Floor Area - 830sqm
Building Height - 20m

Project

Luo Xi Development

05
Szechuan Financial Corporation
2002
Szechuan, PRC
Program - Corporate
Site Area - 3,345sqm
Floor Area - 50,000sqm
Building Height - 130m

06
Government Headquarters
2002
Hong Kong, PRC
Program - Institutional
Site Area - 42,000sqm
Floor Area - 160,000sqm
Building Height - 90m

07
Luo Xi Development
2003
Guangzhou, PRC
Program - Residential
Site Area - 32,090sqm
Floor Area - 90,050sqm
Building Height - 45m

08
San Lin Project
2003
Shanghai, PRC
Program - Residential
Site Area - 100,400sqm
Floor Area - 140,000sqm
Building Height - 45m

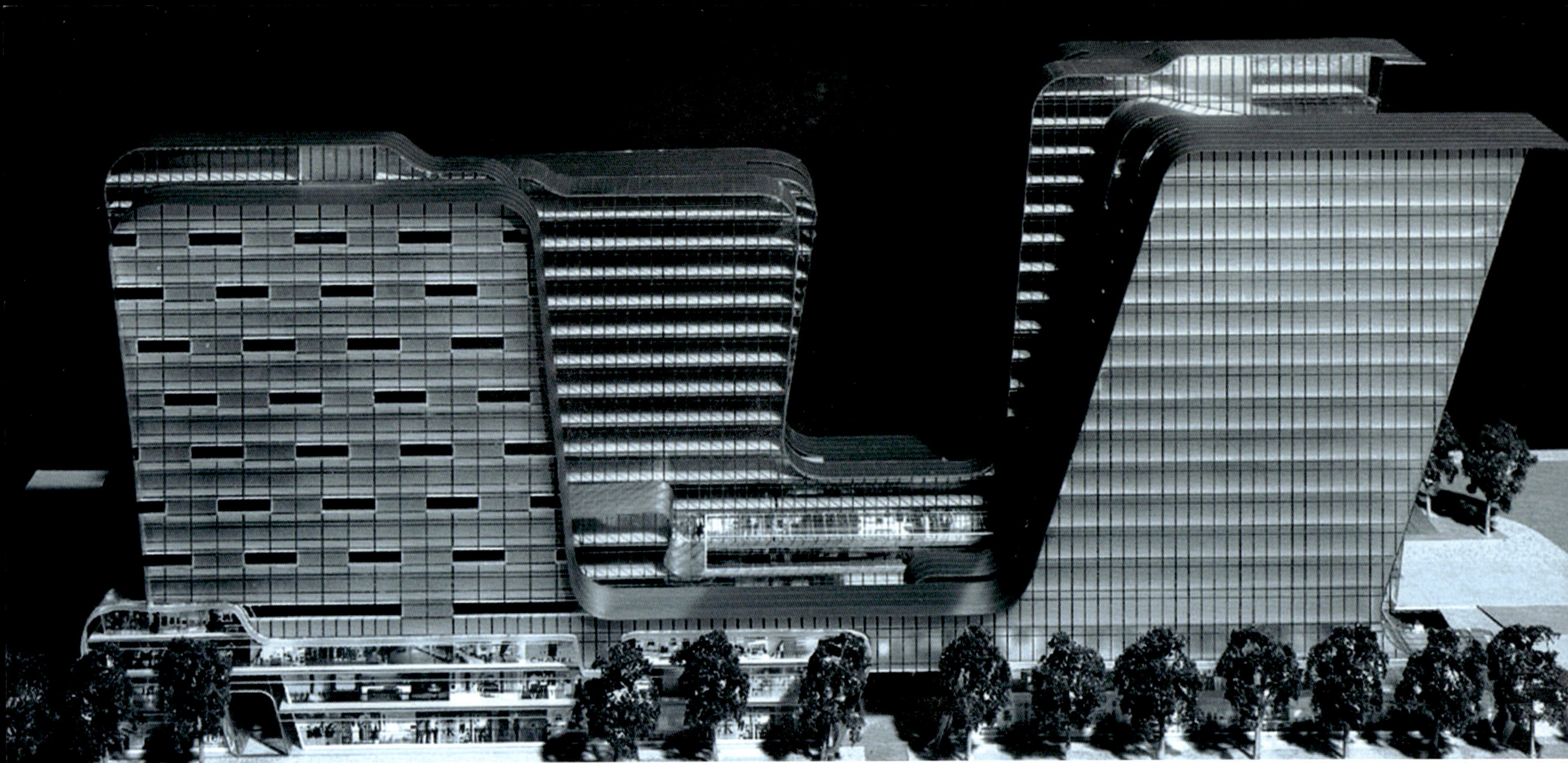

Government Headq

09
HKU Space
2003
Hong Kong, PRC
Program - Institutional
Site Area - 2,077sqm
Floor Area - 15,377sqm
Building Height - 64m

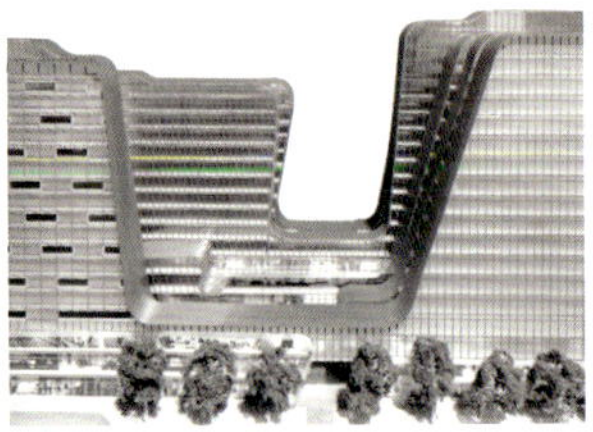

10
Zhongguan Plaza
2003
Beijing, PRC
Program - Mixed Use
Site Area - 12,950sqm
Floor Area - 64,314sqm
Building Height - 79m

11
Foshan Media Center
2003
Foshan, PRC
Program - Media Center
Site Area - 63,600sqm
Floor Area - 87,696sqm
Building Height - 82m

12
North Star
2003
Beijing, PRC
Program - Mixed Use
Site Area - 2,525sqm
Floor Area - 161,780sqm
Building Height - 107m

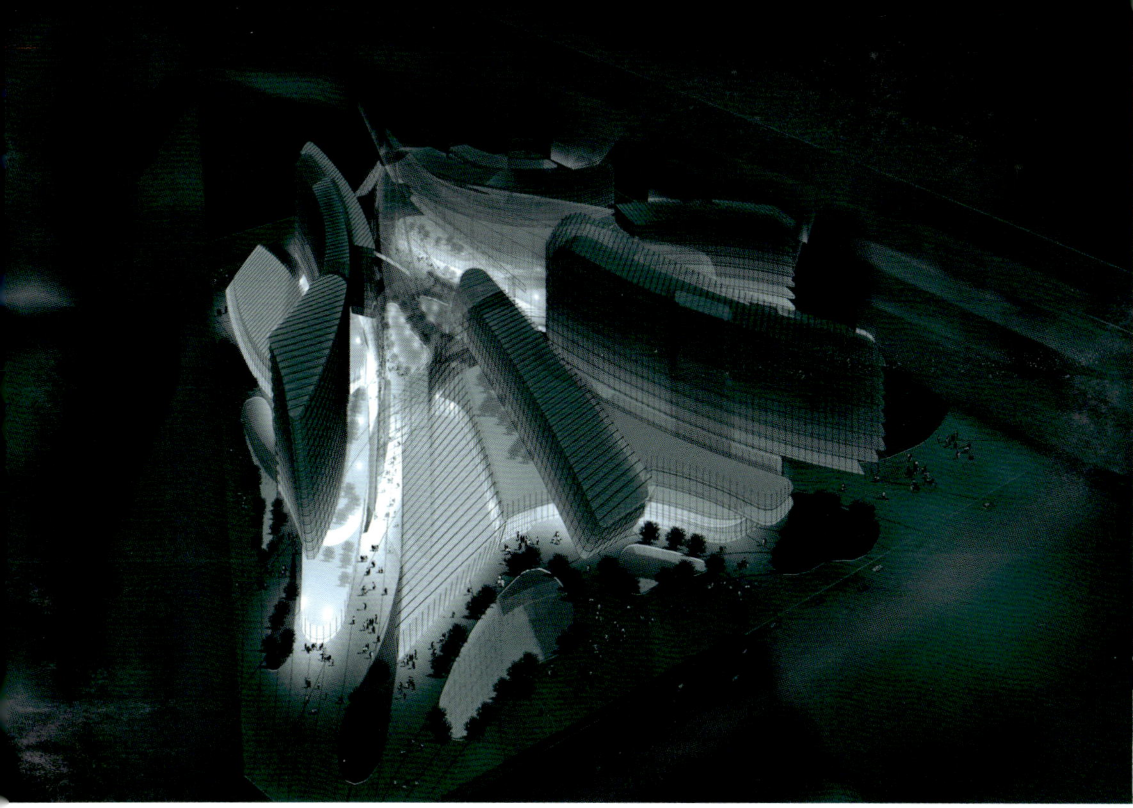

uare

13
Xian Ziwei Mall
2003
Xian, PRC
Program - Retail/Mixed Use
Site Area - 1,800,000sqm
Floor Area - 500,000sqm
Building Height - 80m

14
HKIA Exhibition Center
2003
Hong Kong, PRC
Program - Exhibition
Site Area - 170,000sqm
Floor Area - 151,600sqm
Building Height - 18m

15
West Kowloon Cultural District
2004
Hong Kong, PRC
Program - Cultural
Site Area - 400,000sqm
Floor Area - 1,734,871sqm
Building Height - 155m

16
Union Square
2004
Dubai, UAE
Program - Mixed Use
Site Area - 43,000sqm
Floor Area - 139,641sqm
Building Height - 35m

Dong Zhi Men Dev

17
Headquarters at Media City
2004
Dubai, UAE
Program - Corporate
Site Area - 10,058sqm
Floor Area - 37,170sqm
Building Height - 194m

18
Sunshine 100 Residential Development
2004
Chongqing, PRC
Program - Residential
Site Area - 65,255sqm
Floor Area - 335,500sqm
Building Height - 100m

19
Ocean Heights One
2004
Dubai, UAE
Program - Residential
Site Area - 3,746sqm
Floor Area - 858,655sqm
Building Height - 310m

20
Dong Zhi Men Development
2005
Beijing, PRC
Program - Mixed Use
Site Area - 14,685sqm
Floor Area - 97,860sqm
Building Height - 105m

21
Grand Marco Polo Hotel and Residential
2005
Beijing, PRC
Program - Mixed Use/Hotel
Site Area - 36,000sqm
Floor Area - 112,200sqm
Building Height - 65m

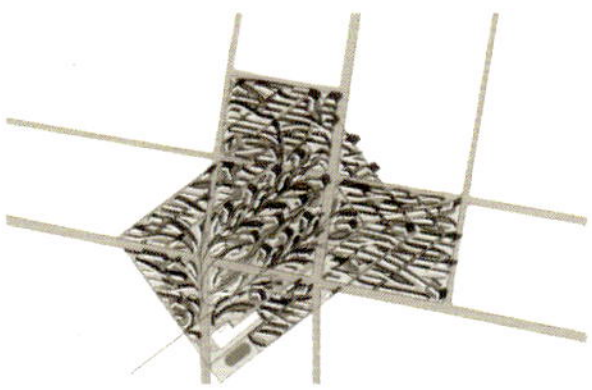

22
Xian Master Plan
2005
Xian, PRC
Program - Residential
Site Area - 2,200ha
Floor Area - 2,000,593sqm
Building Height - Varies

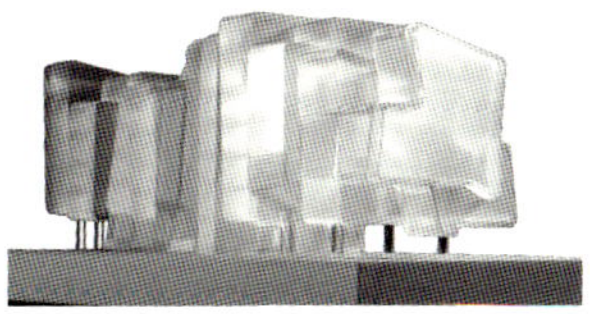

23
Sheth Headquarters
2005
Mumbai, India
Program - Mixed Use
Site Area - 2,651sqm
Floor Area - 4,966sqm
Building Height - 25m

24
The Legs
2005
Abu Dhabi, UAE
Program - Mixed Use
Site Area - 87,420sqm
Floor Area - 232,340sqm
Building Height - 350m

Sorouh

Jet

25
Atlas Mills
2005
Mumbai, India
Program - Residential
Site Area - 40,000sqm
Floor Area - 125,976sqm
Building Height - Varies

26
Sorouh
2005
Abu Dhabi, UAE
Program - Residential
Site Area - 29,356sqm
Floor Area - 330,977sqm
Building Height - 185m

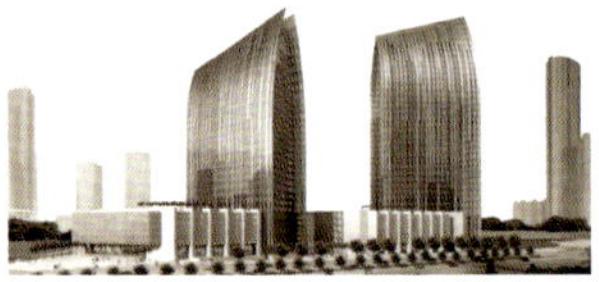

27
Boulevard Plaza
2005
Dubai, UAE
Program - Hotel
Site Area - 17,200sqm
Floor Area - 60,927sqm
Building Height - 174m

28
Crowne Plaza Hotel
2005
Huizhou, PRC
Program - Hotel
Site Area - 9,904sqm
Floor Area - 84,237sqm
Building Height - 97m

Dancing Towers

29
Jebel Hafeet
2005
Abu Dhabi, UAE
Program - Hotel
Site Area - 345,000sqm
Floor Area - 60,927sqm
Building Height - Varies

30
Dancing Towers
2005
Abu Dhabi, UAE
Program - Mixed Use
Site Area - 4,180sqm
Floor Area - 44,235sqm
Building Height - 160m

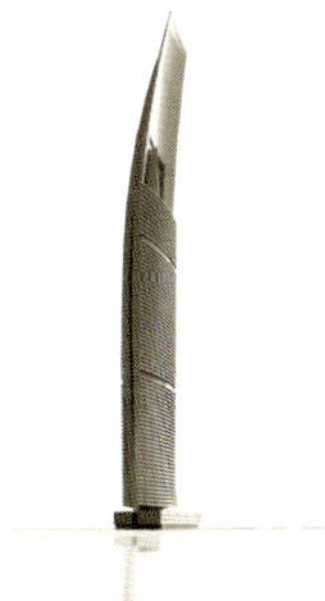

31
Ocean Heights Two
2005
Dubai, UAE
Program - Residential
Site Area - 3,453sqm
Floor Area - 197,975sqm
Building Height - 420m

32
U-Bora Towers
2006
Dubai, UAE
Program - Mixed Use
Site Area - 19,883sqm
Floor Area - 119,298sqm
Building Height - 263m

Med

33
Multaka Master Plan
2006
Abu Dhabi, UAE
Program - Urban Planning
Site Area - 9,795,000sqm
Area - 6,611,625sqm
Population - 50,248

34
Solidere
2006
Beirut, Lebanon
Program - Residential
Site Area - 2,711sqm
Floor Area - 43,987sqm
Building Height - 120m

35
Empire Tower
2006
Abu Dhabi, UAE
Program - Residential
Site Area - 7,007sqm
Floor Area - 90,206sqm
Building Height - 249m

36
Media Tower
2006
Dubai, UAE
Program - Broadcast Studio/Office
Site Area - 39,756sqm
Floor Area - 303,929sqm
Building Height - 300m

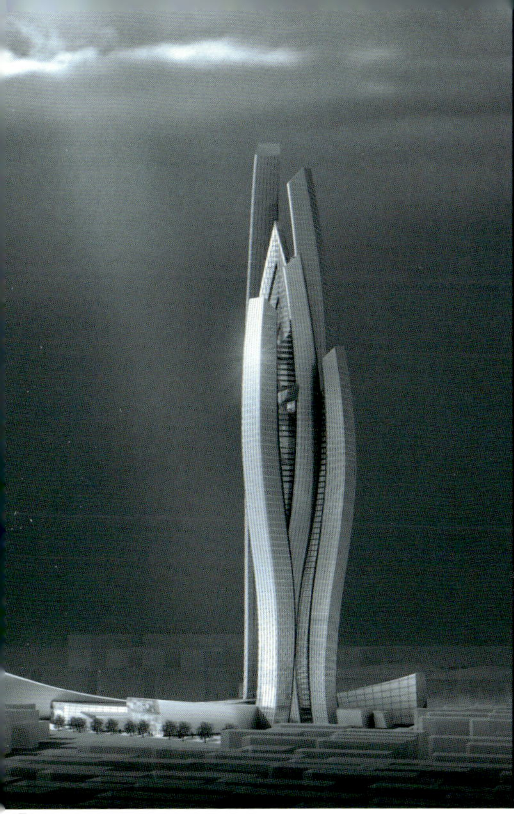

e Towers

37
Corporate Towers
2006
Bangkok, Thailand
Program - Mixed Use
Site Area - 54,519sqm
Floor Area - 351,684sqm
Building Height - 428m

38
Arabian Performance Venue
2006
Middle East
Program - Performance
Site Area - 3,200,000sqm
Floor Area - 650,890sqm
Building Height - 284m

39
Pentominium
2006
Dubai, UAE
Program - Residential
Site Area - 3,500sqm
Floor Area - 114,543sqm
Building Height - 516m

40
Civic, Cultural & Retail Complex
2007
Singapore
Program - Theater/Mixed Use
Site Area - 19,270sqm
Floor Area - 62,000sqm
Building Height - 60m

01

41
Office Park
2007
SE Asia
Program - Mixed Use
Site Area - 54,519sqm
Floor Area - 679,697sqm
Building Height - 420m

42
Corporate Towers 2
2007
Jeddah, Saudi Arabia
Program - Mixed Use
Site Area - 60,000sqm
Floor Area - 194,516sqm
Building Height - 615m

43
Gateway Complex
2007
PRC
Program - Mixed Use
Site Area - 60,267sqm
Floor Area - 195,803sqm
Building Height - 282m

44
Pazhou Exhibition Complex
2007
Guangzhou, PRC
Program - Mixed Use
Site Area - 57,698sqm
Floor Area - 159,329sqm
Building Height - 126,4m

ark tower

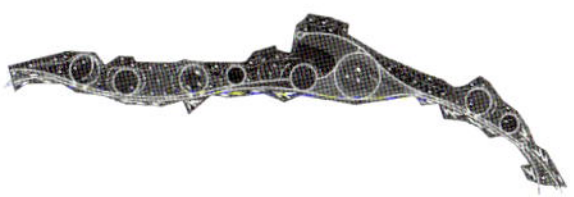

45
Remizovka Master Plan
2007
Almaty, Kazakhstan
Program - Mixed Use
Site Area - 288,650sqm
Floor Area - 184,832sqm
Building Height - Varies

46
Entertainment Resort
2007
Guangdong, PRC
Program - Entertainment
Site Area - 65,745sqm
Floor Area - 609,500sqm
Building Height - 156m

47
Majan Park tower
2007
Dubai, UAE
Program - Office
Site Area - 3,420sqm
Floor Area - 18,453sqm
Building Height - 138m

48
Khor Dubai
2007
Dubai, UAE
Program - Mixed Use
Site Area - 6,000sqm
Floor Area - 49,411sqm
Building Height - 129m

Asia A

49
Kutuzovskiy Prospekt
2008
Moscow, Russia
Program - Mixed Use
Site Area - 71,387sqm
Floor Area - 378,994sqm
Building Height - 98m

50
Asia Asia Hotel
2008
Dubai, UAE
Program - Hotel/Mixed Use
Site Area - 572,000sqm
Floor Area - 20,000,000sqm
Building Height - 245m

51
West Kowloon Terminus
2008
Hong Kong, PRC
Program - Station/Mixed Use
Site Area - 56,712sqm
Floor Area - 674,000sqm
Building Height - Varies

52
Aerovokzal
2009
Moscow, Russia
Program - Mixed Use
Site Area - 57,922sqm
Floor Area - 566,228sqm
Building Height - 90m

vloon Terminus

Towers of Arabia

53

cx-2-1
2009
Singapore
Program - Office/Theater
Site Area - 6,816sqm
Floor Area - 21,460sqm
Building Height - 53m

54

Towers of Arabia
2009
Middle East
Program - Mixed Use
Site Area - 120,000sqm
Floor Area - 293,495sqm
Building Height - 1001m

construction

construction
projects overview

north star | beijing | completion 2009
mixed use

boulevard plaza | dubai | completion 2010
office/retail

u-bora towers | dubai | completion 2010
mixed use

ocean heights | dubai | completion 2010
residential

pazhou exhibition complex | guangzhou | completion 2012
exhibition/mixed use

civic, cultural & retail complex | singapore | completion 2012
theater/mixed use

pentominium | dubai | completion 2013
residential

empire tower | abu dhabi | completion 2012
mixed use

west kowloon terminus | hong kong | completion 2015
civil

beijing north star

office/residential towers/retail

client: beijing north star land company
location: chaoyang, beijing, prc
site area - 2525sqm
floor area - 161.780sqm
building height - 107m

boulevard plaza

plots 12&13
office towers/retail

client: emaar properties pjsc
location: burj dubai, dubai, uae
site area - 17.200sqm
floor area - 60.927sqm
building height - 174m

BARCLAYS

u-bora towers

plots bb.a05.029
mixed use

client: bando engineering & construction co. ltd
location: business bay, dubai, uae
site area - 19.883sqm
floor area - 119.298sqm
building height - 263m

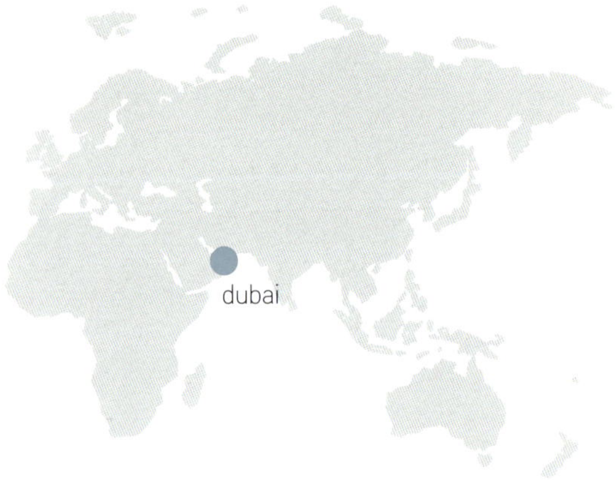

ocean heights

plots 392-188/a27a
residential

client: damac gulf properties llc.
location: marsa dubai, dubai, uae
site area - 3.746sqm
floor area - 858.655sqm
building height - 310m

arabtec

pazhou exhibition complex

plot pzb 1301 pzb 1401
exhibition/mixed use

client: nan fung development ltd.
location: pazhou, guangzhou, prc
site area - 57.698sqm
floor area - 159.329sqm
building height - 126m

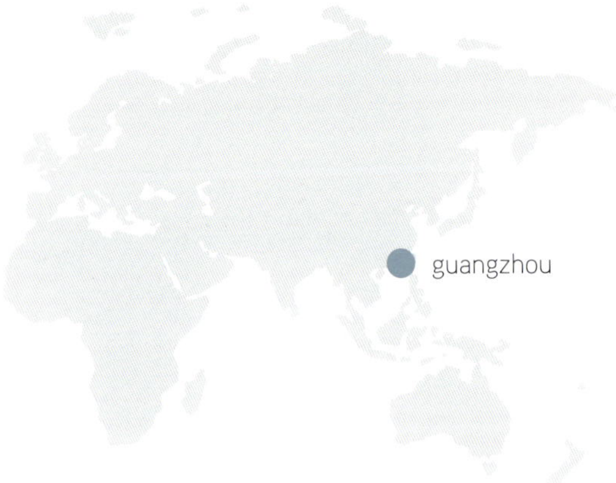

civic, cultural & retail center

cultural/mixed use

client: rock ltd+capitaland ltd
location: one north, singapore
site area - 19.270sqm
floor area - 62.000sqm
building height - 60m

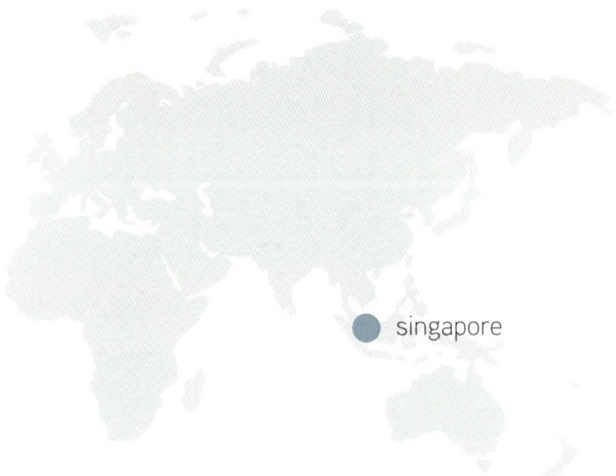

TC3

pentominium

plot 395-567
residential

client: trident international holdings
location: marsa dubai, dubai, uae
site area - 3.500sqm
floor area - 114.543sqm
building height - 516m

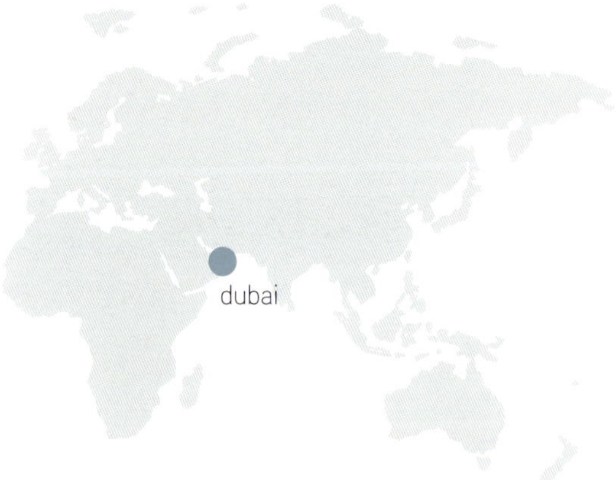

THE PENTHOUSES

empire tower

residential
client: empire holdings
location: shams, abu dhabi, uae
site area - 7007sqm
floor area - 90.206sqm
building height - 249m

SEG

west kowloon terminus

plot 395-567
civil

client: mtr corporation ltd.
location: west kowloon, hong kong, prc
site area - 56712sqm
floor area - 674000sqm
building height - varies

BACHY SOLETANCHE
法國地基建築公司

scale

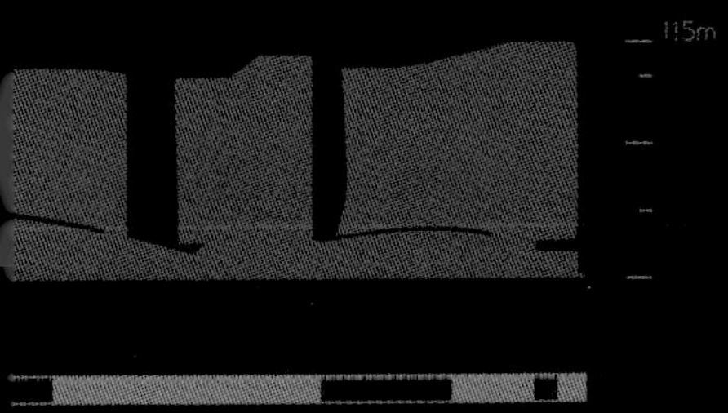

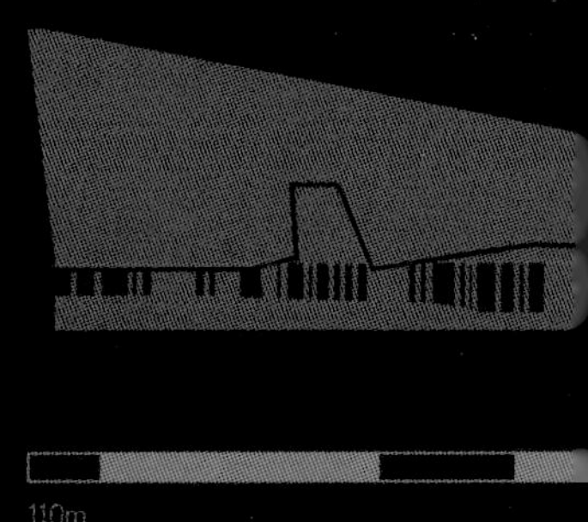

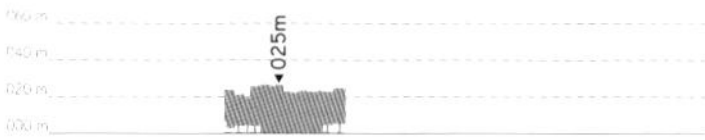

Sheth Headquarters
2005

Mumbai, India
Program - Mixed Use
Site Area - 2,651sqm
Floor Area - 4,966sqm
Building Height - 25m

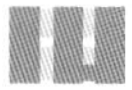

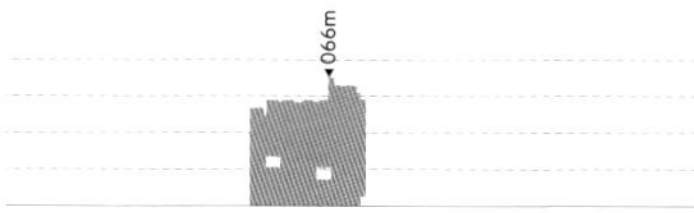

HKU Space
2003

Hong Kong, PRC
Program - Institutional
Site Area - 2,077sqm
Floor Area - 15,377sqm
Building Height - 64m

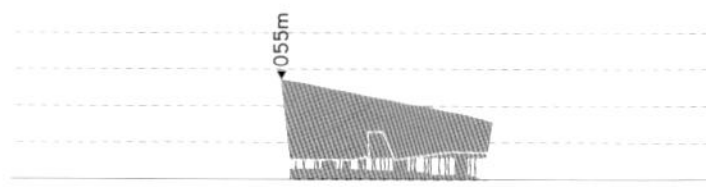

CX-2-1
2009

Singapore
Program - Office/Theater
Site Area - 6,186sqm
Floor Area - 21,468sqm
Building Height - 53m

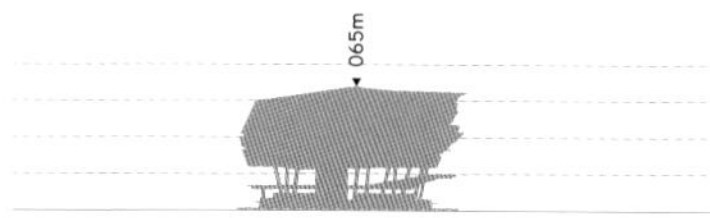

Civic, Cultural & Retail Complex
2007

Singapore
Program - Theater/Mixed Use
Site Area - 19,270sqm
Floor Area - 62,000sqm
Building Height - 60m

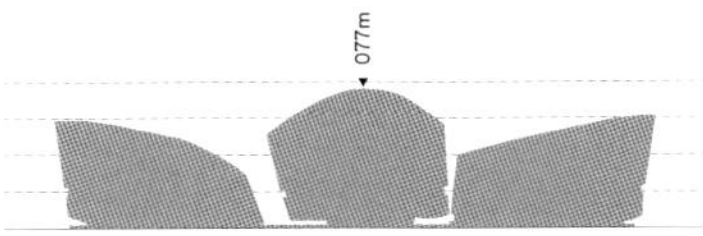

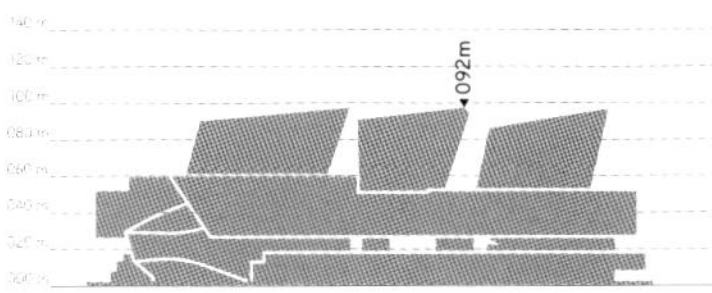

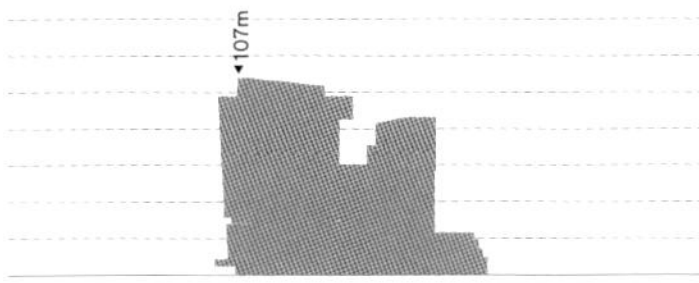

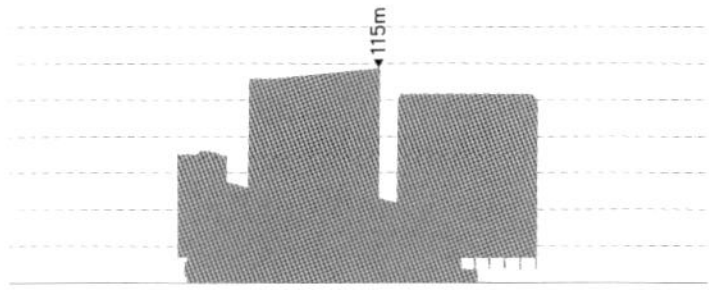

Kutuzovskiy Prospekt
2008
Moscow, Russia
Program - Mixed Use
Site Area - 71,387sqm
Floor Area - 378,994sqm
Building Height - 98m

Aerovokzal
2009
Moscow, Russia
Program - Mixed Use
Site Area - 52,922sqm
Floor Area - 566,228sqm
Building Height - 90m

North Star
2003
Beijing, PRC
Program - Mixed Use
Site Area - 2,525sqm
Floor Area - 161,780sqm
Building Height - 107m

Atlas Mills
2005
Mumbai, India
Program - Residential
Site Area - 40,000sqm
Floor Area - 125,976sqm
Building Height - Varies

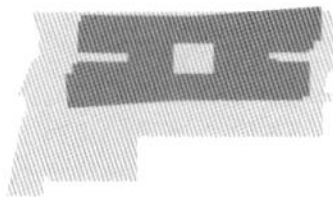

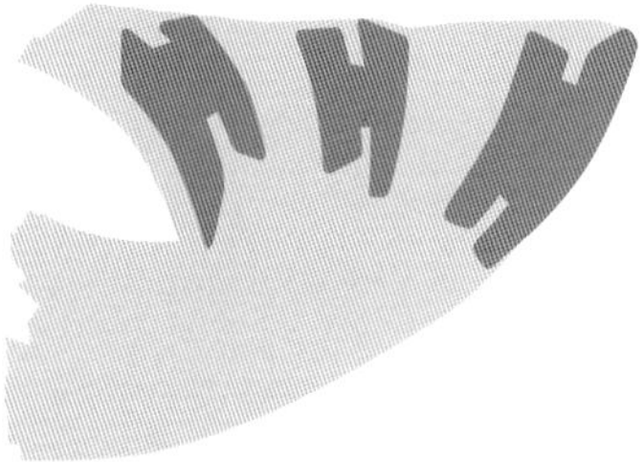

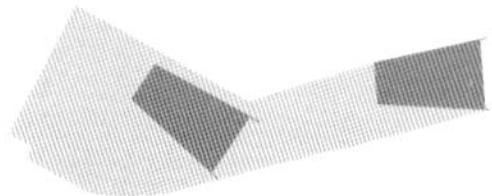

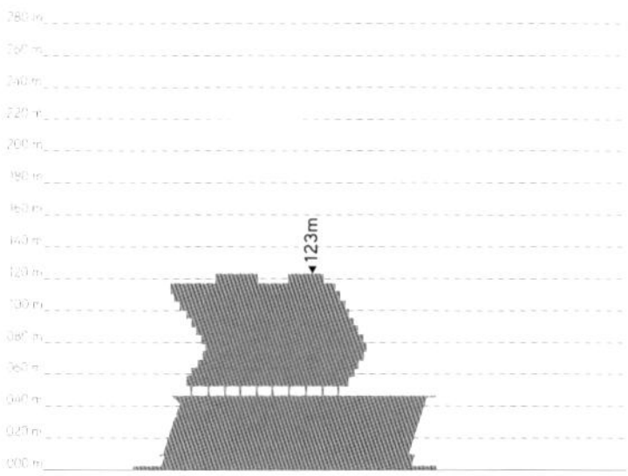

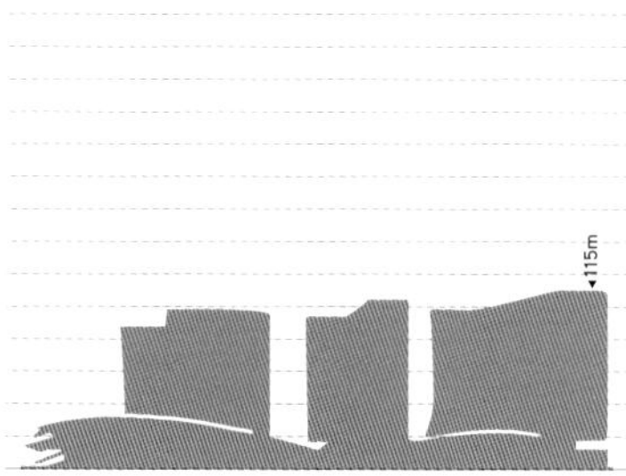

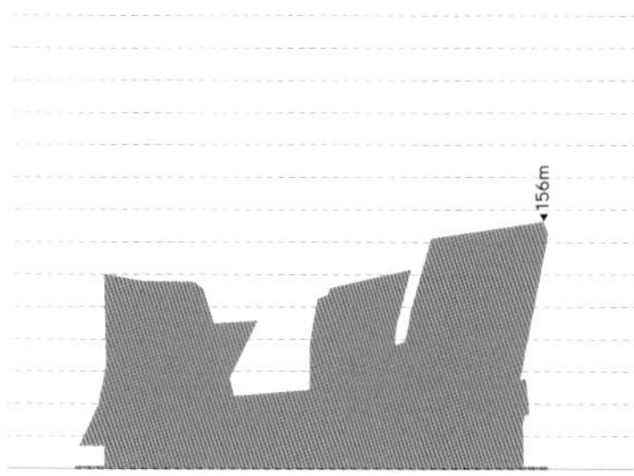

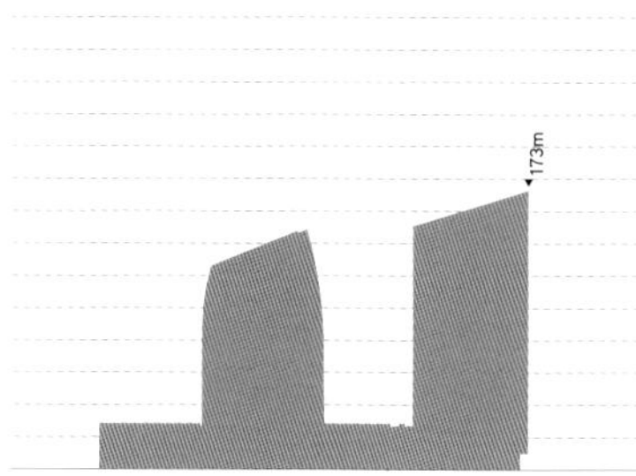

Pazhou Exhibition Complex
2007
Guangzhou, PRC
Program - Mixed Use
Site Area - 57,698sqm
Floor Area - 159,329sqm
Building Height - 126.4m

West Kowloon Terminus
2008
Hong Kong, PRC
Program - Station/Mixed Use
Site Area - 58,800sqm
Floor Area - 674,000sqm
Building Height - Varies

Entertainment Resort
2007
Guangdong, PRC
Entertainment Mixed Use
Site Area - 65.745sqm
Floor Area - 609.500sqm
Building Height - 156m

Boulevard Plaza
2005
Dubai, UAE
Program - Hotel
Site Area - 17,200sqm
Floor Area - 60,927sqm
Building Height - 174m

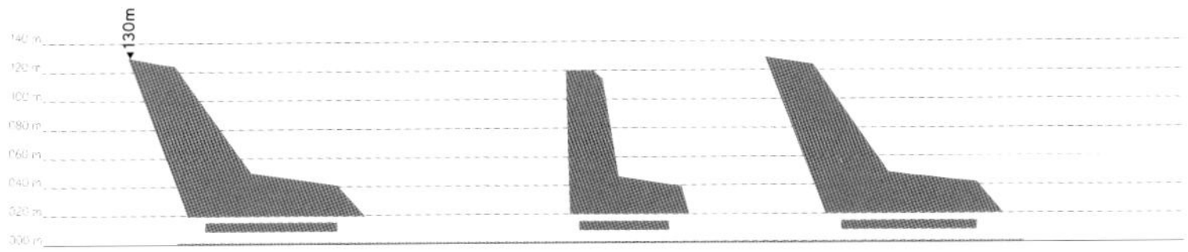

Khor Dubai
2007
Dubai, UAE
Program - Mixed Use
Site Area - 6,000sqm
Floor Area - 49,411sqm
Building Height - 129m

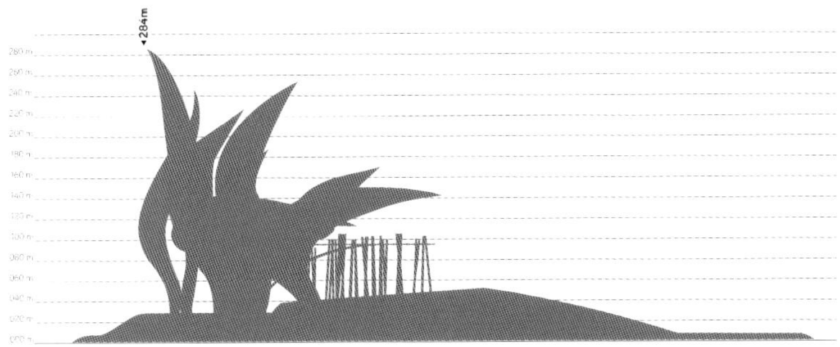

Arabian Performance Venue
2006
Middle East
Program - Performance
Site Area - 3,200,000sqm
Floor Area - 650,890sqm
Building Height - 284m

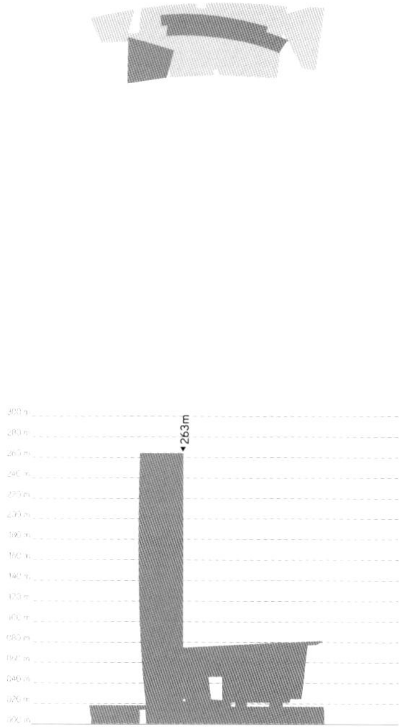

U-Bora Towers
2006
Dubai, UAE
Program - Mixed Use
Site Area - 19,883sqm
Floor Area - 119,298sqm
Building Height - 263m

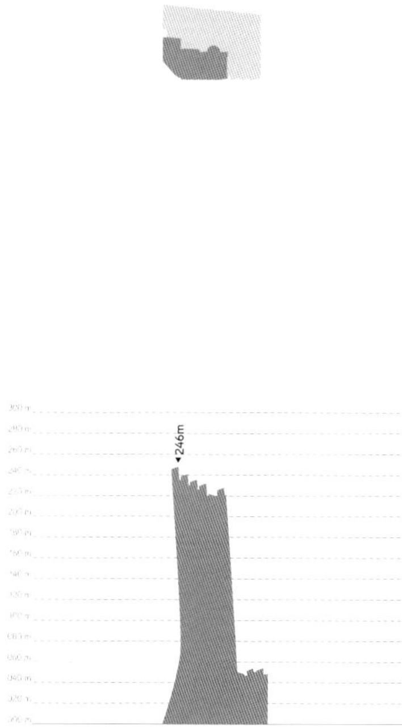

Empire Tower
2006
Abu Dhabi, UAE
Program - Residential
Site Area - 7,007sqm
Floor Area - 90,206sqm
Building Height - 249m

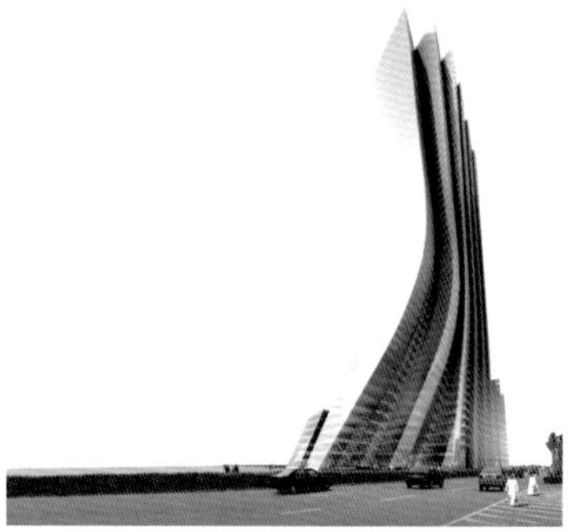

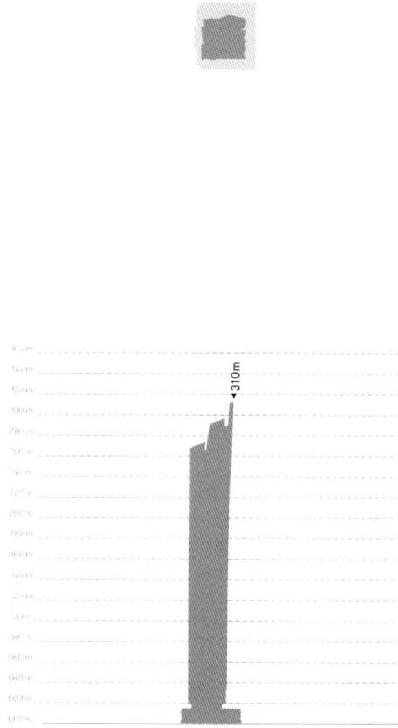

Ocean Heights One
2004
Dubai, UAE
Program - Residential
Site Area - 3,746sqm
Floor Area - 858,655sqm
Building Height - 310m

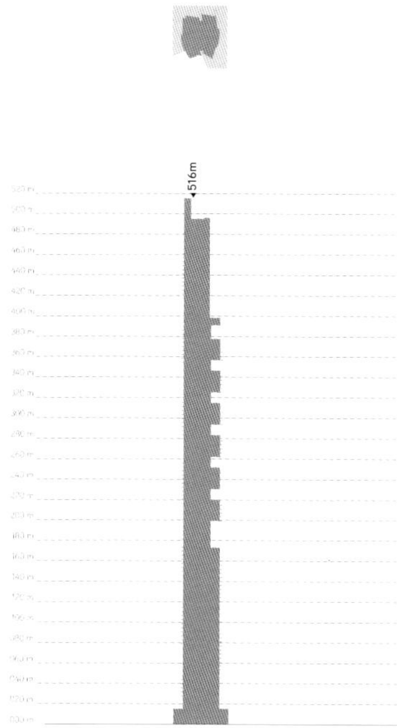

Pentominium
2006
Dubai, UAE
Program - Residential
Site Area - 3,500sqm
Floor Area - 114.543sqm
Building Height - 516m

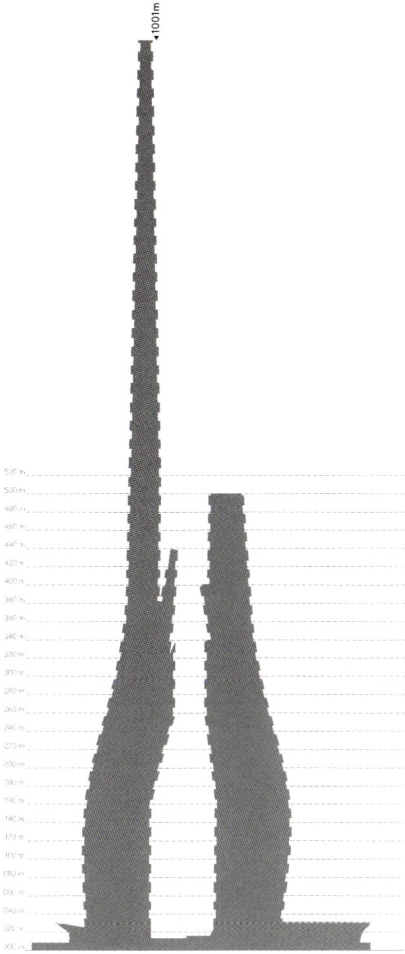

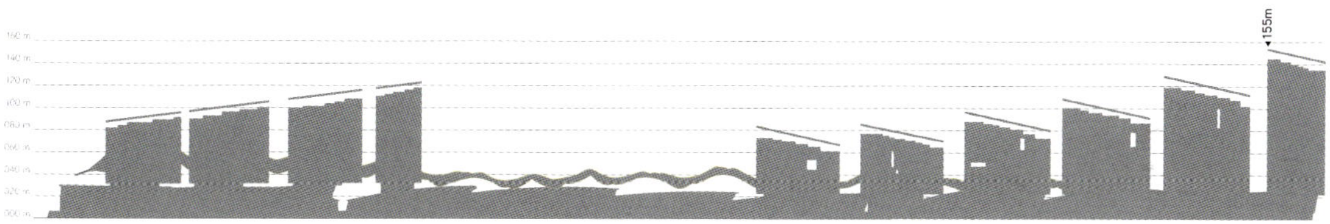

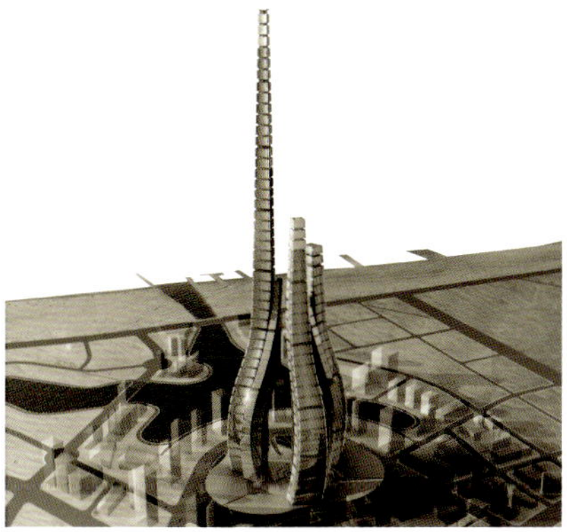

Towers of Arabia
2009
Middle East
Program - Mixed Use
Site Area - 120,000sqm
Floor Area - 293,495sqm
Building Height - 1001m

West Kowloon Cultural District
2004
Hong Kong, PRC
Program - Cultural
Site Area - 400,000sqm
Floor Area - 1,734,871sqm
Building Height – Varies

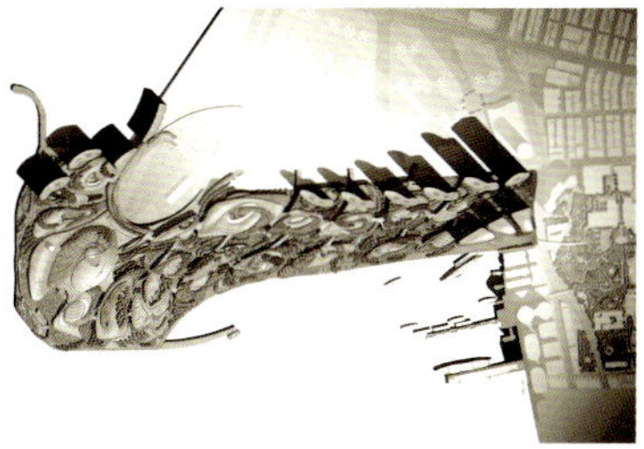

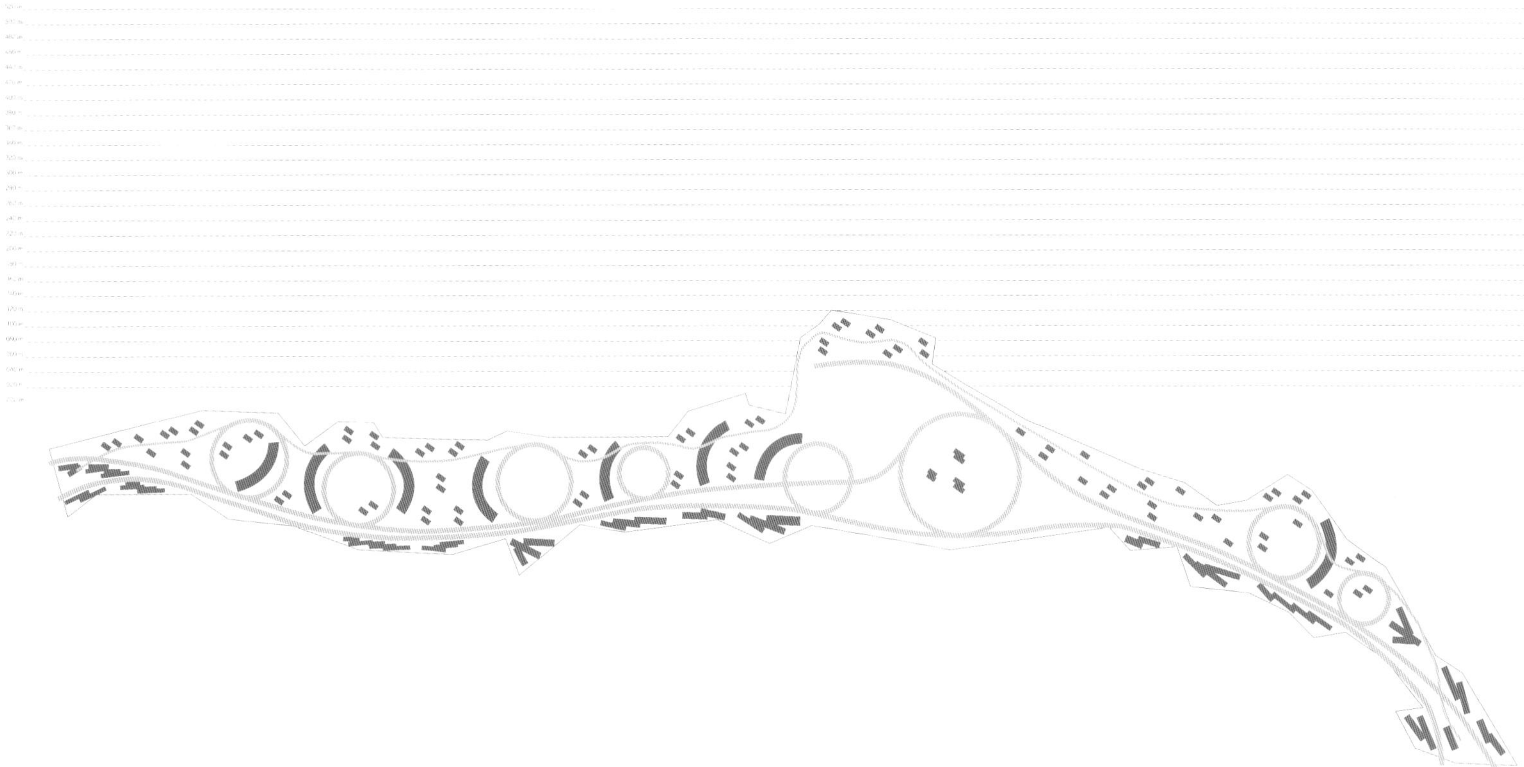

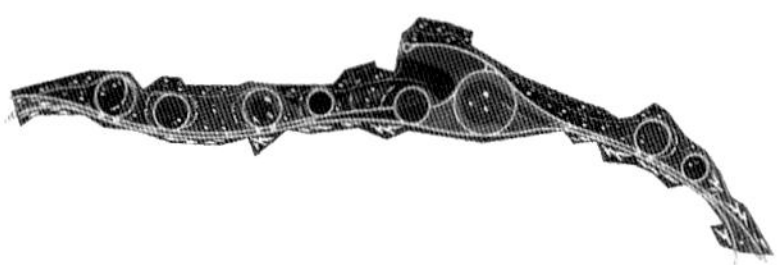

Remizovka Master Plan
2007
Almaty, Kazakhstan
Program - Mixed Use
Site Area - 288,650sqm
Floor Area - 184,832sqm
Building Height - Varies

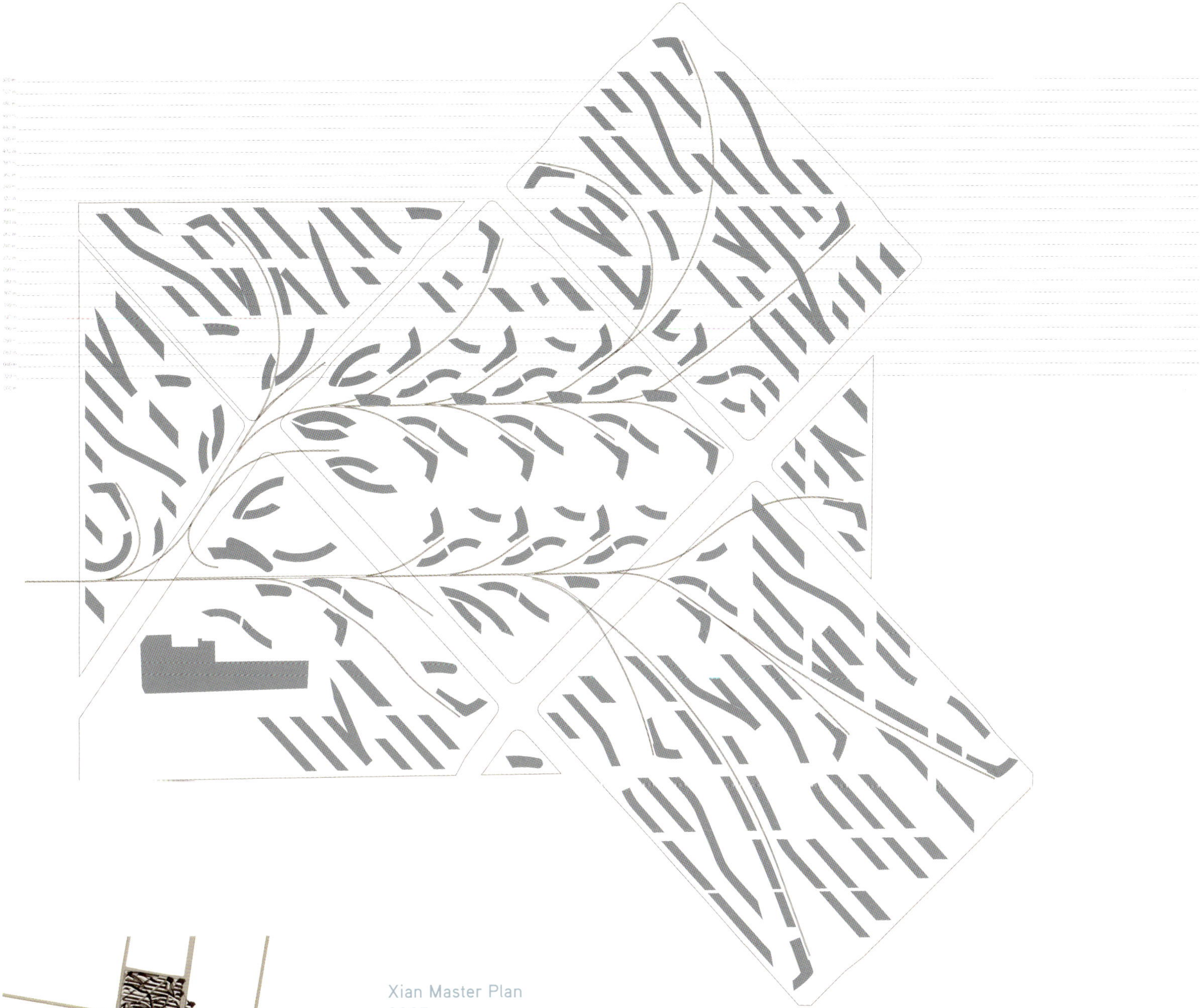

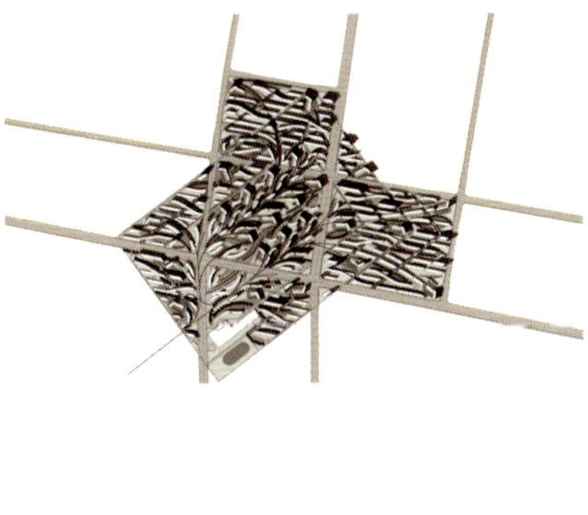

Xian Master Plan
2005

Xian, PRC
Program - Residential
Site Area - 2,200ha
Floor Area - 2,000,593sqm
Building Height - Varies

appendix

education

Bachelor's in Environmental Design
University of Colorado
Arizona State University
(Special Honors)

Master's in Architecture
Southern California Institute of Architecture
University of Washington

As an architect striving for innovation and vision, Andrew Bromberg has led the design on numerous award-winning projects throughout the world. Andrew has over sixteen years of professional experience in Architecture, with the last eight of them in Hong Kong. Andrew is a lead designer for Aedas, recognized for his ability to conceptualize and realize complex designs within a wide range of projects.

competitions

2010
- 1st Prize | World Twin Towers, Chongqing, PRC

2009
- 1st Prize | Express Rail Link West Kowloon Terminus, Hong Kong
- 1st Prize | CX-2-1, One-North, Singapore

2007
- 1st Prize | Pazhou Exhibition Centre, Guangzhou, PRC
- 1st Prize | Civic, Cultural & Retail Complex, Singapore

2006
- 1st Prize | U-BORA Towers Complex, Dubai
- 1st Prize | Oceanscape Shams, Abu Dhabi
- 1st Prize | Solidere Development Block 20, Beirut, Lebanon

2005
- 1st Prize | Ocean Heights Two, Dubai
- 1st Prize | Grand Marco Polo Hotel, Beijing
- 1st Prize | The Legs, Middle East
- 1st Prize | Jebel Hafeet Hotel, Al Ain, UAE
- 1st Prize | Khaldeya Mixed (Dancing Tower), Abu Dhabi
- 2nd Prize | Dong Zhi Men Mixed-Use Development, Beijing
- 1st Prize | Xian Residential Development, Xian

2004
- 1st Prize | Ocean Heights Residential Tower, Dubai
- 1st Prize | Sunshine 100, Residential Development, Chongqing
- 1st Prize | Damac Headquarters, Dubai

2003
- Shortlisted | West Kowloon Cultural District, Hong Kong
- 1st Prize | North Star Mixed-Use Development, Beijing
- 1st Prize | Foshan Media Center, Foshan
- 1st Prize | Goldfield San Lin Residential, Shanghai
- 2nd Prize | Luo Xi Residential Development, Guangzhou
- 1st Prize | Zhongguan International Plaza, Beijing
- 1st Prize | Workers Daily, Beijing

2002
- 1st Prize | Szechuan Financial Corporation, Chengdu
- Shortlisted | Hong Kong Tamar Government Headquarters, Hong Kong
- 1st Prize | Beijing International Plaza, Beijing

2001
- 1st Prize | Chinese Overseas Bank Headquarters, Taipei

awards

2010
- World Architecture Festival (WAF). Winner, Future Projects – Infrastructure | West Kowloon Terminus
- World Architecture Festival (WAF). Winner, Future Projects – Competitions | Dance and Music Center
- Cityscape Awards for Architecture in the Emerging Market. Winner, Commercial/Mixed Use – Future Category | Civic, Cultural & Retail Complex
- Cityscape Awards for Architecture in the Emerging Market. Winner, Tourism, Travel and Transport – Future Category | West Kowloon Terminus
- Cityscape Awards for Architecture in the Emerging Market. Highly Commended – Commercial/Mixed Use Built | North Star
- Cityscape Awards for Architecture in the Emerging Market. Highly Commended – Commercial/Mixed Use Future Category | West Kowloon Terminus
- The International Architecture Award – The Chicago Athenaeum | Empire Tower
- International Property Awards, Global. Finalist – The Architecture Award | North Star
- International Property Awards, Asia Pacific. Winner – The Architecture Award | North Star
- International Property Awards, China. Winner – The Architecture Award | North Star
- International Property Awards, Asia Pacific. Commended – The Architecture Award | Pazhou Exhibition Complex
- MIPIM Architectural Review Awards. Commended – Future Mixed-Use | Civic, Cultural & Retail Complex

2009
- International Property Awards, Global. Finalist – The Architecture Award | Civic, Cultural & Retail Complex
- World Architecture Festival (WAF). Finalist – Future Projects, Commercial | Pazhou Exhibition Complex
- Middle East "Architect of the Year". Finalist, Andrew Bromberg
- CNBC Arabian Property Awards. Winner – Best Architecture (Multiple Residential Units) Dubai | U-Bora Towers
- CNBC Arabian Property Awards. Winner – Best Residential Development Dubai | U-Bora Towers
- CNBC Arabian Property Awards. Commended – The Architecture Award Dubai | U-Bora Towers
- CNBC Arabian Property Awards. Winner – Best Mixed-Use Development in Dubai, Commercial | U-Bora Towers
- CNBC Asia Pacific Commercial Property Awards. Winner – The Architecture Award Asia Pacific | Civic, Cultural & Retail Complex
- CNBC Asia Pacific Commercial Property Awards. Winner – The Architecture Award Singapore | Civic, Cultural & Retail Complex
- Cityscape Middle East Real Estate Awards. Winner – Future Projects Residential | The Pentominium

2008
- CNBC Arabian Property Awards. Commended – Best High-Rise Architecture Abu Dhabi | Empire Tower
- MIPIM Architectural Review Future Project Awards. Commended – Mixed Use | Arabian Performance Venue

2007
- International Design Awards, Architecture – Urban Design, Second Place | West Kowloon Cultural District
- CNBC Arabian Property Awards. Winner – Best Apartment | The Pentominium
- CNBC Arabian Property Awards. Winner – Best Property Dubai | The Pentominium
- CNBC Arabian Property Awards. Winner – Best Architecture | The Pentominium
- CNBC Arabian Property Awards. Commended – Best International Property | The Pentominium
- CNBC Arabian Property Awards. Commended – Best High-Rise Architecture | The Pentominium
- 40 Under 40, Perspective Magazine – Andrew Bromberg

2006
- Cityscape Architectural Review. Commended – Sport & Leisure | Jebel Hafeet
- MIPIM Architectural Review. Commended – Master Planning | West Kowloon Cultural District
- Arabian Property Award – Best Architecture Award | Ocean Heights Two
- Arabian Property Award – Best Development Award. Oceanscape

2005
- Bentley International Award. Commended – Best Architecture | Ocean Heights

2004
- Cityscape Architectural Review. Commended – Master Planning | West Kowloon Cultural District
- Cityscape Architectural Review. Commended – Residential Future Projects | Luo Xi

2001
- American Society of Landscape Architects – Merit Award, Ohio Chapter | Reebok World Headquarters

2000
- American Institute of Architects Seattle – Merit Award | Reebok World Headquarters
- Chicago Athenaeum American Architect Awards | Reebok World Headquarters

1999
- National Association of Industrial and Office Properties – Office of the Year | Adobe NW Headquarters

1995
- American Institute of Architects Seattle Honor Award – Conceptual Work | Four Houses and a Bluff. Selection Juror – Steven Holl

1993
- Rice University Fellowship, by Lars Lerup, Dean.

1989
- American Institute of Architects Colorado Anniversary Fellowship.

1988
- Dana Giffen Soper Memorial Fellowship.

publications

The Emirates Construction Trade Magazine, Empire Tower, Mar 2010
Perspective, Pazhou Exhibition Centre,
Perspective Plus, Pazhou Exhibition Centre, Jan 2010
Unbuilt Masterworks of the 21st Century, Inspirational Architecture for the Digital Age, Arabian Performance Venue, The Legs and West Kowloon Cultural District, Oct 2009
Archiportable.com, Pentominium, Oct 14, 2009
Edilportable.com, Pentominium, Oct 14, 2009
Architecture & Design, Pentominium, Sep 16, 2009
The New Trends of the Creation of High-Rise Building, Empire Tower, Pentominium, North Star Mixed-Use, Ocean Heights 1&2, Sep 2009
Perspective, Singapore Civic and Cultural Centre, Sep 2009
ha+d (hospitality architecture + design), Damac Heights, Sep 8, 2009
Architect's Journal, Pazhou Exhibition Centre, Aug 27, 2009
Journal du Net, Des tours aux allures de jambes aux Emirats, The Legs, Aug 2009
Times House 時代樓盤 , Empire Tower, Volume 51, May 2008
World Architecture News.com, Top 100 Most Viewed Projects in 2008 (5 out of 100 Projects)
Times House 時代樓盤, U-bora Tower, Volume 46, Dec 2008
Hinge Magazine, U-bora Tower and Empire Tower, Volume 161, Building on Sand... Architecture and the UAE, Dec 2008
Ponts & Chaussees Magazine, The Legs and Ocean Heights, No.2-3 of 2008
Lusso & Mercati, Pentominium, Dec 2008
Hinge Magazine, Pentominium, Volume 160, Nov 2008
My Paper, Singapore Civic and Cultural Complex, Oct 31, 2008
The Economic Journal, "Architects' Dream Workshop-Dubai 建築師夢工場 -杜拜 ", Oct 18/19, 2008
HKIA Journal, "Roundtable Forum – Working Outside Hong Kong", Issue 52, Aug 2008
HKIA Journal, Pentominium and Empire Tower, Issue 52, Aug 2008
The Architects Journal, Singapore Civic and Cultural Complex, Jul 2008
MA magazine "Aedas: Metro, Empire and Iris Crystal" featuring David Roberts, Robert Troup & Andrew Bromberg, May 2008
New Architecture in the Middle East, Dancing Towers, The Legs, Pentominium, Ocean Heights Two, Apr 2008
Architecture and Urbanism, Arabian Performance Venue, The Legs, West Kowloon Cultural District, Singapore Civic and Cultural Complex, Feb 2008
Architecture in the Emirates, Dancing Towers & Pentominium, Oct 2007
Urbanism and Architecture 城市建築, Pentominium, Series 8, 2007
Future World Skyline, The Legs, U-Bora, Aug 2007
Perspective, "40 under 40" – Andrew Bromberg, Jul 2007
MGS Architecture, Empire Tower, Jun/Jul 2007
Die Welt, Pentominium, Jun 18, 2007
Architecture Plus, Emaar Towers, May 2007
Ottagano, Dancing Towers, May 2007
World Architecture News.com, Pentominium, May 22, 2007
Mark, Empire Tower & The Legs, Apr/May 2007
MGS Architecture, U-Bora, Apr/May 2007
Sustain Magazine, The Legs, Mar 1, 2007
Interior + Design Magazine Moscow, The Legs, Mar 2007
Hinge Magazine, Ocean Heights One, Feb 2007
The Big Project, U-Bora, Issue 2, 2007
Elle Décor Russia, The Legs, Feb 2007
World Architecture News.com, U-Bora, Feb 26, 2007
Edilportale.com, Emaar Towers, Feb 26, 2007
Edilportale.com, Dancing Towers, Feb 19, 2007
Archiportale.com, Dancing Towers, Feb 16, 2007
Archiportale.com, Emaar Towers, Feb 13, 2007

World Architecture News.com, Empire Tower, Feb 6, 2007
Tall Buildings, Ocean Heights One, Jan 30, 2007
Archiportale.com, The Legs, Jan 22, 2007
BD World Architecture, The Legs, Jan 2007
World Architecture News.com, The Legs, Ocean Heights One & Two, Jabel Hafeet, Jan 2007
Cityscape Dubai Magazine, "Aedas Building Distinctive Skyline", Dec 2006
Costa - Urola, "Bromberg vists Zarautz Y Salberdin", Dec 2006
South China Morning Post, U-Bora, Sept 20, 2006
Gulf News, Ocean Heights Two, Oct 31, 2006
Tall Buildings: Europe, the Middle East and Africa, Ocean Heights One, 2006
Construir Magazine, Dancing Tower, Nov 30, 2006
South China Morning Post, "Hong Kong Architects Reach For The Sky In Dubai", Aug 7, 2006
Construction Week, "Legs project akimbo as client rethinks designs", Jun 24, 2006
Property Weekly, "South Korean Developer Sees Great Promise in Dubai", Jun 14, 2006
Hinge Magazine, The Legs, Mar 13, 2006
101 of the World's Tallest Buildings, Ocean Heights One, 2006
The Architects' Journal, "Zaha and Aedas Think Along Similar Lines In Middle East", Jun 28, 2006
Perspective, North Star, May 2006
Architecture @ 07 BCI Asia, North Star, Mar 2006
Perspective, Ocean Heights One & Two, Apr 2006
Architectural Record, "South Terminal Expansion Project – Seattle Washington", Oct 2005
Architecture China, Ocean Heights One, May 25, 2005
architecture+, Ocean Heights One, May 19, 2005
The Sunday Times, Ocean Heights One, Apr 10, 2005
Construction Week, Ocean Heights One, Jan 29, 2005
BD World Architecture, "Top 200 Architecture Firms", Jan 2005
BD World Architecture, DAMAC Headquarters, Jan 2005
The Standard, "5,000 Luxury Flats For Cultural Hub", Nov 16, 2004
Capital CEO, "West Kowloon", Jul 2004
Architectural Record, "Reebok's New World Headquarters", 2002
Architecture, Reebok World Headquarters, Sep 2000
Seattle Times, "Art Spaces – Davidson Gallery", 1996
Retrospect, "A Prototypical House For Exhibition", 1994
Architecture, Denver International Airport, Aug 1994
Architecture, Boulder Public Library, Oct 1992

Boran Agoston
Aleardo Arenosto
Umesha Barua
Karma Barfungpa
Catharina Behr
Laszlo Berces
Geraldine Borio
Andrew Bromberg
Diarmaid Brophy
Billy Chan
Candy Chan
Darren Chan
David Chan
Gigi Chan
Henry Chan
H.P. Chan
Judy Chan
Thomas W T Chan
Wayne Chan
Julie Cheng
Sam Cheng
Toby Cheung
Jennifer Chik
Sam Cho
Jason Chong
Bosco Chu
Alex Dabringhausen
Marie Von Der Groeben
Bryan Joseph Diehl Jr
Julie Dubois
Felix Fischer
Anthony Fok
Sabine Fuhrer
David Fung
Karen Fung
Eikie Giam
Pauline Gidoin
Katarzyna Gorecka
Konrad Grabczuk
Hemalika Gulati
Candy Ho
Gabrielle Ho
Ka-Ming Ho
Samantha Hu
Sally Hui
Yann Hui
Kyle Hyde
Kevin Kasparek
Eugene Kiang
Marcin Klocek
Willie Kua
Kam Kwan
Sue Kwan
Olivier Lacombe
Andy Lai
Fernie Lai
Lawson Lai
Martin Lai
Edward Lam
Emily Tk Lau
Leo Lau
Wing Lau
Helena Lee
Benjamin Lee
Peter Lee
Raymond Lee
Ada Leung
Henry K.C. Leung
May Leung
Tiffany Leung
Timothy Leung
Wilson Li
Francesco Lietti
Bonnie Liu
Luxiang Liu
Andy Lu
Katherine Luk
Ewa Maciejewski
Alfred Mak
Emma Mak
Boris Manzewski
Derek Mceneaney
Paul Mui
Ewa Niescioruk
Moreno Negri
Max Ng
Lancelot Ng
Wendy Ng
Patrick Nguyen
Maffrine Ong
Tobias Ott
Ying Qing Ou
Karen Pang
Vicky Pang
Garry Phillips
Mirco Pieroni
Karl Poon
Frederico Ramos
Maciej Setniewski
Matthew Shao
Tony Sin
Joshua So
Jason So
Kar Yee Tam
Danny Tang
Jason Tang
Julie Valette
Christoph Vogl
Patrick Wai
Serene Wang
Jeremy Wang
Lukasz Wawrzenczyk
Kenny Wong
Catherine Wu
Lyla Wu
Albert Yu
Jason Yue
Ada Yuen

Bahar Afshar
Rana Al-Sayegh
Hani Alturk
Tony Ang
Caroline Aviles
Jaenes Bong
Addison Chan
Angela Chan
Ethan Chan
Gary Chan
Hei Chan
Katherine Chan
Longkei Chan
Olivia Chan
Tim Chan
Stephen Cheng
Crystal Cheung
William Cheung
Christy Cheung
Jolish Chengammal
Winnie Chiu
Winnie Cho
Alan Chong
Alvin Choo
Mousumi Roy Chowdhury
Kit Choy
Johnny Chung
Wai Chung
Edward Cluer
Muhammad Fadly
Greg Farrell
Santiago Galang
Adrian Geaves
Petrina Goh
Keith Griffiths
Emma Hardy
Shawn Hau
Charles Ho
Tommy Ho
Mantis Hon
Gary Houghton
Stanley Hui
Zaid Ilyas
Isa Imin
Beatrice Ip
Ravi Jaitly
David Knill-Samuell
Koh Thien Nee
Cherry Kwok
William Kwong
Erica Lam
Kenny Lam
Kent Lau
Eric Lee
Grace Lee
Ann Leung
Edward Leung
Lawrence Leung
Kai Li
Jeffrey Lo
Karen Lo
Pong Lo
Andrew Loke
Dominic Mak
Kenneth Man
Uros Markovic
Steve Marsden
Derek McEneaney
Frank McGoldrick
Logan MacWatt
John Minford
Ricardo Monterrubio
Konrad Mueller
Kai Mui
Alberto Munoz
Alen Nikolovski
Louise O'Brien
Adrian Pang
Rose Pattison
Sandra Piesik
Mark Pollard
Iskandar Rahman
Jeremy Richey
David Roberts
Malcolm Sage
Mario Sana
Eugene Seow
Sunny Siu
Yebin Sreenivasan
Kyran Sze
Abigail Tam
Tin Tam
Ambrose Tang
Wai Tang
Serene Toh
Robert Troup
Paul Tse
James Turford
Johnson Wai
Ken Wai
Kent Williams
Brice Wong
Chan Wong
Helen Wong
Gary Wong
Jason CH Wong
Jet Wong
Kam Chan Wong
Samson Wong
Richard Wilkinson
Cora Wu
Frank Yau
Megdaline Yeo
Kenneth Yung
Sharifah Zerdharina

special thanks

acknowledgements:

Beijing North Star Land Company
Bando Engineering & Construction Co. Ltd.
Capitaland
Canela Brown
Capital Investment
China Overseas
City Of Foshan
Damac Gulf Properties
Emaar Properties Pjsc
Empire Holdings
Hong Kong University
Kong Sing Ltd
Mtr Corporation Ltd.
Nameson Group
Nan Fung Development Ltd.
Paliburg Development Consultants Ltd.
Rock Production Ltd.
Sat Zhoi Construction Lip
Sunny Development
Sama-Dubai
Sorouh
Sino-Land
Sheth Development
Trident International Holding
Yin Xin Development

construction consultants:

Adrian L. Norman Ltd.
Aecom
ALT Cladding Inc.
Anthony Hunt Engineers
Artec Consultant Inc.
Arup Engineers
Abhay Wadhwa Associates
BMT Fluid Mechanics Ltd.
Bo Steiber Lighting Design
Brewer Smith & Brewer Gulf
CCP Wind Engineering
De Leeuw Middle East
ECG Engineering Consultant Group
Edaw
Fast Forward BIM Consulting Ltd.
Foresight
Form and Structure
Gallagher and Associates
Group Consult International
GMS Consultants Pty Ltd.
Hanscomb
HBA: Hirsch Bedner Associates
Hyder Consulting Engineers
IBA: Ian Banham & Associates
IMG Artist
James Cubitt & Partners Consultants
Manusell Engineering
Max Fordham Partnership
Meinhardt Engineering
MMC: Museum Management Consultants
Mott Connell Ltd.
Point of Design
Whitby and Bird Engineers
WSP Group

visual consultants:

Crystal Beijing
Imre Solt
King 3d models
Kerun Ip
Francis Leung
Lifang International
RJ Models
Tiko Models
Szczepan Urbanowicz

Book Concept/Design and Layout: Henry Chan, Brian Diehl, Konrad Grabczuk, Kevin Kasparek, Willie Kua, Olivier Lacombe, Francesco Lietti, Leo Malinow, Oscar Riera Ojeda, Vicki Pang, Larry Rouch, Maciej Setniewski, Lukasz Wawrzenczyk, Andrew Bromberg
Graphic Editor/Direction and Production: Oscar Riera Ojeda and Leo Malinow
Copy Editing: Kit Maude

Andrew Bromberg would like to thank:
In producing and achieving this book: Oscar Riera Ojeda, Larry Rouch, Leo Malinow, Lukasz Wawrzenczyk and Maciej Setniewski.
In producing this work: Andrew's Team, our supportive clients and consultants.
In support of our efforts: Everyone at Aedas including the Aedas Board.

Special Thanks to all of our writers: Aaron Betsky, Joseph Giovannini, Ralph Lerner, and Larry Rouch.

Oscar Riera Ojeda Publishers

Singapore
3791 Jalan Bukit Merah,
E-Centre@Redhill #05-27.
Singapore 159471
Telephone: 65 62711708

USA
143 South Second Street, Suite 208,
Philadelphia, PA 19106-3073
Telephone: 1-215-238-1333

Argentina
Conde 2847 D,
C1428DBM. Buenos Aires
Telephone: 54-11-4543-6289

www.oscarrieraojeda.com
info@oscarrieraojeda.com

ISBN 9 788499 361864